3-87

THE ARMY AND CIVIL DISORDER

THE ARMY AND CIVIL DISORDER

Federal Military Intervention in Labor Disputes, 1877-1900

Jerry M. Cooper

Contributions in Military History, Number 19

GREENWOOD PRESS

Westport, Connecticut • London, England

Library of Congress Cataloging in Publication Data

Cooper, Jerry M
    The Army and civil disorder

    (Contributions in military history ; no. 19
ISSN 0084-9251)
    Bibliography: p.
    Includes index.
    1. United States. Army—History—19th century.
2. Labor disputes—United States—History—19th century.
3. Sociology, Military—United States—History—19th
century.   I. Title.   II. Series.
UA25.C66   355.3'4   79-7064
ISBN 0-313-20958-8

Library of Congress Card Number: 79-7064
ISBN: 0-313-20958-8
ISSN: 0084-9251

First published in 1980

Greenwood Press, Inc.
51 Riverside Avenue, Westport, Connecticut 06880

Printed in the United States of America

10 9 8 7 6 5 4 3 2 1

To My Mother and Father

Contents

Abbreviations for Notes and Bibliography

JMSI	*Journal of the Military Service Institution of the United States*
Sec. War Rept.	Will appear with a particular year and denotes the annual report of the Secretary of War which appears regularly as a House Executive Document in the Congressional serial set.
LC	Library of Congress
HQA	Headquarters of the Army
RG	Record Group
NA	National Archives
USA	United States Army
Adj. Gen.	The Adjutant General of the Army

Acknowledgments

The debts one incurs in bringing a scholarly work to fruition become most obvious only after that work is finally completed. It is now time to acknowledge those debts, even if I cannot repay them. This study originated under the tutelage of Edward M. Coffman; his continued encouragement and friendship sustained me through revisions and additions. I am deeply obligated to him.

Dr. Paul Scheips of the Center of Military History, Washington, D.C., provided valuable criticism for a portion of the work. My colleagues in the Department of History, University of Missouri-St. Louis are responsible for creating an atmosphere in which research and writing are viewed as valuable adjuncts to the teaching of history. More specifically, I am indebted to Jim Roark for his advice to sharpen some rather vague contentions in portions of the text. Professor George Rawick read the entire manuscript and gently but persuasively led me out of a conceptual wilderness at a time when I had lost nearly all sense of direction. Their critical advice has surely improved the quality and focus of the work but does not absolve me of responsibility for its content and conclusions.

A variety of institutions have provided assistance as well. The staffs of the Rutherford B. Hayes Library, Fremont, Ohio, and the Idaho State Historical Society assisted in gathering essential material. At the National Archives, the late Mary Johnson extended a friendly welcome and first-class assistance. Members of the staff of the Library of Congress also rendered help. The State Historical Society of Wisconsin and its knowledgeable and efficient librarians provided both the material and the setting for sustained research. I am grateful as well to the librarians of the Inter-Library Loan Department of the Thomas Jefferson Memorial Library, University of Missouri-St. Louis. LABOR HISTORY has kindly given permission to use material from my article, "The Army As Strikebreaker: The Railroad Strikes of 1877 and 1894," which originally appeared in 18, no. 2 (Spring 1977): 179-96.

Richie Martin, Julie Andrew, and Mary Supranowich of the secretarial staff of the Department of History, University of Missouri-St. Louis gamely typed their way through a variety of emendated drafts of this book and always maintained their good cheer. Their work is greatly appreciated.

Finally, and most importantly, I want to thank my family. Christine's good cheer and her loving pride that Daddy was writing a book always seemed to surface precisely when I needed a boost. Ellie was there at the beginning, providing love, support, and, as do most unsung wives of scholars, the money academe seldom concedes is so necessary to the pursuit of scholarship. This book is as much hers as it is mine, the fruit of partnership, friendship, and deep affection.

Jerry M. Cooper

Introduction

The Gilded Age was a time of transition for the U.S. Army. The generation that fought and won the Civil War dominated command positions,
while the generation that would lead the Army in World War I learned
the fundamentals of military leadership through lengthy service in the
junior grades. Superficially, duty in the "Old Army" after Reconstruction resembled antebellum experiences. Promotion came excruciatingly
slowly. Most officers and enlisted men could not avoid long periods of
duty at isolated and uncomfortable frontier garrisons, and the career
soldier continued to face a general civilian dislike for the professional
man-at-arms. Many aspects of the Army had changed considerably since
the prewar years, however. A nascent professionalism made itself evident
in the years after 1877. Political considerations and manpower needs led
to the addition of all-black infantry and cavalry regiments after the Civil
War. The Army's need to devote nearly all of its time and resources to
dealing with the Indians on the frontier eased by the early 1880s as the
remnants of Indian power were broken for all time.

Despite the fact that the Army did not participate in a general war
against a foreign enemy from 1877 to 1898, historians have studied the
post-Reconstruction service extensively from a variety of perspectives.
The recent trend in military history to devote nearly as much effort to
military institutions in time of peace as in war partially accounts for this
attention. But in part historians' interest has been attracted by the specific
nature of the Army's experience in the Gilded Age. These were years of
change for the service; patterns of military thought and relations between
civilians and soldiers that would affect later developments were taking
shape in what Russell Weigley calls the "Twilight of the Old Army."[1]

Evolving professionalism and growing military intellectualism were important trends in the peacetime activity of the Army during the late nineteenth century. They developed, however, with little public awareness or interest. Federal military intervention in labor disputes brought the Army more directly into American life than did any other service activity. President Rutherford B. Hayes's commitment of federal troops to aid state authorities in ending the riotous strikes of railroad workers in July, 1877, was the Army's first involvement in an extensive labor upheaval. In the next two decades, the service intervened in three other major labor disorders and several minor ones. The use of federal troops in industrial upheavals had a qualitative rather than a quantitative importance. In the 1877 intervention, federal troops effectively ended the first labor attempt to act on a nationwide basis. The Army's presence in the 1894 railroad strikes ended Eugene Debs's attempt to create a viable industrial union in the American Railway Union. By quelling strikes in the Coeur d'Alene mining region of Idaho in 1892 and 1899, federal troops contributed substantially to the founding of one of the most radical and militant labor organizations in American history, the Western Federation of Miners.[2]

A narrative of the service's role in the suppression of labor disorders after 1877 makes up a large part of this study. Military records and the papers and writings of Army officers serve as the main sources for the descriptive sections. *The Army and Civil Disorder* seeks not only to describe the activities of federal military forces in labor upheavals but also to assess the impact of the Army's strike duty on the service and dissident workers. Officers did not seek strike duty; it was thrust upon them by civilian superiors. Once assigned the task in 1877 and after, military leaders attempted to exploit civilian fears of a disorderly working class to further the service's interests by calling for increases in manpower and appropriations in order to preserve the civil peace. In this they failed, but in the process deep fears were generated within the labor movement about an expanded Army.

Above all, strike duty involved the service in the most contentious social and economic struggles of the era. Conflicts over the rights of property in contrast to the needs of individuals, and the implementation of a new set of values generated by the onset of corporate industrial capitalism, would inevitably have engendered social turmoil. The advocates of property and the new values, however, controlled the agencies of government and hence the institutions of social control. Police, the National Guard, and the Army were committed to maintaining existing power relationships in the name of law and order. The officer corps discovered a commonality with the social classes that controlled government. Despite the growing sense of professionalism within the service and the military's evident dislike for the grosser aspects of materialism, strike duty revealed that the Army, as represented by the officer corps, was not divorced from middle and upper-class America. Indeed, they shared a common set of values.

Notes

1. The phrase is Weigley's title for chapter 12 in his *History of the United States Army* (New York, 1967); see also his *Towards an American Army: Military Thought from Washington to Marshall* (New York, 1962), chaps. 7, 9; Samuel P. Huntington, *The Soldier and the State: The Theory and Politics of Civil-Military Relations* (Cambridge, Mass., 1957), chaps. 8, 9. Works dealing with professionalism and military reform and focusing on this time period include Stephen E. Ambrose, *Upton and the Army* (Baton Rouge, La., 1964), particularly pp. 96-110, 121-24; Graham Cosmas, *An Army for Empire: The United States Army in the Spanish-American War* (Columbia, Mo., 1971), chaps. 1, 2; C. Robert Kemble, *The Image of the Army Officer in America: Background for Current Views* (Westport, Conn., 1973), section 4, discusses the debate over the Army's place in society. Don Rickey, Jr., *Forty Miles a Day on Beans and Hay: The Enlisted Soldier Fighting the Indian Wars* (Norman, Okla., 1963), and Jack D. Foner, *The United States Soldier Between Two Wars: Army Life and Reforms 1865-1898* (New York, 1970) examine enlisted life. Marvin Fletcher, *The Black Soldier and Officer in the United States Army, 1891-1917* (Columbia, Mo., 1974), and William B. White, "The Military and the Melting Pot: The American Army and Minority Groups, 1865-1924," (Ph.D. diss., University of Wisconsin, 1968), analyze minority groups in the Army.

2. Richard B. Morris, "Andrew Jackson, Strikebreaker," *American Historical Review* 55 (October 1949): 54-68, discusses the earliest instance of the use of the Army in a peacetime labor upheaval. For a brief overview of the Army's strike duty in the late nineteenth century, see Barton C. Hacker, "The U.S. Army as a National Police Force: The Federal Policing of Labor Disputes, 1877-1898," *Military Affairs* 33, no. 1 (April 1969): 255-64.

THE ARMY AND CIVIL DISORDER

Labor, Capital, and Industrial Warfare

During the last two and a half decades of the nineteenth century, the United States experienced many domestic upheavals. The majority of these conflicts was in some way the product of the drastic economic and technological changes taking place in the nation, changes which had important social implications. Some of these violent outbreaks involved groups at odds with the political system, while others concerned racial and ethnic animosities which lurked below the surface of social intercourse. A great many more of these domestic disorders, however, resulted directly from labor protests, at times spontaneous but more often resulting from organized efforts.

Industrial discontent did not reach large proportions in the United States until the early 1870s. The national trade unions in existence before the Civil War lacked sufficient organization and influence to generate effective action. During the war, the efforts of organized labor intensified but remained generally ineffectual. After the war, national trade unions came of age and began to organize workers on a greater scale in an effort to meet corporate bigness with union solidarity. Starting in the 1870s, strikes and boycotts and the employers' strike, the lockout, increased steadily. Statistics on the early strikes are sparse, but by 1877 industrial conflict was a permanent part of the American scene. The trend of conflict after that date was almost steadily upward. Between 1881 and 1900, 22,793 strikes affecting 117,509 establishments and involving 6,105,694 workers took place, with an average duration of 23.8 days. At the same time, 10,005 lockouts affecting 9,933 businesses and 504,307 workers occurred, with an average duration of 97.1 days.[1]

The legal and philosophical milieu of the late nineteenth century severely circumscribed workers in these contests. Both law and tradition emphasized the sanctity of private property, defined in that era as not only the physical property of individuals and corporations but also the intangible property of profits. Workers' demands for higher wages, shorter hours, and better working conditions would inevitably affect profits, and owners and managers had the right—some argued it was a duty—to protect the property of profits from workers' demands. Supply and demand, not the whims of either employees or employers, determined wages, just as they determined profits. Natural law far more than legal provisions determined the market value of everything, including the price of labor. Individual workers and organized labor were challenging timeless law when they demanded the right to interfere with management prerogatives in determining wages, hours, and working conditions, a challenge that property owners, judges, and much of middle-class America would not countenance.[2]

Given these assumptions, the tactics of labor were bound to alienate the propertied classes and violate the law. Strikes, boycotts, picketing, intimidation of strikebreakers, and other methods of pressuring employers inevitably brought down agencies of law upon workers. Each worker's freedom of contract to bargain with his employer set further limits on organized labor. American law accepted the existence of unions, principally as fraternal organizations, but it did not sanction unions as collective voices for their members. A contract existed between employers and employees when workers accepted jobs at prevailing wages and hours. Most states maintained laws which made it a crime "for any person to prevent, or seek to prevent, by means of threat, intimidation, or force, alone or in combination with others, any person from entering into or continuing in the employment of any other person."[3]

The law and employers' conceptions of their rights and responsibilities ruled out collective bargaining and union recognition in almost all circumstances. If workers wanted to organize as a fraternal order, to provide insurance benefits and education for their members, that was acceptable, even laudable. But when they sought to invade the prerogatives of the property owner and dictate wages, hours, and hiring practices, they became "antagonistic to the constitution of the United States" and threatened to "destroy the first principles of free government by restraining freedom of thought and action."[4]

Late nineteenth-century law found strikes to be legal. It was the workers' right to leave their jobs, individually or in concert, in quest of better opportunities or in hopes that their leaving would pressure employers to meet their demands. Beyond the strike tactic, however, there was little workers could do legally to force employers to bargain. Boycotts and picketing were almost universally illegal. Any attempts to coerce or intimidate strikebreakers were banned as well. Strikes, boycotts, and picketing sometimes prevailed despite the law because of local officials' sympathies or the shortage of labor, but more often than not employers had little difficulty in obtaining judicial and executive assistance to protect strikebreakers and their property.[5]

Despite the laws and the implicit right of owners and managers to call upon the state to intervene on their behalf, propertied interests did not always have things their own way. A larger issue than property rights was at stake in labor conflicts of the late nineteenth century, as Herbert Gutman has shown. The impact of industrial capitalism led to a conflict of values beyond the question of who controlled property and involved all members of the community, not just workers and owners. In many instances workers found allies in the local community as they contested the power and values of management. Such alliances often circumscribed and stymied management. They also often led to violent outbursts which local officials could not or would not control. The managers' economic and political power allowed them to go beyond the local area to acquire strikebreakers, private police, state militia, or federal marshals and military forces. In the name of the law, property and management wielded the necessary powers to maintain their dominance.[6]

The powers at the command of property owners allowed them to break strikes with regularity using a variety of means. Poorly organized walkouts often collapsed with the arrest of union officers or clearly visible leaders in the case of nonunion strikes. Injunctions banning picketing and ordering the arrest of strike leaders on disturbance of the peace or conspiracy allegations more fully thwarted labor protests—when workers obeyed the courts. Court orders of this ilk, of course, could be and were enforced by militia and federal troops. The crux of any major strike, however, was the introduction of strikebreakers and management attempts to resume operations of the struck facility. Police, militia, and occasionally federal troops were then needed to protect scabs and property. Police and military protection allowed strikebreakers to enter factories and mines and work them and to operate trains and canal boats. To the average laboring man in the Gilded Age, strikebreaking meant, above all other things, the use of force to allow non-strikers to take their jobs. The appearance of strikebreakers was the most volatile moment in a strike and likely to provoke violence. Management, the public press, and public officials asserted that workers had no right to interfere with another individual's desire to take a job or with the owner's due to use his property as he saw fit.

In this setting, labor found itself continually admonished to obey the law, eschew collective action, and allow the miracle of the American dream to lift them from poverty and impotence. Arguing that strikes may have been justified in Europe, one commentator on the labor scene in the 1880s found that they were "not justifiable in our country. . . . The laboring man in this bounteous and hospitable country has no ground for complaint. His vote is his potential and he is thereby elevated to the position of man."[7] Another observer recommended not only the ballot as a better remedy than the strike but also counseled patience. "Remember that many a present millionaire was not long ago a workman like you; your surest reliance is on the sympathy of your countrymen, on prudent counsels and the rapid march of time."[8]

When workers took collective action the voices of property used the public press to accuse them of many sins. The pursuit, prosecution, and hanging of members of the Ancient Order of Hibernians (the infamous Molly Maguires) in the Pennsylvania coal fields in the early 1870s received extensive press coverage. Eastern newspapers depicted the Mollies as murderous thugs of foreign import involved in a criminal conspiracy to subvert the basic laws and values of the United States. The 1886 Knights of Labor campaign to gain the eight-hour day which culminated in the notorious Haymarket riot received similar treatment. Writers in the *North American Review* depicted the Knights' campaign as "utterly revolutionary" and "completely subversive of social order" and demanded that "the Anarchists, Nihilists, Socialists, and Communists must be disposed of by the police."[9] Harry P. Robinson, editor of the management journal *Railway Age,* saw the Pullman Strike as "nothing less than a general industrial rebellion."[10]

The rhetoric of the popular press helped to create in the public mind an image of labor unions as undemocratic, un-American, revolutionary, and, above all, violent. Given the premises and intent of organized labor, the press implied, labor-management conflict brought on by workers led inevitably to tumult. In assaulting unions, *The Outlook* charged that "The 'solidarity of labor' involves the 'solidarity of capital.' It means all employed and all employers organized into hostile camps. It means chronic suppressed war between the two, breaking ever and anon into open war."[11]

The role of the state in the conflict was quite clear. Law, order, and the rights of property and of individual non-union workers were at stake. The issue was simple, the *Portland Oregonian* editorialized. "The state is bound to afford this protection. It cannot shirk the duty."[12] Few contemporary observers comprehended that this basic legal fact was the source of much of the turmoil. Labor writer Oren B. Taft understood that "all the machinery of State stands ready to protect and further the interests of capital, while labor is left absolutely without law, a law unto itself, save when it commits some act, to be dealt with as a criminal."[13]

Labor also understood well its relationship to the law, as it too indulged in the rhetoric of conflict. *The Iron Molder's Journal* complained in 1877 that the press, the law, and employers persecuted labor, "all having but one object in view, the total destruction of Trade Unions. It can be truly said that the war of capital and labor is now raging as it never did before."[14] Seeing strikes as "industrial wars," the *American Federationist* feared that "like wars between nations, the best disciplined army with plenty of ammunition wins the battle. It is power not justice that wins."[15] Labor journals seldom advocated the use of violence or armed force, but the rhetoric underlined the fact that workers knew that power and force were basic elements in late nineteenth-century American labor relations.[16]

Neither labor nor management consciously opted for violence in dealing with each other, but it came nonetheless. Management fell back on the use of force to preserve the *legal* status quo, even as its economic and administrative policies revolutionized the American economy and the political and social arrangements connected to it. Working people bore the brunt of social change as circumstances forced them to give up or modify old cultural values and work habits. Finding themselves in a legal system that overwhelmingly favored property owners and managers frustrated workers exploded sporadically in violence and destruction against the symbols of industrialism, seeking at times to preserve the preindustrial order or to assert their own interests in the new order.[17]

Despite a long history of individual and group violence, American society in the Gilded Age had not yet developed effective agencies of social control capable of dealing with civil disorder. Invariably, labor upheavals forced public officials to create ad hoc forces to suppress rioting or enforce the law. The informal nature of these forces contributed to the potential for violence. In rural areas, such as the coal fields of Pennsylvania and Tennessee, in the mining regions of Idaho and Colorado, and the small railroad section stations dotted across the trans-Mississippi West, law enforcement fell to the sheriff and the constable. These elected officials were not only subject to strong political pressures during disorders but also had a limited amount of manpower to use when mass violence arose. The sheriff's usual recourse in such circumstances, the *posse comitatus,* did not really serve well. Too often a posse of local citizens quickly took a side in the conflict. The end result was often chaos, violence, and bloodshed.[18]

In urban areas, civic officials usually sympathized with management. Acquiring manpower to confront labor protests was not a problem, but efficient use of that manpower was. Urban police forces lacked professional leadership and techniques. Most urban policemen were not sympathetic to strikers, and when faced with problems of crowd control and rioting they resorted to excessive force and consequently escalated the violence beyond their capacity to control it.[19]

The lack of competent law enforcement agencies led many corporations and businesses to take independent action to protect their property, prevent intimidation of strikebreakers, and eliminate sabotage during strikes and lockouts. Private industrial police forces first appeared in Pennsylvania coal fields, which had a long history of industrial unrest. In order to provide some permanent security force, regional mine owners and railroad corporations sought and obtained from the state the right to raise and arm private police. These officers received all the powers of a sheriff or constable, including the right of arrest. The Coal and Iron Police soon became feared and hated by the coal miners and railroad workers of Pennsylvania. It was the Coal and Iron Police of Franklin Gowen's Philadelphia and Reading Railroad and Coal Company, for example, organized and manned by the Pinkerton Detective Agency, that finally destroyed the Molly Maguires.[20]

The success of Gowen's Coal and Iron Police led other industrialists to create similar forces. The Pinkerton Detective Agency, under the leadership of Allan Pinkerton, became the best-known agency among many to provide private guards and labor spies for management. Had the private corporation guards been used to protect property they would have earned less enmity from organized labor. Corporations, however, used private police not only as security forces but also as a means of harassing unions, to spy and act as agents *provocateurs*. During strikes and lockouts, the Coal and Iron Police often acted with undue severity in dispersing mobs, arresting alleged instigators and securing "evidence" to prove that unions had destroyed property. The presence of these security forces during strikes added one more ingredient to an already volatile mixture of emotion and distrust and certainly contributed to the violence that so often surrounded these disputes.[21]

Most businessmen did not normally employ a large security force, but in times of strikes and lockouts they hired large numbers of private guards. Between 1877 and 1892, the Pinkerton Preventive Patrol provided security forces to corporations in at least seventy strikes. The agency advertised in a circular to business firms that "we respectfully call the attention of those in charge of . . . railroads, and all other corporations who have to deal with large numbers of patrons or disaffected or striking employees, to the advantages of our patrol." Pinkerton never committed his men to a job without receiving police powers from the local government. Thus armed with the law, his men took orders only from the management employing them and arrested union leaders and strikers.[22]

The presence of private industrial guards in any strike contributed greatly to the incidence and intensity of violence in labor-management confrontation. A Senate investigation committee studying the matter in 1892 reported, "Every man who testified, including the proprietors of the detective agencies, admitted that the workmen were strongly prejudiced against the so-called Pinkertons, and that their presence at a strike serves unduly to inflame the passion of the strikers."[23] Eugene Debs characterized the Pinkertons as "a motley gang of vagabonds mustered from the slums of the great cities; pimps and parasites, outcasts, abandoned wretches of every grade; a class of characterless cut-throats who murder for hire; creatures in the form of humans but heartless as stones."[24] Laborers who fought Pinkertons became heroes in the eyes of most workingmen, and corporations employing them were depicted as arrogant plutocrats quite willing to use any method to grind down the workers of America.[25]

It is hardly surprising that laborers disliked Pinkertons and other private guards. What was important was the intensity of that feeling and how these emotions contributed to violence. As the *National Labor Tribune* stressed, "The unwritten law of organized labor is that the employment of Pinkerton means 'war to the knife.' "[26] Labor and reform groups mounted a campaign to have either the states or the federal government place a ban on the use of private guards in industry. The campaign proved effective. In 1892, during congressional investigations, many congressmen voiced approval for outlawing Pinkertons and their like, as did journals such as *Harper's Weekly*. After 1892, a number of states banned the use of all types of private police in labor disputes.[27]

While the private guard system came into disrepute in the early 1890s, the problem of how management could protect its property during labor troubles remained. The *Nation* contended that the property owner had the right to use any means necessary to protect his property when the constituted authorities failed to do so, and a House report on the Homestead affair of 1892 said that in most cases the use of private guards in labor disorders "has largely grown out of the sloth and dilatoriness of the civil authorities to render efficient and prompt protection to persons and property in such cases."[28] If the property owner had a right to protection, yet could not hire private guards, and local officials failed to cope with civil disorder, what recourse was there?

The *Railroad Trainmen's Journal* spoke for many when it pointed out that "The national guard of each state is thoroughly competent to protect the interests of its people."[29] Labor's strong reaction to the Pinkertons' actions at the Homestead strike in 1892 made the use of the National Guard in labor troubles appear attractive. Support for the *Trainmen's Journal* suggestion could be found in many labor journals in 1892. But previous experience had shown that during labor conflicts labor did not always see the Guard in such a favorable light. And what of the future? Robert A. Pinkerton, Allan's son and a partner in the firm, testified during the Homestead investigation that

> the enmity which the labor organizations have against our
> agency would exist against any person attempting to protect the
> property of employers and the lives of nonunion workers.
> Whomever may be thus employed, whether private watchmen,
> or the police, or the militia or the Federal troops, the ani-
> mosity against them will be just as strong as is now shown
> against our agency.[30]

No matter how self-serving Pinkerton's testimony was, his words proved to be correct. The basic legal and philosophical beliefs of late nineteenth-century America, which made the road to economic and political equality so difficult for the laboring man, provided a background predisposed to conflict and often violence, regardless of the peace-keeping agency involved.[31]

The condition of the states' militias in the early 1870s merely enhanced the probabilities for violence, as they were poorly trained, equipped, and organized for riot duty. As late as 1877, one contemporary observed that "the United States militia may be said to be almost valueless in a strictly military point of view." Noting that some states had attempted to refurbish their military forces, he nonetheless concluded that "all these efforts have so far failed of any important success."[32] By the close of the nineteenth century, state militias, most now bearing the name "National Guard," presented a far different picture. Every state had revised its military laws in the interim, giving the state far more control over local volunteer companies, centralizing administrative supervision in the office of the state adjutant general, and increasing state financial support considerably.[33]

The need to supplement public and private police agencies in maintaining or restoring order during domestic disorders spurred the states to show an interest in their state soldiers. Tradition sanctioned the use of the National Guard as a keeper of the civic peace; "its primary object was, and still is, to aid the civil authorities in maintaining the law within the States, in those cases where the ordinary means—the sheriff, the constable, and the police—are insufficient."[34] Since the eighteenth century, both the enrolled militia and the volunteers had acted in times of flood and fire, policed slavery in the South, quelled political riots, and enforced the law when necessary. It was no novel idea in the late nineteenth century to turn to state militias to restore order in civil disturbances.[35]

The postwar organized militia fared little better than local police forces in meeting the first significant outbreak of discontented workers. Most states were unprepared to deal with the widespread disorder during the largely spontaneous railroad strikes of 1877. Some states lacked any organized militia at all, others had extreme difficulty in mobilizing existing forces, while still others, most notably West Virginia and Pennsylvania, found their militiamen openly fraternizing with strikers. In the aftermath of these tumultuous events, the press castigated the militia almost as severely as the strikers. *The Army and Navy Journal* lambasted "the utter hollowness and insufficiency of our whole militia system."[36] *The New York Times* echoed the sentiment when it noted that "under the first serious trial they have endured, apart from the Civil War, they have ignominiously broken down."[37]

A popular clamor for a reorganization of the militia appeared even before the 1877 strikes came to an end. "What is . . . wanted," *Leslie's Weekly* editorialized, "is pluckier men in civil authority, and a militia so organized and drilled and trusted as to be effective in emergency."[38] *Harper's Weekly* demanded "that henceforth the State militia must be an army trained for war, or the security of order is gone."[39] In the years after 1877, the views of the editor of the *United Service* were repeated in various forms as an explanation for the rise of the National Guard:

> The labor riots of 1877, direful as were the events . . . may yet prove a blessing in disguise. In so saying we refer to the unmistakeable change for the better which has taken place within the last two years in the organization and training of the militia in many of the states, and which is directly traceable to the experiences of the eventful summer of the year mentioned.[40]

National Guard advocates, particularly the adjutants general of the states, eagerly seized upon the 1877 riots and other labor disorders to justify to their governors and legislatures the need for more appropriations. Besieged corporate officials added their voices to the call. Local leaders also saw a revived militia as a way out of the politically dangerous business of forcing one's constituents to behave properly. In some states, Pennsylvania and Washington are two well-documented examples, corporate leaders moved to ensure that only the "right stripe" of men commanded and served in the National Guard. In other states, Nebraska and Wisconsin for instance, big businessmen merely supported increased spending on the service without attempting to dominate it directly. Usually National Guard officers did not actively seek strike duty, but political support for increased appropriations came from those who wanted a military force capable of suppressing domestic disorder. Politically wise Guardsmen cultivated that desire.[41]

Furthermore, few National Guard officers had much sympathy for the goals and methods of organized labor or any intuitive feeling for the frustrations of unorganized workers. Most officers, who remained in the service far longer than most enlisted men and controlled its operations, were middle-class professionals, merchants, and politicians. If they were sometimes wary of the more outrageous behavior of big businessmen, they still cherished orderly change, the unfettered movement of the individual in the labor market, and the sanctity of private property, values that so circumscribed industrial workers. *The National Guardsman,* voice of the New York National Guard, stated perhaps overdramatically, the view of many:

> The volcano of Communism burns angrily beneath the thin crust of civil law which holds it in subjection, ready at the slightest provocation to break forth into fiercer flames than ever. It falls to the lot of the young men of the country to stand as a bulwark in times of emergency in defense of liberty and in the preservation of law and order. Their place is in the ranks of the National Guard.[42]

Inevitably, the National Guard took on the image of strikebreaker. Although statistics on strike duty are imprecise, a conservative estimate is that between 1870 and 1900, the National Guard of the several states went on active duty at least one hundred and fifty times to deal with industrial disputes. Many disorders lasted only a short time, and the Guard did little more than parade through the streets or stand by their arms in an armory. In other cases, however, Guardsmen on strike duty spent as much as two months in the field, fought pitched battles with strikers, and in a few instances lost the fight. No other type of domestic disturbance matched the cost, size of force involved, or the intensity of violence as did labor disorders. The states mobilized their military forces for riot duty 328 times in the decade 1885-95; of these instances, 118 involved labor conflicts. The railroad strikes of 1877, the Homestead affair, the coal strike of 1894, and the Pullman strike all brought national attention to the Guard's role in suppressing protesting workers. Lesser known conflicts—the 1886 Milwaukee eight-hour day strike, the Tennessee miners' war of 1891-92, the continual struggle between the Western Federation of Miners and the Colorado National Guard in the late 1890s, or the strike duty records of the Pennsylvania, Ohio, and Illinois National Guards in the Gilded Age—attest to strike duty's central place in the rise of the National Guard.[43]

The press comments of National Guardsmen and some of their supporters enhanced the reality of strike duty, which almost always led to

the workers' defeat. *The National Guardsman* could not refrain from at-
tacking the "lawless demonstrations of ultra-Communism," which it saw
at work in 1877, and continued to fear in 1894, when it pointed out that
labor agitation "not unexpectedly, has called out the worst instincts of the
ignorant unemployed."[44] "Since the railroad, Molly Maguire, and communistic riots, thinking men have been convinced that we need a much
better body of citizen soldier," a Regular Army officer wrote in discussing
"Our Militia."[45] Another Guard supporter declared in 1892 that organized labor within the past six weeks has shown itself to be synonymous
with organized lawlessness," thus justifying in his own eyes the need for
maintaining a well-organized National Guard.[46] Throughout the 1880s
and 1890s, few popular articles discussed the service without at the same
time discussing labor protests generally, and organized labor particularly,
as the source of social disorder.[47]

In the aftermath of the Homestead strike, when 8,000 Pennsylvania
National Guardsmen finished the work begun by Pinkerton guards, labor's
passing support of the National Guard dissolved. *The Cigar Maker's Journal*
bemoaned the fact that "if the Pinkertons were shut out, it seems the
militia steps in . . . to overawe and shoot the men into abject submission."[48]
Justifiably, working people saw the National Guard as a tool of the corporations. Even when no violence attended a strike, the militia's "guns
and bayonets are brought into play for the purpose of terrorizing the
strikers and intimidating them . . . to return to work at the bosses figure."[49]
Most union journals agreed with the *Miner's Magazine* that "the state
militia under present industrial conditions is a weapon of barbarism, wielded
by the employer."[50]

But labor lacked the power to change the way states used the National
Guard. The Knights of Labor called for a repeal of post-Civil War militia
reforms and a return to the antebellum system of a decentralized, locally
controlled, volunteer militia. Barring that, "we demand the abolition of
the militia of the various States." The demand went unheeded.[51]

The most consistent approach that organized labor adopted toward the
National Guard in the 1890s was to mount a campaign urging workingmen to boycott the service. Terence V. Powderly urged workers to "look
carefully through the ranks of the soldiers, scan well the forms and faces
of the men who defend . . . the property of the millionaire, and you will
find no millionaires or sons of millionaires. They are all workingmen, sons
of workingmen and merchants." Powderly then advised, "do not enlist

in either the State militias or regular army."[52] Another union editorialist spoke more strongly: "For myself, I have no patience with, nor respect for, the trade unionist who would attach himself to any branch of the State militia."[53] By the mid-1890s, many unions went beyond exhortation, banning National Guardsmen from joining their organizations and automatically expelling any union members who served in the National Guard.[54]

The union boycott did not affect the National Guard in any substantial way, nor did it succeed in keeping workingmen out of the service. Organized labor represented a very small portion of workers, and its journalistic campaign failed to move most workingmen from quitting their Guard activities. Samuel Gompers may have been correct in branding the National Guard as "a machine of monopolistic oppression against labor," but he also should have recognized that the stokers manning the machine were overwhelmingly workingmen.[55]

As the intensity of the labor effort to get and keep workers out of the Guard indicated, a majority of enlisted Guardsmen came from the working class. Labor journals consistently noted this fact, as did the observations of others writing on the service. Ironically, for example, the Fourteenth Regiment of the Pennsylvania National Guard, which aided in ousting steel strikers at Homestead, was composed mostly of ironworkers. Detailed studies of state military forces are sparse, but the few available substantiate the impressionistic evidence. In the 1880s, 60 percent of Wisconsin National Guardsmen were workers, including machinists, lumber mill workers, iron molders, and railroad men; so, too, were 50 percent of New Jersey enlisted men in 1896. Continued working-class participation in the National Guard, despite that institution's central role in the suppression of labor disorders, suggests that workers found state military service appealing, regardless of the Guard's strikebreaking record.[56]

Commentators on the Guard were nonetheless concerned about the attitudes of workingmen in the rank and file. As demonstrated in 1877, and again in California and Washington in 1894, Guardsmen sometimes displayed sympathy for workers when called out to restore order. Fears that working-class Guardsmen would allow their class feelings to override the demands of law and order were misplaced. The issue was of a different order. "No law or codes can prevent the common soldier from imbibing the principles and prejudices of the men they constantly associate with in their daily walks," Pennsylvania Governor John F. Hartranft pointed out in explaining the behavior of some of his Guardsmen in 1877.[57] It was asking a great deal of men to have them confront their neighbors with guns and bayonets and compel them to accept things as they were. "Such things are not military, they are political and social," Hartranft stressed.[58] Regardless of the advice of Major Winthrop Alexander, District of Columbia National Guard, that "the officer or soldier has no . . . right to question the wisdom or justice of enforcing . . . laws," Guardsmen sometimes could not help but respond first to "the principles and prejudices" of their fellow men. Workers could thus exhibit a lack of class consciousness by joining a military service whose principal raison d'être was to act as an industrial constabulary and yet display considerable sympathy for strikers in certain instances. Although most Guardsmen were workers, their behavior during strike duty was not determined by their sense of class but by circumstances.[59]

Generally the Guard performed effectively as a constabulary force in controlling or suppressing labor disorders in the late nineteenth century. At times, however, the tensions and conflicts of industrial social turmoil overcame the service's ability or willingness to put down disorderly workers. The National Guard was the last organized agency of force within the states to suppress disorder, and when it failed state officials turned to the federal government for military assistance. Except for the direct intervention of the Cleveland administration in the railroad strike of 1894, it was by this process that federal military forces entered the struggle between capital and labor.[60]

The Constitution, Article IV, Section 4, guaranteed federal assistance to the states when the latter could not cope with domestic disorder. Federal law authorized the president to use militia and the land and naval forces of the United States "to suppress such insurrection" when the legislature of a state so requested, or when the legislature was not in session and not easily convened, upon the call of the governor. Precedent had established that a state requesting federal military aid had to exhaust all efforts and resources in quelling the disturbance before turning to Washington. The law did not require the president to respond to a state's call for aid, stating that "it shall be lawful for the President" to do so. The law and the power of the presidency left the matter wholly to the chief executive's discretion.

Federal law also authorized the president to use the militia, Army, and Navy to enforce federal law in the states and territories when riot or rebellion prevented civilian federal officials from doing so. A similar statute gave the same authority to prevent the loss of constitutional rights during domestic violence. In all three cases, the Revised Statutes applying to the suppression of insurrection required, when federal troops were used to aid civil authorities, that "the President shall forthwith, by proclamation, command the insurgents to disperse and retire peaceably to their respective abodes."[61]

Despite the growing frequency of labor disorders after 1877, Congress made no attempt to deal with their underlying causes; neither did it make any effort to provide the executive or the judiciary with general policy guidelines within which to act. The executive developed no consistent practice either and responded to calls for military assistance from state officials and civilian federal officers on an ad hoc basis, in the face of immediate crisis. Sometimes presidents granted the requests; at other times they denied them. In the 1880s and 1890s, the federal judiciary began to formulate a labor policy of sorts in the form of the injunction. The judicial approach did not really solve the problem of labor disorders so much as place greater constraints on organized labor than already existed under state and local laws protecting private property. In effect, there was no federal policy governing the use of federal troops in labor conflicts between 1877 and 1900.

Throughout the late nineteenth century, presidents justified using federal forces in labor disturbances in the name of law and order. Pressured by beleaguered state officials or worried corporate leaders, Presidents Hayes, Harrison, Cleveland, and McKinley reluctantly committed federal troops in the name of the law, making little or no effort to consider the causes of upheaval or to formulate policy that might lessen the likelihood of future outbreaks. In each instance they allowed others—state politicians, corporation officers, cabinet members, congressmen, and senators—to define the necessity for intervention. No president deemed it wise or necessary to send independent observers, be it an Army officer, cabinet member, or other federal officer not immediately located in the disturbed area, to report on the advisability of a federal presence.

The lack of policy and the failure of presidents to scrutinize personally the need for federal intervention did not allow the commander-in-chief to provide military officers with a clear sense of purpose while in the field. No president intended to use the Army as a force of Cossacks to suppress ruthlessly an unwieldy and wild industrial proletariat. Indeed, presidents who authorized federal military intervention generally took great care to ensure that they met the letter of the law and that the responsible military commanders understood the limits of that law. Having no larger intent for intervention than restoring order and enforcing the law, however, meant that presidential commitment of military force inevitably placed the Army on the side of capital in the industrial warfare of the late nineteenth century.[62]

Notes

1. John R. Commons et al., *History of Labour in the United States*, vol. 2 (New York, 1918), pp. 43-47, 86-87, 151-81; U.S. Industrial Commission, *Final Report of the Industrial Commission,* vol. 19 of the Commission's, reports, 57th Cong., 1st sess., House Document 380, pp. 864-65, 877; U.S., Department of Labor, *Strikes in the United States, 1880-1936,* prepared for the Bureau of Labor Statistics by Florence Peterson, Bulletin no. 651 (Washington, D.C., 1938), pp. 18-25. Also see Thomas R. Brooks, *Toil and Trouble: A History of American Labor,* 2nd ed. rev. (New York, 1971), pp. 40-46; Melvyn Dubofsky, *Industrialism and the American Worker, 1865-1920* (New York, 1975), pp. 50-51.

2. For contemporary discussions of the rights of labor in the late nineteenth century, see F. J. Stimson, *Labor and Its Relation to the Law* (New York, 1895), pp. 47-51, 56-59, 80-84, 91-98; and T. M. Cooley, "Labor and Capital Before the Law," *North American Review* 139, no. 337 (December 1884): 503-16. Secondary discussions of value here are John R. Commons and John B. Andrews, *Principles of Labor Legislation* (New York, 1920), pp. 101-13; J. Bernard Hogg, "Public Reaction to Pinkertonism and the Labor Question," *Pennsylvania History* 2, no. 3 (July 1944): 184-85, 195-99; Edward C. Kirkland, *Industry Comes of Age: Business, Labor and Public Policy, 1860-1897* (Chicago, 1967), pp. 353-56, 374-77; Gerald G. Eggert, *Railroad Labor Disputes: The Beginnings of Federal Strike Policy* (Ann Arbor, 1967), pp. 78, 227-28, 236-38; Arnold M. Paul, *Conservative Crisis and the Rule of Law: Attitudes of Bar and Bench, 1887-1895* (Ithaca, N.Y., 1960), pp. 6-18, 105-07.

3. Stimson, *Labor and Its Relation to Law,* p. 56.

4. Rufus Hatch et al., "The Labor Crisis," *North American Review* 142, no. 355 (June 1886): 605. For similar views, see the comments of Henry Clews in the same article, pp. 598-601; Austin Corbin, "The Tyranny of Labor Organizations," *Ibid.* 149, no. 395 (October 1889): 414-15.

5. See note 2.

6. Herbert G. Gutman, "The Worker's Search for Power: Labor in the Gilded Age," in *The Gilded Age: A Re-Appraisal*, ed. H. Wayne Morgan (Syracuse, N.Y., 1963), pp. 39-47, and "Work, Culture, and Society in Industrial America, 1815-1919," *American Historical Review* 78, no. 3 (June 1973): 569-76, 581-85.

7. Clews, in Hatch, "The Labor Crisis," p. 601.

8. David Dudley Field et al., "Solutions of the Labor Problem," *North American Review* 156, no. 434 (January 1893): 63. Also see Corbin, "The Tyranny of Labor Organizations," pp. 415-18.

9. Clews, in Hatch, "The Labor Crisis," p. 598, for the first quotation; *Ibid.*, p. 606 for the second.

10. "Lessons of the Recent Strike," *North American Review* 159, no. 453 (August 1894): 195. On the Molly Maguire affair, see Wayne G. Broehl, Jr., *The Molly Maguires* (Cambridge, Mass., 1964); and Marvin W. Schlegel, *Ruler of the Reading: The Life of Franklin Gowen, 1836-1889* (Harrisburg, Pa., 1947), pp. 97-127, 139-44.

11. Vol. 1, no. 4 (July 28, 1894): 130.

12. July 13, 1894, p. 4.

13. Field, "Solutions of the Labor Problem," p. 66.

14. July 10, 1877, p. 387.

15. Vol. 1, no. 7 (September 1894): 140.

16. Class-conscious language and imagery appeared with increasing frequency in labor journals after 1880. See, for example, *American Federationist* 1, no. 6 (August 1894): 115; *The Altruist* 24, no. 7 (April 1892): 26; *National Labor Tribune* 22, no. 35 (August 1892): 1; *Chicago Labor* 1, no. 41 (April 28, 1894): 4; *Miner's Magazine* 3, no. 1 (January 1902): 32.

17. Gutman, "The Worker's Search for Power," pp. 39-41, and "Work, Culture, and Society," pp. 567-76, 581. On the violence attending labor-management relations in the late nineteenth century, see Philip Taft and Philip Ross, "American Labor Violence: Its Cause, Character and Outcome," in *Violence in America: Historical and Comparative Perspectives*, ed. Hugh D. Graham and Ted R. Gurr, Report to the National Commission on the Causes and Prevention of Violence, June 1969 (New York, 1969), pp. 270-74, 289, 362-65.

18. Bruce Smith, *Police Systems in the United States*, 2nd ed. rev. (New York, 1960), pp. 70-80; Hogg, "Public Reaction to Pinkertonism," pp. 171-72. To date, no adequate history of law enforcement in the United States exists. See also U.S., Congress, Senate, Select Committee, *Facts in Relation to the Employment for Private Purposes of Armed Bodies of*

Men, or Detectives, in Connection with Differences between Workmen and Employers, 52nd Cong., 2nd sess., S. Rept. 1280 (Washington, D.C., 1893), pp. iv-v, on the weakness of the *posse comitatus* in dealing with labor disturbances, hereafter referred to as *S. Rept. 1280.*

19. Smith, *Police Systems in the U.S.,* pp. 105-06; James F. Richardson, *Urban Police in the United States* (Port Washington, N.Y., 1974), chaps. 2, 3, esp. pp. 50-53; Blake McKelvey, *The Urbanization of America, 1860-1915* (New Brunswick, N.J., 1963), pp. 92-96.

20. J. P. Shalloo, *Private Police: With Special Reference to Pennsylvania* (Philadelphia, 1933), pp. 1-3, 28-29, 41-42, 58-61; Schlegel, *Ruler of the Reading,* pp. 91, 139-44, 151-52; Broehl, *The Molly Maguires,* pp. 352-53, 360; *S. Rept. 1280,* pp. 61, 225; U.S., Congress, House, Committee on the Judiciary, *Employment of Pinkerton Detectives,* 52nd Cong., 2nd sess., H. Rept. 2447 (Washington, D.C., 1893), p. 207, hereafter referred to as *H. Rept. 2447.*

21. *H. Rept. 2447;* there is no scholarly treatment of the growth of such detective agencies and the roles they played in the labor troubles of the nineteenth century. James D. Horan has written several popular books on the exploits of Allan Pinkerton and his firm. Most of these are uncritical and border on hero worship. See his *The Pinkertons: The Detective Dynasty that Made History* (New York, 1967), pp. 328-35, on how the agency became involved in labor conflicts.

22. *S. Rept. 1280,* pp. 47-49, 61-62; *H. Rept. 2447,* pp. v-ix; U.S. Ind. Comm., *Final Report,* vol. 19, pp. 890-91.

23. *S. Rept. 1280,* p. xii. There is much evidence to support this contention of the inflammatory effect of these guards. See *Ibid.,* pp. 109-15; *H. Rept. 2447,* pp. xviii-xxvi; Horan, *The Pinkertons,* p. 335; U.S., Justice Department, Attorney General, *Annual Report of the Attorney General of the United States for the Year 1896; Appendix,* 54th Cong., 2nd sess., House Executive Document 9(Washington, D.C., 1896), pp. 118-19.

24. *Locomotive Firemen's Magazine* 16, no. 8 (August 1892): 728. See similar sentiments in *Locomotive Engineer's Journal* 26, no. 8 (August 1892): 751-52.

25. B. O. Flower, "The Menace of Plutocracy," *Arena* 6, no. 34 (September 1892): 513-15; *The Railway Conductor* 9, no. 9 (September 1892): 363-64; *Journal of the Knights of Labor* 13, no. 5 (July 28, 1892): 5 and vol. 13, no. 6 (August 4, 1892): 4; Norman Pollack, *The Populist Response to Industrial America* (New York, 1966), pp. 57-58.

26. Vol. 20, no. 31 (July 23, 1892): p. 1. Also see *Journal of the Knights of Labor* 13, no. 4 (July 21, 1892): 2.

27. *Harper's Weekly* 36, no. 1857 (July 23, 1892): 698; *The Railway Conductor* 9, no. 5 (May 1892): 203; *Railroad Trainmen's Journal* 9, no. 101 (July 1892): 481-82; *United Mine Worker's Journal* 2, no. 14 (July 14, 1892): 2-3; *H. Rept. 2447*, pp. xvii-xxvi. Pinkertons are also condemned in Chauncy F. Black, "The Lesson of Homestead: A Remedy for Labor Troubles," *The Forum* 14 (September 1892): 1-25.

28. *H. Rept. 2447*, p. xv. See *The Nation* 55, no. 1411 (July 14, 1892): 22, and no. 1413 (July 28, 1892): 60.

29. Vol. 9, no. 101 (July 1892): 481.

30. *S. Rept. 1280*, p. 241.

31. For labor and radical support for replacing Pinkertons with the National Guard, see Flower, "The Menace of Plutocracy," p. 515; *Cleveland Citizen* 2, no. 76 (July 9, 1892): 2; *National Labor Tribune* 20, no. 29 (July 9, 1892): 1; *Railroad Trainmen's Journal* 9, no. 101 (July 1892): 482. See also *Harper's Weekly* 36, no. 1857 (July 23, 1892): p. 698; 698: *The Washington Post*, July 7, 1892, p. 4.

32. F. N. Whitaker, "The American Army," *The Galaxy* 24, no. 3 (September 1877): 390-91. On the postwar condition of the volunteers, see William H. Riker, *Soldiers of the States: The Role of the National Guard in American Democracy* (Washington, D.C., 1957), pp. 42-47.

33. Martha Derthick, *The National Guard in Politics* (Cambridge, Mass., 1965), chap. 1; Riker, *Soldiers of the States,* pp. 47-57; Frederick P. Todd, "Our National Guard: An Introduction to its History," *Military Affairs* 5 (1941): 156-63; Louis Cantor, "The Creation of the Modern National Guard: The Dick Act of 1903" (Ph.D. diss., Duke University, 1963), chaps 1, 2.

34. Francis V. Greene, "The New National Guard," *Century Magazine,* n.s., vol. 21, no. 4 (February 1892): 496. Also see H. M. Boies, "Our National Guard," *Harper's New Monthly Magazine* 60, no. 360 (May 1880): 916: Lloyd S. Bryce, "A Service of Love," *North American Review* 145, no. 370 (September 1887): 277; John A. T. Hull, "The Organization of the Army," *North American Review* no. 509 (April 1899): 391; T. F. Rodenbough, "Militia Reform Without Legislation," *Journal of the Military Service Institute of the United States* 2, no. 8 (1882): 390, hereafter referred to as *JMSI*. Colonel Ernest MacPherson, Kentucky State Guard, "Comment and Criticism," *JMSI* 13, no. 60 (November 1892): 1174.

35. On the early uses of the militia in domestic peace keeping, see John K. Mahon, *The American Militia: Decade of Decision, 1789-1800* (Gainesville, Fla., 1960), chaps. 4, 5. Robert W. Coakley, "Federal Uses of Militia and the National Guard in Civil Disturbances," Jim Dan Hill,

"The National Guard in Civil Disorders," and Clarence C. Clendenon, "Super-Police: The National Guard as a Law-Enforcement Agency in Civil Disturbances," all in *Bayonets in the Streets: The Use of Troops in Civil Disorders*, ed. Robin Higham (Manhattan, Kan., 1969), pp. 22-28, 61-79, 85-112, respectively.

36. Vol. 14, no. 51 (July 28, 1877): 816.

37. July 25, 1877, p. 4. Also see *Chicago Tribune,* July 26, 1877, p. 4; *Baltimore American,* July 28, 1877, p. 2; *St. Louis Dispatch,* August 1, 1877, p. 2; *Leslie's Illustrated Weekly,* August 25, 1877, p. 414; *Harper's Weekly,* Aug. 11, 1877, p. 618.

38. August 11, 1877, p. 382.

39. August 11, 1877, p. 618.

40. Vol. 2, no. 3 (March 1880): 394. See also T. F. Rodenbough, "The Militia of the United States," *United Service* 1, no. 2 (1879): 284; National Guard Association, *Proceedings of the Convention of the National Guards, 1879* (Philadelphia, 1879); Henry P. Mawson, "The National Guard," *Harper's Weekly,* September 3, 1892, p. 858, *Leslie's Illustrated Weekly,* October 11, 1894, p. 229; Boies, "Our National Guard," p. 917; Greene, "The New National Guard," p. 486.

41. For examples of state adjutants general seeking additional funds to meet labor disorders, see John G. Westover, "The Evolution of the Missouri Militia" (Ph.D. diss., University of Missouri, 1949), pp. 181-82; Jerry M. Cooper, "The Wisconsin Militia, 1832-1900" (Master's thesis, University of Wisconsin, 1968), pp. 247-49; Joseph J. Holmes, "The National Guard of Pennsylvania: Policemen of Industry, 1865-1905" (Ph.D. diss., University of Connecticut, 1970), pp. 2-10; and Patrick Henry McLatchy, "The Development of the National Guard of Washington as an Instrument of Social Control, 1854, 1916" (Ph.D. diss., University of Washington, 1973), *passim.* Also see Ronald M. Gephart, "Politicians, Soldiers and Strikers: The Reorganization of the Nebraska Militia and the Omaha Strike of 1882," *Nebraska History* 46, no. 2 (June 1965): 93-94, 100-03; Charles A. Peckham, "The Ohio National Guard and Its Police Duties, 1894," *Ohio History* 83, no. 1 (Winter 1974): 51-56.

42. Vol. 1, no. 2 (September 1, 1877): 30. Also see E. L. Molineux, "Riots in Cities and Their Suppression," *JMSI* 4, no. 16 (1883): 335-36.

43. The number 150 was arrived at by using data in the following: U.S., Congress, House, Committee on the Militia, *Efficiency of the Militia,* 52nd Cong., 1st sess., H. Rept. 754, (Washington, D.C., 1892), pp. 16-20, for the years 1870-85; Major Winthrop Alexander, District of Columbia National Guard, "Ten Years of Riot Duty," *JMSI* 19, no. 82 (July 1896), for the years 1885-95; for the years after 1895, see Report AWC 9744-C,

"Duty Performed by the Organized Militia in Connection with Domestic Disturbances from 1894 to 1908, Inclusive," General Staff, War College Division, Record Group 165, National Archives, Washington, D.C. For an account of one of the most blatantly anti-labor National Guards, see George H. Suggs, Jr., *Colorado's War on Militant Unionism: James H. Peabody and the Western Federation of Miners* (Detroit, 1972).

44. Vol. 1, no. 2 (September 1, 1877): 17, for first quotation; vol. 7, no. 11 (June 15, 1894): 163, for the second.

45. Lt. Col. Thomas M. Anderson, 9th U.S. Infantry, "Our Militia, State or National?" *United Service* 5, no. 1 (July 1881): 27.

46. Mawson, "The National Guard," p. 858.

47. For example, see Molineux, "Riots in Cities and Their Suppression," pp. 335-40; George B. McClellan, "The Militia and the Regular Army," *Harper's New Monthly Magazine* 72, no. 428 (January 1886): 297-301; Alexander, "Ten Years of Riot Duty," pp. 27-30; Captain E. L. Zalinski, "The Army Organization Best Adapted to a Republican Form of Government, which will Ensure an Effective Force," *JMSI* 14, no. 65 (September 1893): 940.

48. Vol. 16, no. 11 (August 1892): 6.

49. *United Mine Worker's Journal* 4, no. 15 (July 19, 1894): 7.

50. Vol. 4, no. 6 (June 1903): 13. See also *Locomotive Fireman's Magazine* 16, no. 9 (September 1892): 773; *The Carpenter* 4, no. 5 (May 1894): 8; *Chicago Labor* 2, no. 8 (September 8, 1894): 6; *Railroad Trainmen's Journal* 11, no. 125 (July 1894): 589, 591-92. For general comments on the labor and militia, see David Levin, "Organized Labor and the Military." (Master's thesis, University of Wisconsin, 1950), pp. 89-103.

51. *Proceedings of the General Assembly of the Knights of Labor,* 16th reg. sess., November, 1892 (Philadelphia, 1892), pp. 85, 86. A similar call for the return of the militia to local control in American Federation of Labor, *Proceedings of 12th Annual Convention, 1892* (Philadelphia, 1892), p. 12.

52. *Journal of the Knights of Labor* 13, no. 9 (August 25, 1892): 1.

53. *American Federationist* 1, no. 2 (April 1894): 28.

54. U.S. Industrial Commission, *Labor Organization, Labor Disputes and Arbitration,* vol. 17 of the Commission's reports, 57th Cong., 1st sess., House Document 186 (Washington, D.C., 1901), pp. 78, 151, 168-69, 276, lists a number of unions that banned militiamen. Also see "Labor Unions and the Militia," *Literary Digest* 23, no. 3 (July 20, 1901): 65. Such labor journals as *The Carpenter* and *American Federationist* also called for such a ban.

55. A. F. of L., *Proceedings of 12th Annual Convention,* p. 12.

56. Cooper, "The Wisconsin Militia," pp. 330-32; on the New Jersey Guard, see Derthick, *The National Guard in Politics,* p. 19. See *Twentieth Century* 9, no. 5 (July 28, 1892): 1, on the 14th Regiment, Pennsylvania National Guard. For comments on workingmen in the militia, see, among many, *National Labor Tribune* 22, no. 29 (July 9, 1892): 1; *United Mine Worker's Journal* 4, no. 15 (July 19, 1894): 7; *American Federationist* 1, no. 2 (April 1894): 27-28; Alexander, "Ten Years of Riot Duty," p. 34.

57. Pennsylvania, Executive, "Annual Message of the Governor of Pennsylvania, Jan. 2, 1878," in *Governor's Message and Reports of the Heads of Departments of the Commonwealth of Pennsylvania, 1877-1878,* vol. 1 (Harrisburg, Pa., 1878), p. 23.

58. *Ibid.,* p. 25.

59. "Ten Years of Riot Duty," p. 33. Hartranft's observations made by others, see, for example, Rodenbough, "The Militia of U.S.," p. 285.

60. On the overall effectiveness of the National Guard, see Alexander, "Ten Years of Riot Duty," and Hill, "The National Guard in Civil Disorders," pp. 61-79.

61. The segments of the Revised Statutes cited here are taken from U.S., Executive, War Department, *Regulations of the Army of The United States and General Orders in Force February 17, 1881,* abridged (Washington, D.C., 1881), pp. 87-91. Portions of the laws and a discussion of their meaning are found in Frederick T. Wilson, *Federal Aid in Domestic Disturbances, 1787-1903,* 57th Cong., 2nd sess., Senate Document 209, (Washington, D.C., 1903), pp. 5-12. Also of value, Bennett M. Rich, *The Presidents and Civil Disorder* (Washington, D.C., 1941), pp. 189-206, and Marlin S. Reichley, "Federal Military Intervention in Civil Disturbances" (Ph.D. diss., Georgetown University, 1939), pp. 174-77. The works by Wilson, Rich, and Reichly also give overviews of how and why federal forces have aided civil officials from 1787 to the twentieth century.

62. Eggert, *Railroad Labor Disputes,* pp. 19-22, 224-32. The preceding two paragraphs are a summary of Eggert's conclusions. While his study pertains only to federal policy in railroad labor problems through 1898, Eggert's valuable observations are valid for the occasions when the federal government intervened in other than railroad labor conflicts.

2 The Regular Army

The Whiskey Rebellion was the only instance when a president relied solely on federalized militia to suppress a domestic disturbance. After 1794, presidents preferred regular troops as the focal point of federal efforts in dealing with social upheavals, although they called on state forces at times as well. The militia appeared less and less, however, when the central government intervened in domestic disorders. Regulars, unaided by militia, dealt with the Mormon troubles in Utah and the struggles over slavery in Kansas in the 1850s, while a combined force of soldiers and Marines ended John Brown's uprising at Harper's Ferry in 1859. The Army enforced civil rights and voting laws during Reconstruction without the assistance of federalized militia. In no instance from 1877 to 1900 did militia or National Guard troops serve the federal government in suppressing domestic disturbances.[1]

The presidents' increasing reliance on federal troops and eventual abandonment of militia reflected in part the federal government's growing power and the Army's institutionalization. Militia inefficiency, the probabilities of militia sympathies with the disaffected, and the difficulties of mobilizing state troops were more important in shaping this policy. As the presidents' key instrument in dealing with domestic disorder, the Army gave commanders-in-chief a force at their immediate command which was far less likely than the National Guard to be in sympathy with disorderly protesters. This was particularly the case after Reconstruction, when labor-related disorders came to be the most significant instances of federal military intervention in civil disturbances. Despite the many problems of organization, administration, and manpower with which the Army had to cope in the late nineteenth century, it did meet the demands placed upon it by chief executives to enforce the civil peace.[2]

The service's postwar condition did not make the task easy. The Army after 1876 only faintly resembled the victorious Grand Army of the Republic. Congress had quickly called for the demobilization of the huge volunteer Union Army in 1866, and then gradually reduced the remaining regular force over the ensuing decade. By 1876, twenty-five regiments of infantry, ten of cavalry, and five artillery regiments made up the Regular Army. Congress set the total enlisted strength at 25,000 men, a figure unchanged until 1898. The use of enlisted men as clerks, hospital corpsmen, ordnance men, quartermasters, and in other noncombatant duties left the effective combat strength at 20,000 rank and file. This manpower policy forced the War Department to man only eight of the authorized ten companies of each regiment, and at that the remaining eight companies were grievously understrength for peacetime duties.[3]

A large part of the Army (all of the cavalry and three-fourths of the infantry) moved west of the Mississippi at the close of Reconstruction. The majority of the artillery continued to serve in the East, scattered in two and three-company posts along the Great Lakes and the Atlantic seaboard. Most of the artillery was equipped as infantry because the coastal artillery posts were small and in disrepair. The size of the Army and its widespread distribution created inefficiency, made maintenance of the small force expensive, and taxed the ingenuity of its leaders to meet the demands placed on the service.[4]

Military leaders and their civilian counterparts in the War Department recognized the negative effects produced by widespread distribution. Commanding General William T. Sherman urged the closing of small posts and the concentration of troops in regimental garrisons. Sherman stressed that with the expansion of railroads in the West troops could be concentrated and yet guarantee protection to remote areas. Every secretary of war and commanding general from 1875 echoed Sherman's recommendations. As late as 1892, however, 70 percent of the Army was stationed west of the Mississippi, and the entire force occupied ninety-six posts throughout the country. The War Department finally began to close down some of the smaller posts in 1895, and concentrate many of the regiments in larger garrisons.[5]

Army manpower policy further lessened the service's efficiency. Faced with monotonous garrison duty, inadequate living conditions, low pay, and the Army's notorious caste system which marked off enlisted men from officers, thousands of the former deserted yearly. In 1868, 10,000

of the allotted 35,000 rank and file went over the hill. The desertion rate
declined sharply in the following years, but 1,000 to 2,000 men deserted
every year until the end of the century. War Department officials attempted
to find a means of halting desertion but never discovered a remedy. A mixture of economically desperate native-born whites, black men, and recruits of foreign birth gave little coherence to the enlisted ranks. Society
as a whole—and a significant portion of the officer corps—looked upon
the rank and file of the service with distaste and distrust.[6]

The service's decentralized and antiquated administrative system contributed to its inefficiency. There were three distinct areas of administration or command, and rarely did the men heading them coordinate their
activities. In theory, the secretary of war controlled and coordinated the
troops of the line and the logistics bureaus, but in fact the system did not
work that way. Politically important but militarily ignorant men all too
often assumed the post. Most post-Reconstruction secretaries of war were
honest, intelligent men, and capable administrators. Few, however, had
any conceptual idea of how the War Department ought to operate. Few-
er still devoted much thought to long-range planning or to creating a uni-
fied, coherent command system.[7]

The chiefs of the logistics bureaus tended to set War Department policy
by default. An ignorant or poorly informed secretary of war turned to
them for advice and guidance. With long-term service in Washington, the
bureau chiefs developed lasting relationships with key congressmen and
were more influential than the better-known line generals. Each bureau
chief was more concerned with the business of his own department than
the overall operations and needs of the Army. The adjutant general, because he kept personnel records and oversaw all military correspondence,
probably had the best overview of anyone in the service, but he had no
authority to exploit that purview. A gulf separated the logistics bureaus
and the line; the former was constantly making decisions that materially
affected the latter's welfare while rarely conferring with them.[8]

Despite his title, the commanding general seldom commanded the
Army *in toto* in peacetime. The post was actually a wartime position,
when the commanding general was expected to lead the field forces in
battle. Little of the service's ongoing operations demanded the commanding general's attention, and the institutional division of power between
the bureaus and the line prevented him from exerting overall control.
The fame and prestige of Generals William T. Sherman (1869-83) and

Philip H. Sheridan (1883-88) failed to overcome the power of the staff and the disinterest of Congress. Sherman especially sought to reform the Army's command system, but in this he failed. Lieutenant General John M. Schofield (1888-95) succeeded in at least establishing a policy of funneling all military correspondence from the president, secretary of war, and the bureaus to the field forces through the commanding general's office. This practice did not add measurably to Schofield's power, but it did give him an overview of the Army's condition, location, and ongoing duties. When Lieutenant General Nelson A. Miles (1895-1903) replaced Schofield, he dropped the practice and exerted little effort to guide the Army's operations.[9]

One element of the Army gave it a sense of cohesion that the administrative system was incapable of providing. This was the officer corps. Whether graduated from West Point, transferred from the wartime volunteer service, appointed directly from civil life, or promoted from the enlisted ranks, officers shared a common purview. The routine of paper work, the daily rhythm of post life, and the influence of Army regulations all socialized officers in the customs and traditions of the service. Even when divided by the disparate duties of the staff bureaus, Corps of Engineers, the Eastern artillery, and the Western line companies, officers remained tied together by the common bond of officership. This bond did not create a monolithic conception of what the service ought to be, nor did it erase the resentments and hostilities between the staff and line. But it did create a sense among all officers that they belonged to a particular calling, serving in a special institution, the Army, whose responsibility was to ensure the nation's defense.[10]

Duty in the Civil War enhanced this commonality. Veterans of the great conflict dominated the upper levels of command through the Spanish-American War. Yearly additions of West Point graduates into the junior ranks after 1865 slowly diluted the percentage of war veterans in the officer corps, but even at the turn of the century few of these new men had reached the rank of captain; none served above that rank in the line regiments. The war experience left a lasting impact on the veterans. For most it had meant that the greatest military experience in their lives came at an early stage in their careers. To those who had commanded corps, divisions, and brigades and had helped create and lead the greatest military force in the nineteenth century, all that followed could only be anti-climactic. Regardless of the resentment between West Pointers and volunteer officers who shared the meager number of appointments in the reduced postwar Army, both groups carried with them the conviction that it was they who had preserved the nation after pettifogging and inept politicians had nearly destroyed it. This powerful sense of nationalism and of the Army's special place in the nation's history contributed to the cohesion of the officer corps.[11]

Graduates of the United States Military Academy added to that coherence. Second only to the all-pervasive "customs and traditions of the service," the West Point perspective shaped the officer corps. Academy graduates did not dominate the corps in total numbers until the very close of the century, but their influence was substantial. Of the five commanding generals after 1865, for example, only one, Nelson A. Miles, was not an Academy graduate. The education provided by the Academy was not primarily responsible for this influence. West Point did not teach an overall theory of war nor cultivate introspective thought in cadets. It did teach a highly technical, engineering-oriented curriculum, supported with a heavy dose of company-level tactics. Its emphasis on rote learning and class recitation from memory hardly encouraged intellectual curiosity or the desire to plow new ground in military thought.[12]

What West Point did provide was discipline, a strong sense of order, and a deep commitment to the institution it served, the Army. Cadets were immersed in a routine whereby the Academy determined practically every detail of their daily lives. They were to give obedience to their superiors and all of their time to West Point. The System unquestionably circumscribed the individual cadet's personal impulses and desires, but it also generated an intense loyalty to the service. In its first ninety-four years, only eleven of 3,741 graduates did not take commissions. There were 1,945 living graduates in 1902, and 1,630 of them were still in the Army. It was this sense of commitment and loyalty to the service and to those who had shared the West Point experience that Academy graduates took with them as they entered active duty.[13]

West Point not only inculcated a sense of discipline and order but also reinforced a social point of view. Officers were gentlemen. They did not develop social intimacy with enlisted men. Officers cultivated the manly virtues: physical fitness, cleanliness, frugality, moderation in drink, and Protestant morality. The nineteenth-century conception of the social aspects of officership was quintessentially middle-class. "There are a great many not very genteel people in the army now," Lieutenant Charles

McClure wrote his mother in 1877. "But we hope as time rolls on to
bring the respectability to a higher standard."[14] Respectability was the
key word. Lieutenant McClure was upset with the number of ungentleman-
ly and unrespectable officers brought into the Army from the volunteer
service of the early 1860s. The passage of time and the introduction of
West Point graduates would correct that weakness in the officer corps.[15]

While not colored with the tinge of aristocracy reflected by many mid-
shipmen at the United States Naval Academy, the vast majority of cadets
at West Point came from the middle and upper classes. Sons of merchants,
professional men, businessmen, politicians, and farmers and planters of
varying degrees of success comprised two-thirds of all cadets entering the
military academy in the nineteenth century. Officers commissioned from
West Point as well as those appointed from civil life not only came from
the middle and upper classes, but were overwhelmingly native-born, of
northern European ethnic heritage, and Protestant. Their socioeconomic
background differed little from the men who ran the economic and
political institutions of the nation. Given the fact that appointments to
West Point and commissions from civil life demanded that the prospective
officer have an entree to political influence, it was only natural that the
military elite would reflect the governing classes.[16]

It was evident as well that a West Point education did not alter a graduate's social values so as to make him a stranger in civil society. Much
of the social life at Army posts was a reflection of genteel society. Dances,
theatrical groups, literary readings, teas, and dinners filled the social lives
of officers and their families. When posted to staff headquarters in Washington and other cities, or when detailed to colleges and the National
Guard as military instructors, officers and their wives did not find it difficult to meld into the local social scene. Lieutenant McClure found life at
the headquarters of the Department of Dakota at St. Paul, Minnesota
quite pleasant. "The army people here are refined and very nice, and know
how to entertain nicely. The people look up to them."[17]

Neither did a West Point education educate a man so narrowly that he
could find no civilian employment once he left the service. The majority
of retired Army officers found no difficulty in winning elections, fitting
into corporate business life, or joining the faculties of colleges and uni-
versities. The engineering and managerial skills of West Point-educated
officers were always welcomed in the civilian economy. In reviewing the
Academy's accomplishments in its first one hundred years, one West

Pointer proudly summed up "The Services of Graduates in Civil Life," stating that "we must admit that the mental training which the cadets receive does enable them not only to perform their military duties . . . but also to meet the requirements of civil life in its widest variation in a manner of which we may all feel proud."[18] A fellow graduate believed that these accomplishments in civil life were "a convincing refutation of the assertation that a military education unfits for civil functions and occupations."[19]

The officer corps of the Army may have shared a common social background and perspective with the middle and upper classes of late nineteenth-century America, but it still perceived itself as a group apart from the rest of society. Despite the service's central role in crushing rebellion, the Army lost its sense of identification with the mass of the citizenry in the years after the war. The Army's role in Reconstruction eroded public support, in part because of the cost but more generally because military force was used to support a social and political program most white Americans cared little for. "The grand mistake of the whole reconstruction period as regards the army was that force was used for a purpose foreign to the spirit of a republican government," an otherwise friendly Army supporter concluded.[20]

More importantly, officers felt isolated from civilians because they had committed themselves to a lifetime career in a line of work viewed with distaste by most Americans. The majority of civilians not only feared the threats a standing army posed to a democratic society but also doubted the necessity of supporting a large force of trained military professionals. The old Jacksonian dislike for specialized occupations persisted, supported by the likes of John A. Logan and Ben Butler who tramped the land denouncing aristocratic West Pointers. The long-standing American belief in the efficiency of citizen soldiers over professionals, so well symbolized in the recently demobilized Grand Army, continued to shape American perceptions of the Regular Army.[21]

Conversely, life in the service tended to encourage officers to view their civilian counterparts with a certain amount of envy and dislike. Gone were the war days of public praise and support, Major General O. O. Howard lamented, and "our people, little by little, have fallen back into the old ways of doing and thinking."[22] The postwar Army offered limited opportunity for promotion, glory, or monetary reward. Promotion came slowly in the reduced Army, there being no mandatory retirement age until 1882 (set at 64). Early in the 1890s, Congress attempted to open up promotion by allowing advancement within each branch of the service rather than within each regiment. This did not solve the problem, for the static size of the Army simply did not provide room for promotion. Consequently, "a very large proportion of all the intermediate grades are much too old for their rank."[23]

Officers felt frustrated not only because of stagnant promotion but also because they believed they were not sufficiently rewarded for their services. Basic pay ranged from $1,400 annually for new second lieutenants to $7,500 for a major general. The government also provided officers with quarters, fuel, and forage for horses. One civilian observer believed that officers received an income "reasonably on a par with the professional incomes of other callings throughout the republic."[24] But military pay did not react to inflation, nor was it adjusted to the higher cost of living west of the Mississippi. Officers bore the cost of moving their families when transferred. The quarters provided by the Army at many military posts were often little better than hovels, and few officers could afford to pay the cost of improving them. Above all, a military career promised no opportunity for rapid advancement or a quick increase in wealth. If only a tiny minority of civilians rose from clerk to millionaire in business, no one could expect to do so in the Army.[25]

Thwarted ambition may have been the most gnawing of all the officers' concerns. As sons of the middle class, they were imbued with the gospel of success. But they had also chosen to commit themselves to an institution sharply circumscribed by the rest of society. Officers had chosen a career where glory and advancement came in abnormal times, during war. Paradoxically, men who desired to make a mark in a service governed by tradition, subordination of self, and seniority had to go outside sanctioned channels to do so. The most ambitious of officers sought to use political and social connections to gain transfers from the line to the staff, to receive assignments to college duty, to be detailed as instructors to the National Guard, or other desirable service away from the regiments. "Few out of the military service can form the slightest idea of the fatal blows discipline and efficiency have received" from the quest for political preferment, Brigadier General John Gibbon complained.[26]

The contrasts between a military career in the late nineteenth century and the opportunities for educated men in the burgeoning civilian economy were marked. Indian warfare was often physically taxing and challenging for the moment but rarely offered opportunities to test the managerial skills of most officers. Furthermore, General Sherman reported in 1883, "I now regard the Indians substantially eliminated as a problem of the Army."[27] The monotony of garrison duty induced lethargy and apathy in many of the older officers. Though General Gibbon complained that "requisitions, returns, reports, board proceedings, in duplicate, triplicate and quadruplicate block army administration in every direction," many took comfort in the routinized paperwork. "Most of the older officers scoffed at study," another officer remembered. "They did not believe in books; they claimed that such things were for the ignorant, that they had graduated in the school of war."[28]

While some were content with the status quo, other officers, mindful of dramatic changes taking place in contemporary European armies, were not. The discontented sought to find ways to reform their service so as to give meaning to their work, to make the Army a more effective instrument for waging war, and to provide themselves with greater opportunity for success and achievement. Specifically, Army reformers wanted to professionalize their occupation. Under the tutelage of William T. Sherman and the intellectual stimulation of Colonel Emory Upton, a growing portion of the officer corps came to argue that planning for war and conducting warfare called for an expertise that could be developed only through years of training and study. The need to cultivate this expertise demanded that only those who understood the special nature of warfare, professional soldiers, should control the education, training, and maintenance of the nation's military forces. While not always explicit about it, Army advocates of professionalism believed that they should oversee the internal operations of the service, determine its functions, and reward and punish themselves and their fellow officers according to ethics and rules determined by professional standards. Military reformers continued to defer to their civilian superiors in larger matters of policy but insisted that the nature of warfare had evolved beyond the point where amateur citizen soldiers and make-shift institutional arrangements could cope with it. To deny professional guidance in military matters, they argued, was to court disaster.[29]

The military quest for professionalism paralleled similar developments in medicine, the law, education, engineering, and other specialized occupations in the late nineteenth and early twentieth centuries. Before 1900, however, officers calling for reforms in the Army gained few of their objectives. Latent fears of a standing army were restimulated when it became apparent that many of the reformers' proposals were first adopted in the Prussian army. Part-time citizen soldiers of the newly revived state militia, the National Guard, objected to reforms that would relegate them to a third-line status. Opposition also came from the logistical staff bureaus as staff officers feared a loss of influence. Other Americans objected to the cost of supporting an oversized peacetime officer corps in order to meet what were merely the possible needs of war.

Ultimately, calls for military reform failed; no matter how inefficient and understrength the Army was, it managed to fulfill the assignments society gave it to the satisfaction of the vast majority of Americans. In an age of what Walter Millis has called "isolated security," there was no demonstrable need for a major overhaul of the service. While commanding general, John M. Schofield admitted as much, saying, "Our security against this necessity for a great standing army results from our geographical position, and not from the special loyalty and zeal of our people."[30] The Spanish-American War altered the geographical status of the United States, and military reform followed soon after.[31]

The paucity of military reform created consternation and sometimes even pessimism in the officer corps over the place of a professional soldiery in American society. In part these lamentations on the condition of the service were generated by fears of America's vulnerability to external attack. But invariably military reformers had to place the possibility of attack in the future for they could not point to any likely threat in the present. Stunted careers and thwarted ambitions contributed significantly to the pessimism career officers expressed. Professional soldiers remained on the periphery of American life, with little or no influence in government and politics or even in the shaping of military policy. To them this indicated that most Americans did not take them seriously as professional experts with valuable skills and knowledge to contribute to national life. Russell Weigley has shown graphically how this sense of frustration affected Emory Upton's morose writings on American military policy and created in Upton's followers a despair that the Army would ever have significant influence in the country. Colonel Henry C. Merriam's 1893 query, "What our Army shall do in time of peace is practically a new question," was not merely rhetorical but a genuine plaint about the place of his service in the larger society.[32]

Some officers suggested that one function of a modernized Army would be to add a leaven of discipline to an increasingly disorderly society. "Standing armies are essential to civilization," Captain James Chester asserted. "Without an adequate standing army government becomes impotent, the people effeminate, the nation helpless."[33] Colonial William Ludlow believed that "military training, physical and moral, is valuable *per se.*" It taught self-reliance, built the body and character, and prompted quick action. Ludlow justified widespread military training because

> self-restraint and the practice of a becoming obedience to law, respectful demeanor to those above and about one, and consideration and kindness to those below, these are all military attributes with which every citizen may profitably seek to endow himself.[34]

Other military reformers, conscious of the negative impact of suggesting a dose of military discipline for society, more wisely sought other ways of winning civilian friends to the service. To the *Army and Navy Journal,* the most pertinent question for the Army was "how far it can be popularized without being demoralized and losing its efficiency."[35] Secretary of War Stephen B. Elkins justified removing troops from isolated frontier posts partially on the grounds that "the presence of troops in the States would familiarize the people with the Army, lead them to better understand its operation, and . . . foster a kindlier interest in it."[36]

The Army did not lack civilian supporters. William Conant Church used the editorial pages of the *Army and Navy Journal* to espouse the reform line. Congressmen such as James A. Garfield of Ohio and John A. T. Hull of Iowa supported military revisions in Congress and public print. The influential voices of the *New York Times* and *The Nation* often spoke favorably of needed changes in the service. Through the words and pictures of Frederick Remington and Rufus Zogbaum, *Harper's Weekly* gave attention to the Army. Other national periodicals, particularly the *North American Review,* ran pieces on various aspects of military and naval affairs. Military men themselves had access to the periodical press, often making their arguments forcefully. Military reform failed in the late nineteenth century, but the Army's case had been brought to the public's attention, not only by military men but by civilians as well.[37]

Its close relationship to the presidency contributed to the Army's inability to foster change. The chief executive's post slipped in power after 1865, as Congress temporarily supplanted the office as the source of political power and patronage. As the most evident instrument of the inherent powers of the president, the service was bound to suffer from a temporary eclipse of the presidency. A commentator in the *North American Review* opposed civil service reform because it would enhance the power of the executive, who, in the Army, already controlled a body, which "by organization and discipline" was "welded into one body, one soul—that of its supreme commander." With civil service reform, "the President will have in one hand the army and its adjunct—the navy— obedient to his will; in the other, the far greater army of office-holders . . . a might political power also obedient to his will." This view was not uncommon, and it added to the opposition to modernizing the service.[38]

For career soldiers, however, subordination to the will of the president was their single most important commitment. Service to the nation through the orders of the commander-in-chief governed how officers would act. The post-Civil War Army was deeply committed to civilian control of the military but *through* the chief executive. When given clearly defined orders, officers obeyed them without question. "The only exception we have to the rule of implicit obedience," Colonel Thomas M. Anderson admonished his regimental officers,

> is that the order we decline to obey is an unlawful order. This
> is a question for everyman's conscience. But a too sensitive
> conscience is a dangerous thing for a soldier to cultivate. It too
> often leads to a crown of martyrdom.[39]

When left to their own devices, with ambiguous orders, officers continued to rely on their consciences. They sought to discern in ambiguity what their military superiors and the president intended. This was not always easy in the decentralized Army of the late nineteenth century. The inadequate command system sometimes prevented the distribution of clear-cut orders, and when, as was usually the case in federal intervention in labor disputes, presidential policy and intent were poorly defined, officers were left to contemplate Colonel Anderson's doleful prediction. At that point, officers' fundamental social values, their desire to further the interests of their institution, and their perceptions of the nature of American society influenced their final decisions as much as did military necessity.

Notes

1. A convenient survey of federal intervention in domestic disorders is Frederick T. Wilson, *Federal Aid in Domestic Disturbances, 1787-1903,* 57th Cong., 2nd sess., Senate Document 209 (Washington, D.C., 1903). Also see Robert W. Coakley, "Federal Use of Militia and the National Guard in Civil Disturbances," in *Bayonets in the Streets,* ed. Robin Higham (Manhattan, Kan., 1969), pp. 17-34.

2. Coakley, "Federal Use of Militia and National Guard," pp. 26-27, on the decline in the use of the militia. Wilson, *Federal Aid in Domestic Disturbances,* pp. 206-14, on post-Civil War uses of the Army in non-labor-related domestic disorders.

3. The following secondary works have been used to sketch the history of the Army in the years after Reconstruction. Of most value were Russell F. Weigley, *History of the United States Army* (New York, 1967), chap. 12; Walter Millis, *Arms and Men* (New York, 1957), chap. 3; Joseph C. Bernardo and Eugene H. Bacon, *American Military Policy* (Harrisburg, Pa., 1955), *passim.* On postwar strengths, see William A. Ganoe, *The History of the United States Army* (New York, 1924), pp. 307-08, and Oliver L. Spaulding, *The United States Army in War and Peace* (New York, 1937), pp. 338-41.

4. Brigadier General John Gibbon, "Needed Reforms in the Army," *North American Review* 156, no. 435 (February 1893): 212-14; Rufus F. Zogbaum, "The United States Artillery," *Harper's Weekly* 38, no. 1970 (September 22, 1894): 894; Spaulding, *The U.S. Army,* p. 369.

5. See George B. McClellan, "The Regular Army of the United States," *Harper's New Monthly Magazine* 55, no. 329 (October 1877): 780. The annual reports of the secretary of war for all of the late nineteenth century are of value here, but see particularly *Sec. War Rept. 1875,* p. 21; *Sec. War Rept. 1892,* pp. 5, 7; *Sec. War Rept. 1894,* pp. 9-10; *Sec. War Rept. 1895,* pp. 14-15, 64.

6. For contemporary comments on enlisted men, see Captain George Wilson, "The Enlisted Men of the United States Army," *Cavalry Journal* 4, no. 15 (December 1891): 377; James Parker, *The Old Army: Memories 1872-1918* (Philadelphia, 1929), pp. 17-22; Brig. Gen. A. V. Kautz, "What

the United States Army Should Be," *The Century Magazine* 36, no. 6 (October 1888): 934; Brig. Gen. Henry C. Corbin, "The Army of the United States," *The Forum* 28 (January 1899): 513-18; "The Status of the Non-commissioned Officer in the United States Army," *United Service,* n.s., 9 (April 1893): 340-47. See *Sec. War Rept. 1875,* p. 164, on the 1868 desertion problems. Useful secondary sources include Don Rickey, Jr., *Forty Miles a Day on Beans and Hay: The Enlisted Soldier Fighting the Indian Wars* (Norman, Okla., 1963); Jack D. Foner, *The United States Soldier Between Two Wars: Army Life and Reforms, 1865-1898* (New York, 1970); Marvin Fletcher, *The Black Soldier and Officer in the United States Army, 1891-1917* (Columbia, Mo., 1974), chap. 4, William B. White, "The Military and the Melting Pot: The American Army and Minority Groups, 1865-1924" (Ph.D. diss., University of Wisconsin, 1968), chap. 5; Edward M. Coffman, "Army Life on the Frontier, 1865-1898," *Military Affairs* 20, no. 4 (Winter 1956): 195-201.

7. Weigley, *History of the U.S. Army,* pp. 270-72, and Leonard White, *The Republican Era, 1869-1901* (New York, 1958), pp. 134, 140-44, discuss the command system.

8. Graham Cosmas, *An Army for Empire: The United States Army in the Spanish-American War* (Columbia, Mo., 1971), chaps. 1, 2, is an excellent discussion of the failings of the bureaus. Also see Bernardo and Bacon, *American Military Policy,* pp. 251-56; Spaulding, *The U.S. Army,* p. 395; John M. Schofield, *Forty-Six Years in the Army* (New York, 1897), pp. 469-73.

9. Schofield, *Forty-Six Years in the Army,* pp. 468-83, and Russell F. Weigley, "The Military Thought of John M. Schofield," *Military Affairs* 22, no. 2 (Summer 1959): 77-83. Edward Ranson, "Nelson A. Miles as Commanding General, 1895-1903," *Military Affairs* 29, no. 4 (Winter 1965-66): 179-200.

10. Russell F. Weigley, "The Elihu Root Reforms and the Progressive Era," in *Command and Commanders in Modern Warfare,* ed. William Geffen, 2nd ed., Proceedings of the Second Military History Symposium, United States Air Force Academy (Washington, D.C., 1971), pp. 15-17. Allan R. Millett, *The General: Robert L. Bullard and Officership in the United States Army, 1881-1925* (Westport, Conn., 1975), pp. 47-50, suggests that there were four armies in the late nineteenth century, each distinguished by its peculiar duties.

11. The centrality of the Civil War experience to officers serving in the Army after 1877 is suggested in Weigley, *History of the U.S. Army,* p. 266, and Ganoe, *History of the U.S. Army,* pp. 305-07. The memoirs of war veterans who remained in the Army makes this even clearer.

12. Weigley, *History of the U.S. Army*, p. 272; Millett, *The General*, pp. 34-39; Stephen E. Ambrose, *Duty, Honor, Country: A History of West Point* (Baltimore, 1966), chap. 10; Samuel P. Huntington, *The Soldier and the State: The Theory and Politics of Civil-Military Relations* (Cambridge, Mass., 1957), chaps. 8, 9.

13. *Ibid.* Also see, for the graduation figures, United States Military Academy, *The Centennial of the United States Academy at West Point, New York, 1802-1902* (Washington, D.C., 1904), pp. 481, 876-77.

14. Nov. 19, 1877, lot 4, George W. Getty Papers, Library of Congress, Washington, D.C.

15. On the relations between officers and men, see Foner, *The United States Soldier Between Two Wars*, pp. 59-66. On the social values stressed at West Point, see Millett, *The General*, pp. 35, 41; Heath Twichell, Jr., *Allen: The Biography of an Army Officer, 1859-1930* (New Brunswick, N.J., 1974), chap. 2. See Howard Mumford Jones, *The Age of Energy: Varieties of American Experience, 1865-1915* (New York, 1970), pp. 30-36, 44, 185, and Gilman Ostrander, *American Civilization in the First Machine Age, 1890-1940* (New York, 1970), pp. 45-65, 70-72, on Victorian middle-class values.

16. There is not yet an adequate study of the social backgrounds of officers serving in the nineteenth-century Army similar to Peter Karsten's work on the Navy, *The Naval Aristocracy: The Golden Age of Annapolis and the Emergence of Modern American Navalism* (New York, 1972). Recent biographies of Army officers note the middle-class backgrounds of their subjects in particular and the officer corps in general. See, e.g., Millett, *The General*, pp. 11-12, 27-29; Twichell, *Allen*, pp. 3-12; Donald Smythe, *Guerrilla Warrior: The Early Life of John J. Pershing* (New York, 1973), pp. 4-6. Also see White, "The Military and the Melting Pot," pp. 305-11, and Richard C. Brown, "Social Attitudes of American Generals" (Ph.D. diss., University of Wisconsin, 1951), pp. 1-16, 34-35. On the backgrounds of American business and political leaders, see Frances W. Gregory and Irene D. Neu, "The American Industrial Elite in the 1870's: Their Social Origins," and William Miller, "American Historians and the Business Elite," and "The Recruitment of the American Business Elite," in *Men in Business: Essays in the Historical Role of the Entrepreneur,* ed. William Miller, Harper Torchbook Edition (New York, 1962), pp. 193-211, 309-28, 329-38, respectively. The backgrounds of West Point cadets' fathers in USMA, *Centennial of USMA,* pp. 482-83.

17. The "people" Lieutenant McClure refers to were the civilian citizens of St. Paul. McClure to his mother, Nov. 19, 1877, Getty Papers.

The correspondence from various military posts to the *Army and Navy Journal* written by officers noting the social activities of garrison life in the late nineteenth century supports this view. Also, see Edward M. Coffman, "The Young Officer in the Old Army," in *The Harmon Memorial Lectures in Military History,* no. 18 (United States Air Force Academy, Colo., 1976), pp. 6-7, 10; Millett, *The General,* pp. 61-62, 78-79; Twichell, *Allen,* pp. 26-28; and Smythe, *Guerrilla Warrior,* pp. 30-34, on social activities of officers.

18. Winfield Scott Chaplin, in USMA, *Centennial of the USMA,* p. 892. Chaplin, USMA, class of 1870, was chancellor of Washington University, St. Louis, Missouri, in 1902.

19. *Ibid.,* p. 485.

20. F. Whittaker, "The American Army," *The Galaxy* (September 1877): 395. Also see James Sefton, *The United States Army and Reconstruction, 1865-1877* (Baton Rouge, La., 1967), pp. 252-54.

21. Huntington, *The Soldier and the State,* pp. 155-57, 224-26; and Arthur Ekirch, Jr., *The Civilian and the Military* (New York, 1956), pp. 112-22. C. Robert Kemble, *The Image of the Army Officer in America: Background for Current Views* (Westport, Conn., 1973), section 4, discusses various civilian perceptions of the Army in the post-Civil War era. Russell F. Weigley, *Towards an American Army: Military Thought from Washington to Marshall* (New York, 1962), chap. 8, discusses John A. Logan's views of the regular Army.

22. "A Plea for the Army," *The Forum* 26 (August 1897): 645.

23. Maj. Gen. John M. Schofield to Capt. E. W. War (ret.), November 19, 1894, p. 618, Letters Sent, 1892, Headquarters of the Army, Record Group 108, National Archives, Washington, D.C. See Weigley, *History of the U.S. Army,* pp. 288-89; Downey, *Indian Fighting Army,* p. 22; Ganoe, *History of the U.S. Army,* pp. 324-25, 365, 366.

24. Archibald Forbes, "The United States Army," *North American Review* 135, no. 309 (August 1882): 139.

25. Coffman, "The Young Officer in the Old Army," pp. 3-4. For individual officers' money problems, Millett, *The General,* throughout the book discusses the financial problems of Robert Lee Bullard; and Smythe, *Guerrilla Warrior,* pp. 30-34, on John J. Pershing. Conversely, Henry T. Allen had an outside income which allowed him to keep a black manservant, a personal string of horses, and hunting dogs while on duty as a second lieutenant at Fort Keogh, Montana Territory, in the mid-1880s. See Twichell, *Allen,* pp. 26-36.

26. Brig. Gen. Gibbons, "Needed Reforms in the Army," p. 215. A similar lament in Howard, "A Plea for the Army," p. 644. Also Henry L.

Nelson, "The Army and the Politicians," *Harper's Weekly* 33, no. 1702 (August 3, 1889): 626-27. Ambitious officers discouraged by the monotony of garrison duty and the stagnation of promotion turned readily to politicians for assistance in obtaining detached duty assignments and transfers to the staff bureaus, where promotion was more rapid. See, as examples, Millett, *The General,* pp. 78-79, 81-83; Smythe, *Guerrilla Warrior,* pp. 39-40, 58-60; Twichell, *Allen,* pp. 26-29, 75-77.

27. *Sec. War Rept. 1883,* p. 45.

28. Gibbon, "Needed Reforms in the Army," p. 216, for the first quotation; Parker, *The Old Army,* p. 23, for the second. Also Weigley, *History of the U.S. Army,* pp. 267-70; Ganoe, *History of the U.S. Army,* pp. 335, 348-56; Spaulding, *The U.S. Army,* pp. 356-61.

29. Stephen E. Ambrose, *Upton and the Army* (Baton Rouge, La., 1964), pp. 96-110, 113, 121-24; Weigley, *Towards an American Army,* chaps. 7, 9; Huntington, *The Soldier and the State,* pp. 260-68. Allan Millett's Introduction to *The General* gives an excellent definition and discussion of military professionalism and its development in the late nineteenth-century Army.

30. Schofield to Charles F. W. Archer, July 20, 1894, Headquarters of the Army, Letters Sent, 1894, pp. 154-55, Schofield Papers, Library of Congress, Washington, D.C.

31. Ambrose, *Upton and the Army,* p. 105. See comments of Russell F. Weigley, in *Soldiers and Statesmen,* Proceedings of the Fourth Military Symposium, United States Air Force Academy, 1970 (Washington, D.C., 1973), pp. 47-53; Walter Millis, ed., *American Military Thought* (New York, 1966), pp. xxviii-xxxii.

32. Merriam's comment in *Army and Navy Journal,* December 2, 1893, p. 242. On pessimism in the officer corps, see Weigley, *History of the U.S. Army,* chaps. 7, 9. As only one of many examples of officers positing the possibility of a British invasion, see Lt. George B. Duncan, "Reasons for Increasing the Regular Army," *North American Review* 166, no. 497 (April 1898): 448-59.

33. "Standing Armies A Necessity of Civilization," *United Service* 9, no. 6 (December 1883): 658.

34. "The Military Systems of Europe and America," *North American Review* 155, no. 458 (January 1895): 82. Also see Howard, "A Plea for the Army," pp. 650-51, and Hugh L. Scott, *Some Memories of a Soldier* (New York, 1928), pp. 134-35, for similar comments.

35. April 15, 1893, p. 565.

36. *Sec. War Rept. 1892,* p. 7.

37. This public interest and support for the Army is discussed in

Lester D. Langley, "The Democratic Tradition and Military Reform 1878-1885," *Southwestern Social Science Quarterly* 48, no. 2 (September 1967): 192-200; Bernard L. Boylan, "The Forty-fifth Congress and Army Reform," *Mid-America* 41, no. 3 (July 1959): 173-86; and Kemble, *The Image of the Army Officer in America*, pp. 134-40, chap. 14. Both general officers and junior officers authored a variety of articles on the service for popular journals. Rather than list these, I suggest that the periodicals mentioned in the text as well as others referred to in these notes would support this view.

38. See William M. Dickson, "The Political Machine," *North American Review* 134 (1882): 41-42. Also, White, *The Republican Era,* chap. 2, pp. 134-37.

39. "Duties in Connection with the Enforcement of Civil Law," *JMSI* 11, no. 89 (September 1897): 275-76. Also see Lt. Richard Young, Fifth Artillery, "Legal and Tactical Considerations Affecting the Employment of the Military in the Suppression of Mobs; Including an essay on Martial Law," *JMSI* 9, no. 33 (March 1888): 70.

3 1877—The Great Strike

In the late spring of 1877, eleven Molly Maguires convicted of plotting to destroy local government in the state went to the gallows in Pennsylvania. Many native Americans found the existence of foreign secret societies in their midst disquieting but ignored the crushing poverty of the Pennsylvania coal fields that produced the Mollies. It was not easy for Americans of either native or foreign birth to ignore poverty in 1877. The depression that followed the Panic of 1873 deepened during the year; more businesses failed, great railroads went into receivership, wages shrank, and unemployment rose. Industrial workers in particular bore the brunt of the economic downturn. Those railroad workers who retained their jobs nonetheless faced several pay cuts prior to 1877, and in June of that year many of the large roads enacted yet another 10 percent reduction. The unemployed and underpaid had neither unions nor social agencies to turn to for assistance in times of economic distress. The lack of any means of ameliorating poverty and hard times created a great deal of discontent and a large floating population of idle men, particularly in the cities where the depression was especially severe.[1]

Beginning on July 17, thousands of angry railroad workers unexpectedly left their jobs in a spontaneous protest against the June wage reduction. There was little direction to the strike because few local unions existed among the railroad workers and none on a national scale. The railroad strike began in West Virginia and spread north, and then west, from trunk line to trunk line, until it virtually halted all rail traffic east of the Mississippi. Soon other discontented workers left their jobs. Coal miners in West Virginia, Pennsylvania, Ohio, and Illinois, some laid off by the rail strike, made common cause with the railroaders. In the cities, the unemployed and underpaid gathered in the streets and railroad yards to

give moral and physical support to the strikers. In St. Louis, the Workingmen's Party of the United States, a Socialist group, engineered a successful general strike and virtually ruled the city for three days. The con-
flagration reached San Francisco, where irate workers took out their
frustrations on hapless Chinese in three days of murder and arson. Other
great cities, most notably Baltimore, Pittsburgh, and Chicago, experienced
violent rioting, arson, and killing in the streets.[2]

The extent and intensity of the upheaval surprised and frightened many
observers. James Ford Rhodes later recalled:

> The action of the mob in Baltimore, Pittsburg, [sic] Reading,
> Chicago and Scranton seemed to threaten the chief strong-
> holds of society and came like a thunderbolt out of a clear
> sky, startling us rudely. For we had hugged the delusion that
> such social uprisings belonged to Europe.[3]

As disconcerting as the turbulence and violence was the collapse of law enforcement. Except in Chicago, police and sheriff's departments either
proved incapable of coping with the widespread disorder or displayed sympathy for the strikers. Appeals to governors for aid brought the National
Guard on the scene, but this did not always lead to a restoration of order.
Often, as at Martinsburg, West Virginia, scene of the first strike, militiamen
who responded to the call for active duty fraternized with strikers. Fraternization between Guardsmen and strikers also occurred in Ohio and New
York. In Maryland, many National Guardsmen refused to turn out, and the
severe handling the Fifth and Sixth Regiments received at the hands of a
Baltimore mob destroyed the only effective force that state possessed.
For a time, Pennsylvania's National Guard almost collapsed when local
Guardsmen refused to disperse crowds in Pittsburgh, and Philadelphia units
sent in to relieve them caught the fury of a mob partially armed with
weapons from the local units. In one instance, at Reading, Guard units
faced each other at gunpoint and almost came to blows.[4]

While some states discovered that their Guard units were inefficient
or prone to side with the strikers, others found themselves with little or
no Guard organization at all. The Illinois National Guard was in the process
of reorganization when the disturbances began, and it took several days to
get the few existing regiments into the field. Indiana and Missouri possessed
no organized militia at all and had to depend upon hastily formed citizens'

volunteer companies and committees of safety to supplement the beleaguered local law officers. Even in states with some militia, volunteer
groups were formed, often made up entirely of Civil War veterans. Until
these emergency groups perfected their organization, the threat of another
Pittsburgh hung over such cities as Cleveland, Philadelphia, Louisville, and
Cincinnati.[5]

The strike developed so unexpectedly and so rapidly that state and
local officials failed to react promptly. The failure of law enforcement
agencies and the militia often resulted from indecision on the part of
state and local executives. Once these leaders developed a set policy and
gained control of the situation, both police and militia managed to restore
order. The governor of Pennsylvania, John F. Hartranft, absent when the
strike began, provided guidance upon his return and put to good use many
of the militia units that had failed earlier. Much the same transpired in
New York and New Jersey. States without militia organizations eventually
restored order with their volunteer groups. While civil officials were concerned mainly with keeping or restoring order, they found themselves
constantly under great pressure from railroad officials and the press to
open rail traffic and break the strike. This action only provoked further
violence and disorder.[6]

Press coverage of the strike, especially of the violence in Baltimore
and Pittsburgh, created fears of revolution, as newspapers made allusions
to the Paris Commune of 1871. The trumpeting from the front pages of
the nation's most influential dailies about the widespread nature of the
strikes and attendant disorders engendered fears that things had gotten
out of hand. The fact that the strike assumed national rather than local
scope intensified this feeling. Almost from the beginning many railroad
officials and much of the press demanded that federal troops be ordered
out to quash the disorder.[7]

The first governor to find himself subjected to insistent demands that
he request federal troops, Henry M. Mathews of West Virginia, acceded
rather quickly. John W. Garrett, president of the Baltimore and Ohio
Railroad, and his vice-president, John King, Jr., pelted Mathews with demands that both militia and federal troops be sent to Martinsburg to
break the strike. The B & O exerted tremendous power in West Virginia
and Maryland, and Mathews found he could not ignore these demands.
The failure of the West Virginia militia to open traffic at Martinsburg
gave Mathews the opportunity, on July 17, to wire a request for federal

troops to President Hayes. Mathews had hardly exhausted all his powers to open traffic at Martinsburg. Although no extensive disorder had yet occurred in that village, he shaped his request to Hayes in words which led the president to believe that regulars were needed. On July 18, Secretary of War George W. McCrary ordered Colonel William H. French, Fourth Artillery, commandant at the Washington Arsenal, to take his small command to Martinsburg and report to the governor "in connection with the existing riots."[8]

While French prepared his meager force of seventy artillerymen, the adjutant general wired Fort McHenry, Baltimore, Maryland, for more troops. French's move to Martinsburg by rail was delayed on the afternoon of July 18, until Hayes could issue a proclamation commanding all persons engaged in unlawful and insurrectionary proceedings to disperse and retire peaceably. At six thirty in the morning, July 19, the federal force moved into Martinsburg. Colonel French, however, discovered no disorder and at noon reported, "At present everything seems quiet and I doubt whether anything more than a demonstration will be required."[9] He added that he would not act without first consulting with the governor or his aides. Later in the day, the force from Fort McHenry, seventy-six artillerymen, arrived. Because there was no disorder, and because Governor Mathews had no plan for using federal forces, having merely given in to railroad pressures in requesting them in the first place, French and his men did nothing on their first day in West Virginia. The *Baltimore American* reported that on the 19th the soldiers lounged about the village and "were treated civilly, the strikers merely expressing the opinion that there was no occasion for their presence. . . . Good humor appeared to prevail and groups of officers and strikers could occasionally be seen together talking and laughing."[10]

The movement of federal troops into Martinsburg marked the beginning of a new experience for the nation and the Army. From July 18 until the middle of August, federal troops acted in West Virginia, Maryland, Pennsylvania, Indiana, Illinois, and Missouri to restore order and open railroad traffic in the territory east of the Mississippi. President Hayes ordered troops to the first three states in response to the requests of governors. In Indiana, Illinois, and Missouri, the president sent troops to protect government property and aid United States marshals in enforcing court orders. The first troops to be used came from coastal artillery installations located in and around Maryland, Virginia, and the District of Columbia. The artillery companies, woefully understrength, averaging only thirty enlisted men and two officers, took the field equipped as infantry. As the strike spread from West Virginia to Maryland and Pennsylvania and disturbances threatened in New York, the War Department came to realize most of the troops in the Military Division of the Atlantic would be needed to meet governors' requests. Troops from all the New England and New York Harbor artillery posts, recruits and engineers from Willet's Point, New York City, and infantry regiments in the South eventually played a part in the strike. Since the Army was unable to meet all the demands for manpower in this crisis, they were supplemented by Marines and sailors stationed along the Atlantic coast.[11]

The secretary of war, through the adjutant general's office, directed the first troop movements. From the time that Colonel French's troops marched out of the Washington Arsenal to entrain for Martinsburg until July 25, no concise plan of organization existed for the use of federal forces in the railroad strike. The orders given by McCrary and his subordinates created a piecemeal movement of troops commanded by officers with no clear knowledge of their duties. For example, the commander of the Subsistence Department wrote to the adjutant general, E. D. Townsend, that he could not supply the troops unless he knew where they were and was relying on newspaper reports to find out about troop movements. Would the adjutant general please inform him of these movements? he asked. Townsend replied that he would try his best, but "the troops have been so constantly and so rapidly moved in the past three days, the usual routine has been necessarily interrupted. The officers and clerks have been incessantly at work night and day."[12]

The Army was totally unprepared for strike duty. It had no mobilization plan to meet the demands for troops along the trunk lines of the eastern railroads, nor did it have a well-conceived policy to guide officers in the field conducting strike duty. The condition of the service in 1877 added to the difficulties the War Department faced in developing a coherent approach to the crisis after it began. Because of congressional politics surrounding Reconstruction, the Army operated for most of the year without appropriations, and at the time of the strike it had gone months without pay. Although the Army no longer enforced Reconstruction in the South, troops remained scattered all over the region. As of June 30, 3,052 officers and men served in the Division of the Atlantic at thirty-nine posts spread over eighteen states. In the West, regulars were involved in a major campaign against the Nez Perce Indians, while several hundred troops patrolled the Mexican border. Stretched to the limits of its manpower capability before the strike, the Army faced inevitable confusion until the War Department mobilized sufficient troops, corrected the command problem, and developed a firm policy to guide federal forces in the field.[13]

The old problem of poor coordination between the bureaus and the field commands cropped up immediately. The commanding general, William T. Sherman, was in the Dakotas inspecting forts and had nothing to do with the strike at any time. Major General Winfield Scott Hancock, commander of the Division of the Atlantic, played no role in the first troop movements to West Virginia. Almost as an afterthought, the adjutant general informed Hancock of the use of his troops there under Colonel French. Then, on July 21, as the disorders spread into Maryland and Pennsylvania, the secretary of war gave the adjutant general authority to order troops anywhere he deemed necessary, an extraordinary power for a bureau officer. Hancock, the field commander, had no control over his troops for a day or two. On the same day, the secretary wired Hancock, "The President suggests that it might be well for you to go to Baltimore to confer with the Governor and advise us."[14]

A native of Pennsylvania, Winfield S. Hancock earned a reputation during the Civil War as a steady, courageous combat leader. As commander of the II Corps of the Army of the Potomac, he directed the fierce Union resistance on Cemetery Ridge and the Round Tops during the first two days of the Battle of Gettysburg. He brought the same calmness and determination to the direction of the Army's effort to restore order in West Virginia, Maryland, and Pennsylvania. Hancock was the only federal official, civilian or military, who attempted to centralize and rationalize the government's efforts to aid civil authorities in 1877, or to ponder the implications of federal military intervention in industrial disputes. He eagerly accepted the secretary of war's order to assume command of troops in the East.[15]

Once he arrived in Baltimore Hancock began to assume the power a field commander ought to have over his troops. On July 22, the adjutant general informed Hancock that he should consider himself in command of the units on duty in Maryland and West Virginia. Just as the general began to coordinate operations in this area, the president ordered him to Philadelphia as conditions in Pennsylvania grew steadily worse. Hancock

arrived there late on the afternoon of the 23rd, bringing with him one
hundred Marines and more than three hundred artillerymen who had
originally gone to Baltimore from their New England posts. Upon his
arrival in Pennsylvania, the adjutant general informed Hancock that "the
Secretary of War directs me to say that the President desires you to understand that you have full authority to move any troops within your division as you may think necessary during these disturbances." This order
gave Hancock full control of the federal military effort in the East during
the strike.

The general and his staff spent two sleepless days and nights concentrating troops and sending them into the disturbed regions while formu-
lating a plan of action. They discovered a bewildering array of problems.
Troops in upstate New York ordered to Philadelphia had to be held up
as it appeared for a time that New York militia would lose control of
strikers at Buffalo. Treasury officials in New York City demanded protection of government property. The interior of Pennsylvania was almost
completely cut off from the East as strikers controlled all rail lines and
insistent demands for immediate military action came into Hancock
from railroad officials there. At the same time, Hancock and his staff
had to bring some order to the chaos created by the adjutant general's
piecemeal direction of troops to Baltimore and Philadelphia. Further to
the West, disorder threatened at Cleveland, Louisville, and Indianapolis,
all of which fell within Hancock's jurisdiction.[16]

General Hancock arrived in Philadelphia before Pennsylvania authorities
requested U.S. troops. President Hayes sent the general and his force there,
ostensibly to protect U.S. property, but the president fully expected a
formal request for troops from Governor Hartranft at any moment. However, confusion surrounded the relationship between federal military
forces and the state authorities. Soon after Hancock arrived, Pennsylvania
National Guard officers began reporting to him for orders and supplies.
Hancock was perplexed by this and wired one Guard general, "I am not
controlling the measures for the preservation of peace in this or other
states."[17] He then asked Washington for a clearer definition of his position in Pennsylvania. By this time, Governor Hartranft had made the
proper requests for federal aid, and the president ordered Hancock to
report to the governor for orders.[18]

With the command problem settled for the time being, Hancock returned to the problem of distributing troops to points of disorder. By

July 25, most of the troops in his division had been gathered in from the scattered posts and placed where they would be most effective. On this day, Hancock reported, "Reports received from all points today within reach of my troops indicate that matters are very quiet—it may be the lull before the storm elsewhere, or that the backbone of the disorders within these limits is broken."[19] Although the latter prediction proved to be correct, Hancock still found himself without enough troops to meet all the demands of railroad and state officials, but he refused to break up his troops into small units. Hancock's cardinal principle throughout the strike was to concentrate sizable numbers of troops at key points and operate from those points with battalion-sized units to open rail traffic. For example, on July 28, Hancock had the following troop distribution:

	no. of officers and men
Philadelphia, Pa.	293
Reading, Pa.	214
Pittsburgh, Pa.	644
Cumberland, Md.	204
Grafton, W. Va.	80
Martinsburg, W. Va.	46
Baltimore, Md.	421
Newport Barracks, Ky.	220
Indianapolis, Ind.	271
Louisville, Ky.	220
Jeffersonville, Ind.	94

The general consistently admonished his subordinates to keep the troops in large detachments and under no circumstances allow the Army to be disgraced or defeated, even in the smallest skirmish. "We have not made much noise it is true," he wrote Major General John M. Schofield, "nor did we enlarge on our numbers." Hancock asked Adjutant General Townsend to stop the Signal Corps from telegraphing daily troop strengths. "We have a small number of troops and it is best to let human nature exaggerate our numbers instead of stating them accurately."[20]

The troops operating under General Hancock and the staff of the Division of the Atlantic performed various duties during the railroad strike. Early in the strike, the main objective was to restore or maintain order. For example, on July 24, Hancock sent two hundred men under Major

John Hamilton to Reading to prevent the outbreak of a threatened riot. In Washington, where the *New York Times* reported ugly crowds at the B & O depot, Marines and sailors who came up from Norfolk by ship were used to protect important government buildings and guard railroad bridges, tunnels, and other property in and around the capital. Eventually, President Hayes placed Major General John M. Schofield in charge of the Washington forces. Marines and sailors performed similar services in New York City, guarding government property.[21]

The most extensive action by U.S. troops to preserve the peace was taken in Baltimore. Late on the evening of July 20, angry strikers and their supporters assaulted the militia and attacked and burned B & O property at Camden Station. Governor John Lee Carroll then requested federal troops. President Hayes complied and issued the required proclamation. Orders went out to the Marine force in Washington and to General Hancock to send all available troops from New York Harbor. At Fort McHenry, Colonel William F. Barry, Second Artillery, was ordered to report to the governor for duty. Barry began to receive a bewildering array of telegrams. Wires came from Governor Carroll, the adjutant general, and B & O officials, while the collector of customs in Baltimore urgently asked for troops to protect the Customs House. Just as these efforts were to culminate in action, Governor Carroll cancelled his request for troops. The War Department immediately cancelled the troop movements, but Barry reported on the afternoon of the 21st, "I am again called upon by Gov. of Md. for troops and field guns. In consequence of the draft made on this garrison for Martinsburg I have only enough men left to man three guns and none to serve as infantry."[22]

This time the orders went out and were not rescinded. One hundred Marines left Washington for Baltimore while Hancock sent three hundred fifty artillerymen from New York Harbor. On Sunday morning, July 22, the troops arrived. When the soldiers entered the city they were met with a few jeers and stones from a crowd at Camden Station, but the regulars executed a port arms with fixed bayonets, and the mob quickly dispersed. Hancock commented on the day's events, "Everything here seems quiet. It is generally believed that the presence of the U.S. troops has had a salutary effect here."[23] By the time the federal forces reached Baltimore the riot had spent its force. Again, as in Martinsburg, it was not clear what the regulars were to do. For the next few days they patrolled the riot district and ensured the maintenance of peace in the city. General

Hancock, in Baltimore on July 21, left for Philadelphia two days later and turned over command to Colonel Barry. Hancock told Barry to remain in the city and informed him, "About five hundred troops are en-route for Fort McHenry from the north. If not stopped you will put them in order on their arrival and organize them and all other troops here."[24] This became Barry's primary duty for the rest of the strike, as troops from both the North and the South passed through Fort McHenry for transfer to other points of duty.[25]

The second task performed by regulars on strike duty concerned opening the blockaded rail lines. In effect, this amounted to strikebreaking, for the strikers and their sympathizers refused to allow trains to be operated by strikebreakers unless military or police protection prevented the strikers' interference. Colonel French began this process at Martinsburg on July 20, by sending out a force of ten men under a lieutenant on a westbound freight. As this train passed through Cumberland, Maryland, it was stoned , and when it reached Keyser, West Virginia, angry strikers drove off the engineer and fireman. The lieutenant believed his force too small to deal with the obstructors so he returned to Martinsburg. Because French was operating with no guidance from his superiors at this time, he improvised. First he issued a notice which stated in part that "strikers impeding the passage of United States troops in any manner whatsoever, do so at their own peril," and then he beefed up his train guards.[26] The colonel also discovered that the worst trouble was at Cumberland, where he was not authorized to operate, as Governor Carroll had not yet asked for federal aid. The spread of the strike to Baltimore halted all rail traffic for a time anyway, although this brought federal troops into Maryland and ended the jurisdictional problem.[27]

Confusion and a lack of coordinated efforts to open the railroads caused Colonel French a good deal of difficulty. On July 22, Hancock ordered French to Cumberland to report to Governor Carroll's representative and to open the B & O. French reached Cumberland with his force the next day, saw that things were quiet there, and proposed to move on to Keyser, West Virginia. At this point, Governor Carroll's representative and the B & O officials refused to provide the Colonel with a train. This problem arose because French was operating under both Governor Carroll and Governor Mathews of West Virginia. Mathews wanted the federal forces returned to his state, and French was inclined to listen to him. The railroad officials, however, did not want the forces moved, and since they worked closely with the Maryland authorities, the train did not move. French believed it was all the railroad's fault and wired the War Department. "If my operations are dependent upon the ideas of petty officials of the railroad, it had better be turned over to them, and relieve myself from any responsibility."[28]

When Thomas R. Sharp, superintendent of the B & O refused to provide a train, the crusty French lost his temper. A major general of volunteers during the war and for a time commander of the III Corps of the Army of the Potomac, Colonel French understandably was not used to having his authority, and therefore the Army's authority, questioned by civilians. An argument ensued, in full view of the Cumberland strikers. French publicly damned Sharp and ordered his arrest. With this threat, Sharp and the Maryland officials agreed to release the train, and it moved on to Keyser. Reverberations from this affair travelled back to Washington. French fired several strongly worded telegrams to the War Department, while B & O officials charged that French had been drunk and lacked self-control. The unseemly affair came to an end when French requested to be relieved and the War Department gladly obliged him. There is no evidence to support the contention that the colonel had been in his cups, although he later admitted, "I have a peculiar kind of temper, and when I am roused I might create the impression that I had consumed thirty gallons of proof."[29] From newspaper reports and descriptions of the affair submitted by French's fellow officers, it appears that Sharp and other B & O officials were insolent enough towards the old soldier to warrant a display of temper. The War Department, however, had no desire to create more bad feelings among the railroads, Maryland officials, and the Army by demanding public apologies to French. No public statement was made by the Department exonerating the colonel, nor was he disciplined.[30]

It soon became evident that the key to opening B & O rail traffic in Maryland and West Virginia was Cumberland. But Colonel George W. Getty, Third Artillery (French's replacement), discovered that the number of troops—a few more than two hundred—in the region was not sufficient to preserve peace in the railroad towns and at the same time guard trains. For the time being, then, Getty's command remained stationed at the key trouble spots, at Cumberland, Maryland, and, in West Virginia, at Martinsburg, Keyser, and Grafton, making no effort to move trains. A Civil War veteran suffering from rheumatism and a bad cold, Getty found strike duty tedious and disagreeable. Nonetheless, duty in the region was not totally devoid of social amenities. Local citizens held dances and dinners for his officers, and Getty wrote his wife, "The girls all about this region are wild about the young officers. They cannot do too much for them and I tell them that they are spoiling the officers and will soon have them beyond my control."[31]

Although the local girls were wild about the soldiers, striking railroadmen, coal miners, and canal boatmen were not, and conditions remained tense in the area through the rest of July. Hancock continually pressed Governor Carroll to send the Baltimore troops to open the B & O in other parts of Maryland. The governor was reluctant to have troops leave Baltimore. He demanded five hundred more soldiers to open the rail lines. General Hancock did not have five soldiers to spare, and seven hundred were already in Maryland. Finally, on July 28, Carroll ordered a simultaneous movement of trains from Baltimore, heading west, and from Getty's headquarters at Cumberland, heading east. Federal troops rode as train guards both ways, and in Baltimore Colonel Barry reported "considerable crowd but no rioting or material opposition. Have five hundred foot troops and two guns in position at this station."[32] The maneuver succeeded without opposition, and on July 30, twenty-two freight trains under the guard of a Marine battalion, left Baltimore for Martinsburg. The B & O was open for good, and a day later Colonel Getty reported that trains ran from Baltimore to the Ohio line without opposition.[33]

Pennsylvania suffered more disorder and destruction from the railroad strike than any other state. All rail communication between Philadelphia and the industrial cities to the west was severed. Early in the strike this had hindered the movements of the National Guard, and now it affected the use of federal troops. Governor Hartranft, after some difficulties, finally submitted the correctly worded request for federal troops to President Hayes on July 23. Hartranft reached Philadelphia from his hurriedly cancelled Western trip on the 24th, and went into consultation with Hancock the next day. After showing some indecision, the governor proposed a plan to Hancock that would open the Pennsylvania Central Railroad between Philadelphia and Pittsburgh. Hancock reported to McCrary, "I will send not less than four hundred troops, more if possible, and he will take two thousand (militiamen). Pittsburgh is the main objective point." Governor Hartranft and General Hancock determined that until they opened the Pennsylvania Central, little could be done to restore

order in the state. Accordingly, they decided to send their strong force on
a series of troop trains to Pittsburgh, opening the railroad and restoring
civil authority along the way.[34]

The expedition left Philadelphia on July 26, with Major John Hamilton
in command of the regulars, 577 officers and men. Hamilton soon discovered that Hartranft and his National Guard force preferred caution
to alacrity. The major decided to move his two troop trains to the head
of the expedition and push on quickly to Pittsburgh. When the federal
force arrived in Altoona, it found an ugly crowd of strikers which forcefully removed the engineers and firemen from the trains. Hamilton quickly
solved this problem by impressing the necessary crewmen from the crowd
surrounding his trains. Then he had problems with railroad officials. He
needed extra engines to pull his trains over a steep grade outside Altoona.
The Pennsylvania Railroad agent refused to give up the engines because
he did not want the regulars to leave. Hamilton reacted in much the same
way as had Colonel French. Since forceful and angry arguments got him
nowhere, Hamilton seized three passenger trains passing through the city
and refused to allow them to continue until he got his engines. The railroad officials finally gave in to the major's demands.[35]

When Hamilton's force passed through Johnstown, a large crowd met
it at the station. The mob showered the first train, carrying Hamilton
and ten companies of regulars, with stones. The rocks broke many windows
on the train and bruised and cut several of Hamilton's soldiers. The major
ordered the train to stop and back up, intending to teach a lesson to the
strikers, but before his order was carried out, the train jumped the tracks
and was wrecked. Later investigation showed that the tracks had been
tampered with. Despite a broken rib, Hamilton took immediate action.
He ordered skirmishers out around the wrecked train, then led some of
his troops back into Johnstown and arrested every man in sight. At this
time, the second troop train arrived, and Hamilton had the situation well
under control. The major supervised the repair of the track and train,
took his one hundred prisoners aboard, and moved on. He placed a guard
and an officer in each engine to protect the train crew, "with orders to
slow on approaching every crowd, and at the first stone, to reverse the
engine and to commence firing."[36] There was no cause to act on these
orders during the rest of the trip to Pittsburgh. On July 28, the combined
relief expedition of regulars and National Guard reached the city. Hamilton
reported, "The quiet occupation of Pittsburgh and opening of the Penn-

sylvania Railroad settles the question in this Division, of order."[37] This brought an end to the railroad strike in Pennsylvania. However, federal troops remained in Pittsburgh, Reading, and Philadelphia until the end of August to ensure unobstructed operation of the railroads.[38]

Troops from Hancock's division also saw service in Indiana. On July 26, the governor of Indiana requested federal assistance to maintain order, but Hayes denied his request due to its improper wording. Even before this appeal, a detachment of fifty recruits and two officers from the recruit barracks in St. Louis went to Indianapolis to protect a large government arsenal. A day later, July 23, the secretary of war ordered three companies of the Eighteenth Infantry, on duty in the South, to Jeffersonville, Indiana, to protect a large quartermaster depot. Although Governor James D. William never did receive federal troops, five companies arrived in Indianapolis to help protect the arsenal. This brought the total number of troops there to 250. Several of the railroads operating in Indiana were in federal receivership, and on at least one occasion federal troops aided the U.S. marshals in opening one of these roads. Other than that, the troops in Indiana did very little in an active way to end the strike. Undoubtedly, however, their presence served to warn strikers that force would be used if necessary. Assisting marshals to open railroads under protection of U.S. courts broadened the ways in which the Army could be used to end the strike, and the walkouts in Indiana ended quickly and without violence. Troops remained in the state until the end of August.[39]

Action pertaining to the railroad strike also took place in the Military Division of the Missouri, commanded by Lieutenant General Philip H. Sheridan. In this division, the administrative weaknesses of the Army quickly came to light, hence the use of troops, particularly in Chicago, is difficult to follow. When the strike broke out, General Sheridan was in Montana superintending the reinterment of Custer's command at the Little Big Horn battlefield. It took some time to communicate with Sheridan and order him back to Chicago. In the interim, the direction of troops fell to Colonel R. C. Drum, adjutant general of the division, and to Brigadier General John Pope, commander of the Department of the Missouri, within whose jurisdiction lay Illinois and Missouri. Because Drum was at divisional headquarters in Chicago, he handled most of the troop movements and informed Pope, at Fort Leavenworth, Kansas, of each action. Adjutant General E. D. Townsend, in Washington, communicated daily with Drum and transmitted all orders to Sheridan and Pope through Drum's office.

Decisions made by the president and the secretary of war went from Townsend to Drum to the field commanders involved. In effect, this made Drum the key man in the Division of the Missouri, for he often had to act quickly without communicating with Sheridan or Pope.[40]

The first military activity in the division took place on July 22, when the secretary of war ordered Drum to stop units of the Twenty-second Infantry in Chicago. Coming from the Dakotas, they were on their way to new duty stations in the East. As affairs began to assume a more threatening tone in the city, both Drum and General Pope became increasingly concerned. They wired the adjutant general several times suggesting that more troops be sent to Chicago before railroad traffic in and out of the city was shut down completely. If a shutdown occurred, they noted, it would be impossible to get soldiers to Chicago for several days. Since there were no troops near the city, reinforcements had not yet arrived when rioting broke out in Chicago and railroad traffic momentarily came to a halt. Only two companies of the Twenty-second were present. Adjutant General Townsend wired Drum that day, "The Secretary authorizes you, if emergency requires, to order such infantry to Chicago as you think General Sheridan would approve."[41] Drum immediately ordered six companies of the Ninth Infantry at the Rock Island, Illinois, Arsenal and three companies of the Fifth Cavalry at Fort McPherson, Nebraska, to Chicago.[42]

The municipal authorities did not want federal troops in Chicago, for they feared that the arrival of troops would aggravate existing troubles. The mayor of Chicago also resisted demands to make more use of local militia units. But the rioting increased during the 25th, and Mayor Monroe Heath first asked Drum for weapons to arm volunteers and later for use of federal troops. Drum gave out the rifles but could not order out the troops. Finally, late in the day, Governor Shelby M. Cullom wired President Hayes, requesting federal aid. On July 26, the War Department ordered Drum to report to the governor, who in turn asked Drum to report to Mayor Heath. By this time, twelve companies of regulars were in the city. On the 26th, violent rioting erupted, and clashes between mobs, police, and militia left several dead and many wounded in the working-class sections of the city. Throughout these troubles, the federal troops were used only to protect government property.[43]

Although it is not clear why, on July 27, President Hayes and Secretary of War McCrary decided to reappraise the use of federal troops in Illinois.

They were reluctant to give troops to Governor Cullom in the first place and on the 27th asked Drum if their use in Chicago was necessary. Drum wired back that local and state officials were handling the disturbances with vigilance and energy, and "I have to express the opinion there does not now exist an emergency requiring the interposition of U.S. troops." He went on to say, however, that thousands were unemployed, many of whom were of the "communistic element," and "I therefore think the regular troops should be retained here until all appearance of disturbance ceases."[44]

The query from Washington concerning the use of federal troops created questions in Drum's mind. It was not at all clear to him just what authority he possessed and what was expected of him. He wired the adjutant general, expressing these doubts and confusions. The secretary of war ordered Drum to use troops only to protect U.S. property and to enforce court orders. Only in an emergency, he said, should Drum aid state and local officials. It is impossible to determine why this reversal in policy was made. Later, when General Sheridan arrived, the question remained un-settled. Sheridan wanted the troops under the authority of the governor, as they were in the East, but McCrary told him on July 30, that "the President has hoped that a necessity would not arise for him to issue a proclamation putting the troops under the governor unless the governor and you deem it necessary." The secretary told Sheridan to use troops in Chicago in the same way as Drum and "to display such strength as to serve moral purpose of keeping the peace."[45]

To add to the confusion, Drum had already given troops to Mayor Heath to guard the gas and water works in the city and the Chicago, Burlington, and Quincy roundhouse when the new orders arrived. The colonel attempted to find out if these orders were to be cancelled but was advised to leave the troops on duty until peace returned to Chicago. While Colonel Drum attempted to make sense out of this, he began to receive advice and orders from General Pope. The general opposed, as did Hancock, the use of troops as mere policemen. He told Drum, "The regular troops ought not be divided or scattered on any account. They are so few in number that they can only act effectively in a body and will be thoroughly lost or scattered about amongst militia and police."[46]

Generally the people of Chicago welcomed the troops. Most of the city's newspapers hailed the arrival of the regulars and predicted that the federals would quickly and ruthlessly put down the riots. Actually the regulars never came in contact with angry mobs. Over 650 officers and men came to Chicago between July 25 and July 30. Except for the duty of guarding city utilities on July 27, these troops did not serve under state or local officials. The soldiers sent to Chicago had come directly from Indian country by forced march, and they looked it. "The men were all tanned and grizzled, and with unwashed faces and unkempt hair, and their clothes covered with dust an inch thick in some places."[47] Some of the veterans, especially the Twenty-second Infantry, were in poor physical condition after months of frontier campaigning. All welcomed duty in Chicago as a relief from life on the frontier. The soldiers craved fresh vegetables, and the Chicago Board of Trade managed a campaign that raised one thousand dollars to buy vegetables and other fresh foods for the regulars.[48]

The crisis passed quickly in Chicago, and on July 30, a day after he arrived, General Sheridan reported, "I do not regard the trouble here as fully settled, but affairs have an improved look today."[49] The general and the soldiers remained in the city until mid-August, guarding government property and ensuring peace by their presence. An increase in Indian troubles necessitated their return to the Western posts.[50]

Powerful political figures in Missouri, especially railroad magnate James Harrison Wilson, insistently demanded that the administration put troops in St. Louis. The government yielded rather quickly to this pressure, and on July 24, Colonel Jefferson C. Davis, Twenty-third Infantry, Division of the Missouri, arrived in the city with six infantry companies. Davis's force was to "go to St. Louis to protect the property of the United States and by their presence to promote peace and order."[51] Missouri officials had not asked for troops, and this was the only legal way in which Hayes could send federal forces to the state. Brigadier General Pope, Davis's immediate superior, closely supervised the actions of federal forces in St. Louis. He cautioned Davis to take no action without orders from departmental headquarters and to maintain a low profile in the city.[52]

For four days the troops in St. Louis guarded government property. A total of 536 officers and men served in the city, some coming from as far as Fort Lyon, Colorado. On July 28, Colonel Davis used his troops to assist U.S. marshals in opening railroads under receivership of the U.S. court in East St. Louis, Illinois. The soldiers met no resistance to this movement, and they speedily restored rail traffic across the Mississippi

River. Regulars guarded trains, bridges, and railroad property in East St. Louis, from July 28 to August 2. They returned to St. Louis on the 2nd, and remained there until August 11, when Colonel Davis took his command back to its regular posts.[53]

The Hayes administration committed federal troops in aid of civil officials under three legal justifications in 1877: to aid state officials in suppressing domestic insurrection; to protect federal property; and to assist federal marshals in enforcing the orders of federal courts. In West Virginia, Maryland, Pennsylvania, Indiana, Illinois, and Missouri, the Army contributed to the restoration of order princiaplly by their mere presence. Regulars never confronted an uncontrollable mob, nor were they forced to use violence to end a riot. Civic officials in Baltimore and Chicago quelled rioting with police and militia, while the destructive riot in Pittsburgh burned itself out several days before regulars arrived. Only at Johnstown, Pennsylvania, did the Army come close to a confrontation with an angry mob, where quick action by Major Hamilton ended the possibility of violence.

The Army's major effort under the rubric of aiding the states to suppress domestic disorder came in the opening of the struck railroads in West Virginia, Maryland, and Pennsylvania. By providing train guards and protecting strikebreakers and railroad property, federal troops allowed the railroad corporations to overcome the deep hostility of strikers and their supporters. In effect, this was strikebreaking, but it fell within the laws protecting private property and the individual right to work of strikebreakers. The Army guaranteed railroad management the protection it needed to operate and that state and local officials could not or would not provide.[54]

Hayes and his cabinet used the justification of protecting federal property to get troops into potentially explosive situations without the specific request of state officials. Troops went to New York City, Philadelphia, Indianapolis, Chicago, St. Louis, and Washington, D.C., for this purpose. The need was probably justified in New York and Washington, but served more as a pretext in the other cities. Troops in Indianapolis and St. Louis eventually aided federal marshals in opening struck railroads under the receivership of federal courts.

However they were used, regulars proved effective. Their discipline at Johnstown, for example, prevented a potentially bloody outcome, and in most instances the knowledge that federal troops accompanied a

train automatically forestalled the strikers' attempts to halt it. Regulars
were never seriously challenged wherever they appeared. This was quite
remarkable given the intensity of the riots in Pittsburgh, Baltimore, and
Chicago, when mobs clashed with police and militia. Undoubtedly tension and feelings were high, but the appearance of federal troops (perhaps
national troops is a more accurate term) invariably brought order with
little use of force. In West Virginia, Maryland, and Pennsylvania, trains
escorted by regulars were sometimes met by rocks and curses, but any
demonstration of a serious intent to counter violence with violence
brought an end to resistance. The steady leadership of Colonel William F.
Barry in Baltimore, and Colonel George W. Getty in outstate Maryland
and West Virginia, prevented open conflict between strikers and regulars.
Both men had served as brigadier generals of volunteers in the late war,
with commensurate responsibilities of command. That experience provided them with the confidence to meet the widespread demands of
strike duty without losing control. A third veteran artilleryman, Major
John Hamilton, exhibited that same steadiness and assurance when avoiding bloodshed at Johnstown, Pennsylvania. Most certainly the coolness of
the regulars under pressure impressed protesters, but strikers seemed
just as impressed by the fact that the soldiers were federal troops.

General Hancock perceived this fact in praising his men's performance.
"The troops have lost the government no prestige," he stressed. Their appearance "had a powerful effect. It was the moral force of the United
States government that was displayed—not its physical force."[55] Just as
important to Hancock was the fact that "not a drop of blood has been
shed—nor as far as I know, has a shot been fired by our troops."[56] As
Hancock saw it the restraint of regulars in the delicate task of policing
civilians was the Army's signal success in 1877. Colonel Getty shared the
general's sense of relief in a more personal vein, being pleased with the
fact that there was no loss of blood or property "at any point over which
I have control."[57] Whatever their personal views on the morality of the
strikers' actions, neither man lusted for blood.

As Hancock well knew, the Army did not accomplish its assignment
easily. The widespread distribution of regulars hampered early, effective
action. First the War Department, and then Hancock, had to gather troops
from far-flung posts and consolidate them in temporary battalions. Company E, Third Infantry, traveled 1,082 miles from its home station at
Mobile Barracks, Alabama, to Louisville, Kentucky, then to Indianapolis,

and finally to Scranton. Other companies, from the Sixteenth and Twenty-second Infantries, came from Western posts to St. Louis and Chicago, respectively.[58]

The inadequate command system contributed to the confusion. Commanding General William T. Sherman had nothing to do with the operation. On July 25, President Hayes requested that Sherman return to Washington from his inspection tour of Western posts. Sherman demurred, and when he finally agreed to come East the crisis had passed. Consequently, Secretary of War George McCrary and Adjutant General E. D. Townsend directed the military aspects of strike duty. This led to a piecemeal application of troops and ad hoc command assignments in the field. General Hancock eventually established a rational policy for distributing troops in the Division of the Atlantic, but at no time during the strike did a general officer of the line supervise the operations of all the troops on strike duty, regardless of division or department.

A larger problem than the administrative one of troop distribution was present throughout the strike. From the first commitment of troops under Colonel French at Martinsburg through the end of the strike and beyond, ultimate tactical control of federal forces belonged to state officials. French was ordered to proceed to Martinsburg and report to Colonel Robert Delaplaine, aide-de-camp to Governor Mathews, "in connection with the existing riots." French found no riots and an unsure Colonel Delaplaine. Rather quickly, B & O officials took charge, Delaplaine and Mathews deferred to them, and French lost his command because he refused to follow their orders. His replacement, Colonel Getty, made no complaints and acceded to the railroad's requests.

Colonel Barry in Maryland, and General Hancock in Pennsylvania, were also ordered to report to the governors of those states and to act under their orders. Governor Carroll of Maryland consistently bent to the will of the B & O and while Hartranft of Pennsylvania was more his own man, he was nonetheless solicitous of the Pennsylvania Road's needs. Besides, Thomas Scott of the Pennsylvania did not need a governor as a go-between. He was the first civilian to meet Hancock when the general first passed through Philadelphia on July 21. Whatever Hancock's personal feelings, he apparently accepted Scott's requests as if they came from Hartranft. The railroad owners, through state officials, directed the tactical operations that reopened the struck lines. On occasion, as with Colonel French in West Virginia, and Major Hamilton at Johnstown, officers protested the railroads' interference in the purely military aspects of operations. Otherwise, they deferred. Some cooperation between the roads and the Army was necessary in making up trains and deciding when and where to begin opening rail traffic. But the Army never had overall tactical control of operations.[59]

Officers in command of troops sent to states to protect federal property or aid federal marshals were often confused as to their relationship with local and state officials. The commander of regulars sent to Indianapolis to guard an arsenal, Lieutenant Colonel Henry A. Morrow, arrived in the city on July 27. He immediately contacted the mayor and local militia commander and then reported to Governor James D. Williams for orders. When he learned of Morrow's actions, Hancock ordered him to work only with federal marshals. The anomalous position of Colonel Drum in Chicago was even more confusing. At one time or another, Drum collaborated with the mayor of Chicago, the governor, and certain railroad officials. He also had to respond to orders and suggestions from Generals Sheridan and Pope and the War Department.[60]

Hancock came to recognize fairly early in the crisis that the Hayes administration's policy of turning troops over to state officials created both legal and tactical problems. Tactically, as late as July 24, no one seemed to know who was to command the Army in the field. Hartranft wanted the general to command his National Guardsmen as well as regulars but Hancock correctly rejected the offer, pointing out that *he* was to serve under the governor. Nonetheless, Hancock objected to the practice of placing federal troops under the orders of state officials. He argued that when a governor asked for federal military assistance he was admitting the failure of civil authority. "From that time commences a state not of peace but of war," and "the only outcome is to resort to force through the federal military authorities . . . until lawful order is restored." Unless the Army oversaw the tactical suppression of disorder, "there can be no complete exercise of power in a military way within the limits of the states by the federal officers."[61]

The general was also concerned with the legal problem of removing officers and men on strike duty from the chain of command. The president ought not to put troops under the command of governors, he argued, but "it should be alone by the intervention of federal authority by military force and by the President exercising control."[62] In order to solve both the legal and tactical problems, Hancock urged that all federal troops serving in a domestic disturbance be under the command of a single military officer of high rank who was directly responsible only to the president. The Hayes administration considered Hancock's objections but decided that a change in practice while the strike continued would create only more confusion and hence made no changes.[63]

Fundamental to the problems of command that concerned General Hancock was the fact that the Hayes administration developed no clear-cut policy to govern the actions of federal forces. Perhaps such a policy was not possible. The strike was something new and wholly unanticipated for the nation. Hayes and his advisers were forced to deal with an immediate crisis, and despite tremendous pressures from a wide variety of places and persons they acted with restraint. On July 22, Hayes and his cabinet decided against a call for volunteers or federalizing the militia, suggestions which came from many quarters. The administration also became increasingly wary of state calls for troops and rejected appeals from the governors of Indiana, Michigan, Wisconsin, and California. Reports from Signal Corps weather stations in key cities gave Hayes an overview of conditions far sounder than reports coming from harassed state officials and corporate leaders.[64]

For all his restraint, Hayes erred in two basic decisions in the early days of the strike. He allowed the governors to define the conditions for intervention without investigating the necessity for federal troops. The visit of an experienced military officer to Martinsburg, for example, would almost assuredly have prevented Hayes's assent to Governor Mathews's request for federal troops. None of the states requesting federal assistance had exhausted all efforts to deal with strikes and rioting before calling on the president. Secondly, Hayes too readily gave tactical control of the Army to the governors. This not only hindered efficient military conduct in reopening the railroads but allowed the governors to determine how troops would be used and made it extremely difficult for the administration to get the governors to relinquish use of the troops.[65]

The only policy governing Hayes, then, was to suppress disorder as defined by the governors. Underlying his actions was a basic commitment to the legal and economic status quo. Hayes was not a harsh, brutal man indifferent to workers' needs or bent on crushing the working class. "The railroad strikers, as a rule, are good men, sober, intelligent, and industrious," he confided to his diary.

The mischiefs are:
1. Strikers prevent men willing to work from doing so.
2. They seize and hold the property of their employers.
3. The consequent excitement furnishes an opportunity for
    the dangerous criminal classes to destroy life and property.[66]

Given these assumptions, Hayes's acceptance of the governors' and rail-road officials' definition of the crisis was quite logical, and the use of federal troops to assist in breaking the strikes inevitable.

It was possible for the federal military presence to affect the course of the strike without the Army being identified immediately as a tool of the railroads. Brigadier General John Pope and Colonel Jefferson C. Davis, the former the inept commander of Union forces at the second Battle of Bull Run, the latter a Civil War brigadier general of volunteers of moderate ability, managed to do so in St. Louis. Davis arrived in the city with orders from Pope to keep his troops at Jefferson Barracks and out of the city. The colonel was to make a personal survey of the situation in St. Louis, confer with local officials, and inform Pope as to whether the constituted civil authorities could handle things without military help. Davis was not to act without first conferring with General Pope.[67]

Colonel Davis met with the mayor of St. Louis and a hastily organized "Committee of Safety." He urged the civilians to raise an emergency militia force and provided federal arms for their use. In every possible way, Davis attempted to encourage the civil authorities to meet the threats of disorder on their own. He wanted then to exhaust all their re-sources "before calling upon Federal aid, in suppressing such insurrec-tions, etc. That not until such action has been taken, could Federal aid be properly rendered."[68] Pope deliberately remained out of the city so that he would not discourage civilian efforts to cope with disorder. Pope could supervise Davis's activities by telegraph easily enough and yet not find himself subjected to great personal pressure for military ac-tion by remaining at department headquarters in Omaha.[69]

Pope's approach proved effective. Supplied with weapons by Davis, St. Louis civic leaders organized a make-shift militia force which prevented disorder and effectively ended a general strike. Unquestionably, the pres-ence of Davis's fourteen companies of infantry at Jefferson Barracks en-couraged the forces seeking to end the strike and discouraged the strikers, but federal troops never confronted the latter in the city. Strikebreaking prevailed in St. Louis, as elsewhere, but the federal role in it was far more muted than in the East. Pope summed up the effect of his approach: "The conduct of officers and men was excellent throughout. They neither did too much nor too little, and I think all concerned will cheerfully testify to the immense service they rendered directly and indirectly."[70]

Conditions in St. Louis were peculiarly well suited to General Pope's methods. Colonel Davis's force was sent to the city under the pretext of guarding federal property and was therefore not at the command of state officials. While a general strike was underway and tension between strikers and the forces of order was high, there was no rioting, mainly due to the efforts of the general strike leaders. Pope's approach, however, indicated the value of keeping federal forces under the command of the Army. Once tensions eased, Davis's troops were quickly returned to station. Such was not the case in the East, where the governors clung to federal troops long after the crisis had subsided.

Notes

1. For a superb account of the events and their causes in 1877, see Robert V. Bruce, *1877: Year of Violence* (New York, 1959), pp. 19-21, 27, 33-34, 38-39, and *passim.* Also see Samuel Rezneck, "Distress, Relief and Discontent in the United States during the Depression of 1873-1878," *Journal of Political Economy* 58, no. 6 (December 1950): pp. 502-09; Philip S. Foner, *History of the Labor Movement in the United States,* vol. 1 (New York, 1947), pp. 463-88; Clifton K. Yearly, Jr., "The Baltimore and Ohio Railroad Strike of 1877," *Maryland Historical Magazine* 51, no. 3 (September 1956): 188-89; Samuel Yellen, *American Labor Struggles* (New York, 1936), chap. 1.

2. See Bruce, *1877,* chaps. 6, 8 and 9, 12, on Baltimore, Pittsburgh, and Chicago, respectively, for detailed information on rioting in those cities, and *passim* for other cities. J. T. Headley, *Pen and Pencil Sketches of the Great Riots,* 2nd ed. (New York, 1882); J. A. Dacus, *Annals of the Great Strike* (New York, 1877); and Edward W. Martin [pseud. for James McCabe], *The History of the Great Riots* (Philadelphia, 1877), are contemporary accounts emphasizing lurid aspects of the upheavals. Other scholarly treatments are David T. Burbank, *Reign of the Rabble: The St. Louis, and General Strike of 1877* (New York, 1966), pp. 59-60, 90-91; Russell M. Nolen, "The Labor Movement in St. Louis from 1860-1890,"

Missouri Historical Review 24 (January 1940): 160-61. *Harper's Weekly* 21, no. 1076 (August 11, 1877): 626-28, has word and pictures stories of these riots.

3. *History of the United States from Hayes to McKinley 1877-1896* (New York, 1919), p. 46.

4. On militia fraternization in the states named in the text, see Bruce, *1877*, pp. 76-80, 100-10, 127-40; Foner, *History of Labor in the U.S.*, p. 466; Yearly, "The B & O Strike of 1877," pp. 196-205; Maryland, Executive, *Annual Report of the Adjutant General of Maryland for the Year 1877*, document E in *House and Senate Documents for Maryland, 1878* (Annapolis, Md., 1878), pp. 4-5, 34-35; Pennsylvania, Executive, *Report of the Adjutant General of Pennsylvania for the Year 1877* in *Governor's Message and Reports, 1878* (Harrisburg, Pa., 1878), pp. 3-20.

5. Emergency volunteer groups were formed in almost every city that experienced strike trouble; see appropriate places in Bruce, *1877*, for all the cities mentioned in the paragraph. On Illinois, see Illinois, Executive, *Biennial Report of the Adjutant General of Illinois, for 1877 and 1878*, vol. 2, document E, in Reports to the General Assembly of Illinois, 1879 (Springfield, Ill., 1879), pp. 3-4, 103-07. For Missouri, see Missouri, Executive, *Report of the Adjutant General, State of Missouri, for the Years 1877 and 1878*," in Appendix to the Senate and House Journals, Missouri, 1879 (Jefferson City, Mo., 1879), pp. 3-7; *St. Louis Dispatch*, July 24, p. 1, July 25, 1877, p. 1; Burbank, *Reign of the Rabble*, pp. 44-46, 115-16.

6. See *Report of the Adj. Gen. of Pennsylvania, 1877*, pp. 3-10; Bruce, *1877*, pp. 162-64; Dacus, *Annals of the Great Strike*, pp. 52-53, 222-33.

7. See *New York Times*, July 19, p. 4, July 24, p. 4, July 26, 1877, p. 4; *Philadelphia Inquirer*, July 19, 1877, p. 4; *The Nation* 25, no. 630 (July 26, 1877): 49; *The Christian Union* 16, no. 4 (July 25, 1877): 61-63; *The Army and Navy Journal* 14, no. 50 (July 21, 1877): 801, 14, no. 51 (July 28, 1877): 813.

8. Adjutant General to French, July 18, 1877, in consolidated file no. 4042, Letters Received, Adjutant General's Office, Record Group 94, Old Military Records Division, National Archives, Washington, D.C. On microfilm, this consolidated file contains all the correspondence relating to the Army's role in the 1877 strikes. The file is arranged chronologically and geographically. All materials relating to the Army's action in West Virginia, for example, are in one place, arranged by date. This file will be referred to throughout as AGO no. 4042. Individual file numbers on correspondence will not be used as its location is easily found by date and

place. For pressures on Mathews, see Bruce, *1877*, pp. 76-77, 80-84; Yearly, "The B & O Strike of 1877," pp. 196-97, 206-08; Gerald G. Eggert, *Railroad Labor Disputes: The Beginnings of Federal Strike Policy* (Ann Arbor, 1967), pp. 26-27. See Bennett Rich, *The Presidents and Civil Disorders* (Washington, D.C., 1941), pp. 189-95, for the constitutional and legal provisions governing the use of federal troops in aid of state governments.

9. French to Adj. Gen., July 19, 1877, AGO no. 4042.

10. July 20, 1877, p. 1. For the movement and arrival of troops at Martinsburg, see series of wires between French and Adj. Gen., dated July 18 and 19, in AGO no. 4042, and in *The Army and Navy Journal* 14, no. 50 (July 21, 1877): 796.

11. See Bruce, *1877, passim*, on the requests from the governors; Rich, *The Presidents and Civil Disorders*, pp. 80-82; Eggert, *Railroad Labor Disputes*, pp. 24-27; Richard S. Collum, *History of the United States Marine Corps* (Philadelphia, 1890), pp. 203-16; Capt. H. C. Cochrane, U.S.M.C., "The Naval Brigade and Marine Battalion in the Labor Strikes of 1877," *United Service* 1, no. 1 (January 1879): 616-34; *Sec. War Rept. 1877*, pp. 87-89, 92-98.

12. R. McFeely to Adj. Gen., July 25, AGO no. 4042. See *Army and Navy Journal* 14, no. 51 (July 28, 1877): 812-13, for a description of multiple troop movements.

13. See *Sec. War Rept. 1877*, pp. xiv-xv, 87-89, 99-100; Woodward, *Reunion and Reaction*, pp. 6-8, 239-240; U.S., Congress, House, *Distribution of United States*, 45th Cong., 2nd sess., *House Executive Document 55* (Washington, D.C., 1877), pp. 2-3.

14. McCrary to Hancock, July 21, Letters Received, 1877, Military Division of the Atlantic, Records of United States Continental Army Commands, Record Group 393, Old Military Records Division, National Archives, Washington, D.C. Also, Adj. Gen. to Hancock, July 18, in AGO no. 4042.

15. Hancock to Adj. Gen., July 21, in AGO no. 4042. The only recent biography on Hancock, Glenn Tucker's *Hancock the Superb* (New York, 1960), has nothing on the 1877 railroad strikes. See pp. 69-70, on Hancock's character. *Sec. War Rept. 1877*, p. 5.

16. Adj. Gen. to Hancock, July 22, three wires; series of wires between Hancock and Adj. Gen., July 23; Hancock to Sec. of War McCrary, July 23, three wires; Hancock to Adj. Gen., July 24, two wires, all in AGO no. 4042. Col. Elwell S. Otis, U.S.A., "The Army in Connection with the Labor Riots of 1877," *The Journal of Military Service Institution of the United States* 5, no. 19 (September 1884): pp. 301-04, hereafter

referred to as *JMSI;* Mrs. Almina Russell Hancock, *Reminiscences of Winfield Scott Hancock* (New York, 1887), pp. 162-63.

17. Hancock to Adj. Gen., July 24, AGO no. 4042.

18. Adj. Gen. to Hancock, July 22; Hancock to Adj. Gen., July 24; Adj. Gen. to Hancock, July 24, in AGO no. 4042.

19. Hancock to Adj. Gen., July 25, AGO no. 4042.

20. Hancock to Schofield, July 30, for first quotation; Hancock to Adj. Gen., July 31, for second, both in AGO no. 4042. For continuing troop demands, see Hancock to Adj. Gen., July 26, two wires, and July 31. For troop disposition, Hancock to Adj. Gen., July 28; on Hancock's policy of using large units, Hancock to Sec. War McCrary, July 23, and to Adj. Gen., July 30 and 31. All in AGO no. 4042.

21. See Hancock to Adj. Gen., July 24, two wires, on Reading, *Ibid.* On the activities at Washington, see *New York Times,* July 23, 1877, p. 5; Schofield to Sec. of Navy, July 28; series of wires between Adj. Gen. and Capt. James Forney, U.S.M.C., July 28; Schofield to Capt. E. Barrett, U.S.N., July 29, three wires. All in AGO no. 4042. On the Marines in Washington and New York, Collum, *History of the U.S. Marine Corps,* p. 211; Cochrane, "The Navy and Marines in 1877 Riots," pp. 119-22; *Army and Navy Journal* 15, no. 2 (August 18, 1877): 22.

22. Barry to Adj. Gen., July 21, 1:30 P.M., William F. Barry Papers, Maryland Historical Society, Baltimore, Maryland. See, also, Yearly, "The B & O Strike of 1877," pp. 202-05; Bruce, *1877,* pp. 101-02, 110-11; Carroll to Hayes, July 20; Sec. of War McCrary to Carroll, July 21; series of wires between Sec. of War and Adj. Gen., July 21, for troop orders; Adj. Gen. to Barry, July 21; Adj. Gen. to Hancock, July 21; Carroll to Sec. of War, July 21; all in AGO no. 4042. In the Barry Papers, there is a series of telegrams, some undated, others dated July 20 and 21, but all pertaining to efforts of B & O agents and Gov. Carroll to obtain Barry's assistance.

23. Hancock to Adj. Gen., July 23. These events may be traced through Hancock to Adj. Gen., July 21; Adj. Gen. to Barry, July 21; Adj. Gen. to Hancock, July 21; Hancock to Sec. of War., July 21; Barry to Adj. Gen., July 22; Hancock to Adj. Gen. and to Sec. of War, on July 22, all in AGO no. 4042. See *Baltimore American,* July 23, 1877, p. 1, and Otis, "The Army in Riots of 1877," pp. 297-98, on the arrival of troops in Baltimore.

24. Hancock to Barry, July 23, Barry Papers.

25. The Barry Papers contain numerous telegrams between Barry and Hancock's headquarters from July 23 to August 15, pertaining almost wholly to this administrative and logistical function. See Cochrane, "The Navy and Marines in 1877 Riots," for peacekeeping duties in Baltimore.

26. French to Adj. Gen., July 20, five wires, AGO no. 4042. *Baltimore American,* July 21, 1877, p. 1.

27. French to Adj. Gen., July 20, two wires; Adj. Gen. to French, July 20, written report, French to Adj. Gen., July 20; French to Adj. Gen. and Adj. Gen. to French, July 21; *Baltimore American,* July 21, 1877, p. 2; *Philadelphia Inquirer,* July 23, p. 4.

28. French to Sec. of War, July 22. See also Adj. Gen. to French, July 21; Hancock to Adj. Gen., July 22; French to Adj. Gen., July 22, in AGO no. 4042.

29. *Baltimore American,* July 24, 1877, p. 4.

30. French to Adj. Gen., July 22, three wires; French to Sec. of War, July 22; Adj. Gen. to Hancock, July 22; Hancock to Adj. Gen., July 22, two wires; Adj. Gen. to Hancock, July 23; Hancock to Adj. Gen., July 23, two wires; French to Adj. Gen., July 23; Lt. R. Kilbourne to Adj. Gen., July 23, all in AGO no. 4042. Several letters in French's personnel file are from his subordinates, all attesting to the Colonel's soberness, in 3318ACP77, Appointment, Commission and Personal Branch, Adjutant General's Office, Record Group 94, National Archives. The *Baltimore American* gave the event a good deal of coverage, all in the favor of French; see July 23, pp. 1, 4; July 24, p. 4; July 29, p. 4; July 21, p. 4. See also Martin, *The History of the Great Riots,* pp. 36-40.

31. Getty to his wife, August 4, 1877. See also Getty to his wife, July 25, 27, August 7, August 17; in George W. Getty Papers, Library of Congress, Washington, D.C. Hancock to Adj. Gen., July 22, two wires, AGO no. 4042.

32. Barry to Adj. Gen., July 28, AGO no. 4042.

33. Carroll to Sec. of War McCrary, July 26; Adj. Gen. to Hancock, July 27; Carroll to McCrary, July 27, Hancock to Adj. Gen., July 30, two wires, on the consultations with Carroll, Hancock to Adj. Gen., July 28, two wires; Getty to Hancock, July 28; Adj. Gen. to Barry, July 28, Barry to Adj. Gen., July 28; Barry to Adj. Gen., July 30; Carroll to McCrary, July 30; Hancock to Adj. Gen., July 31, on conditions in western Maryland and the opening of the B & O. More on this in Getty to his wife, July 29 and August 1, Getty Papers; Otis, "The Army in Riots of 1877," pp. 309-10; Cochrane, "The Navy and Marines in 1877 Riots," pp. 618-20.

34. Hancock to McCrary, July 25, AGO no. 4042. Hartranft to Hayes, July 22, in Rutherford B. Hayes Papers, Hayes Library, Fremont, Ohio. The Hayes Library has collected all the telegrams and correspondence dealing with the strike from the president's point of view. Hereinafter,

these will be referred to as Strike Wires, Hayes Papers. The library also has a microfilm on the strike, containing newspaper clippings and miscellaneous correspondence. This will be referred to as Microfilm, Hayes Papers. See also Hartranft to Hayes, July 23, two wires, pp. 234-36; book 1, Executive Mansion Telegrams, Hayes Papers. See Hancock to McCrary, July 25, AGO no. 4042; and *Report of the Adj. Gen. of Pennsylvania, 1877,* p. 17.

35. *Report of the Adj. Gen. of Pennsylvania, 1877,* pp. 16-18; Hancock to Adj. Gen., July 26; Hancock to Sec. of War, July 26, two wires; Hancock to Adj. Gen., July 27, two wires; report of Major John Hamilton to Hancock, July 29, all in AGO no. 4042. *Army and Navy Journal* 15, no. 1 (August 1, 1877): 13, has a description of the Altoona incident.

36. Hamilton's report to Hancock, July 29, AGO no. 4042.

37. Quoted in Hancock to Adj. Gen., July 28, *Ibid.*

38. Hamilton's report to Hancock, July 29; Hancock to Adj. Gen., July 28, four wires, Hancock to Adj. Gen., August 3, *Ibid. Army and Navy Journal* 15, no. 1 (August 11, 1877): 304-05, also discusses the events at Johnstown.

39. See Adj. Gen. to Col. Thomas Ruger, 18th Inf., July 23; Hancock to Adj. Gen., July 23; Hancock to Adj. Gen., July 24; Walter Q. Gresham to Hayes, July 25; Adj. Gen. to Hancock, July 25; Gov. James D. Williams to Hayes, July 26; Sec. of War to Hancock, July 28; Hancock to Adj. Gen., July 31; written report of Lt. Col. Henry A. Morrow, 13th Inf., to Hancock, Aug. 26, all in AGO no. 4042. Quartermaster General to Sec. of War, July 23, no. 6022, Letters Received, Office of Secretary of War, Record Group 107, National Archives. Otis, "The Army in Riots of 1877," pp. 300, 310; *Sec. War Rept. 1877,* pp. 93-98, 108-09.

40. See *Sec. War Rept. 1877,* p. 56. On Sheridan's activities in the Dakotas, see folder of communications for July 19-25, container 17, Philip H. Sheridan Papers, Library of Congress.

41. Townsend to Drum, July 25, AGO no. 4042.

42. Townsend to Sheridan, July 22; Drum to Townsend, July 24, two wires; Pope to Townsend, July 24; Townsend to Pope, July 24; Pope to Townsend, July 25; Townsend to Drum, July 25, in *Ibid.* See, also, Drum to Pope, July 25, no. 639, Letters Sent, 1877, Military Division of the Missouri, Record Group 393, National Archives. On the same date, see no. 643 and no. 645, for orders of troop movements.

43. See Drum to Townsend, July 25; Collum to Hayes, July 25; Collum to McCrary, July 25; Townsend to Drum, July 26, AGO no. 4042. Drum to Pope, July 24, no. 619; Drum to Pope, July 25, no. 636; Drum to

Pope, July 25, no.646; Drum to Major Heath, July 25, no. 636, Letters Sent, 1877, Military Div. of the Missouri, RG393, NA. *Biennial Report of the Adj. Gen. of Illinois, 1877 and 1878,* pp. 103-05.

44. Drum to Adj. Gen. Townsend, July 27, no. 692, Letters Sent, 1877, Military Div. of the Missouri, RG393, NA.

45. Townsend to Sheridan, July 20, no. 8709, Letters Received, 1877, Military Div. of the Missouri, *Ibid.* Also Adj. Gen. to Drum, July 27, no. 4233, in *Ibid,* and Drum to Townsend, July 27, no. 692; Sheridan to Adj. Gen., July 30, no. 723, Letters Sent, 1877, *Ibid.* See McCrary to Drum, July 27, AGO no. 4042.

46. Pope to Drum, July 27, no. 4245, Letters Received, 1877, Military Div. of the Missouri, RG393, NA. Drum to Mayor Heath, July 27, no. 700, Drum to Adj. Gen., July 27, no. 701, Drum to Heath, July 27, no. 702, Drum to Adj. Gen., July 27, no. 705, all in Letters Sent, 1877, *Ibid. Chicago Tribune,* July 25, 1877, p. 4; *Chicago Times,* July 27, 1877, p. 6.

47. *Chicago Tribune,* July 26, 1877, p. 3.

48. *Ibid.,* July 25, p. 4, July 26, pp. 3-4, July 27, pp. 1, 4; *Chicago Times,* July 27, pp. 3, 6. *Sec. War Rept. 1877,* p. 97, on the number of troops. See Sheridan to Adj. Gen. August 2, AGO no. 4042, and *Army and Navy Journal* 15, no. 1 (August 11, 1877): 5, on the condition of the Twenty-second Infantry. See *Chicago Times,* July 28, p. 3, and July 29, p. 1, and Lt. Col. M. V. Sheridan to Charles Randolph, Sec., Chicago Board of Trade, July 28, 1877, container 17, Sheridan Papers, on the vegetables.

49. Sheridan to Adj. Gen., July 30, no. 720, Letters Sent, 1877, Military Div. of the Missouri, RG393, NA.

50. Sheridan to Townsend, August 17, no. 806, *Ibid.*

51. Adj. Gen. Townsend to Gen. Pope, July 24, AGO no. 4042.

52. See Department of Missouri to Davis, July 23, no. 482, Department of Missouri, Letters Sent, 1877, RG393, NA. Also series of wires, Pope to Townsend, July 23, 24, 25, 26, in AGO no. 4042; Pope's comments in his annual report in *Sec. War Rept. 1877,* pp. 62-63; Davis's final report on duty in St. Louis, August 30, 1877, in AGO no. 4042.

53. The activities of federal troops in St. Louis may be followed in AGO no. 4042; Pope to Sec. War McCrary, July 28, two wires; Pope to Adj. Gen., July 28; Davis to Adj. Gen., July 28, all in AGO no. 4042. Pope to Sheridan, August 2, no. 4431, and Pope to Adj. Gen., August 8, no. 4543, Letters Received, 1877, Military Division of the Missouri, RG393, NA. *St. Louis Post-Dispatch,* July 25, 26, 27, 28, 30, 31. Burbank, *Reign of the Rabble,* pp. 153-55, 157-60.

54. Eggert, *Railroad Labor Disputes,* pp. 30-33.

55. To. Gen. Schofield, July 30, in AGO no. 4042.

56. *Ibid.*

57. To his wife, July 27, 1877, Getty Papers. Secretary of War McCrary noted with emphasis in his annual report for 1877 that federal troops inflicted no wounds nor killed anyone, *Sec. War Rept. 1877,* p. xiii.

58. See July and August reports of the Third Infantry, Returns of Regular Army Infantry Regiments, AGO RG94, NA. See July and August Reports for Thirteenth, Sixteenth, Eighteenth, and Twenty-second Infantries, *Ibid.*

59. Orders to officers going to the aid of state officials found in AGO no. 4042: see, Adj. Gen. to Commanding Officer, Washington Arsenal, (Col. French), July 18; Adj. Gen. to Capt. John J. Rodgers, 2nd Artillery, July 18; Col. French to Adj. Gen., July 19, two wires; Adj. Gen. to Col. Barry, July 21; Adj. Gen. to Hancock, July 21, and July 24; Hancock to Adj. Gen., July 24, July 26. Evidence of the relationship between field commanders and the railroad officials in *Ibid.,* e.g. on Hancock and Scott, see Hancock to Adj. Gen., July 22, 25, 27; on Hancock and Franklin Gowen of the Reading Railroad, Hancock to Adj. Gen., July 24, *Ibid.,* and Hancock to Gowen and Gowen to Hancock, in "Telegrams, Riots of Pennsylvania," Military Division of the Atlantic, RG393, NA. The pervasive influence of the railroads in the affected states is discussed in Bruce, *1877,* pp. 76-77, 101-02, and *passim;* Eggert, *Railroad Labor Disputes,* pp. 25-27, 48-50; Rich, *The Presidents and Civil Disorders,* pp. 77-81; Yearly, "The B & O Strike of 1877," pp. 196-207.

60. Report of Lt. Col. Morrow to Military Division of the Atlantic, August 26, 1877, AGO no. 4042.

61. Hancock to Sec. War McCrary, July 24, 1877, *Ibid.*

62. *Ibid.*

63. *Ibid.* Also see McCrary to Hancock, July 25; Hancock to McCrary, July 25, 26, 27; McCrary to Hancock, July 28, all in *Ibid.* Otis, "The Army in Riots of 1877," pp. 297-99.

64. The deliberations of Hayes and his cabinet are contained in Hayes's own handwriting for July 24 through July 28, in Hayes Papers. The Signal Corps reports are collected under the name Strike Wires, in the Hayes Papers. Requests from and answers to governors in AGO no. 4042. *New York Times,* July 23, 1877, p. 5, and Harry Barnard, *Rutherford B. Hayes and His America* (New York, 1954), pp. 446-47, are also of value. Also, Bruce, *1877,* pp. 278-79; Eggert, *Railroad Labor Disputes,* pp. 47-49; Rich, *The Presidents and Civil Disorder,* pp. 80-85.

65. Eggert, *Railroad Labor Disputes,* pp. 50-53.

66. In Charles R. Williams, ed., *Diary and Letters of Rutherford Birchard Hayes,* vol. 3 (Columbus, O., 1924), pp. 440-41. Similar sentiments in Sec. War McCrary to F. L. Wood, Batavia, N.Y., August 13, 1877, Hayes Papers.

67. Headquarters, Department of the Missouri, to Davis, July 23, no. 482, Department of the Missouri, Letters Sent, 1877, RG393, NA.

68. *Ibid.*

69. Pope to Adj. Gen., July 25 and 26, *Ibid.*

70. In Pope's annual report for 1877, in *Sec. War Report 1877,* p. 63.

4 1877—The Aftermath

By the end of July, the combination of federal troops, state militia, and hastily organized citizens' posses had put an end to disorder and re-opened rail traffic in the disturbed states. The Army did not return to station immediately, however. Federal forces remained in Chicago and St. Louis to watch over an uneasy peace until mid-August. Once it became apparent that the workers' protest had run its course, the War Department sent these troops back to their regular duties. The Hayes administration discovered that in West Virginia, Maryland, and Pennsylvania, states where troops had been given to the governors to suppress domestic insurrection, it was difficult to gain a release of the Army. Having allowed the governors to define the necessity for federal intervention in the first place, the administration now allowed them to determine when the insurrection was over. Hayes's acquiescence to the governors' retention of troops placed the Army in the position of being an obvious instrument of strikebreaking.

Both Colonel Getty in West Virginia, and Colonel Barry in Maryland, were reporting peace on the Baltimore and Ohio by August 1. Trains were running in and out of Baltimore without military guards, and Barry suggested that troops were no longer needed in Maryland. Getty told his wife that his command had seen no trouble since he had relieved the irascible Colonel French. Even Governor John L. Carroll of Maryland conceded that the "impression prevails that the end is near."[1] Hancock's headquarters ordered the federal commands in the two states to begin packing up and prepare to move to Pennsylvania. It seemed to be all over in Maryland and West Virginia.[2]

Then, canal boatmen went on strike in Maryland, and coal miners walked off their jobs in West Virginia. In neither case did the strikers go on a riotous rampage, although they did harass B & O rail traffic to an extent. Governor Carroll appealed to Hancock for federal military assistance, and after some hesitation the general granted the request. Carroll sent two regiments of state militia to the disturbed area but contended he also needed regulars. On August 11, three companies aided the Cumberland sheriff in arresting strike leaders in the canal walkout. The troops performed no other duty than to maintain order by their presence. Federal troops also kept a watchful eye on striking coal miners in West Virginia, where Governor Mathews made no effort to raise state militia to deal with the problem. Carroll and Mathews simply relied upon the Army as the main instrument of law and order in the disturbed regions of both states.[3]

No one at either the state or federal levels questioned the legality, let alone the propriety, of using federal troops to intimidate strikers. Neither Carroll nor Mathews made any attempt to exhaust state and local resources in coping with the strikes. There was no disorder to suppress, but the fear that these strikes would rekindle the flames of protest seen in July impelled the governors to hang on to the federal troops despite the absence of widespread disorder. Colonel Getty shared these fears, sensing a depth of resentment "through the mountain region, which is liable to break out into violence at any moment."[4] While he disliked strike duty, Getty believed it was necessary to keep troops in Maryland and West Virginia. "The civil authorities are utterly powerless or sympathize with the rioters," he told his wife.[5]

Federal troops would remain until industrial peace returned. "Tomorrow will determine whether the miners and canal men go to work or not," Getty wrote on August 12. "Should they go to work there will be an end to the strike for the present and the troops withdrawn."[6] The strikers soon went back to work, and the War Department began earnest efforts to have federal forces released in Maryland and West Virginia. By August 17, Getty noted that "everything is working nicely now both on the railroad and canal—so I suppose the war is over and we may go home very soon."[7] Pressures from Hancock and Secretary of War McCrary finally brought official requests from Governor Mathews and Governor Carroll for a withdrawal of troops. They left the two states on August 25. From the beginning of the month until their departure, federal troops in Maryland and West Virginia served not as force to restore order but as a threat to compel strikers to return to work.[8]

The clearest incident of strikebreaking through intimidation by the Army took place in Pennsylvania. The railroad strike spawned a series of other strikes in the state, with iron workers and coal miners quitting work during the railroad shutdown and often joining the railroaders in blocking traffic. When the railroad men returned to work, however, the coal miners in the eastern part of the state refused to do so. The strike occurred in the region of the Molly Maguires, and the miners were in an ugly mood. On August 1, the coal strike reached the crisis stage at Scranton when angry miners precipitated a riot in which several of them were killed by a citizens' posse. In this city, and at Wilkesbarre, Reading, and Easton, striking miners attacked freight trains hauling coal and damaged mining property. Soon all of the coal mines in Luzerne County were shut down. Local law enforcement agencies proved unable to cope with the disorders. Once again, Governor John F. Hartranft appealed to Hancock for federal troops.[9]

Hancock knew as early as July 30, that he might have to send troops to the coal region. Several railroads and coal companies operating there were in federal receivership, and U.S. marshals had already made requests for troops to protect these properties. The general faced two problems in meeting the demands for troops from the marshals and Governor Hartranft. His main problem was manpower. All of the troops in the Military Division of the Atlantic were in use, and he was not sure where to obtain the necessary men for the coal region. The general was aware of the mood of the coal miners and did not want to send his troops there until he could put together a force large enough to ensure success once they entered the area. The second problem Hancock faced related to control of the troops. All the troops in Pennsylvania were under the orders of Governor Hartranft, and Hancock was not sure if he could take troops away from the Governor and lend them to U.S. marshals. Hancock's earlier fears of divided authority proved to be correct, but he eventually solved the problem by working out a *modus vivendi* with Hartranft.[10]

Hancock and Governor Hartranft agreed to a joint movement of state and federal troops into the disturbed coal region. The general brought the Twenty-second Infantry from Chicago and gathered spare troops from his command in Pennsylvania, Maryland, and West Virginia, and from the infantry regiments in Indiana and Kentucky. Hartranft reactivated the National Guard First and Sixth Divisions, which had performed so poorly at Pittsburgh. The Guard command, totalling nearly 5,000 men and personally led by Hartranft, arrived in Scranton on August 2. The first contingent of federal troops arrived the same day. During the next three days, regulars moved to Wilkesbarre, Easton, and Mauch Chunk, where striking miners continually interrupted rail traffic. The presence of state and federal troops restored order and railroad travel to these regions, but by no means did it bring complete peace.[11]

When the troops first arrived in the coal region, there was much interference with rail traffic and sabotage to mining property. The local governments seemed unable to guarantee protection for the railroads or mining companies. The regulars' first duty, then, was to aid marshals and sheriffs in preventing miners from interfering with the operations of railroads and mines. On August 7, federal troops assisted the U.S. marshal in opening traffic on the New Jersey Central Railroad at Mauch Chunk. At the time, the Central was in receivership to the United States district court. Again on August 7, Lieutenant Colonel Elwell S. Otis, Twenty-second Infantry, gave a posse of thirty men to the sheriff at Wilkesbarre to protect a train leaving there with a load of coal. The soldiers rode on the cars, and their presence prevented any interference. When the troops first went in, Hancock had authorized the commanders to respond to sheriffs' and marshals' requests for troops to act as posses whenever trouble seemed imminent. He soon found out that this sort of duty could continue all fall, as the law officers sought troops at the first hint of trouble. Some of their demands were ridiculous. The marshal at Wilkesbarre requested 1500 troops at one time, which amounted to half of Hancock's entire command. He was refused.[12]

Eventually, General Hancock evolved a policy which severely limited the use of federal troops as a *posse comitatus*. He informed all troop commanders that they could aid U.S. marshals only when they presented a court order specifically stating the need for a posse. Officers were not to aid local sheriffs until they had exhausted all their resources, including the militia. "It is not desirable," Hancock wrote, "that the U.S. troops shall be used except when necessary. The troops ought not to be sent about in small detachments and only when the necessity for a large force is apparent should they be used."[13] The general not only disliked this police work but also feared that a small detachment of federals might be overpowered by a mob. The Army, he believed, could not take that sort of disgrace.[14]

The harassment of trains and sabotage to mining property ended, as did the need for posses, but Governor Hartranft showed no desire to let the federal troops leave. On August 15, he wrote to the secretary of war,

> The emergency for which federal troops were brought into
> this State is over, but the situation in the mining regions is
> still very critical and for prudential reasons I request the re-
> tention for the present of such forces as are not needed else-
> where.[15]

So the Army settled down to an occupation of the coal region of eastern Pennsylvania. By mid-August, Hancock concentrated troops in large numbers at Mauch Chunk, Scranton, and Wilkesbarre, with a smaller detachment at Reading.[16]

Although the miners were well organized and determined to stay out until they achieved a victory, the presence of federal troops ensured their defeat. The civil authorities used the threat of regulars to keep the miners quiet and prevent even peaceful demonstrations. Living conditions among strikers and their families deteriorated. Hancock reported that almost 100,000 men were idle and that they and their families lived on potatoes, wild blackberries, and whortleberries. The miners had little influence with the federal officers but made some attempts to win the sympathies of the enlisted men. Although some officers scoffed at this, Hancock ordered that

> localities for summer camps of our troops in the disturbed
> regions should be somewhat removed from the influence of the
> strikers and persons in sympathy with them in the recent dis-
> orders whose influence might be brought to bear on their fellow
> foreign countrymen.[17]

General Hancock was ambivalent about keeping the Army in Pennsylvania after the railroad strikes. He particularly disliked remaining there under the orders of Governor Hartranft, and continually pressed the governor for a release of federal troops. On August 11, Hancock wired Secretary of War McCrary, asking if there was some way to get Hartranft to agree to a withdrawal, for "the Federal troops should not be permitted to remain in the localities of serious disorder unless the Governors should continue steadfastly to assert that their presence is necessary for the purpose for which they were originally ordered therein."[18] In September, Hartranft took the unprecedented move of enrolling two full-time state regiments of volunteers to relieve National Guard units on duty in the coal region. Nonetheless, he refused to agree to a withdrawal of the regulars. Hancock bitterly complained that the Army "should not be made a police force for the State in a matter which incidentally belongs to the state instead of the General Government."[19]

At the same time, Hancock suggested to the adjutant general that semi-permanent camps be established at Scranton, Wilkesbarre, and Mauch Chunk, or some other suitable place. In part he was concerned that the troops would be caught in winter with no quarters. But, more importantly, he would not "advise a reduction of the force in the mining district. It would not have a good effect to move troops from there unless replaced. This condition of affairs will not, I think, continue long. It will exist, however, practically until the miners go to work."[20] He even suggested reorganizing the Division of the Atlantic so as to place more troops in the North and close down many of the posts in the South. He recommended keeping troops in the disturbed states for some time to come, concentrated in large garrisons which would have ready access to the strike regions. General Sherman rejected the proposals as unnecessary. The only new troop disposition made after the strike was the stationing of four artillery batteries at Carlisle Barracks, Pennsylvania, through December of 1877.[21]

Civilians in Pennsylvania attempted to get the Hayes administration to establish permanent garrisons in the state. A petition from Scranton argued that "our people feel that their property and interests will never be safe here without a permanent standing army force," and offered to help bear the cost of supporting such a force.[22] At Reading, the Pennsylvania Railroad offered to provide quarters for any troops kept there during the winter. Hancock may have succumbed to these pressures in his overall assessment of the situation in Pennsylvania. The coal strike sputtered out in mid-October, and, on October 19, Governor Hartranft informed Hayes that the troops could be withdrawn. By October 30, all troops had returned to station except the artillery batteries at Carlisle Barracks.[23]

Hancock's ambivalence was due in part to his desire to retain military control of federal forces in the state and yet at the same time prevent the striking miners from fomenting trouble. The establishment of semi-permanent posts would have given control of the troops back to the Army but also would allow, as Hancock cryptically put it, "for an intelligent disposition of them with a view to future operations of a public nature of one kind or another."[24] He was willing to have the Army serve as an intimidating force to prevent future labor-related rioting but not under the control of state officials.

Hancock's officers reflected a similar concern for maintaining industrial peace. Lacking any substantive guidance from the War Department as to their duties except to follow the dictates of Governor Hartranft, the field commanders were left on their own. Hancock instructed them as to when and how to aid sheriffs and marshals but provided no other direction. Almost immediately, the officers' middle-class respect for order, the sanctity of private property, and distaste for working-class action surfaced. The military commanders at Wilkesbarre, Scranton, and Mauch Chunk established direct and daily contact with mine owners, railroad officials, and local civic leaders as soon as they moved in. They also kept a close watch on the activities of strikers and their leaders. Lieutenant Colonel Henry A. Morrow reported from Scranton, "I am promptly informed of all that is doing here, so thoroughly indeed, that it would be next to impossible for 50 men to be assembled with bad intentions without the fact being immediately communicated to me."[25] Lieutenant Colonel Otis found the miners at Wilkesbarre sullen, "but they have little idea of resisting U.S. troops."[26]

Exhibiting a decided dislike for unions, Colonel Otis believed that without union threats of revenge the strike would collapse in a day. Army officers asserted that federal troops were essential to the peace of the region. "Many conservative citizens feel grave apprehension of trouble unless strikers resume work," Colonel Morrow noted. "At present there is no prospect of an immediate resumption of labor and until labor is resumed I regard an armed force of some kind in or near Scranton necessary."[27] Major Richard Arnold of the inspector general's department also found support for the Army among "the better class," and concluded that "the presence of the Federal troops has invariably restored and preserved order, and given a confidence that could not have been reached in any other way."[28]

Officers in the strike region were pleased to discover the interest the "better class" displayed in the service. Otis promised to "make the Army popular . . . among all classes," but spent all his time with the mine owners.[29] Hancock proudly forwarded to the War Department an excerpt from the *Scranton Republican* describing the troops' departure which praised the regulars and concluded, "Their brief residence among us has revolutionized our views and opinions of army men in general, and henceforth we shall always feel that we have friends among the national defenders."[30]

Strike duty brought the Army temporarily out of its physical and psychological isolation and into contact with social groups which valued its duty and with which the officer corps shared values. Officers did not lust for strike duty; indeed many found it disagreeable. Neither did they pursue a harsh policy while in the field. For the most part, the Army was quite restrained during the railroad strike and the occupation of the coal region. Unnecessary or uncontrolled violence, which so often marked the appearance of the National Guard in 1877, was not part of the Army's performance. Nonetheless, many officers found it pleasurable to make contact with civilians who appreciated their existence and their duty. Other professional soldiers, a minority, saw in strike duty an opportunity to further the interests of their service. In both cases, officers serving in the strike-bound regions in 1877 would not forget this new experience of the U.S. Army.[31]

In the immediate aftermath of the 1877 strikes, some elements in the country called for an increase in manpower and an expansion of the Army's authority in coping with civil disorders. Congress did not respond to the calls. In the long run the antipathies left over from Reconstruction and well-ingrained dislike for a large standing army proved far stronger than any fears generated by the labor riots. When Congress met in October of 1877 to act on the long-deferred Army appropriations bill, it left the service at 25,000 enlisted men. In the debates on the bill, Democrats attempted to reduce the force, relying primarily on the Reconstruction experience as an example of the misuse of the military in civil affairs. Condemnation of the Army's role in the labor upheavals of the summer was a minor theme in the debate and attracted little attention. Strike duty did not alter the service's material condition.[32]

General Hancock's worries about the proper relationships between state and federal military forces during civil disturbances, a concern far more relevant to the experience of 1877 than the need to enlarge the Army, went unresolved. Hancock had believed the issue of utmost concern, even during the strike, as he noted to General Schofield.

"This thing" will appear again, and at that time, it will be
necessary that the States should have a well organized
militia, of force and power, that it be used promptly, or
that the Federal Government shall have the means of commanding or—for the next time this comes, I judge from the
passions I have seen outcrop, society may be shaken to its
foundations.[33]

Few in the national government heeded Hancock's warning or contemplated the possibilities of resolving the dilemma of the proper command relations between federal troops and state officials during civil
tumult. Neither the legislature nor the executive attempted to digest the
1877 experience in terms of remedies for the basic causes of the outbreak.
Nor were preparations made for future disorders. Only by accident did
Congress pass a law which would affect the later conduct of federal forces
in suppressing domestic disorder. This act of serendipity was the *posse
comitatus* law of 1878. A Democratic Congress seeking to redress what
they saw as the abuse of federal military power during Reconstruction
forbade the use of the Army as a posse to aid local officials in dealing
with domestic turmoil without the express order of the president, and
only then for very specific purposes. During Reconstruction, and coincidently during the 1877 strikes, federal troops had assisted local law
officers and federal marshals in enforcing a variety of laws simply upon
the request of a civil law officer to the local military commander. The
1878 act stipulated that all appeals for federal military aid had to go to
the president first, and all orders to carry out such assistance had to be
issued through the military chain of command down to the local commander. Army regulations implied that the chain of command had to be
maintained even when troops were sent to assist governors.[34]

The Reconstruction experience influenced the perceptions and ex-
pectations of officers who served on riot duty. Above all, in light of that
experience, they were concerned about their legal liabilities when aiding
civil officials to enforce the law. During Reconstruction officers had often
been left to their own devices to interpret and carry out the vaguely defined intents of both presidential and congressional policy in the South.
The frequent use of troops as a *posse comitatus* by local, state, and federal
civil officers, often for conflicting purposes, not only engendered great

hostility toward the Army but led to civil suits against officers and some-times even arrest. The government did little to aid the officers' legal de-fense in these cases.[35]

Consequently, in the aftermath of the 1877 upheaval and the passage of the *posse comitatus* law, officers sought precise definitions of their legal rights and responsibilities when aiding civil officials. Colonel Elwell S. Otis recalled that strike duty in 1877 had been unpleasant "because of the exceeding delicacy of the duty and the vagueness of expressed law to guide action under the circumstances that existed."[36] Since neither Congress nor the War Department made any effort to fill the legal void, Otis and other officers attempted to do so. The officers' major concern was the questionable legality of being placed under the command of a state governor, or his aides, or other local officials. Otis concluded, "We cannot discover any authority for this proceeding. Neither the Constitu-tion nor Congress ever expressly authorized the President to turn over troops to the governors of States."[37] Officers clearly wanted the security, both legal and military, of remaining directly within the federal chain of command. A military force acting in support of civil officials, Captain James Regan argued, "is to remain under the direction and orders of the President, as commander-in-chief and his military subordinates, it cannot be placed under the direct orders or exclusive disposition of the Governors of a State."[38]

Officers dealing with this issue were attempting to incorporate the implications of the *posse comitatus* law, delineate their legal responsibili-ties, and determine precisely the extent of tactical control they exercised when in the field in support of civil officials. It was not an easy task, given the lack of direction from above, and officers themselves did not agree on the meaning of law and precedent. Lieutenant Richard Young, Fifth Artillery, took issue with the argument of General Hancock and Colonel Otis that governors could not command federal troops. Young maintained that a governor "exercises a general supervision indicating the objects to be attained," while the Army officer in command com-plied within the Articles of War and prevailing regulations.[39] Colonel John Hamilton, Fifth Artillery, argued that the military suppression of riots was such a volatile and unpredictable duty that no set of laws or regulations could guide the soldier. In Hamilton's eyes, "an anti-mob-commander" should "be blind to courts and newspapers," and merely do what was necessary to suppress the mob. "The reason there are no laws to govern the officer in quelling a riot is that none can be written. Write one, and in five minutes I can put enough ifs and buts into it to rob it of all force."[40]

Officers of both the Army and National Guard also gave attention to the purely tactical demands of riot duty. Both services had discovered in 1877 that they had no tactical guides for operations during riot duty. Articles in service journals and popular magazines, as well as books on the topic, discussed in detail the methods of dealing with urban mobs. Most of these works were aimed primarily at the National Guard, and there is little indication that the Army altered its basic post drill to incorporate training for domestic disorder.[41]

That the question of civilian command of troops in civil disorder remained unresolved and that the Army made little effort to train for riot duty reflected the failure of Congress and the executive to set any policy to govern future federal military intervention in domestic disorders. A few officers in the Army considered future possibilities of duty in this area. At least one general officer, Major John M. Schofield, took action to prepare his command for service in domestic upheavals. In 1883, Schofield assumed command of the Military Division of the Missouri, with headquarters in Chicago, a city branded by many Americans as the seedbed of radicalism and labor agitation in the 1880s. Once stationed in Chicago, Schofield put his staff to work preparing contingency plans for moving federal troops quietly but quickly into the city in the event of a large strike or riot. The General's aide-de-camp, Captain J. P. Sanger, consulted with officials of the chief railroads in the city and rode about on these railroads, taking notice of important strategic points. In 1885, when a labor riot threatened, Sanger met with the Chicago chief of police and discussed the possibility of the need for federal troops.[42]

After the Haymarket Riot in 1886, Schofield played a central role in establishing Fort Sheridan at Evanston, some twenty miles north of Chicago. Schofield's predecessor, Philip H. Sheridan, had tried for several years to locate a large garrison near Chicago but had failed. The Haymarket Riot stirred businessmen and industrialists of the city to action. A group of these influential men, including George Pullman, Marshall Field, and Cyrus McCormick, donated a large sum of money for the purchase of a suitable land site. Schofield, working with Sheridan who was now commanding general, selected the Evanston site. The Chicago group purchased this land for $156,890, and in 1887, the government accepted the gift and built Fort Sheridan. By 1892, an entire regiment, the Fifteenth Infantry, was stationed there.[43]

Schofield's activities in Chicago are the clearest indication of an important Army officer directly involving himself in preparations for riot duty. There is some evidence that others made similar preparations. For example, in his 1893 report, Major General Oliver O. Howard, commander of the Department of the East, reported that several large strikes had taken place in his department in 1892, "were intently observed by officers of the regular Army," and close contacts were maintained with officers of the National Guard in the affected states.[44]

The labor turbulence of the 1880s, however, found the government and the Army singularly unprepared. While there was no general labor outbreak in the decade necessitating federal intervention, there were calls from states and territories. The responses to these calls indicated that neither civilian nor military leaders at the national level had taken the 1877 strike as a harbinger or that they anticipated the use of federal troops in disorders after that event. What marked the 1880s interventions was the lack of planning involved. The federal executive, both the president and the War Department, reacted to each request on an ad hoc basis, making policy as crises developed.

A call from Governor Albinus Nance of Nebraska on March 9, 1882, upon President Chester A. Arthur led to a commitment of federal troops in Omaha. Neither the city nor the state had exhausted its resources in dealing with the disorder, and Governor Nance had succumbed quickly to pressures from Omaha businessmen to obtain federal assistance. Despite the observation of General George Crook, commanding the Department of the Platte headquartered in Omaha, that "thus far [March 9] there has been no necessity for interference of military," Arthur granted Nance's request.[45] Federal troops served in Omaha from March 11 to the 21st. The *Army and Navy Journal* reported that "the United States troops had little to do with the riots."[46] The incident indicated the propensity for federal officials to take state pleas for military assistance at their face value without attempting to discern the actual need for federal troops.[47]

Three years later a justifiable call for federal assistance in a labor-related upheaval was temporarily forestalled because neither the governor of Wyoming Territory nor members of the Cleveland administration had a clear idea of the legalities governing federal military assistance to states and territories. The disturbance in Wyoming involved white and Chinese miners employed by the Union Pacific Railroad at Rock Springs. The Chinese miners refused to join the whites in a strike, and consequently, on September 2, 1885, white miners attacked the Chinese, killing over twenty men and driving the remainder into the hills surrounding the Rock Springs mines. Another fifty Chinese died of exposure and starvation. Rock Springs was a small, isolated mining town, and the rampaging whites were in total control. Wyoming had no militia, and Governor Francis E. Warren immediately appealed to General Oliver O. Howard, commanding the Department of the Platte, for military assistance.[48]

Under the *posse comitatus* act, Howard could not respond to Warren's request, but he did send it on to Washington. From September 2 through the 7, Warren attempted to get the properly worded request to President Cleveland. Only on September 8 did the Cleveland administration finally decide upon a proper legal justification for committing troops in Wyoming. Much of the confusion and delay was not Warren's fault. In Washington, Adjutant General R. C. Drum first handled the requests. He was in a difficult position. President Cleveland was in Buffalo, New York; Secretary of War William Endicott was in Salem, Massachusetts; the attorney general was out of the capital as well. Drum conferred with Endicott by telegraph, and met personally with Secretary of State Thomas F. Bayard. With Bayard's approval, Drum ordered Major General John M. Schofield, commanding the Division of the Missouri, to send troops to Wyoming on the pretext of protecting the Union Pacific as a military road and mail route. By patrolling the UP near Rock Springs, Drum hoped "the mere presence of troops will prevent further trouble and restore order."[49]

Secretary of War Endicott gave little help to General Drum in the early stages of the crisis. Endicott thought Governor Warren's need for help "sufficient" but did not want to act without the president's approval. "I hesitate to do it on my sole responsibility," he told Drum. "Consult with Secretary of State and other members of the Cabinet in Washington. I will act with them or issue orders if they approve."[50] Finally, on September 7, the Cleveland administration moved beyond the protection of mails and a military route for justifying the presence of troops in Wyoming. Drum notified General Schofield that his troops were to operate in enforcing a treaty between the United States and China which guaranteed protection of Chinese aliens and their property. This gave Schofield and his officers the authority to take whatever action was necessary to suppress disorder. By early October, an officer at Rock Springs reported, "the troops here are fully occupied in guarding mines and machinery and protecting the Chinese. It is not a pleasant duty, nor is Rock Springs especially desirable as an abiding place." But the trouble was over. A small contingent of troops remained there for several years afterward.[51]

The episode was not of the kind that could be easily anticipated or prepared for, but the confusion on the part of both Governor Warren and Secretary of War Endicott indicated the weakness of having no policy whatsoever to govern federal military aid to states and territories. Warren had assumed from the outset that since Wyoming was a territory it was not necessary for civilian territorial officials to make the same kind of formal request for federal assistance that the statutes demanded of state governors. The failings of the Army's command system, particularly when neither the president nor the secretary of war were present in Washington, contributed to the confusion as well. Adjutant General Drum overcame these liabilities with the exercise of a little imagination and a willingness to act on his own responsibility, qualities which his civilian superior Endicott seemed to lack. Above all, the absence of any general policy contributed to the indecision of the Cleveland administration.[52]

Perhaps this indecisiveness led Cleveland to respond quickly to a call from the governor of Washington Territory later in the same year. Again, conflict between organized white labor and Chinese workers was the underlying cause of disorder. In an effort to rid themselves of a despised racial minority, which they believed undercut their economic well-being, and to confront openly a politically conservative business community in the territory's cities, organized labor in Washington attempted to expel forcibly Chinese workers. They succeeded in Tacoma on November 3, 1885, and appeared to be ready to do the same in Seattle. In anticipation of the latter action, territorial officials requested federal troops on November 5. Cleveland denied the call but gave in to a more urgent request from Governor Watson Squire on the following day. On November 8, Brigadier General John Gibbon, Department of the Columbia, accompanied ten companies of the Fourteenth Infantry into Seattle. Gibbon found complete order, but remained there ten days, "during which no action of any kind was called for."[53]

The fact that there was no demonstrable need for the U.S. troops in Seattle in November, 1885, undoubtedly created skepticism in Washington when another request for troops came from the territory on February 7, 1886. Labor's threat to force Chinese workers out of the city became reality. Seattle leaders quickly put together a force of militia, temporary home guards, and a sheriff's posse to protect the Chinese and arrest the leaders of the anti-Chinese movement. The entire affair was highly tense, pitting organized labor against the city's leading property owners and employers, who were prominent in the militia and home-guard leadership. On February 7, and for the next two days, Governor Squire appealed to President Cleveland for federal troops. He declared martial law in Seattle on the 8th, after a group of home guards protecting the Chinese had fired upon a crowd of workers, killing four men and wounding another. Cleveland finally acceded to the demands of key political figures in Washington and ordered troops to Seattle later on February 9, simultaneously issuing a proclamation demanding that the rioters disperse.[54]

Unquestionably, Seattle faced a serious problem of disorder. It is doubtful, however, that federal military assistance was needed to control the disorder. General Gibbon, commanding eight companies of the Fourteenth Infantry from Vancouver Barracks, which moved into Seattle on the 10th, discovered,

Everything was perfectly quiet and peaceful. There was no "domestic violence" to suppress, and no civil authorities to aid in overcoming obstruction to the enforcement of the laws. The city was in possession of the militia organizations, with a provost marshal appointed by the governor in charge.[55]

Despite the apparent peace and civil control of the city, Gibbon wrote Governor Squire on February 12 and urged him to take advantage of the state of martial law "to arrest every known leader of the late outrages. . . . I consider that the welfare of society demands that these men be at once arrested." Gibbon offered to oversee these arrests, and Squire accepted the offer.[56]

The War Department took a dim view of a department commander personally supervising the arrest and incarceration of leaders of a riot in a local situation. Gibbon justified the action on the grounds that he was sent to aid the civil authority in the territory and that since martial law was in effect, Governor Squire was the only civil official to be aided. He argued that martial law was justified, that those in favor of law and order were a minority, and sympathy for the anti-Chinese was so widespread that no civil official was willing to arrest them. Gibbon's deep concern for law and order led him to accept the role of arresting law breakers because "the lawless element shows that it feels perfect immunity from any punishment by the courts."[57] The general interjected himself into a social-political struggle between contending economic classes, and he did little to hide his antipathies towards "the shiftless and improvident, largely composed of foreign elements."[58]

Once order was restored, Gibbon discovered that his advocacy for law and order and the security his troops offered made it difficult to obtain their withdrawal. Governor Squire lifted martial law on February 22, and four of the eight companies of infantry returned to Vancouver Barracks. In the ensuing five months, Gibbon repeatedly attempted to have the remaining troops relieved, arguing that Seattle police and the territorial National Guard were more than sufficient to maintain order. Ironically, he contended that the continued presence of federal forces in Seattle sapped the will of civil authorities to deal with the problem. The Cleveland administration did not withdraw troops from the city until August 19, 1886.[59]

The Seattle experience indicated once again the liabilities of committing federal troops to suppress disorder upon the appeal of state or territorial officials without first attempting to investigage the nature of the disorder and the efforts of state and local forces to deal with it. As in 1877, Gibbon had been ordered to report to Squire "to aid civil authorities in overcoming obstruction to the enforcement of the laws."[60] The vagueness of such an order invariably gave the immediate military field commander the opportunity to act as he saw fit. Gibbon did not have to suppress disorder in Seattle for, as he reported, there was none. But he immediately aligned himself with one side of a serious social-political-economic conflict. This was probably inevitable given the nature of the legal system and the fact that the propertied classes controlled local and territorial government. The general made no effort to appear merely as a force for order, however, and exhibited an open commonality with the middle and upper-class elements of Seattle.[61]

In the aftermath of the tumultuous riots of 1877, the Army remained substantially unchanged. The service, with no guidance from Congress or the executive, did little to prepare for future domestic duty. Few officers in either the staff or the line had any real interest in preparing the service for riot duty. The thrust of professional concerns at the newly established Infantry and Cavalry School at Fort Leavenworth, and in the service journals appearing in the 1870s, was on making the U.S. Army an efficient and modern instrument for war. A few officers expressed interest in the legal and tactical problems in suppressing domestic disorder, but this was a limited concern. The Army would be called upon again in the 1890s to deal with labor-related disorders, however, and its failure to give serious attention to such duty would then become evident.[62]

Unlike the Army, the National Guard underwent substantial changes in the decade and a half after 1877. The public press had excoriated the state soldiers' performance during the great railroad strikes. "The country must be pretty well convinced by this time," *The Chicago Times* editorialized, "that people who play soldier under the name of militia . . . are rather worse than no soldiers at all for the purpose of quelling insurrection."[63] Practically every public comment echoed the criticism, as did regular officers who wrote about the disturbances. Guard critics argued that part-time soldiers lacked the preparation and discipline needed to quell large-scale riots.[64]

The criticisms annoyed National Guard officers but spurred state legislatures to refurbish their state military systems. Supporters of the Guard as a domestic peace-keeping force argued that, given enough money, the militia could be well equipped and properly trained for riot duty. National Guard advocates contended that if the militia was not improved regulars would have to be used, and the frequent use of the Army in civil disorders would lead to unwarranted federal interference in local affairs. Fears of a national constabulary and the ability of the Guard to handle most labor disorders in the late nineteenth century contributed to the Army's tendency to slight the possibility of its future use in domestic disturbances.[65]

The federal government's failure to develop a position on labor-management relations after 1877 left labor policy in the hands of state and local officials or the owners and managers of industrial capitalism. Federal labor policy was created through acts of omission. Labor troubles were seen as private problems or issues for state and local government. With the keeping of the industrial peace left to local agencies like the National Guard, only on rare occasions would the Army be used to police labor. Unlike Europe, national forces could not be easily used to cow an industrial proletariat. But federal neglect led to haste and improvisation when the call came for national action. The onus of policy making then fell on Army officers, a task for which they were neither prepared to fulfill nor legally qualified to carry out.

Notes

1. Carroll to Sec. War George W. McCrary, July 30, 1877, consolidated file no. 4042, Letters Received, Adjutant General's Office, Record Group 94, Old Military Records Division, National Archives, Washington, D.C., hereafter referred to as AGO no. 4042.

2. See series of wires from Hancock to Adj. Gen., July 31 and August 1; Colonel William F. Barry to Adj. Gen., July 31, August 1 and 2, all in *Ibid.* Headquarters, Military Division of the Atlantic, to Barry, August 1, in William F. Barry Papers, Maryland Historical Society, Baltimore, Maryland. Colonel George W. Getty to his wife, July 29, August 1, 1877, in George W. Getty Papers, Library of Congress, Washington, D.C.

3. Conditions in West Virginia and Maryland in August, 1877, and the activities of the commands of Colonel Getty in the former and Colonel Barry in the latter may be followed in wires from and to the colonels and General Hancock and the War Department in AGO no. 4042. Getty to his wife, throughout August, in Getty Papers also helps to reconstruct events in West Virginia. Also see, Maryland, Executive, *Annual Report of the Adjutant General of Maryland for the Year 1877,* document E in House and Senate Documents for Maryland, 1878, (Annapolis, Md., 1878), pp. 20-21; Col. Elwell S. Otis, 20th Inf., "The Army in Connection with the Labor Riots of 1877," *JMSI* 5, no. 19 (September 1884): 314-15.

4. To his wife, August 2, Getty Papers.

5. August 3, Getty Papers.

6. To his wife, *Ibid.*

7. *Ibid.*

8. Getty's letters to his wife are most helpful here. On the withdrawal of troops from West Virginia and Maryland, see Sec. War McCrary to Governors Carroll and Mathews, both dated August 21, Letters Sent, 1877, Office of the Secretary of War, Record Group 107, National Archives; *Sec. War Rept. 1877,* pp. 93-97; Otis, "The Army in Connection with the Labor Riots of 1877," pp. 309-10, 314-15.

9. See Edward W. Martin, *History of the Great Riots* (Philadelphia, 1877), pp. 189-95, 202-11, on the background of the coal strike. *Philadelphia Inquirer,* front-page stories, August 6, 7, 8, 1877, and *Philadelphia Public Ledger,* August 1, 2, 3, 1877, for the violence and disorder attending the coal strike.

10. Hancock to Sec. of War McCrary, July 30, James W. Kerns, U.S. Marshal, to Hancock, July 31, Hancock to Kerns, August 1, Hancock to Adj. Gen., July 31, AGO no. 4042; Otis, "The Army in Riots of 1877," pp. 311-14.

11. Hancock to Adj. Gen., July 31, Hancock to Adj. Gen., August 1, two wires; Hancock to Adj. Gen., August 2, two wires, in AGO no. 4042; Pennsylvania, Executive, *Report of the Adjutant General of Pennsylvania for the Year 1877,* in Governor's Message and Reports, 1878 (Harrisburg, Pa., 1878), pp. 44-48, 115-23; *Philadelphia Public Ledger,* August 3, p. 1, August 4, p. 1, August 6, p. 1, August 7, 1877, p. 1; Martin, *The History of the Great Riots,* pp. 211-14.

12. Hancock to Adj. Gen., August 2, two wires; F. S. Lathrop, receiver, New Jersey Central Railroad, to Hancock, August 7; Hancock to Lathrop, August 7; Hancock to Adj. Gen., August 7; Lt. Col. Otis to Hancock, August 7, all in AGO no. 4042. Otis, "The Army in Riots of 1877, pp. 317-18; Martin, *The History of the Great Riots,* pp. 211-14.

13. Hancock to Samuel Dickson, receiver for New Jersey Central, August 11, AGO no. 4042.

14. See Hancock to Adj. Gen., August 7; Hancock to Dickson, August 11; Lt. Col. Otis to Hancock, August 16; Hancock to R. H. McKune, Mayor of Scranton, August 20; Lt. Col. H. A. Morrow to Hancock, September 21, all in AGO no. 4042. Hancock to Lt. Col. Otis, August 8, Letters Received, 1877, U.S. Troops at Wilkesbarre, Pa., Records of U.S. Army Continental Commands 1821-1920, Record Group 393, National Archives. Hancock to Lt. Col. R. B. Ayres, August 2, at Mauch Chunk, in "Telegrams, Riots of Pennsylvania," Military Division of the Atlantic, RG393, NA.

15. Hartranft to McCrary, AGO no. 4042.

16. Hancock to Adj. Gen., Aug. 29, *Ibid.*

17. Hancock to Maj. John Hamilton, August 8. Letters Received, 1877, Allegheny Arsenal, Pittsburgh, Pa., RG393, NA. Marked "Confidential," this letter was also sent to Army commanders at Cumberland, Maryland, Mauch Chunk, Wilkesbarre, Easton, and Reading, Pennsylvania. See Lt. Col. Otis, at Wilkesbarre, to Hancock, August 10, AGO no. 4042, for a report on strikers' attempts to win over Irish enlisted men.

18. AGO no. 4042.

19. To the Adj. Gen., Sept. 9, *Ibid.*

20. To the Adj. Gen., Aug. 29, *Ibid.*

21. On fears of the cold weather and its effects on the troops, see Lt. Col. Henry A. Morrow to Hancock, September 19, and Hancock to Gov. Hartranft, October 9, 15, AGO no. 4042. On considerations of semi-permanent posts in West Virginia, Maryland, and Pennsylvania, and re-organization of the Division of the Atlantic, see series of wires from Hancock to Col. Getty, the Adj. Gen., Gov. Hartranft, and Brig. Gen. C. C. Augur, commanding general, Department of the South, the first two

weeks of August, *Ibid.* Hancock to Sherman, October 25, Sherman to
Hancock, October 27, *Ibid.*, deal with Sherman's rejection of the idea.

22. E. B. Sturges to McCrary, August 29, *Ibid.* Also see W. A. Herren,
Pittsburgh, to President Hayes, August 8, in "Papers Pertaining to the
Railroad Strike of 1877," Rutherford B. Hayes Library, Fremont, Ohio,
on microfilm.

23. On the Pennsylvania Railroad's offer at Reading, see Maj. John
Mendenhall to Headquarters, Military Division of the Atlantic, September
22, Records, U.S. Troops at Reading, Pa., 1877, RG393, NA. On troop
withdrawals, see Hancock to Adj. Gen., September 9, October 20, 21,
24, Hancock to Sherman, October 25, Hartranft to Hayes, October 19,
all in AGO no. 4042; Lt. Col. Morrow to Headquarters, Military Division
of the Atlantic, October 30, in Records, Headquarters, U.S. Troops at
Scranton, Pa., RG393, NA.

24. To McCrary, August 11, AGO no. 4042. Similar views in Hancock
to Adj. Gen., October 18, *Ibid.*

25. Morrow to Headquarters, Military Division of the Atlantic, October 15, Records, Headquarters, U.S. Troops at Scranton, Pa., RG393,
NA.

26. To Hancock, August 10, AGO no. 4042. The commanders at
Scranton, Wilkesbarre, and Mauch Chunck kept a close watch on the
strikers, constantly attempting to assess support for the strike and to
determine when it would end. Lieutenant Colonel Otis at Wilkesbarre,
Lieutenant Colonel Morrow at Scranton, and Lieutenant Colonel R. B.
Ayres at Mauch Chunk reported regularly to Hancock on these assessments, as seen in a series of wires to Headquarters, Military Division of
the Atlantic, throughout August, September, and October of 1877, in
AGO no. 4042. Hancock himself kept in touch with the situation by
personally discussing the strike with mine owners and managers, as seen,
e.g., in Hancock to Adj. Gen., September 9, *Ibid.* and Hancock to Franklin
Gowen, August 2, in "Telegrams, Riots of Pa.," Military Division of the
Atlantic, RG393, NA.

27. To Headquarters, Military Division of the Atlantic, September 21,
AGO no. 4042.

28. In Inspector General to Gen. Philip Sheridan, October 29, *Ibid.*

29. To Hancock, August 10, *Ibid.*

30. October 22, 1877, in Hancock's collection of newspaper clippings
dealing with the strike, in *Ibid.*

31. The letters of Colonel Getty to his wife, August, 1877, in Getty
Papers, indicate his strong dislike for strike duty. Also see Col. Otis,

"The Army in Riots of 1877, *passim*. See below, Chapter Nine, for officers'
reactions to the import of strike duty.

32. For debates on the Army bill, see U.S., Congress, *Congressional
Record,* 45th Cong., 1st sess., 6, pp. 415-23, and pp. 288-300, 306-26,
333-35, on the Senate and House debates, respectively. For later efforts
to reduce the Army, see U.S., Congress, *Congressional Record,* 45th Cong.,
2nd sess., 7, pt. 4; 3534-55, 3669-84, 3715-30. Also of value, *The Nation*
25, no. 646 (November 15, 1877): 293, and no. 647 (November 22, 1877):
309; and *Army and Navy Journal* 15, no. 23 (January 12, 1878): 360-61,
and no. 25 (January 26, 1878): 392-93.

33. Emphasis in the original, July 30, 1877, AGO no. 4042.

34. U.S., War Department, *Regulations of the Army of the United
States and General Orders in Force, February 17, 1881,* abridged (Washington, D.C. 1881), article LIX, pp. 87-91, and Otis, "The Army in Riots
of 1877," 6, no. 22 (June 1885): 117-18.

35. James E. Sefton, *The United States Army and Reconstruction,
1865-1877* (Baton Rouge, La., 1967), pp. 25, 226, 252-54. See the comments of General Sherman on the vagueness of the law providing for the
use of the Army as a *posse comitatus* in Reconstruction, *Sec. War Report
1870,* p. 4.

36. "The Army in Riots of 1877," vol. 5, p. 323.

37. "The Army in Connection with the Labor Riots of 1877, *JMSI* 6,
no. 22 (June 1885): 123.

38. *Military Duties in Aid of the Civil Power: for the Regular Army,
National Guard, etc., and Police Forces Generally* (New York, 1888), p.
25. Similar conclusions in Capt. George F. Price, 5th Cavalry, "The
Necessity for Closer Relations Between the Army and the People, and the
Best Method to Accomplish the Result," *JMSI* 6, no. 24 (December 1885):
305, and the comments of Colonel Romeyn B. Ayres, 2nd Artillery, in
E. L. Molineux, "Riots in Cities and their Suppression," *JMSI* 4, no. 16
(1883): 361.

39. "Legal and Tactical Considerations Affecting the Employment of
the Military in the Suppression of Mobs, Including an Essay on Martial
Law," *Journal of the Military Service Institution of the United States
(JMSI)* 9, no. 33 (March 1888): 76, hereafter referred to as "The Mob
and the Military."

40. In General E. L. Molineux, "Riots in Cities and Their Suppression,"
JMSI 4, no. 16 (1883):370. Also see Major Robert N. Scott, Third Artillery,
"Martial Law in Insurrection and Rebellion," *JMSI* 4, no. 16 (1883): 408-
10.

41. Col. David Austen, New York National Guard, *Manual for Street Fighting* (New York, 1877); Brig. Gen. William H. Brownell, New York National Guard, *Formations for Street Riot Duty* (New York, 1888); M. D. Leggett, "The Military and the Mob," *Sketches of War History,* vol. 1 Ohio Commandery, Military Order of the Loyal Legion (Columbus, O., 1883), pp. 188-97; Brig. Gen. Albert Ordway, District of Columbia National Guard, *Drill Regulations for Street Riot Duty* (Washington, D.C., 1891); Fitz-John Porter, "How to Quell Mobs," *North American Review* 141, no. 347 (October 1885): 351-60; Major Edward G. Sprowl, California National Guard, *Street Tactics, Armory Formation and Street Marches* (San Francisco, 1889); Russell Thayer, "Movements of Troops in Cities in Cases of Riots or Insurrection," *United Service* 1, no. 1 (January 1879): 92-99; Molineux, "Riots in Cities and Their Suppression," pp. 335-60; Regan, *Military Aid to the Civil Power,* the bulk of the book deals with tactics; Young, "The Mob and the Military," pp. 257-89.

42. See Sanger to Schofield, November 11, 1884; January 15, 1885, January 24, 1884, in Letters Received, 1876-88, series II, John McAllister Schofield Papers, Library of Congress.

43. See John M. Schofield, *Forty-Six Years in the Army* (New York, 1897), pp. 454-55; Capt. H. R. Brinkerfoff, "Fort Sheridan," *United Service,* n.s., 8, no. 3 (September 1892): 271-77; "Our Military Posts: Fort Sheridan," *Leslie's Weekly* 79, no. 2039 (October 11, 1894): 233.

44. *Sec. War Rept. 1893,* p. 107.

45. In, *Use of United States Troops in Nebraska,* 47th Cong., 1st sess., House Executive Document 127 (Washington, D.C., 1882), p. 3.

46. March 25, 1882, p. 764.

47. This overview drawn from *Use of United States Troops in Nebraska,* pp. 1-5; *Army and Navy Journal,* March 18, 1882, p. 737, March 25, 1882, p. 764; *New York Times,* March 10-22, 1882; Ronald M. Gephart, "Politicians, Soldiers and Strikers: The Reorganization of the Nebraska Militia and Omaha Strike of 1882," *Nebraska History* 46, no. 2 (June 1965): 94-118.

48. The following sources provide the background for federal military intervention in Wyoming Territory in 1885: U.S., Department of the Interior, "Report of the Governor, Territory of Wyoming," and "Special Report of the Governor of Wyoming to the Secretary of the Interior Concerning Chinese Labor Troubles, 1885," in *Report of the Secretary of the Interior, 1885,* vol. 2 (Washington, D.C., 1885), pp. 1218-22, 1225-34, respectively; U.S., Congress, House, Committee on Foreign Affairs, *Providing Indemnity to Certain Chinese Subjects,* 49th Cong., 1st sess.,

H. Rept. 2044 (Washington, D.C., 1886), pp. 1-66; Paul Crane and Alfred Larson, "The Chinese Massacre," *Annals of Wyoming* 12, no. 1 (January 1940): 47-55, and no. 2 (April, 1940): 153-61.

49. To Endicott, September 4, 1885, series 2, reel 18, microfilm, Grover Cleveland Papers, Library of Congress, Washington, D.C. Warren's attempts to gain federal assistance seen in "Special Report of the Governor of Wyoming," pp. 1225-29. See series of wires between Drum and Endicott, September 4, Cleveland Papers; *New York Times,* September 4, p. 1, 5, 1885, p. 5.

50. September 5, 1885, Cleveland Papers.

51. *Army and Navy Journal,* October 10, 1885, p. 203. See "Special Report of the Governor of Wyoming," pp. 1230-32; Frederick T. Wilson, *Federal Aid in Domestic Disturbances, 1787-1903,* 57th Cong., 2nd sess., Senate Document 209 (Washington, D.C., 1903), pp. 215-18; *Army and Navy Journal,* September 12, 1885, p. 128, and October 24, 1885, p. 237.

52. "Special Report of the Governor of Wyoming," p. 1229.

53. In "Report of Brigadier General Gibbon," *Sec. War Rept. 1886,* p. 185. The following provide the background for the Seattle episode: Patrick H. McLatchy, "The Development of the National Guard of Washington as an Instrument of Social Control, 1854-1916" (Ph.D. diss., University of Washington, 1973), pp. 128-35, 141-43; Jules A. Karlin, "The Anti-Chinese Outbreaks in Seattle, 1885-1886," *Pacific Northwest Quarterly* 39, no. 2 (April 1948): 103-14; James F. Grant, ed., *History of Seattle, Washington* (New York, 1891), pp. 187-92.

54. McClatchy, "The National Guard of Washington," pp. 147-64; Karlin, "The Anti-Chinese Outbreaks in Seattle," pp. 119-24.

55. "Report of Brigadier General Gibbon," p. 186.

56. *Ibid.,* pp. 186-87. Also see Frederick T. Wilson, *Federal Aid in Domestic Disturbances, 1787-1903,* 57th Cong., 2nd sess., Senate Document 209 (Washington, D.C.), pp. 220-22.

57. To Adj. Gen. R. C. Drum, February 16, 1886; also see Drum to Gibbon, February 16, 1886, in "Report of Brigadier General Gibbon," pp. 187-88.

58. "Report of Brigadier General Gibbon," p. 189.

59. Karlin, "The Anti-Chinese Outbreaks in Seattle," pp. 126-29; McLatchy, "The National Guard of Washington," pp. 169-70.

60. Drum to Gibbon, Feb. 9, 1886, in "Report of Brigadier General Gibbon," p. 186.

61. The socioeconomic nature of the struggle is emphasized in McLatchy, "The National Guard of Washington," pp. 111-20, 170.

62. See Russell F. Weigley, *History of the United States Army* (New York, 1967), pp. 273-80.

63. July 25, 1877, p. 6.

64. As examples of this criticism, see *The Nation* 25, no. 631 (August 2, 1877): 68; *Harper's Weekly* 21, no. 1076 (August 11, 1877): 618; *Army and Navy Journal* 14, no. 52 (August 4, 1877): 832; *New York Times,* July 19, 1877, p. 4; *Chicago Tribune,* July 26, 1877, p. 4. These are merely samples of a caustic press attack on the militia. Professional military men were also critical of the militia. See, e.g., Capt. H. C. Cochrane, U.S.M.C., "The Naval Brigade and the Marine Battalion in the Labor Strikes of 1877," *United Service* 1, no. 1 (January 1879): 116; Young, "The Mob and the Military," p. 255; Captain James Chester, Third Artillery, "Standing Armies a Necessity of Civilization," *United Service* 9, no. 6 (December 1883): 665; Captain Otho E. Michaelis, Ordnance Department, "The Military Necessities of the United States and the Best Provisions for Meeting Them," *JMSI* 5, no. 19 (September 1884): 290 as samples.

65. For supporters of the National Guard, see Lt. Col. James M. Rice, Illinois National Guard, "The Proper Military Support to the Civil Power," *United Service* 11, no. 2 (August 1884): 114-17; Leggett, "The Military and the Mob," pp. 192-95. The refurbishment of the state military systems after 1877 has been discussed in Chapter One, but also see Samuel Rezneck, "Distress, Relief and Discontent in the United States During the Depression of 1873-1878," *Journal of Political Economy* 58, no. 6 (December 1950): 510-12.

5 1894—Miners, Tramps, and the Western Proletariat

The year 1894 was a most difficult one for the American people. The Panic of 1893 had precipitated a severe depression which led to bankruptcies, wage reductions, and massive unemployment. The fact that the nation lacked a relief system for the unemployed and the poor created discord, a discord compounded by the efforts of organized labor to counter wage reductions and layoffs. An assault on the established two party political system by the vociferous and seemingly radical Populist Party further contributed to the sense of fear and doom often expressed by the middle and propertied classes. Expressions of sympathy for strikers and the unemployed by Populist office holders and newspapers and by thousands of ordinary citizens heightened the latter's despair.

A succession of industrial upheavals in the first half of the year seemed to threaten the nation's very existence. Early in April, Eugene Debs's American Railway Union (ARU) struck James J. Hill's Great Northern Railway. Soon after, the United Mine Workers declared the first nationwide coal strike. While the coal strike continued, Jacob Coxey's march on Washington movement began. This movement spawned a series of similar marches in the West and peaked in late April and early May. The year of discontent ended with the tumultuous Pullman strike in July. Disorder and violence inevitably attended these upheavals.[1]

A massive breakdown of local, state, and federal law enforcement took place, and on a far wider geographic scale than in 1877. On the federal level, marshals and a large number of special deputies proved incapable of enforcing federal laws and court orders. On the state and local level, a mixture of inefficiency and sympathy for the dissidents led to another collapse of law enforcement. Sheriffs, mayors, and governors then turned to the National Guard. By the end of the year, over 32,000 National Guardsmen had served on active duty. In some instances, however, such as in California and Washington, the state soldiers refused to use force against strikers. In California, the National Guard verged on collapse during the early days of the Pullman strike. Washington state Guardsmen returning from summer camp refused to ride on trains operated by strikebreakers and were arrested and later dismissed from the state service. Community pressures as well as personal beliefs governed the Guardsmen's actions. In Washington "it was said that the fathers of the cavalrymen would disown them if they rode with non-unionists, and the entire community supported them."[2]

The collapse of both the civil agencies of law enforcement and of many Guard units, the extent of disorder, and the popular sympathy expressed for Coxeyites and strikers eventually brought out the Army in aid of the civil authorities. From April through the middle of September, federal troops were in the field dealing with the turbulence attending the coal strike, the Coxey movement, and the Pullman strike. Six of the eight geographical military departments placed troops in the field, with close to two-thirds of the Army on active duty.

To contemporaries, the 1894 experience was far more shattering than the upheavals in 1877. Secretary of State Walter Q. Gresham reflected with dismay and confusion that "the laboring men of this country—I mean the honest ones . . . firmly believe that the powers of Government have been perverted to their injury, in the interest of the rich."[3] Gresham did not believe this was so, but he dreaded the future because working men so firmly believed it. "What caused the most profound alarm in all thinking minds," another contemporary asserted, "was not any individual incident of the uprising, so much as the fact that the spirit of discontent and despair should have so far saturated large masses of the people of our country as to make such things possible."[4] Given these perceptions by the governing class, it was inevitable that, once called to active duty, the Army would be used to crush working-class protests.

The first violent labor disturbance of 1894 was connected with the coal strike called by the United Mine Workers. The strike began on April 21, with most of the walk-offs occurring in Ohio, Illinois, Pennsylvania, and West Virginia. For some time the strike remained peaceful, but the importation of strikebreakers precipitated violence in many places and brought the National Guard to active duty. In Ohio and Illinois, particularly, governors repeatedly called Guardsmen to duty to deal with rioting miners. Militia forces also served in Alabama, Indiana, Iowa, Maryland, Pennsylvania, and West Virginia. Guardsmen performed adequately throughout the strike.[5]

The Army's first active duty in 1894 was during the coal strike, in the Indian Territory. On May 19, Major General John M. Schofield, commanding general, notified Major General Nelson A. Miles, commander of the Department of the Missouri, to send troops into the Choctaw Nation, Indian Territory, to remove striking miners. The Interior Department oversaw the operation of privately owned mines in the Territory, and, at the request of the coal companies, defined strikers as intruders in the Territory and ordered their removal. The Department acquired the use of the Army to ensure the strikers' departure. Lieutenant Colonel John N. Andrews took a force from Fort Leavenworth, Kansas, for this purpose. Andrews expected to find single men living in bunkhouses, but he reported, "I find these people all own their houses, have gardens and most of them families, which kind of complicates matters."[6]

It is evident from his reports that Colonel Andrews did not like this duty. In his final report he said, "This intruder business has been a rather singular one, and strikes me as only a pretext to get troops in this country, as a man is an intruder if he does not work, and not one if he works." He went on to say, "I think it is very hard on these people," and "I do not think this matter was very thoroughly understood, if it had been I do not think troops would have been sent here."[7]

Nonetheless, beginning on June 15, Andrews's troops began removing the miners, their families, and household goods from the Choctaw Nation and unceremoniously dumping them off in Arkansas. When the coal strike came to an end in July, the Interior Department immediately halted the evictions. This ended an unseemly affair labeled by the *United Mine Workers' Journal* as "Siberia in America." Overshadowed by the Coxey movement and the Pullman strike, the eviction of striking coal miners from the Indian Territory indicated the Cleveland administration's sympathies for property owners and its intention to act quickly and forcefully when it saw fit to do so.[8]

The coal strike had not yet ended when industrial armies began harassing the major railroad lines west of the Mississippi. Just as these episodes were brought under control, Debs's ARU began a boycott of the

Western roads in support of the Pullman strike in Chicago. In his memoirs, General Schofield saw a good deal of similarity between the industrial army episodes and the general railroad strike. Both movements indicated a strong general dislike for the railroads, substantial public discontent, and mass sympathy for both the train stealers and the strikers. There was considerable insight in Schofield's observation. Strong public support for Coxeyites and strikers appeared in the same places as did resistance to law enforcement measures taken against both movements. Schofield observed that the ARU strike was the more effective because it had a central leadership.[9]

As the industrial armies moved eastward, they were met in town and city by welcoming committees and offered food and shelter. In Oregon, Texas, and Colorado, governors ignored railroad officials' demands for use of state troops to capture stolen trains. The outbreak of the Pullman strike brought forth an even greater outpouring of sympathy for those combating the railroad corporations. Although feelings in California were the most intense against the railroads, they were representative of attitudes throughout the West. Afterwards, one Californian noted that the strike brought a total halt to business, industry, and farm marketing in the state. Yet, he recalled,

> While the people of California were suffering these things . . .
> their sympathy was almost unanimously with the strikers.
> I mean not only the sympathy of what are commonly called
> the working classes, but . . . (farmers, businessmen, profes-
> sional men, manufacturers) hosts of persons who ordinarily
> have no direct relations with "organized labor" or much sym-
> pathy with it.[10]

In the industrial army disturbances, interference with railroads in federal receivership usually provided the basis for federal intervention. In the Pullman strike, interference with the mails and interstate commerce more often justified intervention. In the beginning of both affairs, the Justice Department attempted to enforce court orders through the use of marshals and hundreds of special deputies. But public sympathy, the vast regions traversed by the railroads, and the inefficient deputies hindered law enforcement. Then, primarily through the efforts of Attorney General Richard Olney, the Justice Department requested troops from President

Cleveland. The formula developed for obtaining troops followed a certain pattern. Federal judges issued injunctions to prevent interference with the mails, interstate commerce, or railroads in federal receivership. When Coxeyites or strikers ignored injunctions and marshals proved unable to enforce them, the district judge, marshal, and U.S. attorney notified the attorney general and requested federal troops. Olney presented the requests to President Cleveland, who almost always ordered out the troops.[11]

The most pernicious aspect of this policy was that it gave officials of the Justice Department a splendid opportunity to avoid their responsibilities. The Justice files on the Coxey affair and the Pullman strike are filled with correspondence from marshals and judges suggesting to Olney that use of the Army in these disturbances would save the Department a good deal of money. Economy was not the only reason for requesting troops. Often, the Justice Department could not obtain reliable special deputies due to local sympathies for the dissidents. This popular support also influenced the actions of the regular marshals who, fearing economic and social sanctions, attempted to have the onus of enforcement pushed off onto the Army. During the Coxey affair, the Army officer in command at Helena, Montana, reported that the marshal there, William McDermott, was an important property holder in Butte, and

> he dreads the ill will of the citizens of his town, who from all accounts are in sympathy with the industrial army people. . . . the marshal would be glad in every instance, whether an emergency or not, to have the troops of the Army do all the work."[12]

Sometimes, as happened during the Great Northern strike in late April, the appeals of the marshal in North Dakota brought the Army in when no disorders actually existed.[13]

Although the role of the Justice Department and Attorney General Olney is tangential to this investigation, it is important to point out that Olney, his subordinates, and the managers of the affected railroads were the central figures in setting the conditions under which troops were committed to field service. In 1877, some confusion existed over the legality of using troops in the railroad strike. Now, however, the situation seemed clear-cut. Federal laws were violated, marshals could not enforce them, and so the Army was called in.

In all the legal and political maneuverings carried on by Olney, his subordinates, and the railroad officials to get the Army involved, little was said to the commanding general, Major General John M. Schofield. Schofield's main concerns throughout 1894 were to ensure the correct legal use of the Army, especially strict adherence to the *posse comitatus* act of 1878, and to maintain military control over troops in the field. Because of steps taken by Schofield when he assumed the post of commanding general, he had effective direction of the field troops. Orders went from the president to Secretary of War Lamont, and then to Schofield. The general personally supervised the manner in which department commanders carried out their orders, and he had them report directly to him, bypassing the adjutant general. Because of Schofield's central direction and control, the use of the Army in 1894 was much more orderly and efficient than it had been in 1877.[14]

Early in the disorders, Schofield discovered that many officers were ignorant of the restrictions placed on the Army by the *posse comitatus* act of 1878 and had only the vaguest ideas of the responsibilities of military commanders in aid of civil officials. During the industrial army disturbances he had to inform his field commanders as to the limits within which they could operate. He later complained that "distinguished commanders in the field seemed strangely ignorant of both constitutional and military laws." Schofield conceded that the situation was confusing and unexpected but maintained that part of an officer's responsibility was to be prepared for the unexpected, "especially in those things which army officers are not habitually required to know," when commanders must "be intrusted with great responsibilities and discretionary authority."[15]

Because he was immediately in control of the field operations of the Army in 1894, Schofield was able to clear up confusions and ignorance by telegraphic orders. Though he sent many wires to individual commanders outlining their responsibilities, Schofield relied on general orders to educate the entire Army. In General Order No. 15, issued on May 25, General Schofield stated that, whenever the Army went to the aid of the civil authorities,

the troops are employed as a part of the military power of the United States, and act under the orders of the President . . . and his military subordinates. They cannot be directed to act under the orders of any civil officer. The commanding officers

of the troops so employed are directly responsible to their
military superiors. Any unlawful or unauthorized act on their
part would not be excusable on the ground of any order or request received by them from a marshal or any other civil officer.[16]

Schofield expanded on the responsibilities of military commanders in
General Order No. 26, of July 24, again emphasizing the point that officers
could act only within the chain of command.[17]

General Schofield's insistence upon retaining control of troops in the
field placed the Army in an entirely different position from that which it
held in 1877. All orders for the use of troops came through the military
chain of command. Troops could not take orders from civilians, nor
could they make arrests. This latter factor made it necessary for each contingent in the field to be accompanied by one or more marshals or deputies.
"The duty of the Army is," Schofield wrote, "when so ordered by the
President, to overcome and suppress lawless resistance to civil authority.
There military duty ends, and the civil officers resume their functions."[18]
This arrangement was administratively awkward and time consuming for
each individual request for aid from the Justice Department had to go
through the president, to the War Department, and back down the Army
chain of authority. In July, when the disorders attending the Pullman
strike became so widespread, six of the eight department commanders
were given authority to respond to individual requests on their own responsibility.[19]

Another important General Order sent by Schofield in 1894, No. 23,
went out on July 9. This order attempted to tell officers when to fire on
a mob. "A mob, forcibly resisting or obstructing execution of the laws
of the United States," the order stated, "or attempting to destroy property
belonging to or under the protection of the United States, is a public
enemy." It went on to say that a mob usually contained women, children,
and the curious. An officer should attempt to warn these people to disperse. Then, the bayonet should be used to break up an unruly crowd. If
this failed,

the actions of the troops should be governed solely by tactical
considerations. . . . They are not called upon to consider how
great may be the losses inflicted upon the public enemy except
to make their blows so effective as to promptly suppress all resistance to lawful authority.[20]

Schofield's many efforts to ensure that his officers complied with the law, Army regulations, and common sense indicated how ill-informed the majority of the officer corps, including general officers, was on the proper conduct of the Army during the suppression of civil disorder. The service was obviously not prepared for riot duty. Each labor crisis called for a re-education of the officer corps in its legal responsibilities and, as General Order 23 indicated, even in its tactical obligations. It was apparent that the Army spent little time or study on the question of the maintenance of civil order. Schofield's vigorous efforts gave the Army's efforts in 1894 coherence and also kept the service under federal military command. His task was made easier by the fact that the federal government, through the Justice Department, initiated the use of federal troops.

Although the guidelines set down for officers in the general orders made it fairly clear as to when and how the Army could be used in civil disorders, General Schofield found that officials in the Justice Department did not understand the limits placed on the Army. This was especially true during the industrial army disorders. In several instances, judges and marshals attempted to deputize or make posses out of regulars, only to be thwarted by Schofield and his department commanders. The clearest example of this took place in Wyoming, where Judge John A. Riner continually pressed Brigadier General John R. Brooke, Department of the Platte, for such a use of his troops. Riner appealed to Attorney General Olney, who in turn sought support from General Schofield. The General notified Olney that Riner seemed to exaggerate the disorders in Wyoming and overestimated the necessity for troops. Schofield's adamant stand on this point eventually ended most judicial requests for military posses.[21]

The Industrial Armies

The "army" of Jacob Coxey, a mixture of charlatans, comics, utopian reformers, and ordinary workmen, was treated by the nation's press with a mixture of humor and contempt. The Army played no part in the dispersal of Coxey's Army. The Eastern press and the Cleveland administration came to see Western industrial armies in a different light from Coxey's outfit. Unlike the latter, the industrial armies that formed on the Pacific Coast and moved eastward along the transcontinental railroads were truly proletarian in nature. The Western armies were made up of unemployed miners and railroad workers. The propensity for these men to steal trains or obtain free riders by coercion angered editorial writers imbued with respect for the rights of private property. As prospects of thousands of unemployed Western workers flooding into Eastern cities appeared more likely, the press grew more strident in denouncing the industrial armies. *The Independent* saw the movement as "an incentive to lawlessness, laziness, vagabondage," and *Leslie's Weekly* predicted, "From these acts it will be but a short step to downright pillage and murder."[22]

Both the railroads and the Justice Department took a similar view. The department first became involved in dealing with the industrials because the harassed railroads were under the receivership of U.S. courts. Receivers called upon federal judges and marshals to protect railroad property, recover stolen trains, and capture and punish train stealers. Ultimately, the tacit policy of the Justice Department went beyond the protection of property in U.S. receivership, and was aimed at preventing the unemployed bands from reaching the East and making an example of those who would defy private property laws. Richard Olney stressed that the train stealing not only was stopped but also "very large numbers of almost desperate men who would otherwise have found their way to Washington were compelled to remain at home."[23]

General Schofield did not like the idea of using the Army to prevent the eastward movement of the Coxeyites, believing they had "the same right as other citizens to go West or come East at their pleasure, provided they do it in a lawful way." While he conceded that the government could find several pretexts under which it could harass the industrial armies, he believed,

> It seems at least probable that many of the "Commonwealers" are only actuated by the laudable desire to get out of a country where they are no longer able to obtain subsistence. Would it not be better to let them quietly, slowly and laboriously make their way whither they wish to go, while the necessary precautions are taken to prevent their seizing trains, destroying property or otherwise violating the law?[24]

The matter was not within Schofield's province, however, as the Justice Department prepared requests for troops and presented them to President Cleveland. The president more often than not heeded the advice of his attorney general over that of his commanding general.[25]

The industrial army upheavals began in the West in late April and did
not end until the first part of June. These upheavals involved three military
departments of the Army. The Department of Dakota, commanded by
Brigadier General Wesley Merritt, covered the disorders in Montana and
the Dakotas. Brigadier General Brooke of the Department of the Platte
supervised action in Wyoming and southern Idaho. In the Pacific Northwest, where the disorders were the worst, troops in the Department of
the Columbia under Brigadier General Elwell S. Otis saw a good deal of
field duty. Each department carried out similar types of duties. At first,
troops were used to capture stolen trains, while later they guarded bridges,
tunnels, and captured Coxeyites. In some cases, they were stationed at
key points along the various railroads to prevent the capture of trains.

Although the first train stealing by the industrials took place in California in early April, the federal government did not act until April 24
in Montana. A band of unemployed miners called Hogan's army stole a
Northern Pacific train at Butte and began running the train eastward on
April 21. In the next three days, officials of the Justice Department attempted to recapture the train, and when this failed they called on Attorney General Olney for troops. Troops were ordered out on the 24th, and
though the governor of Montana made an official request for regulars the
next day, the April 24th order marked the beginning of a purely federal
effort to control the Coxeyites.[26]

The evidence surrounding the Hogan army affair suggests that the federal
marshal, William McDermott, did not make very strenuous efforts to capture
the stolen Northern Pacific train. The railroad company tore up tracks
and caused a landslide in attempts to halt the train, but in both instances
the miners repaired the track and continued their trek. Meanwhile, Colonel
P. T. Swaine, substituting for General Merritt, ordered six companies of the
Twenty-second Infantry at Fort Keogh to prepare to capture the Coxeyites. At Fort Keogh, Lieutenant Colonel John H. Page had been eaves-
dropping on the telegraph and was aware of the developing events. Antici-
pating a call for troops, Page readied his command for field service. When
the order came, it was expected that the troops would not have to leave
Keogh, as the tracks ran by the fort. Page had the tracks torn up, to wreck
the train if necessary, and prepared an ambush for the train stealers. He
sent four troops of cavalry into the surrounding hills to cover a retreat
of the industrials.[27]

All these preparations went for nought. The Coxeyites got wind of the trap and stopped the train near Rosebud, Montana. Now Page was delayed as the tracks around Fort Keogh were repaired for the troop train. The track mending was done quickly, and soon the infantry troops were racing to Rosebud at sixty miles an hour, with the cavalry traveling overland. The federal forces caught up with Hogan's army at Forsyth, Montana, on April 26, and captured them easily. Despite reports that the industrials were heavily armed and ready for battle, Page discovered only three pistols among the 331 prisoners. The Army now found itself with over three hundred prisoners and no marshal to take them into custody. When Marshal McDermott arrived, he arrested the leaders and set out to take them to Helena for trial, intending to leave the rest with Colonel Page. The marshal refused to assume custody of all the prisoners unless the Army would supply a guard. Schofield reluctantly agreed, and Page's command provided an escort for the marshal to Helena, remaining there until the court disposed of them. McDermott did not fear the prisoners so much as the people in Helena, who exhibited much support for the Coxeyites.[28]

Although the Army did not physically guard the prisoners at Helena, its presence there ensured that McDermott would maintain control of the situation. On May 15, the leaders of Hogan's army were sent to jail and the others released. General Merritt, now back in command of the department, asked Schofield if the troops should return to Fort Keogh. Secretary of War Lamont believed that the situation was so explosive in Helena that the troops should remain. Conditions in Montana remained tense throughout May, and train stealing in Washington, Oregon, and Idaho made it prudent to keep Merritt's troops in Helena and in the field throughout the state. General Merritt was not sure what his duty was and asked Schofield, "Shall steps be taken to prevent the flow of these people eastward?"[29] The commanding general replied,

It is generally desired to prevent, as far as may lawfully be done, the drift of unemployed and lawless persons toward the East; but no law is known which would justify the arrest of such a movement, so long as the parties commit no crime.[30]

Merritt's forces were not used again against the industrials.

Operations in General Brooke's Department of the Platte closely resembled those in Merritt's department. On May 14, Brooke was ordered to send troops to recapture a stolen Union Pacific train traveling east from Idaho. The troops made the capture and then aided marshals in guarding the prisoners. General Brooke did not like the business of referring each request for aid from Justice officials back to Washington, but General Schofield firmly informed him, "It is necessary in such matters to have the orders of the War Department in each specific case before decisive action can be taken in response to the demands of the marshal."[31] In Idaho, conditions deteriorated to the point where Brooke was authorized to aid marshals "when satisfied of the necessity from a full statement of the circumstances in each case."[32] It soon appeared, however, that Justice Department officials overstated the need for troops there. Brook's forces remained in Idaho, patrolling the Union Pacific tracks until June 12, but encountered no opposition.[33]

The most extensive disorders occasioned by the industrial army movement took place in the Department of the Columbia, which included Washington, Oregon, and northern Idaho. Several "armies" appeared in this region and stole trains belonging to the Northern Pacific Railroad and the Union Pacific line. The people in this region strongly supported the train stealers, and the governors of Oregon and Washington refused to call out their National Guards. Several days before the War Department ordered General Otis's troops out, the General was in contact with officials of the Northern Pacific and had the garrisons under his jurisdiction on the alert and ready for field duty. The cooperation between Otis and the railroad was so close that the Northern Pacific had a troop train made up before Otis received word from Washington to use his troops to aid marshals.[34]

On April 28, the Portland industrial army boarded a Union Pacific train and headed eastward. Schofield immediately instructed Otis to aid Marshal Henry C. Grady in recapturing the train. The Department Commander ordered the garrison at Fort Walla Walla, under Colonel E. C. Compton, into Oregon to stop the train and capture the industrials. The Walla Walla force moved into Oregon by train, established themselves at a convenient point to intercept the stolen train, and awaited the Coxeyites. Compton blocked the track with his troop train, hiding his men in the grass, weeds, and buildings around the junction. When the Coxeyites appeared with their train and saw the tracks blocked, they quickly ground the train to a halt. As the Colonel reported, instantly the engine was secured by a Sergeant and three men, previously detailed for this duty, and six of the thievish gang, controlling the movements of the engineer and brakeman. . . . were brought to the ground and placed under guard, at the same time all other parts of the train was [sic] seized by the command.[35]

In all, Compton's command captured just over five hundred men and, at the insistence of Marshal Grady, escorted them to Portland. Grady wanted the troops kept in the city because, as Otis reported, "undue excitement prevails in Portland, on account of arrest and detention of prisoners."[36] On April 30, the industrials went to trial, and Marshal Grady deputized twenty-five soldiers to guard the prisoners at court. When Otis discovered what the marshal had done, he immediately ordered Compton to remove the soldiers from the court and instructed the colonel that he should obey orders only from Otis himself. The court failed to convict any of the Coxeyites and released them on May 1. This action cooled tempers in Portland, and on the same day the Walla Walla troops returned to their garrison.[37]

The industrial army disturbances soon became widespread in Washington and Idaho. Although Otis could not yet aid marshals, he could dispose his troops so as to exert "moral force" upon the dissident train thieves. On April 29, therefore, he ordered troops from Fort Sherman, Idaho, into Spokane. The troops arrived the next day, spent an uncomfortable twelve hours in the troop train, and then camped along the Northern Pacific in and around Spokane. Later, on May 12, Otis sent troops to Seattle to carry out the same duty. Forces stationed all along the Northern Pacific and the Union Pacific, Otis reported, would "render impossible any illegal interference with rolling stock or property."[38] Inevitably, the industrial armies of Washington and Oregon were forced eastward as federal troops attempted to break them up. General Otis eventually sent a force into northern Idaho to protect the Northern Pacific from interference there. The regulars' presence in Idaho broke up the large bands of industrials and pushed them into Montana. On May 22, these smaller groups reassembled and captured a train just inside Montana. Troops from Otis's department pursued the train and "seized cars and placed them in possession of railway authorities, remained in that locality until the mob dispersed, then returned to Idaho."[39]

By the end of May, the industrial army movement died out in the Pacific Northwest. On May 31, Otis reported, "Affairs in the Department have assumed accustomed quiet and all detached troops have joined their permanent stations."[40] The manner in which Otis's troops were sometimes used, that is, guarding property, violated the *posse comitatus* act. The pressure from Justice officials and officers of the Northern Pacific, however, was so strong that Schofield could not prevent this. During the crisis, James McNaught, counsel for the Northern Pacific, wired Olney, "The fact that the troops have not been used in the state of Washington has induced the mob to believe that they will not be used and they therefore more freely oppose by violence the efforts of the marshal."[41] Judges and marshals in this region joined McNaught in strong pleas to use troops to break up the industrial bands before they began moving East. An officer serving in the Fourth Infantry, Lieutenant George B. Duncan, later recalled the extensive preparations taken to prevent the capture of the trains. Soldiers were located along the track and were to wave a flag and fire in the air if a stolen train appeared.

> If the train failed to stop, then a switch would turn the train into a side trace and precipitate it from the bluff into the river. The thought of dire consequence from such a catastrophy [sic] filled me with apprehension. Fortunately, no trains were stolen and the method of teaching a lesson not put into practice.[42]

Regulars from the Department of the Columbia performed one other duty during the industrial army upheavals. Again, this was at the insistence of the Justice Department. Two hundred prisoners who had been arrested in Idaho were tried in Judge James A. Beatty's court at Boise and sentenced to sixty days imprisonment. No facilities existed for imprisoning these men. Therefore, Beatty wanted a prison camp constructed along the Snake River, at the boundary of Oregon and Idaho, and he wanted troops to guard the prisoners. "The design in sending them to Snake River," he argued, "is to push them backward, also by having troops stationed there to deter others who it is rumored are coming from Portland."[43] Secretary of War Lamont authorized Beatty's proposal and the Army escorted the train of prisoners to the Snake River and set up their own camp near the prison. Otis was cautioned by the adjutant general,

> It is to be distinctly understood that the troops are not to be
> used to assist in guarding the prisoners either on the train or
> during confinement at destination, but simply to meet any
> emergency that may arise should the prisoners attempt to
> escape.[44]

No such emergency arose and although the Army was not directly responsible for maintaining the prison camp, in fact they served as prison guards.

Although General Schofield had little control over the commitment of troops to aid marshals, he attempted to limit the extent of military activity in the industrial disorders. Beyond his vague sympathies for the Coxeyites, Schofield believed the Justice Department rarely exerted a full effort to cope with the problem and turned too quickly for assistance from the Army. In memos to Secretary of War Lamont and Attorney General Olney, and in communications with federal judges and his department commanders in the West, the commanding general insisted on strict adherence to the *posse comitatus* law. The basic problem was that federal marshals had to exhaust all available resources before calling for military aid. More often than not, the marshals made only perfunctory efforts to capture stolen trains or arrest train stealers, then quickly called for troops. Schofield insisted that marshals exert greater efforts. In a note to Olney referring to troubles in Wyoming, for example, he pointed out that the "Department [War] is not advised of such a state of defiance to the judicial authority of the United States" as to justify military action.[45] Furthermore, Schofield had to stress continually that troops could neither arrest nor guard train stealers but merely provide sufficient force to prevent disorderly persons from interfering with the marshals' duties. Only in these ways could the commanding general blunt the use of the Army in breaking up the industrial armies.[46]

Some of Schofield's department commanders, especially Generals Brooke and Otis, viewed the Coxey movement as a problem of law and order which justified military action. Brooke contended that the Coxeyites were merely "bands of tramps" out for a free train ride. It mattered little, however, as to the perceptions of Schofield or his field commanders, for the Justice Department under the astute leadership of Richard Olney ultimately controlled the commitment of troops. The use of the Army, the *Army and Navy Journal* boasted, led to "the defeat of the Coxey movement. . . . the date when the hoboes were placed in jail by the

United States troops can safely be looked upon as the time Coxeyism began to decline." It would be difficult to disagree with that assessment.[47]

The Railroad Strike in the West

As the last vestiges of the industrial army movement faded away, the nation and the Army faced a new and larger crisis. The Pullman strike concerned working conditions at the manufacturing plant and company town of Pullman, Illinois. When Eugene Debs's American Railway Union came to the support of the Pullman workers, however, the dispute turned into a general railroad strike from Chicago to the West Coast. The ARU declared a boycott of Pullman cars on June 26. Union members refused to handle the cars or trains pulling them. When men who objected to working trains with Pullman cars were fired, other railroad workers walked off the job. The rapidity with which the strike spread illustrated the deep bitterness and resentment of Western workers. The unpopularity of the railroads among the general populace in the West enhanced the strikers' cause, as mass sympathy hindered the enforcement of federal law. Under the rubric of interference with the U.S. mails, or interstate commerce, or interference with railroads in the receivership of the United States, the Justice Department enjoined the strikers. The inability of marshals to recruit deputies and enforce injunctions brought appeals for troops through procedures developed during the Coxey disorders.

The powerful General Managers' Association of Chicago (GMA) sought from the first day of the strike to gain the support of the Justice Department. Attorney General Olney acceded to the GMA's demands, not because he was their toady, although it is clear the railroads pressured Olney and the rest of the Cleveland administration for decisive action, but because he interpreted the strike as an insurrection. As seen by Olney, the strike was essentially a contest between the ARU and the federal government, not a general strike against the railroads. From the outset, the attorney general intended to use the Army to break the strike and ensure the protection of railroad property and imported strikebreakers and the transcontinental operation of the roads.[48]

Hundreds of special deputy marshals and thousands of National Guardsmen failed to stem the strike west of the Mississippi. Unlike the industrial army disorders, federal marshals' reports that they were unable to handle the strikers were not exaggerations. Army officers' reports from the field corroborated the marshals' difficulties. In many places the marshals and their deputies were manhandled, disarmed, and ostracized. According to Brigadier General Alexander McCook, the federal marshal and his deputies in Raton, New Mexico "could not get food at the hotel. The grocers and merchants will not sell them provisions. The Sheriff of Colfax County, New Mexico, ordered the Marshal not to set foot in town."[49] Again and again, Army officers discovered a deep-seated sympathy for the strikers. General John R. Brooke concluded, "The facts regarding the conditions along the Union Pacific are that a general sympathy with the strikers exists at all points."[50] At Winnemucca, Nevada, Colonel J. S. Poland, Seventeenth Infantry, found "citizens feeling intensely in favor of strikers."[51] In Butte, Montana, Colonel J. C. Bates, Second Infantry, reported that "labor unions were so thoroughly organized and embraced so large a percentage of the population here that they met with practically no opposition."[52] Local communities' open support for the strikers meant that in many places in the West there was only the Army to enforce federal court orders.

On July 1, 1894, General Schofield ordered Brigadier General Thomas H. Ruger, Department of California, to send the First Infantry to Los Angeles "to enforce mandates and warrants of the United States Court and to prevent any obstruction of the United States Mails."[53] Schofield sent another order that day to Brigadier General Alexander McD. McCook, Department of the Colorado, directing him to provide troops to aid federal marshals protecting railroad property in receivership of the U.S. Court at Trinidad, Colorado. From the first of July through the middle of September, troops from the military departments in the West were in the field supporting federal marshals in opening rail traffic, protecting railroad property, and restoring order. Duty in the railroad strike involved almost two-thirds of the Army and brought about the most extensive field service for the regulars since the Civil War. Through the first days of July, General Schofield attempted to maintain direct control over the Army's activities by issuing orders to the appropriate department commander as specific events arose. The upheavals became so extensive, however, that on July 7, Schofield directed department commanders in the West "to employ the military force under your command" to aid marshals whenever they called upon the commanders.[54]

In general, troops in the departments covering the Rocky Mountain states performed similar duties. Many of the troops guarded bridges and tunnels, as the strikers recognized their importance in the region and attempted to burn or dynamite them. In the Department of the Platte, Brigadier General John R. Brooke stationed troops at important points along the Union Pacific from Cheyenne to Ogden. General Elwell S. Otis of the Department of Columbia made similar troop dispositions to cover the Northern Pacific in Washington and Idaho, as did General McCook in Colorado, New Mexico, and Arizona. Other forces rode as train escorts, first to ensure that trains left their respective freight yards and, second, to afford protection to trains and their crews while traveling through rural areas. Finally, troops served as guards over railroad property in the various sectional and divisional towns and cities. All departments carried on these duties for the entire month of July. General Otis's troops returned to station at the end of July, but regulars remained on duty in Brooke's department until August 17, while some of McCook's forces remained in the field until September 12. Limited harassment of the railroads continued after those dates, as Brooke reported, "in the way of uncoupling cars, cutting the airbrakes connections, etc., which could not in any event be provided against by the use of troops."[55]

The resentment of the general populace and the strikers' hostility to any force attempting to open rail traffic hampered the Army's effectiveness. The expedition of a military command from the Department of the Platte to open the Central Pacific Railroad between Ogden, Utah, and Truckee, California, illustrated the challenges the Army faced. General Brooke did not order the movement of the expedition until July 11, as "press despatches satisfy me that an earlier attempt on that road could not have been effective with the force I could have sent earlier."[56] Colonel J. S. Poland commanded the force and left Ogden on the 12th with four companies and dropped off troops at all divisional terminals along the way. The command experienced no difficulty except that it had to repair several damaged bridges. It reached Carlin, in eastern Nevada, at seven in the evening, July 12. Poland reported, "The strikers [at Carlin] are a vicious lot."[57]

The Colonel not only discovered vicious strikers at Carlin but also a lack of U.S. marshals and therefore no one to arrest the trouble makers. Futhermore, seventy-five strikebreakers were brought in from the East, and there was no one to protect them. General Brooke and General

Schofield made efforts to have reliable marshals sent to Nevada but this delayed operations, since Poland did not want to leave Carlin until some arrangements were made to protect bridges and tracks from sabotage. Finally, Brooke told the Colonel that obstructors "are to be treated as public enemies, and may be held as prisoners until they can be turned over to United States marshals."[58]

General Brooke attempted to pressure the Central Pacific to use its powers to obtain deputies. A. N. Towne, general manager of the railroad, replied to Brooke, "We are doing all possible to impress upon the U.S. Marshal and U.S. district attorney to act at once. The marshal has been unable to get more than half a dozen marshals appointed."[59] Eventually, the marshal deputized loyal railroad employees and scraped up other men wherever he could. Poland remarked, however, that "the deputies are worthless. They haven't the nerve and cannot get good men."[60] The intense dislike for the railroads in Nevada continually hampered this aspect of the federal effort.[61]

As affairs quieted down in Carlin, Colonel Poland pushed his command on toward California. On July 13, he passed through Winnemucca, Nevada, continued on to Wadsworth on the 14th, and reached Reno on the 15th. Again he discovered much support for the strikers and much hostility to the Army. At Reno the colonel reported some eggs thrown at a sentinel, who fired in return but hit no one. General Brooke, twice wounded during the late war and a former division commander with a well-earned reputation as a fighter, was not happy with Poland's slow progress to the West, interpreting the slowness as overcautiousness. Brooke apparently did not understand fully the amount of acrimony and obstruction Poland faced in the railroad towns of Nevada. Affairs at Reno were particularly tense. Poland noted that the troops there protected stations, engine houses, depots, and even train crews, who were imported strikebreakers. He reported on the 16th,

> The mob [at Reno] was repeatedly forced back from engineers
> and trains today. Insults nearly drove engineers into refusal to
> take trains out. . . . I promised them every protection I could
> give. . . . This assurance decided them to remain at work.[62]

The work carried on by this command was very arduous. According to Poland, "My men have been on guard duty sixty hours with never a mur-

mur. I have never seen better soldiers than these companies of the Sixteenth, sober, cool, patient and brave. They cannot keep this up much longer."[63]

Poland's men did not have to keep it up much longer. They made contact with General Ruger's men at Truckee on July 16, and, soon after, traffic was running regularly between San Francisco and Ogden. A sufficient force of marshals finally arrived and began arresting strike leaders. Reno remained something of a trouble spot, however, and, on the 21st, Poland reported. "Thus far no blood has been shed. A few bayonet punctures have been made and while the toughs have begun to wear six shooters all have learned that we are here to discharge our duty and intend to do it if it costs life."[64] On the 24th, Poland removed train guards from Central Pacific freights and only maintained guards in and around the stations and depots along the line. Soon he recommended a reduction of troops in Nevada, but the Central Pacific balked at this. However, Brooke approved reductions on August 7, with more on the 10th, leaving one company at Carlin and one at Wadsworth. These outfits withdrew on August 17, and operations ended in the Department of the Platte.[65]

Hostility toward the Army and the railroads and sympathy for the strikers was nowhere stronger than in California. The strike began at Oakland on June 27, and spread throughout the state a day later. On July 1, federal troops went to Los Angeles, where they met no overt opposition and soon had the local trains running. Thereafter, troops "were employed as escorts on outgoing and incoming trains and guard duty in and around roundhouses and depots in Los Angeles from July 4 until July 28.[66]

The strikers in Los Angeles accepted these developments placidly. In other parts of the state, especially at Oakland and Sacramento, the strikers were not in such an accepting mood. From July 1 to July 3, U.S. Marshal Barry Baldwin and his deputies attempted to get trains running in these two cities. Failing to do this, he asked for state troops to assist him. The National Guard was mobilized and, on the morning of July 4, confronted the strikers at the roundhouse of the Southern Pacific in Sacramento. The meeting was noisy, the Guardsmen hot, tired, and ill-prepared. The strikers shouted and screamed at the soldiers, and when Baldwin ordered them to clear out the strikers the militiamen refused to act. "The strikers knew personally every man in the front ranks of the troops," reported the *San Francisco Chronicle.* "Many of the militiamen were railroad hands themselves."[67]

This led to the collapse of the National Guard in Sacramento, and a day later, at Oakland, a similar collapse occurred. A curious situation developed in both cities, as an undeclared truce prevailed. Between July 4 and July 11, the Guard units at Sacramento and Oakland guarded bridges and railroad property outside the railroad yards but made no attempt to remove the strikers or start up trains. As rumors of the use of federal troops grew stronger, all sides bided their time in anticipation of federal intervention.[68]

The federal effort to break the railroad strike in California succeeded only after considerable difficulty. The collapse of the California National Guard came as a surprise and a blow to General Thomas H. Ruger, for he was depending on them to augment his own small force. Ruger had only twenty-two companies totalling 1,469 officers and men, 300 of them already in Los Angeles. His manpower problems were surmounted eventually when Secretary of War Lamont obtained the use of Marines and sailors from Mare Island, near San Francisco. These 500 men proved invaluable to Ruger. The regulars boosted the Guardsmen's morale, and once the two forces joined efforts the state soldiers performed satisfactorily. The regulars, the naval battalion, and the National Guard gave Ruger a force of about 3,500 men but the workers' adamant refusal to work for the Southern Pacific and its subsidiaries and the continual harassment of the railroads in the rural areas kept California in a state of agitation throughout July and August.[69]

On July 7, Ruger received orders from General Schofield to cooperate with General Brooke in opening the Union Pacific and the Central Pacific from San Francisco to Omaha. These orders specifically advised Ruger to consult with the governor of California to gain the aid of the state's National Guard. Ruger "determined to first begin action at Sacramento . . . as that was the point where the strikers were in greatest force and had assumed the most belligerent attitude."[70] A mixed force of infantry, artillery, cavalry, and Marines, numbering 540, left San Francisco for Sacramento on July 10. From the time of the failure of the National Guard, on the 4th, the strikers had grown more belligerent in their public pronouncements, and the regulars fully expected to be met with force. The command, under Colonel William M. Graham, went to Sacramento by boat, arrived on the 11th,

and without serious trouble took possession of the railroad station, yards, shops, etc., clearing them of what strikers were present, without necessity for firing other than advancing companies with bayonets at the charge and the cavalry troops with sabers drawn.[71]

Colonel Graham was under orders not only to clear the Central Pacific yard but also to open up the line to local traffic and to the East. He set up Gatling guns and pickets to keep strikers away from the yards and made contact with the National Guard units still in the city. The governor of California placed the Guard forces under Graham's command, the only instance during the strike where state troops took orders from a federal officer. In the ensuing weeks, the California National Guard aided the regulars in all operations. With this combined force, Graham immediately set about forming a train guard of regulars, and, early in the afternoon of the 11th, he sent out a passenger-mail train for San Francisco. The train jumped the tracks three miles out of Sacramento. Unknown persons had removed the spikes from the rails, and in the wreck that followed, four enlisted men of Battery L, 5th Artillery, were killed.[72]

The wreck of the Sacramento train prevented traffic from going to San Francisco, so Colonel Graham turned his energies to opening communications with the East. On July 13, he sent a force in that direction to open the Central Pacific. This force reached Truckee, at the state line, on the 14th; two days later, troops from the Department of the Platte arrived, and the line was completely open. Graham had to place guards all along the Central Pacific from Sacramento to Truckee to protect bridges and tunnels, and military escorts had to ride with all trains. Because of the shortage of federal troops, California National Guardsmen performed many of these duties.[73]

Meanwhile, on July 12, Ruger sent a force of 370 sailors and Marines to Oakland to break the blockade there. Over 1500 Guardsmen were already in the city. The arrival of the naval force seemed to give new heart to the Guardsmen, who took the lead in clearing the railroad yards and acting as train guards. On the 14th, local trains began to run out of Oakland. The only incident of violence here occurred on July 14, when a mob attempted to prevent a freight train from leaving the city. Guardsmen used bayonets to disperse the crowd and ended the resistance in Oakland.[74]

The bad blood created between soldiers and strikers in Sacramento as a result of the train wreck on the 11th came to a head on the 14th, when regulars fired into a crowd at the freight yards and killed two men.

Soldiers riding guard on a switch engine in the yards became involved in an argument with strikers and hangers-on. The troops ordered the crowd to disperse and then used bayonets when it moved too slowly for the soldiers' liking. Some of the strikers threw rocks, and then the troops fired, apparently without orders. "The scene that followed the shooting was one of wild disorder and almost insane excitement," reported one newspaper. "People were running in all directions, pushing each other aside and even throwing each other down" in an attempt to avoid bullets, bayonets, and the charging cavalry.[75] The outburst of violence in Sacramento on the 14th was not repeated. By the 19th, military protection restored travel within the state, but sabotage to the overland Central Pacific continued, and General Ruger maintained train, bridge, and tunnel guards even after the strike was called off in Sacramento on July 22. He withdrew the troops slowly after that date, but it was not until September 3 that they finally left their posts along the Central Pacific in eastern California.[76]

In many respects, strike duty in Brigadier General Wesley Merritt's Department of Dakota differed little from that in the other departments. His troops, however, remained on duty after the industrial army movement, and Major E. H. Liscum's command was still in Helena when the railroad strike began. Merritt ordered Liscum to take his command back to post on June 28, but the shutdown of the Northern Pacific prevented him from returning. Despite Liscum's pleas, the ARU adamantly refused to haul the troops. General Merritt told the Major to obtain a train and use his troops as engineers, firemen, and brakemen if necessary, "requiring at the same time the most discreet conduct of all your officers and men, so that there may be no conflict."[77]

The Northern Pacific management suggested that Liscum's troops merely board a regular passenger train and travel in that manner, but Merritt told Liscum to ignore the plan. "Do not confound instructions for protection of your own troops and government property on train bearing you . . . with instructions which cover the ordinary traffic of the road."[78] The growing disorders surrounding the strike made it prudent to retain Liscum and his force at Helena.[79]

The Northern Pacific strike affected all of Merritt's forces in Montana. The railroad was the main communications network supplying the forts in the state, many of which were located along the road's right of way. Merritt was unable to pay his troops or resupply them. The worried commander at Fort Assinniboine commented, "It is useless to disguise the fact that we are at the mercy of these men, and if they see fit can isolate us."[80]

The situation grew worse as the strike on the Northern Pacific continued. On July 6, Merritt reported to Secretary of War Lamont,

> Nothing in the way of railroad traffic is being done west of Fargo. I can reach no post by that line. . . . I cannot move the troops by this road from Helena to [Fort] Keogh nor to any point on the line where their services might be needed.[81]

Fearing that if he waited much longer it would be impossible to get his troops into the field, Merritt strongly recommended using troops immediately. Finally, on July 7, Merritt received orders to cooperate with General Otis in opening the Northern Pacific.[82]

The Third Infantry at Fort Snelling, Minnesota, was the only force in Merritt's command with access to an open rail line. Hastily recalled from an encampment with the Minnesota National Guard, two companies of the Third left St. Paul on the night of the 7th, and proceeded west. "No serious trouble was encountered between St. Paul and Fort Keogh," reported *The Army and Navy Journal*, "although angry crowds of strikers were assembled at every station."[83] Merritt recognized that military escorts could push trains through, but the many bridges and tunnels along the Northern Pacific in Montana were very vulnerable. He ordered out all his spare troops to protect these important structures. By July 9, Merritt had ten troops of cavalry and nine companies of infantry, totalling just over 1,000 officers and men, in the field. Soon a pattern developed. Guards rode on trains between towns and cities, as far as Idaho, where troops from the Department of Columbia assumed protection. Department of Dakota troops took over eastbound trains at these points. Strikers and their sympathizers often jeered at the troops when the trains they escorted passed through a railroad town. The fact that some of these trains carried strikebreakers from the East did not increase the Army's popularity in Montana.[84]

From the beginning, Livingston had been the hotspot of resistance in Montana. The town, with its railroad repair shops and warehouses, was an important point on the Northern Pacific. The vast majority of the townspeople worked for the road and were extremely hostile toward the company. The first federal force to reach Livingston arrived on July 10, under the command of Captain Benjamin C. Lockwood. The train under escort was in two sections, and as the first section pulled into town, a crowd of 600 people met it with hoots, boos, and curses. The mob displayed particular animosity toward strikebreakers working on the train. They threw stones at the train and strikebreakers and exchanged harsh words with the soldiers. One private later testified that "just as we pulled in they called us cock sucking sons of bitches and shook their fists at us and said that we were nothing but thirteen dollars a month scabs." Another soldier recalled the threats swapped between strikers and soldiers, in which a striker said, "I'll make him eat that gun or stick it up his arse as soon as the train stops. I told him that if he wanted to do that to just come up a little ways and I will give you a chance."[85]

Just as tempers began to explode, the second section of the train came into Livingston, which pushed the first section away from the depot and the military guard. The mob attacked the crew of the first section. Captain Lockwood appeared on the scene and attempted to bring about order. He ordered his men to push everyone away from both sections. The soldiers found it necessary to use gun butts and bayonets. Then, the Captain recalled, "They still resisted and a great many refused to move, using the most violent and vulgar language to myself and my men." Lockwood moved into the crowd.

> Seeing that if force was not used bloodshed would probably
> follow, I struck at the ringleader with my sword and hit him on
> the head, then this crowd commenced giving way, cursing and
> still using the most profane and vulgar language.[86]

The captain had the bad luck to strike one of the ARU leaders, which only angered the crowd more. This show of force, however, proved sufficient, and the train left Livingston. Lockwood left four officers and ninety-five men in the town to ensure peace.[87]

The Livingston affair immediately became a *cause célèbre* in Montana. Newspapers in the state screamed of military brutality, and strike leaders sent complaints to Washington. The citizens of Livingston reported the use of force by Lockwood and also complained, "The Captain used vile and profane language in the presence of ladies and publicly insulted our Mayor. Our community feels greatly outraged."[88] The governor of Montana sent a protest to the president and demanded that Captain Lockwood be punished.[89]

General Schofield, who assumed that Lockwood had lost control of himself, wired General Merritt and ordered an immediate investigation, commenting, "Of course such isolated cases of wrong cannot always be prevented, but the guilty should be punished with severity."[90] An officer from General Merritt's staff conducted the ensuing investigation. He went to Livingston and took testimony from strikers, soldiers, officers, and anyone else who had witnessed the affair. Predictably, all the Livingstonians testified that Lockwood was at fault, that he had called the mayor a "son-of-a-bitch," as well as striking an innocent old man. Just as predictably, the soldiers and officers swore that Lockwood had acted as an officer and a gentleman and had used only the necessary force to ensure protection of the train and its crew. Captain Mott Hooten testified that "in all his experience with mobs, in the White League riots of New Orleans in 1874, and in the labor riots in Chicago and Wilkesbarre in 1877, he has never seen a more foul-mouthed, blatant and despicable mob."[91] The complainants never did explain why "ladies" were part of a rock-throwing crowd of strikers, while the investigating officer's contention that no officer would use the language attributed to Captain Lockwood bordered on the absurd.[92]

The affair sputtered to an end with this investigation. General Merritt commented that he believed Lockwood should have watched his language, but his use of force was justified. General Schofield, upon learning all the facts, gave full support to Captain Lockwood, holding that the troops were in conditions that "were no less than actual insurrection against the Government of the United States." He concluded, "If these men suffered some violence at the hands of the troops because the latter could not discriminate between the innocent and the guilty, they have nobody but themselves to blame for their misfortune."[93] This ended the Lockwood case. Although no further confrontations between troops and strikers took place there, Livingston remained *the* trouble spot in Montana until the end of the strike.[94]

Although violence and obstruction along the Northern Pacific came to an end during July, the strikers and their sympathizers remained antagonistic towards the railroad and strikebreakers. Troops remained on duty throughout August to protect bridges, tunnels, and railroad property in towns and cities along the railroad. Train guards were eliminated, but the Northern Pacific strongly resisted any efforts to withdraw troops. Despite officers' reports of peace and quiet in Montana, the troops remained on duty in some places until September 1.

As in the Coxey movement, the Justice Department used the Army in the railroad strike to break up a popular movement. Attorney General Olney was motivated in both cases by more than a concern for enforcing federal laws. He accepted fully the railroads' position that the Pullman strike was a conspiracy against not only the railroads but also the federal government. The strongest justification given both by Olney and the railroads for the use of troops in the strike was that the American Railway Union conspired to use intimidation and violence to prevent the operation of the railroads. They charged that the ARU coerced the majority of railroad workers into not reporting for work, that if such coercion had not been used, most workers would have gladly returned to their jobs. If troops were sent in to protect threatened workers, they argued, rail traffic would resume.[95]

This was not the case. The railroad strike was effective, not because the ARU was so well organized as to intimidate thousands of workers in the trans-Mississippi West, but because the workers supported the strike so ardently. The arrival of federal troops did not mean the automatic resumption of rail traffic. General McCook noted that his troops easily removed obstructions from both the Union Pacific and Santa Fe lines in his department, but rail traffic remained stalled because "crews to operate trains could not be obtained."[96] J. B. H. Hemingway, U.S. Attorney for New Mexico, confirmed McCook's observation, reporting to Olney, "I am advised that there is no positive obstruction of mails, but only a refusal of employees to work."[97] Similar conditions prevailed in other parts of the West. Colonel William R. Shafter, First Infantry, found no violence when he arrived in Los Angeles, and after three days there explained the lack of rail traffic, "The difficulty is in getting men to man the trains." In northern California, General Ruger reported as late as July 18, that only a limited number of trains were running on the Central Pacific "owing to the lack of workers, as strikers still cohere." Reports from General Brooke's Department of the Platte, and General Merritt's Department of the Dakota reflected the same problem.[98]

General Schofield seemed to be aware of this possibility early in the strike and directly asked S. H. H. Clark, receiver for the Union Pacific, to what extent forcible obstruction stopped rail traffic "and to what ex-

tent it is due to inability to obtain train crews who are willing to serve."
Clark replied evasively, "Difficult to state what extent blockade is due
to forcible obstruction. We have no doubt of our ability to secure train
crews if protection can be afforded."[99] What Clark had in mind was the
importation of strikebreakers from the East, a policy all the struck roads
were forced to adopt. James McNaught, counsel for the receivers of the
Northern Pacific, informed Schofield that he "found it necessary to send
a large number of men, principally engineers and firemen, from St. Paul
last night to operate the road in Montana. We expect trouble when they
go to work."[100] Colonel Poland's movement on the Central Pacific in
Nevada was met with hostility because the troop train also carried seventy-five strikebreakers. The importation of Italian laborers to work on
the Northern Pacific contributed to the uproar at Livingston, Montana.
Lack of strikebreakers kept the strike alive in California after it collapsed
elsewhere.[101]

Neither General Schofield nor his department commanders questioned
the railroads' assumption that the Army would assist them in introducing
strikebreakers. The effectiveness of the strike demanded importing nonunion men, and throughout the late nineteenth century the appearance
of scabs was the crucial point of a strike. If employers could get strikebreakers to work without precipitating violence or secure the aid of local,
state, or federal law enforcement agencies to quell violence and protect
scabs, the strikers' cause was lost. This is precisely what happened in
1894. Indeed, McNaught of the Northern Pacific specifically promised
federal protection to strikebreakers. "We rely upon the President and
you," he wired Schofield, "to assist in making good this guarantee."[102]

Cleveland and the Army did not disappoint McNaught. It was not so
much that either Cleveland or Schofield were the abject tools of McNaught
and the other railroad managers and counsels as that neither man saw the
situation any differently than the railroads did. This was evident as well
in the relationships that developed between the department commanders
and railroad officials in the West. Between July 1 and July 7, General
Schofield sent generally worded orders to the department commanders
to aid marshals in enforcing the injunctions that forbade the ARU from
interfering with the transport of the mails, interstate commerce, roads in
receivership of the U.S. courts, or roads designated as military roads. Of
necessity, Schofield informed each department commander, "All details
of the execution of these orders are entrusted to your judgement."[103]

Upon receipt of Schofield's instructions, the department commanders contacted the responsible federal judges and railroad managers in their departments. For all intents and purposes, the generals worked with the railroad managers. Their subordinate field commanders also worked closely with railroad officials to determine when and where trains would begin operating.[104]

It was necessary, of course, for department commanders and subordinates in the field to work to some extent with railroad officials. All too often, however, the officers were far too deferential to the railroads' wishes. Colonel Zenas R. Bliss, in command at Trinidad, Colorado, reported frequent meetings with representatives of the Santa Fe and Denver and Gulf lines, "and all assistance offered that they desired."[105] The general manager of the Central Pacific complained to General Brooke about Colonel Poland's caution in opening the Central Pacific.

> We have a tremendous volume of traffic forced upon us at
> the present time. . . . if not inconsistent with your policy may
> we feel free to ask you to instruct the Colonel to be as considerate
> as possible to the end that we may move through his protection
> more than one freight and one passenger train per day?[106]

Despite the protestations of Colonel Poland, who feared sabotage of the freight trains, General Brooke ordered him to step up traffic on the Central Pacific.[107]

The department heads were most deferential about troop withdrawals, usually letting the railroads set the times and conditions for the relief of troops. General Brooke determined that troops no longer need serve in his department but nonetheless requested the views of the general manager of the Union Pacific, noting "that anything you have to suggest will, as in the past, receive due consideration."[108] General Merritt tendered the same consideration to the Northern Pacific. "You will understand that it is my desire to relieve the troops as soon as practicable," he wrote the Northern Pacific's general manager, "but that I want to do nothing in this direction without consulting with the railway authorities."[109]

The close cooperation between military commanders and railroad officials led to military duties clearly not implied in the general directions Schofield sent out. In almost all places, Army elements guarded railroad property. The protection of bridges and tunnels was absolutely essential to the restoration of railroad traffic, but it is not clear how military protection of railroad property fit into restoring the movement of the mails and interstate commerce. Troops nevertheless spent a great deal of time doing so. In Merritt's Department of the Dakota, local commanders were ordered to "consult with the local Railroad authorities" in order to determine what property needed protection.[110] Lieutenant Edgar Hubert's company of the Eighth Infantry, stationed at Rawlins, Wyoming, not only guarded incoming and departing trains, but "sentinels over property are also ordered to protect all men working for Ry. Co."[111]

At Newcastle, Colorado, the regular force's duties "consisted solely in 'guard duty, guarding the railroad bridges and keeping the yards clear.' "[112] Captain George Palmer, Sixteenth Infantry, used fifty men in the day and sixty men at night "to guard the vast amount of property consisting of one thousand freight cars" belonging to the Union Pacific and Central Pacific railroads at Ogden Utah.[113] Company A, Twenty-fifth Infantry, spent the month of August "guarding grounds, work shops, rolling stock, bridges, tunnels and contents of Northern Pacific Railway between Big Timber and Muir, Mont."[114]

Indeed, guard duty of this sort constituted the most common activity for regulars serving in the West in 1894. Only rarely, as at Tacoma, Washington, did a regular officer refuse to carry out this duty. Colonel T. M. Anderson refused the request of a U.S. marshal to guard railroad property there, as Anderson informed the marshal "it is not his duty to guard either prisoners who may be arrested or property, except moving trains."[115]

Perhaps as an intuitive reaction to the Army's direct protection of railroad property and interests, hostility rowards regulars on strike duty in 1894 was much sharper than in 1877. When Colonel Zenas R. Bliss's command left Fort Bayard, New Mexico, for duty at Trinidad, at least two futile attempts were made to wreck the troop train. The arrival at Trinidad of Bliss's all-black Twenty-fourth Infantry occasioned bad feelings. The movement of the First Infantry from San Francisco to Los Angeles caused similar difficulties. Despite the presence of guards on the engine, strikers tampering with the engine halted the train at Bakersfield for four hours. Californians booed the First at every stop on the way to Los Angeles.[116]

In Trinidad, an unknown assailant threw a coupling pin at a soldier on night guard duty. The commanding officer at New Castle, Colorado, reported "two attempts of assassination of soldiers on duty. One man shot through the wrist while posted as sentinel."[117] Lieutenant George B. Duncan, stationed at Hope, Idaho, during the strike, later recalled "strikers and their families were hostile in their attitudes" towards his soldiers.[118] In his final report on strike duty, General Brooke summed up the problem the Army faced in the West in 1894:

> Not only were the striking employees in an attitude of hostility, but it seemed about the entire population along the line of [the Central Pacific] . . . . The troops were met with a considerable degree of hostility . . . there being a great deal of vociferation and annoyance.[119]

The experience of Colonel Poland's command in Nevada, the bitterness between the troops of Colonel Graham and the strikers at Oakland, and the contretemps between Captain Lockwood and the people of Livingston confirmed Brooke's observation.

As in 1877, the Army did not seek strike duty, not did it particularly relish the task. Lieutenant George B. Duncan was most uncomfortable with a standing order that his company should reply to sniping with volley fire into the town of Hope, Idaho. "Such a drastic reply to the act of a fanatical or drunken man appalled me, and I did not propose being a party to it." Duncan managed to have his unit moved out of the railyard in Hope, to the edge of town. "I just had to get away from that railroad yard."[120] General Merritt carefully instructed his officers in the field that they and their men "must be prudent and cool in the discharge of this delicate duty. . . . Let them be cautioned as to this and that while they are soldiers under important orders they are not the less citizens of the Republic, with the first interest in its welfare."[121]

Prudence and coolness marked the Army's behavior in the trans-Mississippi West in 1894. While often overextended, overworked, and met with open hostility, military discipline prevailed. The potential for great bloodshed at Livingston, Sacramento, Oakland, Reno, and several other places in the West was very real, but it did not occur. This was due both to the Army's restraint and to the striker's obvious reluctance to combat federal soldiers. Strikers had the advantage of numbers, and, as military reports indicated, many were armed. But no great calamity took place. Despite Olney's contention that the strike was an insurrection, it is obvious that the railroaders had no intention of engaging the federal government and the U.S. Army in armed rebellion. While regulars were met very often with jeers, catcalls, curses, even rocks, eventually the strikers gave way. The appearance of federal troops, whatever the short-term difficulties, guaranteed an end to the strike.

The conduct of the departmental commanders and their subordinates in the field contributed significantly to the absence of violence and bloodshed. They were all men tested and seasoned by war. Generals McCook and Merritt served as major generals of volunteers, the former as a corps commander in the Army of the Cumberland, the latter as Philip Sheridan's cavalry commander. Brooke and Ruger commanded infantry divisions with the rank of brigadier general of volunteers in the latter stages of the Civil War. General Otis had obtained the rank of lieutenant colonel of the 140th New York Volunteer Infantry by the end of the war. The colonels in the field had not served as general officers, but all had seen combat duty. The responsibilities of command in time of war had tempered the likes of Brooke, McCook, Merritt, Otis, and Ruger to react to crisis and challenge with care and restraint.[122]

Commanding General John M. Schofield set the tone for the Army's performance in 1894. His orders to field commanders were never inflammatory, and he continually advised department commanders to act with caution. He was most insistent that officers and soldiers not do the duties of marshals, that is, arrest individuals, serve warrants, accept custody of prisoners, or perform other such legal duties. He demanded compliance with the *posse comitatus* act of 1878 and maintained the military chain of command. Nonetheless, Schofield was as solicitous of the railroad's interests as any department or field commander. Throughout the industrial army and railroad strike upheavals, he maintained communications with railroad authorities, particularly James McNaught, counsel for receivers of the Northern Pacific. The general not only kept McNaught and others informed of the Army's activities and intentions, he presented their requests with his endorsements to Secretary of War Lamont and Attorney General Olney. Schofield's respect for property and the economic status quo came through clearly in these correspondences and shaped the Army's approach to strike duty in 1894, as much as did his evident concern for avoiding violence.[123]

As the great strike sputtered to a close in late July, Judge Peter S. Grosscup, one of the authors of the wide-ranging injunction used to destroy the ARU, complained to Secretary of State Walter Q. Gresham that the injunction method of suppressing labor involved federal judges too deeply in labor-capital conflicts. The injunctive process pulled judges "into the midst of such a turmoil and compel [s] them, apparently, to take sides. It identifies them personally with the one side, and no amount of argument or enlightenment will ever teach the other, that they are not partisan."[124] Grosscup was about as partisan as a judge could be in 1894, and it is indicative of the social and economic attitudes of the time that he saw himself as an impartial upholder of law and order. But he nonetheless recognized that the role of the federal bench in 1894 destroyed the ideal of the law as a neutral arbiter of conflict. Neither General Schofield nor his officers expressed a similar concern for the part the Army played in 1894.

Notes

1. Background for the chapter and the upheavals of 1894 come from the following: John R. Commons et al., *History of Labour in the United States,* vol. 2 (New York, 1923), pp. 501-08; Philip S. Foner, *History of the Labor Movement in the United States,* vol. 2 (New York, 1947), pp. 235-50; Matthew Josephson, *The Politicos 1865-1896* (New York, 1938), chap. 16; Samuel Rezneck, "Unemployment, Unrest and Relief in the United States During the Depression of 1893-97," *Journal of Political Economy* 61, no. 4 (August 1953): 324-25, 329-36; H. Wayne Morgan, *From Hayes to McKinley, National Party Politics 1877-1896* (Syracuse, N.Y., 1969), pp. 447-48, 460-65; Gerald Eggert, *Railroad Labor Disputes: The Beginnings of Federal Strike Policy* (Ann Arbor, 1967), chaps. 6-8; Almont Lindsey, *The Pullman Strike* (Chicago, 1942), *passim;* Donald L. McMurry, *Coxey's Army: A Study of the Industrial Army Movement of 1894* (Boston, 1924); Howard M. Jones, *The Age of Energy: Varieties of American Experience, 1865-1915* (New York, 1971), chap. 9, on the middle and upper classes' fears of revolt. Eggert was particularly valuable in understanding the development of federal strike policy during 1894.

2. *Army and Navy Journal* 21, no. 47 (July 14, 1894): 812. On National Guard duty for the entire year, see Major Winthrop Alexander, District of Columbia N.G., "Ten Years of Riot Duty," *Journal of the Military Service Institution of the United States (JMSI)* 19, no. 82 (July 1896): 2-26; *The National Guardsman* 7, no. 11 (June 15, 1894): 163; U.S., War Department, *The Organized Militia of the United States, 1894,* AGO, Military Information Division, *report no. 5* (Washington, D.C.,

1895), pp. 269-75, hereafter referred to as MID, *Organized Militia, 1894.* For extensive descriptions on the use of federal marshals, see U.S., Department of Justice, Attorney General, *Fees and Expenses of U.S. Marshals, 1894,* 53rd Cong., 2nd sess., Senate Executive Document 120 (Washington, D.C., 1894), and idem, *Annual Report of the Attorney General of the United States, 1896, Appendix,* 54th Cong., 2nd sess., House Executive Document 9 (Washington, D.C., 1896), hereafter referred to as Atty. Gen., *Appendix to 1896 Report.* Attorney General Richard Olney did not publish any of the correspondence dealing with the use of marshals in 1894 in his annual report for that year.

3. To Colonel John L. Cooper, July 26, 1894, Letterbrook, Walter Q. Gresham Papers, Library of Congress, Washington, D.C.

4. Harry P. Robinson, "The Humiliating Report of the Strike Commission," *The Forum* 18 (January 1895): 523.

5. On the coal strike, see Commons, *History of Labour in the U.S.,* pp. 501-02, and Foner, *History of Labor in the U.S.,* p. 245; Alexander, "Ten Years of Riot Duty," pp. 2-24; Illinois, Executive, Adjutant General, *Biennial Report of the Adjutant General of Illinois, 1893-94* (Springfield, Ill., 1894), pp. vi-vii; Ohio, Executive, Adjutant General, *Report of the Adjutant General, State of Ohio, 1894* (Columbus, O., 1894), pp. 368-70, 564-70.

6. Andrews to Headquarters, Department of the Missouri, June 1, in consolidated file no. 1767, Letters Received 1894, Department of the Missouri, Records of United States Army Continental Commands 1821-1920, Record Group 393, National Archives. The entire episode may be followed in: a series of wires between U.S. Marshal J. J. McAlester and Attorney General Richard Olney, in *Fees and Expenses of U.S. Marshals, 1894,* 53rd Cong., 2nd sess., Senate Executive Document 120, (Washington, D.C., 1894), pp. 8-11, hereafter referred to as *Senate Document 120* and in consolidated file no. 6091, Principal Record Division, 1894, Records of the Adjutant General's Office, 1800-1917, Record Group 94, National Archives, hereafter referred to as PRD no. 6091.

7. Andrews to Headquarters, Department of the Missouri, June 29, no. 1767, Letters Received 1894, Department of the Missouri, RG393, NA.

8. See correspondence in PRD no. 6091; and *United Mine Workers' Journal* 4, no. 12 (June 28, 1894): 7.

9. On Schofield's views, see his *Forty-Six Years in the Army* (New York, 1897), pp. 490-91.

10. Thomas R. Bacon, "The Railroad Strike in California," *The Yale Review* 3 (November 1894): 244-45, and *passim.* On local sympathy for

the Coxeyites, see W. T. Stead, "Coxeyism: A Character Sketch," *Review of Reviews* 10, no. 1 (July 1894): 47-56, and H. L. Stetson, "The Industrial Army," *The Independent* 46, no. 2374 (May 31, 1894): 681. On general discontent in the West, see Lindsey, *The Pullman Strike*, pp. 12-15, 131-35, 240-67, and Eggert, *Railroad Labor Disputes*, pp. 153-54.

    11. Eggert, *Railroad Labor Disputes*, pp. 139, 145-47, 149-66; Bennet Rich, *The Presidents and Civil Disorders* (Washington, D.C., 1941), pp. 87-90; Lindsey, *The Pullman Strike*, pp. 109-25, 174-75, 241-45; Ray Ginger, *The Bending Cross: A Biography of Eugene Victor Debs* (New Brunswick, N.J., 1949), pp. 92-107, 116-27.

    12. Major E. H. Liscum to Brig. Gen. Wesley Merritt, June 6, no. 1849, Letters Received, 1894, Department of the Dakota, RG393, NA.

    13. This paragraph is constructed mainly from a reading of the Justice Department consolidated file on the Coxey affair, year file 4017/1894, Records of the Department of Justice, Record Group 60, National Archives, and Atty. Gen., *Appendix to 1896 Report, passim*. Both of these files are filled with representations from Justice officials in the field calling for troops. The Army's viewpoint is found scattered through consolidated file no. 6370, Adjutant General's Office, Record Group 94, National Archives. AGO no. 6370 is a consolidated file containing the principal correspondence among General Schofield, the War Department, and the field commanders involved in dealing with the industrial army troubles. On the Pullman strike, see consolidated file no. 10, AGO RG94, NA. On the Great Northern Strike, see Col. P. T. Swaine, to Gen. Schofield, April 28, April 29, May 3, in AGO no. 6370, and *The Army and Navy Journal* 31, no. 37 (May 5, 1894): 629, and no. 38 (May 12, 1894): 652.

    14. On Schofield's leadership, see his comments in *Sec. War Rept. 1894*, pp. 57-58. On orders to department commanders to report directly to him, see Circular Letter, July 11, Letters Sent, 1894, Headquarters of the Army, (HQA), pp. 337-38, Record Group 108, National Archives.

    15. *Forty-Six Years in the Army*, pp. 534-35. Also, *Sec. War Rept. 1894*, p. 58.

    16. *Forty-Six Years in the Army*, pp. 505-06.

    17. General Order No. 26 in container 78, John McAllister Schofield Papers, Library of Congress.

    18. *Forty-Six Years in the Army*, p. 508.

    19. Schofield continually stressed to his field commanders the limits to which the Army could be used. Schofield to Secretary of War Daniel S. Lamont, May 18, 1894, Official Endorsements, HQA, 1893-94, 508, Schofield Papers. Schofield to Brig. Gen. John R. Brooke, May 16; to Brig. Gen. Wesley Merritt, May 23; Sec. War Lamont to Governor J. E.

Rickards, Montana, May 19, 1894, all in AGO no. 6370. The depart-
ment commanders were General Merritt, Department of the Dakota;
Gen. Brooke, Department of the Platte; Brig. Gen. Elwell S. Otis, Depart-
ment of the Columbia; Brig. Gen. Thomas H. Ruger, Department of
California; Brig. Gen. Alexander McD. McCook, Department of the
Colorado; Maj. Gen. Nelson A. Miles, Department of the Missouri. See
Schofield's comments, *Sec. War Rept. 1894*, p. 57.

20. In Letters Sent, 1894, HQA, pp. 329-30, RG108, NA.

21. See Brooke's August 1 report to the Adj. Gen., in AGO no.
6370, pp. 1-8; Brooke to Schofield, May 16, 19; Schofield to Brooke,
May 14, 15, 16, all in *Ibid.* Schofield to Olney, May 31, no. 471, Letters
Sent, 1894, HQA, RG108, NA; Brooke to Judge Riner, May 14, no. 252,
May 16, no. 268, Brooke to Schofield, May 24, no. 345, vol. 1, Letters
Sent, 1894, Department of the Platte, RG393, NA. Brig. Gen. Otis also
experienced similar difficulties with Justice officials in Washington and
Oregon. See Otis to Schofield, April 29, Schofield to Otis, April 30, Otis's
May 1 report to the Adj. Gen., all in *Ibid.*

22. For the first quotation, "The Coxey Crusade," *The Independent*
46, no. 2370 (May 3, 1894): 558; *Leslie's Weekly* 78, no. 2017 (May 10,
1894): 302, for the second. Also see *The National Guardsman*, 7, no. 8
(May 1, 1894): 115. On the proletarian nature of the Western industrial
armies, see McMurry, *Coxey's Army*, pp. 127-28, and Eggert, *Railroad
Labor Disputes*, pp. 139-40. On the fate of Coxey himself, see *Washington
News*, April 17, 23, 1894; *Washington Evening Star*, April 18, 23, 1894;
Washington Post, April 24, 1894; Eggert, *Railroad Labor Disputes*, p. 146.

23. As quoted in Henry James, *Richard Olney and His Public Service*,
(Boston, 1923), p. 39. For examples of federal judges and railroad officials
calling for action to make examples of Coxeyites, see Judge James A.
Beatty to Olney, May 23, Ellery Anderson and Oliver W. Mink, receivers
for the Union Pacific to Olney, June 7, 1894, in year file 4017/94, Department of Justice, RG60, NA. James McNaught, receiver for the Northern Pacific, to A. H. Garland, April 24, James J. Hill to Pres. Cleveland,
April 25, 1894, in Grover Cleveland Papers, series 2, reel 84, microfilm,
Library of Congress.

24. To Sec. War Lamont, May 18, 1894, in AGO no. 6370. In *Forty-
Six Years in the Army*, Schofield expressed some sympathy for the industrials, pp. 490-91. For expressions of doubt about using the Army in the
episode, see Schofield to McNaught, April 24, 26, and to Lamont, April
28, letters no. 397, no. 407, no. 413 respectively, in Letters Sent, HQA,
RG108, NA.

25. Eggert, *Railroad Labor Disputes*, p. 146; James, *Richard Olney*,
pp. 37-40.

26. McMurry, *Coxey's Army*, pp. 127-28, 201-04; Eggert, *Railroad Labor Disputes*, pp. 140-42; *Senate Document 120*, p. 3; G. E. Rickards, Gov. of Montana, to Pres. Cleveland, April 25, series 2, reel 84, Cleveland Papers.

27. See Schofield to Swaine, April 24, Swaine to Schofield, April 25, Schofield to Swaine, April 25, Page's written report to Headquarters, Department of the Dakota, May 1, all in AGO no. 6370.

28. See Page's May 1 report, Swaine to Schofield, April 26, three wires, April 27, April 28; Schofield to Swaine, April 28, all in AGO no. 6370. McDermott to Olney, April 27, year file no. 4017/94, Department of Justice, RG60, NA.

29. May 22, in AGO no. 6370.

30. *Ibid.*

31. May 16, *Ibid.*

32. In Brooke to Schofield, May 19, *Ibid.*

33. The best source for operations in the Department of the Platte is in Brooke's special report to the Adj. Gen., August 30, in *Ibid.* See also Schofield to Brooke, May 14, 15, 16, Brooke to Adj. Gen., June 9, 13, all in *Ibid.*

34. See Otis's remarks in *Sec. War Rept. 1894,* pp. 152-53; Otis, May 1 report, pp. 1-5; McMurry, *Coxey's Army,* pp. 216-18, and the *Portland Oregonian,* April 29, 1894, p. 4, on the governors.

35. Enclosure to Otis's May 1 report, AGO no. 6370. See also pp. 8-18 of that report. Schofield to Otis, April 28, Otis to Schofield, April 28, three wires, in *Ibid.*

36. Otis to Adj. Gen., April 29, *Ibid.*

37. Otis's May 1 report, pp. 30, 36, Otis to Schofield, April 29, 30, May 1, *Ibid.*

38. To Schofield, May 17, *Ibid.*

39. Otis to Schofield, May 23, p. 181, Letters Sent, 1894, Department of the Columbia, RG393, NA. For a general account of operations in this department, see Otis's May 1 report, AGO no. 6370. The day-to-day activities are best seen in Otis's orders to his field commanders and their reports to him, in Letters Sent and Letters Received, 1894, Department of the Columbia, RG393, NA, between April 27 and May 20. See also April and May returns, Fourth Infantry, Returns of Regular Army Infantry Regiments, AGO, RG94, NA.

40. Otis to Schofield, May 31, p. 196, Letters Sent, 1894, Department of the Columbia, RG393, NA.

41. May 12 in year file 4017/94, Department of Justice, RG60, NA.

42. Duncan, "Reminiscences 1882-1905," manuscript in the possession of Henry T. Duncan, Lexington, Kentucky, p. 54. The efforts to have

troops in the Department of the Columbia committed to break up the industrials completely is clearly seen in the following correspondence: James McNaught to A. H. Garland, April 26, Judge C. H. Hanford to Pres. Cleveland, April 27, McNaught to Schofield, May 1, Hanford to Olney, May 2, McNaught to Schofield, May 5, all in AGO no. 6370.

43. Beatty to Olney, June 7, 1894, year file 4017/94, Department of Justice, RG60, NA. See also Olney to Sec. War Lamont, June 6, 1894, Richard Olney Papers, Library of Congress.

44. June 7, in AGO no. 6370. See also Otis to Adj. Gen., June 8, Letters Sent, 1894, Department of the Columbia, 205, RG393, NA.

45. May 31, 1894, Letters Sent, 1894, HQA, RG108, NA.

46. See Schofield to Lamont, May 18, to Gen. Brooke, May 16, to Gen. Merritt, May 23; also, Gen. Otis to Adj. Gen., June 8, all in AGO no. 6370.

47. Vol. 31, no. 37 (May 5, 1894): 629. See Brooke's August 30, 1894, report to the Adj. Gen., pp. 8-9, in AGO no. 6370. Otis's views in *Sec. War Rept. 1894*, p. 155.

48. Background on the government's policy in the Pullman strike taken from: Eggert, *Railroad Labor Disputes*, pp. 153-66; Lindsey, *The Pullman Strike*, pp. 109-25, 142-55, 171-75; Ginger, *The Bending Cross*, pp. 116-27; James, *Richard Olney*, pp. 45-54, 201-04; Rich, *The Presidents and Civil Disorder*, pp. 94-97.

49. To Sec. War Lamont, July 3, 1894, no. 4444, AGO 10, RG94, NA. AGO 10 is a large consolidated file on the Army's role in the Pullman strike. Within that file, correspondence from each military department is collected under a single file number. For example, no. 4444 contains all the correspondence between HQA and McCook's Department of the Colorado and all other messages pertaining to operations in that department.

50. Brooke to Brig. Gen. Thomas H. Ruger, July 16, 1894, Letters Sent, 1894, Department of the Platte, vol. 2, RG393, NA.

51. To Headquarters, Department of the Platte, July 13, no. 4747, in AGO 10.

52. To Headquarters, Department of the Platte, July 25, *Ibid.* Comments on the hostility of local communities towards both the Army and federal marshals and the concomitant sympathy for the strikers present in all the sources used here. Of particular value here are the statements of U.S. marshals and U.S. attorneys from the field, in *Fees and Expenses of U.S. Marshals, 1894, passim*, and Atty. Gen., *Appendix to 1896 Report, passim*. It is also evident in the many comments of military field commanders in the various sub-files of AGO 10.

53. In no. 4447, AGO 10.

54. To Generals Brooke, Ruger, and Otis, in Atty. Gen., *Appendix to 1896 Report,* pp. 230, 231, 233. This paragraph drawn from sources in AGO 10, *Fees and Expenses of U.S. Marshals, 1894,* Atty. Gen., *Appendix to 1896 Report,* and *Sec. War Rept. 1894.*

55. Brooke to Adj. Gen., July 17, AGO no. 6370. This summary paragraph fails to convey the extensive use of troops in the Rocky Mountain region. A recitation of detail, however, would be boring and redundant. Sources for this summary are Department of the Platte, no. 4443, AGO 10, containing all of General Brooke's reports to Schofield and the Adjutant General. Brooke's August 30 special report on strike duty to the Adj. Gen., Letters Sent and Letters Received, 1894, Department of the Platte, RG393, and no. 4747, AGO 10 were surveyed from July 5 through August 17, and contain the day-to-day reports and orders to and from the officers in the field. Similar sources were used for the Department of the Colorado, including no. 4444, AGO 10; McCook to Adj. Gen., September 14, no. 5736, *Ibid.,* reports trooop withdrawals. Report of Col. Zenas R. Bliss, reporting on duty at Trinidad, Colorado, and forwarded to the Adj. Gen., by McCook dated September 6, no. 5864, *Ibid.* Letters Sent and Letters Received, 1894, Department of the Colorado, also used, as were McCook's remarks in his annual report, found in *Sec. War Rept. 1894,* pp. 137-40. See also July, August, and September returns, Twenty-fourth Infantry, in "Returns of Regular Army Infantry Regiments," AGO, RG94, NA. For General Otis and the Department of the Columbia, see no. 4445, AGO 10, and Letters Sent and Letters Received, 1894, Department of the Columbia, for July, RG393, NA.

56. Brooke to Schofield, July 11, no. 112, vol. 2, Letters Sent, 1894, Department of the Platte, RG393, NA.

57. Poland to Headquarters, Department of the Platte, July 12, no. 30004, Letters Received, 1894; *Ibid.* See also Headquarters, Department of the Platte, to Poland, July 11, no. 112, vol. 2, Letters Sent, 1894, *Ibid.* Brooke to Schofield, July 12, no. 124, Letters Sent, 1894, *Ibid.;* Brooke to Schofield, July 11, 12, 13, in no. 4443, AGO 10.

58. Headquarters, Department of the Platte to Poland, July 13, no. 133, vol. 2, Letters Sent, 1894; Brooke to U.S. Judge, Carson City, Nevada, July 13, no. 138, and to U.S. Marshal, Carson City, July 13, no. 140, Brooke to Poland, July 13, no. 139, *Ibid.;* Poland to Headquarters Department of the Platte, July 12, no. 3004, July 13, no. 3005, Letters Received, 1894. *Ibid.,* RG 393, NA.

59. Towne to Brooke, July 16, no. 3105, Letters Received, 1894, *Ibid.,* RG393, NA.

60. Poland to Headquarters, Department of the Platte, July 15, no. 3071, *Ibid.*, RG393, NA.

61. On the deputies, see Headquarters to Poland, July 14, no. 151; Brooke to A. N. Towne, July 15, no. 153; Brooke to Gen. Thos. H. Ruger, July 15, no. 156; Brooke to Schofield, July 16, no. 158, July 17, no. 176, Letters Sent, 1894, *Ibid.*, RG393, NA. Poland to Headquarters, July 16, no. 3088; Gen. Ruger to Brooke, July 16, no. 3099; A. N. Towne to Brooke, July 16, no. 3105, Letters Received, 1894, *Ibid.*, RG393, NA.

62. Poland to Headquarters, Department of the Platte, July 16, no. 3088, Letters Received, 1894, Department of the Platte, RG393, NA.

63. *Ibid.* See Brooke to Schofield, July 14, no. 4443, AGO 10, Headquarters, Department of the Platte, to Poland, July 14, no. 151; Brooke to Gen. Ruger, July 15, no. 156; Brooke to Schofield, July 16, no. 158; Brooke to Gen. Ruger, July 16, no. 160, all in vol. 2, Letters Sent, 1894, *Ibid.* Poland to Headquarters, Department of the Platte, July 15, no. 3071, July 16, no. 3088, Letters Received, 1894, *Ibid.* In Poland's final report, pp. 2-5, August 30, in no. 747, AGO 10.

64. Poland to Brooke, July 21, no. 3321, Letters Received, 1894, Department of the Platte, RG393.

65. Poland to Headquarters, Department of the Platte, July 19, no. 3172, no. 3184; July 20, no. 3194; July 21, no. 3321; July 22, no. 3233; July 24, no. 3314; Gen. Ruger to Brooke, July 22, no. 3259, all in *Ibid.* Brooke to A. N. Towne, August 1, no. 270, August 3, no. 286, August 7, no. 302; Brooke to Ruger, August 5, no. 294; August 7, no. 303; August 10, no. 336, all in vol. 2, Letters Sent, 1894, *Ibid.* See also August returns, Sixteenth Infantry, in Returns of Regular Army Infantry Regiments, AGO RG94, NA.

66. In July returns, First Infantry, *op. cit.* The full information on federal troops in Los Angeles is in no. 4447, AGO 10, see especially Schofield to Ruger, July 1; Ruger to Adj. Gen., July 2; Col. Wm. R. Shafter to Sec. of War Lamont, July 5, 7, 8; Ruger to Adj. Gen., July 9, 10, in *Ibid.* Also *San Francisco Chronicle*, July 6, 1894, p. 4, July 7, p. 2; and Grace Stimson, *Rise of the Labor Movement in Los Angeles* (Berkeley, 1955), pp. 168-69.

67. July 5, 1894, p. 1, also July 4, p. 1.

68. Daily issues, July 4-11, front page. *Army and Navy Journal* 31, no. 47 (July 14, 1894): 812-13; MID, *Organized Militia, 1894,* pp. 269-70; Calif. Adj. Gen., *Biennial Report, 1893-1894,* pp. 11, 217-22; Atty. Gen., *Appdx. to 1896 Report,* pp. 22-32.

69. Schofield to Ruger, July 7; Ruger to Schofield, July 8; Schofield

to Sec. of War Lamont, July 8; Lamont to Schofield, July 8; Schofield to
Ruger, July 8, all in no. 4447, AGO 10. Ruger's comments in *Sec. War
Rept. 1894*, pp. 112-15; Ira B. Cross, *A History of the Labor Movement
in California* (Berkeley, 1955), pp. 164-67.

    70. *Sec. War Rept. 1894*, p. 112.

    71. *Ibid.*, p. 113. See also Schofield to Ruger, July 7; Ruger to Scho-
field, July 10, 11, no. 4447, AGO 10; *San Francisco Chronicle*, July 11,
1894, pp. 1, 2, July 12, p. 1; Capt. J. J. O'Connell, U.S.A., "The Great
Strike of 1894," *United Service*, n.s., vol. 15, no. 4 (April 1896): 310-
13. O'Connell was in the federal force that went to Sacramento.

    72. Ruger to Schofield, July 10, 11, no. 4447, AGO 10; Ruger's com-
ments in *Sec. War Rept. 1894*, pp. 113-14; *San Francisco Chronicle*,
July 12, 1894, p. 1; July Returns, Fifth Artillery, Returns of Regular
Army Artillery Regiments, AGO, RG94, NA.

    73. Ruger to Schofield, July 13, 14, 16, no. 4447, AGO 10; July re-
turns, Fifth Artillery, *op. cit.;* July and August returns, First Infantry,
op. cit., on the day-to-day guard duty on bridges, tunnels, and trains. On
the California National Guard, see California, Adjutant General, *Biennial
Report, 1893-94*, pp. 223-31, and MID, *Organized Militia, 1894*, p. 270.
Much of this duty was occasioned by intermittent sabotage against the
railroads in the rural areas of California. See the *San Francisco Chronicle,*
July 16, p. 1, for a description of this type of action.

    74. O'Connell, "The Great Strike of 1894," pp. 313-14; *San Francisco
Chronicle*, July 13, 1894, p. 1, July 14, p. 1, July 17, p. 1; California,
Adjutant General, *Biennial Report, 1893-94*, pp. 223-31.

    75. *San Francisco Chronicle*, July 14, 1894, p. 1.

    76. *Ibid.*, July 18, p. 2; July 19, pp. 3, 5; July 20, p. 3; July 22, pp.
12, 14; Ruger to Adj. Gen., August 10, no. 4447; Adj. Gen. to Ruger,
August 16, no. 3364; Ruger to Adj. Gen., September 3, no. 4758, all in
AGO 10; *Sec. War Rept. 1894*, p. 116.

    77. Merritt to Liscum, June 28, no. 466. Letters Sent, 1894, Depart-
ment of the Dakota, RG393, NA.

    78. July 2, no. 475, *Ibid.*

    79. Besides the above, see Merritt to Adj. Gen., June 29, no. 471;
Merritt to Liscum, July 2, no. 486, in *Ibid.;* Liscum to Headquarters,
Department of the Dakota, July 1, no. 2080, Letters Received, 1894,
Ibid.

    80. Col. Wm. H. Penrose to Merritt, July 5, no. 2166, Letters Re-
ceived, 1894, *Ibid.*

    81. No. 502, Letters Sent, 1894, *Ibid.*

    82. See Merritt to Adj. Gen., June 29, no. 471 and July 3, no. 491;

Merritt to Lamont, July 6, no. 502, *Ibid.;* Merritt's comments in *Sec. War Rept. 1894,* p. 125; Schofield to Merritt, July 6; Schofield to Merritt and Otis, July 7, both in no. 4446, AGO 10.

83. Vol. 31, no. 50 (August 4, 1894): 859.

84. On the Third Infantry, see Merritt to Schofield, July 6, 7, no. 4446, AGO 10; Merritt to Colonel E. C. Mason, 3rd Inf., July 7, no. 503, Letters Sent, 1894, Department of Dakota, RG393, NA., and Capt. Charles Hobart, 3rd Inf., to Headquarters, Department of the Dakota, July 9, no. 2414, Letters Received, 1894, *Ibid.* On bridge and tunnel duty and train escorts, see as examples: Headquarters, Department of the Dakota to Comdg. Officer, Fort Missoula, Mont., July 7, no. 508; Hdqtrs. to Comdg. Officer, Fort Custer, Mont., July 7, no. 509, no. 510; Headquarters to Comdg. Officers Fort Keogh, Fort Buford, Fort Yates, and Fort Yellowstone, no. 515, no. 516, no. 517, no. 521, respectively, all in Letters Sent, 1894, Department of the Dakota; on general developments in the Department, see Merritt to Schofield, July 8, 9, two wires, July 10, all in no. 4446, AGO 10.

85. In special report of Capt. E. F. Glenn, Acting Judge Advocate General, Department of the Dakota, August 6, 1894, no. 5779, AGO 10, pp. 361, 373, respectively. Similar description on p. 366. In the report, pp. 5-9 describe Livingston as a railroad town and the arrival of Lockwood's command.

86. *Ibid.,* pp. 182-83.

87. *Ibid.,* pp. 182-84; Lockwood to Headquarters, Department of Dakota, July 10, no. 2241, Letters Received, 1894, Department of the Dakota, RG393, NA.

88. Citizens of Livingston to Sen. Thomas C. Power, July 11, in no. 5770, AGO 10.

89. J. E. Rickards to Pres. Cleveland, July 11, no. 1869, AGO 10. On newspaper complaints, see Capt. Glenn's report, pp. 396-98, no. 5799, AGO 10.

90. July 11, in no. 5799, AGO 10.

91. Capt. Glenn's report, in *Ibid.,* p. 223. For other officers' support of Capt. Lockwood, see testimony of 2nd Lt. Thomas M. Moody, p. 227, and 1st Lt. Joseph P. O'Neill, p. 226; Capt. Geo. S. Andrews to Headquarters, Department of the Dakota, July 15, no. 2332; Lt. Col. John H. Page to Headquarters, July 24, no. 3180, Letters Received, 1894, Department of the Dakota, RG393, NA.

92. See Capt. Glenn's report, pp. 12-18, no. 5779, AGO 10.

93. In no. 5295, AGO 10. Merritt's comments on p. 1, Capt. Glenn's report, in no. 5779, *Ibid.*

94. See report of Capt. Mott Hooten to Headquarters, Department of the Dakota, July 14, no. 2334; Capt. O. J. Sweet to Headquarters, July 27, no. 2777, Letters Received, 1894, Department of the Dakota, RG393, NA. Merritt to Schofield, July 16, 21, in no. 4446, AGO 10.

95. Lindsey, *The Pullman Strike,* pp. 142-55; Eggert, *Railroad Labor Disputes,* pp. 153-66; Ginger, *The Bending Cross,* pp. 116-27; James, *Richard Olney,* pp. 45-54, 201-04; Rich, *The Presidents and Civil Disorder,* pp. 94-97.

96. In *Sec., War Rept. 1894,* p. 138.

97. July 1, 1894, in Atty. Gen., *Appendix to 1896 Report,* p. 155.

98. For the first citation, Col. Shafter to Sec. War Lamont, July 5, in no. 4447, AGO 10, and for the second, Ruger to Schofield, *Ibid.* See Brooke's final report to Adj. Gen., August 30, 1894, no. 4747, in AGO 10, and Merritt's comments in *Sec. War Rept. 1894,* pp. 127-28. Also, Atty. Gen., *Appendix to 1896 Report,* pp. 27, 33-34, 51, 225; Capt. S. H. Lincoln, at Las Vegas, New Mexico, to Adj. Gen., Department of the Colorado, July 8, no. 2040A, Letters Sent, 1894, Department of the Colorado, RG393, NA.

99. Both wires dated July 6, no. 4443, in AGO 10.

100. July 17, no. 4446, in *Ibid.*

101. On the Italians, see Capt. Mott Hooten to Headquarters, Department of the Dakota, July 21, no. 2651, Letters Received, 1894, Department of the Dakota, RG393, NA. For more on the need of importing workers, see W. P. Clough, vice-president, Great Northern RR, to General Merritt, July 10, no. 2231, and J. W. Kendrick, gen. manager, Northern Pacific to Merritt, July 14, no. 2328, *Ibid.* The violence federal marshals met throughout the West was generally precipitated by marshals' attempt to replace union members with nonunion men. See Atty. Gen., *Appendix to 1896 Report, passim.*

102. July 13, no. 4446, in AGO 10.

103. To Gen. Brooke, July 7, no. 4443, AGO 10. Similar orders were sent to the other department commanders in the West.

104. The substance and nature of Schofield's orders to his department commanders may be seen in *Report of Attorney General, 1894,* pp. 57, 111-12, 136-37, 156; Atty. Gen., *Appendix to 1896 Report,* pp. 230-36; Schofield to James McNaught, July 7, no. 520, and to Gen. Ruger, July 7, no. 522, in HQA, Letters Sent, 1894, RG108, NA. Also see Gen. Brooke's comment on Col. Poland to Brooke, July 11, no. 2966, Letters Received, 1894, Department of the Platte, RG393, and Gen. Merritt to Maj. Liscum, at Helena, Mont., June 28, 1894, Letters Sent, 1894, Department of Dakota, RG393, NA.

105. In Bliss' final report to Gen. McCook, September 6, 1894, no. 5864, in AGO 10.

106. A. N. Towne to Gen. Brooke, July 18, no. 3129, Letters Received, 1894, Department of the Platte, RG393, NA.

107. On this, Poland to Headquarters, Department of the Platte, July 19, no. 3184, *Ibid.* For other examples of the close cooperation between the railroads and the department heads, see Gen. Merritt's comments in *Sec. War Rept., 1894,* pp. 127-28; Gen. Otis to Superintendent of Northern Pacific, July 7, p. 234, Letters Sent, 1894, Department of the Columbia; Gen. Brooke to A. N. Towne, Gen. Manager, Central Pacific, July 9, no. 78, and July 18, no. 200, vol. 2, Letters Sent, 1894, Department of the Platte, both in RG393, NA.

108. To E. Dickinson, August 7, 1894, no. 290, vol. 2, Letters Sent, 1894, Department of the Platte, *Ibid.*

109. Merritt to J. W. Kendrick, July 26, no. 714, Letters Sent, 1894, Department of the Dakota, *Ibid.* Similar letters sent by General Brooke to A. N. Towne, August 16, no. 364, and E. Dickinson, August 4, no. 290, Letters Sent, 1894, Department of the Platte; Gen. McCook to D. B. Robinson, vice-president of the Santa Fe Road, August 24, no. 603, Letters Sent, 1894, Department of the Colorado, all in RG393, NA.

110. Headquarters, Department of the Dakota to Commanding Officers, Fort Missoula and Fort Custer, July 7, 1894, no. 508, no. 509, Letters Sent, 1894, Department of the Dakota, *Ibid.*

111. Hubert to Headquarters, Department of the Platte, July 9, no. 2902, Letters Received, 1894, Department of the Platte, *Ibid.*

112. Capt. F. M. H. Hendrick, Seventh Infantry, to Adj., Fort Logan, Colorado, August 28, 1894, no. 1751, Letters Received, 1894, Department of the Colorado, *Ibid.*

113. Palmer to Headquarters, Department of the Platte, July 9, no. 2911, Letters Received, 1894, Department of the Platte, *Ibid.*

114. In Returns of Regular Army Regiments, Infantry, Twenty-fifth Infantry, microfilm M-665, roll 257, August returns. RG94.

115. U.S. Marshal, Tacoma, Washington, to Olney, July 10, 1894, Atty. Gen., *Appendix to 1896 Report,* p. 203. Anderson was apparently following the orders of Gen. Otis, who reported to the Adj. Gen., July 27, no. 4445, AGO 10, that his officers were "not to guard railway property generally, except in aid of elective civil officers acting under orders of United States court." The extent of "guard duty" over railroad property is best followed in the correspondence of field commanders to their departmental headquarters, contained in Letters Sent and Letters Received, RG393, NA, for the various departments. This duty is also in-

dicated in the various subfiles of AGO 10. In both cases the correspondence relating to guard duty is too extensive to cite specifically. The duty is also clearly indicated in the regimental returns for the months of July and August for all the units on active duty, as seen in Returns of Regular Army Regiments, Infantry, microfilm M-665, RG94, NA.

116. See Bliss to Headquarters, Department of the Colorado, July 31, no. 1459A, Letters Received, 1894, Department of the Colorado, RG393, NA; Bliss to McCook, September 6, no. 5864, in AGO 10. On the First Infantry, see *San Francisco Chronicle,* July 3, 1894, p. 2, July 4, p. 4; and July returns, First Infantry, Returns of Regular Army Regiments, Infantry, microfilm M-665, RG94, NA.

117. Quoted in McCook to Adj. Gen., August 9, no. 3043, in AGO 10.

118. Duncan, "Reminiscences," p. 56.

119. Brooke to Adj. Gen., final report on strike duty, August 30, no. 4747, in AGO 10.

120. Duncan, "Reminiscences," p. 56.

121. Merritt to C. O., Fort Missoula, July 8, 1894, no. 535, Letters Sent, 1894, Department of the Dakota, RG393, NA. Similar orders sent to all commands under Merritt, as seen in letters no. 534, no. 540-43, no. 568, *Ibid.*

122. Convenient sketches of the Civil War service of Brooke, McCook, Merritt, and Ruger may be found in Ezra J. Warner, *Generals in Blue: Lives of the Union Commanders* (Baton Rouge, La., 1964), pp. 46, 294, 321-22, 415-16, respectively. Information on General Otis from his personnel file 2462-ACP80, AGO, RG94, NA. As samples of the war records of some of the field commanders, see the personnel files of Colonel William M. Graham, 1718-ACP72; Lieutenant Colonel John H. Page, 2632-ACP71; Colonel John S. Poland, 4871-ACP81, in *Ibid.;* and the entries in William H. Powell, *List of Officers of the Army of the United States from 1779 to 1900* (New York, 1900), pp. 162-63, 264, 581, on Colonel Thomas M. Anderson, Colonel Robert E. A. Crofton, and Colonel William R. Shafter, respectively.

123. McNaught's correspondence with Schofield scattered throughout AGO 10, for the month of July.

124. July 26, 1894, in Gresham Papers.

6 1894, Chicago—
The ARU and General Miles

In the eyes of the men who managed federal intervention in the Pullman strike, events in the West were peripheral. From the outset, Attorney General Richard Olney saw Chicago as the key to the strike. It was here he concentrated his energies and the power of the Justice Department. Olney's policy and the Army's role in the West were to restore order and enforce court orders. Breaking the strike there was incidental to those purposes. In Chicago, however, Olney consciously worked to break the strike and the power of the ARU and remove Eugene Debs from the leadership of the outbreak. Federal intervention in the strike in Chicago was hampered by the difficulties of dealing with thousands of strikers in an urban area. The opposition of Governor John P. Altgeld to Olney's intentions and the lukewarm reception the Army received from the municipal authorities of Chicago also made the federal effort more difficult. Finally, General Schofield confronted a new problem, an uncooperative department commander, Major General Nelson A. Miles of the Department of the Missouri.

On June 30, Olney wired Edwin Walker, a prominent railroad attorney:

It has seemed to me that if the rights of the United States were vigorously asserted in Chicago, the origin and center of the demonstration, the result would be to make it a failure everywhere else. . . . I feel that the true way of dealing with the matter is by a force which is overwhelming and prevents any attempt at resistance [1]

Olney eventually appointed Walker as special counsel to operate in conjunction with U.S. Attorney Thomas Milchrist. Throughout the strike, Walker and Milchrist worked closely with the railroads' General Managers' Association (GMA) in determining policy and strategy. Olney consistently accepted the advice of these two men.[2]

At first, close to 3,000 deputy marshals attempted to enforce court orders enjoining interference with rail traffic. Often these deputies proved to be more of a liability than an asset. Some were loyal railroad employees, mainly white collar workers sent to the federal marshal by the GMA. Many others were obtained through newspaper advertisements and hardly represented the best that Chicago had to offer. Edwin Walker wired to Olney, "I suggest that the marshal is appointing a mob of deputies that are worse than useless."[3] The use of railroad employees and disreputable men off the streets as deputies increased the probabilities of violence. The quality or objectivity of the deputies did not particularly bother Olney, however, for he did not want to rely on them to break the strike anyway. Furthermore, under the influence of Walker, Milchrist, and the GMA, the attorney general had no desire to turn to municipal or state officials for aid in enforcing the laws or maintaining order. Very early, Olney determined to use federal troops to do this job. He later stated, "The Department of Justice, in order to be prepared . . . took measures to put itself in the position which had induced the President to authorize the use of troops as against the Coxey movement."[4]

The decision to send federal troops to Chicago came on July 3, a day after the Chicago federal court enjoined Debs and the ARU from interfering with the mails and interstate commerce and conspiring to do so. U.S. Marshal John W. Arnold and his deputies attempted to enforce these court orders and remove obstructions and picketers blocking trains. Their efforts failed, as the Chicago strikers adamantly refused to leave the railyards, although up to this point they had not been violent. It is not clear how genuine Arnold's efforts to enforce the court orders were, but the men he had to work with certainly did not help. On July 3, Marshal Arnold, Attorneys Walker and Milchrist, and Federal Judge P. S. Grosscup wired Olney requesting troops.[5]

Cleveland placed the request before a cabinet meeting on the 3rd, attended by Olney, Secretary of War Daniel S. Lamont, Secretary of State Walter Q. Gresham, and Generals Miles and Schofield. Although

Olney made a smooth and well-argued presentation for troop commitment, some at the meeting opposed it, most particularly General Miles
and Secretary of State Gresham. President Cleveland rather quickly over-
rode their objections and ordered General Miles to return immediately
to Chicago, his headquarters, and assume leadership of the military strike
effort. Meanwhile, Schofield ordered troops from Fort Sheridan, Illinois,
into the city.[6]

Miles's mere presence in Washington irritated General Schofield. General Miles was in the East on vacation, and only after some difficulty had
he been contacted for the emergency cabinet meeting. Schofield believed
Miles was derelict in his duty by not returning voluntarily to Chicago as
the crisis grew. When Miles expressed the opinion that troops were not
needed in Chicago, Schofield became upset. He later recalled that when
President Cleveland suggested that Miles return to Chicago, General Miles
"merely replied with marked indifference that he was subject to orders."[7]

Relations between Miles and Schofield had been strained throughout
1894. One of the "boy generals" of the Civil War, aged but 25 when promoted to brigadier general of volunteers in 1864, the egocentric Miles
resented any direction from Schofield. His excellent combat record in
the war and his fame as an Indian fighter of significant ability during the
postwar years apparently encouraged Miles to ignore orders from Washington with impunity. When Schofield ordered troops from the Department of the Missouri to strike duty in the Choctaw Nation earlier in the
year, Miles took two weeks to carry out the order. He not only delayed
sending troops to the Indian Territory but also modified the orders under
which they operated. This precipitated an exchange of sharp telegrams
between the two generals. Schofield dressed Miles down for failure to
obey orders. In return, General Miles fired back several wires justifying
his behavior, some of which bordered on insubordination. Miles's tendency
to modify and alter his orders was evident again during the Pullman strike.
His defiance of the commanding general exacerbated the tension between
him and Schofield and ultimately weakened the federal effort in Chicago.[8]

At the time Cleveland ordered troops to Chicago, the city was relatively
quiet, although no trains were moving. Press reports on the situation indicated a great deal of disorder due to the strike, but such was not the
case. Conditions in the city and the reasons for the presence of federal
troops were further distorted when Olney stated to reporters that the
Army was going to stamp out "anarchy" in Chicago. The belief that riot

and anarchy ruled in Chicago created the impression that federal troops were sent there to restore order. Furthermore, the press and many federal officials made Eugene Debs and the ARU appear as fomentors of revolution.[9] This distortion not only affected the general public's attitude towards the strike but also General Miles's conception of his role in Chicago. For some time, he believed he was to restore order in the city, while his real job was to open rail traffic.[10]

As Miles returned to Chicago, the entire Fifteenth Infantry from Fort Sheridan moved into the city on the morning of July 4. Colonel J. P. Martin, adjutant general of the Department of the Missouri, and Colonel R.E.A. Crofton of the Fifteenth, distributed troops according to previous arrangement with Marshal Arnold, Attorneys Walker and Milchrist, and John M. Egan, of the General Managers' Association. Crofton sent his infantry to Blue Island and Grand Crossing, while the small cavalry and artillery units of the command went to the stockyards. Colonel Martin reported, "cannot learn that anything definite has been accomplished, but there has been no active trouble."[11]

From July 4th through the 8th, the federal military effort in Chicago lacked direction and force, despite General Miles's arrival on the 4th. Requests for troops poured in from Marshal Arnold and the railroad managers. On the 5th and 6th, Colonel Crofton sent out small units to act as train guards on the various lines, but in most instances, the troops experienced great difficulty in moving trains. The fact that the railroads were spread throughout the south side of the city and ran through several residential areas, primarily working-class, hindered effective action. The situation posed an extremely difficult tactical problem because Miles's forces were too small to provide train guards for every railroad. Once the troops cleared tracks of obstructions and forced a train through, crowds swarmed over the tracks again, constructed new barriers, and blocked the next train. Crowd dispersal proved extremely difficult. Cavalry moved into the mobs and pushed them off the tracks, but the strikers disappeared down alleys, into homes and warehouses, only to reappear once the troops left.[12]

Particular points of disorder and resistance were the stockyards and the depot and freight yards at Blue Island. On July 5, troops went into the stockyards and attempted to move a freight train. A crowd of about 5,000 met the two companies of infantry and one troop of cavalry. The officer in command reported "promiscuous mob following train hooting and jeering."[13] Repeatedly the troops guarding the train pushed strikers off the tracks and off the train itself. Despite these efforts, the outnumbered regulars could not move the train and withdrew. General Miles reported later that only the firm discipline of the troops prevented bloodshed.[14] At Blue Island, the strikers and their sympathizers displayed an extraordinary amount of venom toward the Rock Island Railroad. Hostile crowds and obstructions on the tracks thwarted the regulars' attempts to move trains on that line through Blue Island. The mob overturned freight cars and prevented passage of trains despite the presence of two companies of regulars, scores of marshals, and city and county police.[15]

In these early attempts to break the strike, both the troops and the strikers refrained from violence but continued confrontations increased the tension. From the day the troops arrived in Chicago, strikers and crowds displayed hostility towards them. Time and again, troops were met with boos, jeers, and curses. An officer reported, "While we were not assaulted nor were the switches interfered with, the men bore patiently the vilest abuse and vilification."[16] One newspaperman said later that the crowds disliked anyone attempting to break the strike, but "they seemed to take it as a personal insult that the soldiers were there."[17] Frederic Remington, covering the strike for *Harper's Weekly,* wrote that the soldiers resented being used as police and disliked even more being restrained from using strong force against the mob. "When infantry must walk through a seething mass of smells, stale beer and bad language . . . they don't understand. The soldier's idea would be to create about eleven cords of compost out of the material at hand."[18]

General Miles took one measure to cope with this situation by obtaining more men. Between July 6 and July 10, 1,000 additional troops arrived in Chicago. Infantry, cavalry, and artillery troops from Fort Leavenworth, Kansas, and other Western posts and the entire Ninth Infantry from Madison Barracks, New York, reported for duty. With these added forces, Miles developed

> a system of placing companies of troops at each of the six great depots where the twenty-two lines concentrate. At each of these depots trains were provided with locomotives and cars sufficient to carry a small body of U.S. deputy marshals, a company of infantry, with track repairers, and these were ordered to fight their way out and back.[19]

This system, put into operation on July 7, provided the necessary manpower to guard the trains and cope with the crowds. On July 8, for the first time since troops entered Chicago, Miles could report some trains moving.[20]

Critics of the use of the Army in Chicago were quick to point out the inability of the regulars to open rail traffic. *The Chicago Times,* a staunch supporter of Governor Altgeld, led the press attack against the Army. *The Times* contended that regulars were not needed in the first place and stressed the troops' early failures to resume traffic. For several days, *The Times* reported that most of the regulars did nothing but lounge around camp and play baseball. When they were unable to open the Rock Island Railroad, *The Times* headlined: "REGULARS WERE USELESS."[21] Justice Department officials, particularly special counsel Edwin Walker, were dismayed with this development. The argument for using regulars had been that their presence would quickly end the blockade. This proved to be a miscalculation.[22]

There were several reasons why the early effort failed. The nature of riot and crowd control proved to be a problem for regular officers. The lack of troops and the congested condition of the area surrounding the railroad yards and tracks contributed to the tactical problem. Another problem was divided command. By July 7, there were 2,000 regulars, 4,000 National Guardsmen, nearly 5,000 deputy marshals, and about 3,500 city and county police on duty. Each of these forces operated under its own command system and seldom coordinated efforts with other forces. In some cases, units from each force responded to a reported disturbance. Marshals, police, militiamen, and regulars would arrive at approximately the same time, but no single person had the authority to command all the units.[23]

The logical thing to do would have been to place all the forces under General Miles's command, but Altgeld's and the municipal authorities' opposition to the presence of the Army prevented this. On July 7, Secretary of War Lamont asked Miles, "What are your relations now to the city and state military authorities. Are you acting in concert?"[24] Miles answered that he had not met with the mayor but intended to do so. However, "I did not inform him of my opinion or recommendation regarding federal troops. I regard that a federal question."[25] The problem was never solved, although eventually the police and militia concentrated on maintaining order, while the federal forces worked on opening interstate railroad traffic. The antipathies between the federal and local forces were never overcome. In his 1894 report, the adjutant general of the Illinois National Guard maintained that his forces, not the regulars, had broken the strike and restored order.[26]

Most of the blame for the regulars' ineffectiveness must be assigned to General Miles. His dilatoriness and misconception of duty weakened the federal effort and prolonged the need for troops in Chicago. When Miles returned to the city from Washington, he found the forces from Fort Sheridan distributed about in small units, acting as posses for U.S. deputy marshals. He made no effort to alter this distribution. Although Schofield sent Miles a wire directly ordering him to concentrate his troops and not to place them under the command of marshals, the erratic Miles ignored the order and continued to disperse regulars at the marshal's call. Schofield became extremely angry, believing that the action violated the *posse comitatus* act and that Miles disobeyed the guidelines in General Order No. 15. Miles further angered his superior when he wired, "Shall I give the orders for troops to fire on mob obstructing trains?"[27] Schofield reacted to the query with incredulity. He noted later, "It could only be conjectured what explanation could possibly be given of that request for orders in respect to a plain duty which every educated officer is supposed to fully understand." The commanding general went on to say that it was difficult to believe that a "Major General of the Army could be so ignorant of the duty devolved upon the troops when ordered by the President to enforce the laws of the United States."[28]

Miles made greater mistakes than violating tactical guidelines, orders, and military common sense. He became convinced that revolution was at hand and only he could save Chicago from a bloodbath. As a result, he tended to ignore his responsibility to open the railroads and wasted a good deal of his time and energy attempting to ferret out and destroy anarchical and revolutionary conspirators. Miles distrusted labor in general and the ARU in particular, and belief in a conspiracy fit neatly into these predelictions. As early as July 7, Miles notified Schofield, "The masses want peace but the agitators very ugly and say they may have to have civil war."[29] Threats of a general strike in Chicago as a display of support for the ARU struck Miles as proof of the existence of a planned uprising. He sent spies to union meetings in the city, including a Polish-speaking private from the Fifteenth Infantry, and established a special fund of $1000 to expand his spy network. At one time he reported to Secretary of War Lamont

"There is a report . . . that rioters or anarchists have 6000 Winchester rifles and bushels of dynamite bombs."[30]

Miles's belief that Chicago harbored more socialists and anarchists than any other city on earth and that the vilest sort of foreigners roamed through the city's streets not only consumed his energies but determined his use of troops in Chicago. The general believed that the state and municipal authorities could not be trusted to put down the pending revolution and therefore regulars must be ready at any time to meet the threat. This explains in great part why he agreed so readily to the marshals' and the railroads' requests for the use of small troop units. This facet of Miles's conduct in the Chicago strike is best seen in his relationship with John Egan, strike marshal for the General Managers' Association. Egan had the responsibility of obtaining assistance for the railroads from the various law enforcement agencies. Although Miles later testified to the U.S. Strike Commission that he had no relations with the GMA or Egan, the files of the Department of the Missouri show that Miles and Egan communicated daily, both by memo and telephone. Egan informed Miles of the need for troops at different locations in the city, provided the general with reports from labor spies, and indicated the railroads' distrust of the city police. In almost every instance, Miles complied with Egan's requests, and his reports to Washington echoed information and ideas from Egan.[31]

Miles's tendency to exaggerate the amount of disorder in the city, his desire to hold federal troops in readiness to deal with disorder, and his fears of impending revolution all blunted the federal effort. Olney later stated that the troops in Chicago were

> not to preserve the peace of the city nor to enforce any State
> laws or discharge any State functions whatever, but for the ex-
> press purpose exclusively of preventing any obstructions of the
> mails and any interference with interstate commerce.[32]

General Miles never understood this.

While the federal forces found it extremely difficult to open rail traffic through Chicago, city police lost control of rioting mobs on July 5 and 6. On the 6th, Governor Altgeld ordered the entire Illinois National Guard into the city to cope with the rioting, for federal troops could not be used to end rioting. The day after the Guard went on active duty, it fired on a mob, killing one person and wounding several. Tensions that had been

building between the federal troops and the rioters reached a peak on
July 8 when regulars sent to Hammond, Indiana, fired on a mob, again
killing one person and wounding several. The troops went to Indiana
at the request of its governor, for the disorder and traffic stoppage
had spread there. *The Chicago Times* and many Hammond citizens charged
that the soldiers had shot into a peaceful crowd indiscriminantly and
without provocation. The coroner of Lake County, Indiana, declared at
an inquest on the shooting that one Charles Fleischer "came to his death
by accident, caused by soldiers of Company D, 15th Infantry Regiment,
United States Army shooting wantonly and carelessly into a peaceable
crowd."[33]

The charge that the regulars fired indiscriminantly contains some truth.
The commanding officer's report suggests that he lost control of his men
for a time. Captain W. T. Hartz later described the action:

> About 4:30 in attempting to get a mail train to Chicago, the
> mob endeavored to throw a Pullman car in front of the train with
> which I was patrolling the track to keep it open. The men sta-
> tioned on the engine to guard it seeing the danger, opened fire
> and dispersed the crowd. One man was killed and three wounded.
> ... About 30 shots were fired before I could get the engine to a
> standstill and get control.[34]

Captain Hartz never gave an order to fire. The men of the Fifteenth had
been on duty since July 4 with little or no relief; they were tired and had
had more than enough boos, curses, and obstructions. A similar incident
with similar results occurred on July 10, again involving the Fifteenth
Infantry, at Spring Valley, Illinois.[35]

The use of firearms was not tactically necessary in either incident,
and in both cases the shooting was spontaneous. Animosities had been
developing between the regulars and strikers during the early days of the
strike, and the bad feelings came out in these shooting incidents. Press
coverage of the strike and later testimony at congressional hearings on
the strike indicated a high level of mutual dislike between strikers and
soldiers. What is most impressive in hindsight, however, is that even in
the volatile confines of the railroad districts of Chicago, as in the railroad towns of the West, there was no massive outbreak of violence between the two groups.[36]

Under the prodding of General Schofield, Miles finally concentrated some of his troops at a large military camp at the Lake Front Park, on the shores of Lake Michigan, after July 8. The arrival of reinforcements from the Western posts and the Ninth Infantry from New York on the 9th and 10th also encouraged Miles to concentrate his troops. The Lake Front troops guarded government buildings in downtown Chicago and acted as a reserve for the units stationed at the various depots. The troops at the Lake Front camp attracted a good deal of attention from newspapermen and curious civilians. The troops followed the daily routine of military camp life, which reporters found dull and monotonous. On Sundays, large crowds came to see the soldiers, although the camp remained off limits to civilians. *The Chicago Tribune* reported that on one Sunday "there must have been at least 15,000 people staring at the soldiers and sentinels and tents in the Lake Front-Park."[37]

The infantrymen stationed at the depots also assumed a routine, but a more strenuous one. At the Union Depot, for example, Captain Henry H. Humphreys, 15th Infantry, maintained two trains with steam up at all times to rescue any threatened freight train. "When used, no less than four men, good shots, rode on the tender, two men for each car, occupying the platform and the company divided [in] the three day coaches half on one side and half on the other."[38] Despite the use of troops in large numbers, some of Miles's regulars continued to act in small units, often guarding railroad property. Major C. M. Bailey, 15th Infantry, caustically noted the work of his command when he reported that it was divided into small detachments and "the duty required of these . . . by the Railroads consists in a great measure in guarding their round houses, or in other words making policemen of the command."[39]

The presence of large numbers of federal troops in Chicago and the fact that Miles began to concentrate on the railroads while state and local forces sought to restore order finally brought results. On July 12, he reported to Schofield, "Everything quiet today. Have received no reports of hostilities. Railroads have made no appeals for protection. Their mail, passenger and freight trains are moving thus far without obstruction."[40] Continued reports of quiet from Miles and the arrest of Debs and other leaders of the ARU caused Secretary of War Lamont, Attorney General Olney, General Schofield, and others in Washington to consider a speedy withdrawal of troops from Chicago. Once again, Miles's obstinance complicated the situation.[41]

On July 14, Schofield informed Miles that Secretary of War Lamont wanted troops removed from Chicago as soon as possible. The commanding general asked Miles to confer with Marshal Arnold, U.S. Attorney Milchrist, the mayor, and others to ascertain the necessity of retaining the regulars. Miles curtly replied, "I have considered the subject of withdrawing troops and the method. The time has not yet arrived."[42] He then insisted that he be allowed to send an aide to Washington with secret information before troops were removed. Apparently he wanted to show Lamont and Schofield the evidence he had gathered concerning the possibility of revolution. He made the request twice, and twice Lamont informed him, firmly, that it was not necessary to send the aide. Finally, on July 17, Lamont sent Miles a stiff telegram ordering the removal of troops from Chicago. To ensure Miles's compliance with this command, Schofield sent a direct order to him on the 18th, ordering the Ninth Infantry back to Madison Barracks and the remaining troops to Fort Sheridan.[43]

Even these orders did not completely deter the self-willed Miles. Although he began to prepare his command for withdrawal, he sent off a long report, in cipher and marked confidential, outlining the possibilities of revolution, the presence of foreign anarchists and revolutionaries in Chicago, and the chances of a bloodbath against hundreds of imported strikebreakers upon the withdrawal of troops. He then cited the opinions of all Justice Department officials, who wanted the troops retained. Miles concluded, "I believe that the duty of the United States government is to maintain its well defined authority and discharge its duties, whether it be in the State of Illinois, City of Chicago, or any other part of the United States."[44] The implication was, of course, that certain parties in Washington were not concerned with discharging these duties.

The source of Miles's objection to a troop withdrawal, besides his own peculiar logic, is not too difficult to find. On the 18th, both Marshal Arnold and Special Counsel Walker wired Olney, stating categorically that troops could be relieved. On the next day they reversed this opinion and told the attorney general they feared new violence once the troops left. It is clear that the Chicago railroad managers brought pressure to bear on these men and General Miles. As in the West, the railroad managers argued that once the troops left, strikers and other malcontents would take revenge on strikebreakers and special deputies.[45]

Despite these objections, federal troops left Chicago on July 19. Except for the Ninth Infantry, the troops went into garrison at Fort Sheridan and remained there through August, in case trouble recurred in the city. Strike duty in Chicago was a trying experience for the regulars. No soldiers were killed by strikers or the mobs, but on July 16, an artillery caisson blew up during a practice march, killing five artillerymen and one trooper of the Seventh Cavalry. Defective ammunition, not sabotage, proved to be the cause of the accident. Miles's desultory leadership, the lack of co-operation between the several law enforcement agencies present in Chicago, and the tactical difficulties of dealing with disorderly crowds in the city made the Army's performance in Chicago less effective than in the West. In the end, however, as in the West, the Army played the central role in bringing the American Railway Union to its knees and breaking the strike.[46]

The Army could not avoid serving as strikebreaker in Chicago in 1894. President Cleveland ordered federal troops to the city to aid in enforcing court orders so strict that ARU leaders were enjoined from verbal attempts to encourage strikers or recruit strikebreakers to the union cause. Given the nature of court orders and Attorney General Olney's intent to use all the resources of the federal government to break the strike, the Army's role was inevitable and unavoidable. Furthermore, unlike the strike in the West, strikebreakers were more readily available in Chicago, and they needed protection from angry strikers. The actions and statements of General Miles, however, tainted the service of federal troops in the city. Miles's slavish concern for the interests of the GMA, his close working relationship with John Egan, and his inclination to see revolutionaries and revolution in every striker placed his forces at the service of the railroads in a manner not contemplated even by Richard Olney. Miles's fear of a mass outbreak of violence never occurred, partly because no such outbreak was ever contemplated by Debs and the ARU. The material was present for such an outburst, and the perceptions of Miles and some of his officers, as well as many of the railroad officials, added to the atmosphere of po-tential cataclysm. The discipline of the regular troops held, however, and neither the strikers nor the floating mobs of hangers on that accompanied them tested the army's mettle.

If there was hostility towards the service expressed in the streets of Chicago, in other places it received praise and support. This was seen in newspaper editorials, in front-page coverage of the strike and in letters to Cleveland and his cabinet from middle-class business and professional men. Furthermore, as in 1877, strike duty once again brought the Army off the plains and in from the isolated posts and into contact with many civilians, not all of whom were directly involved in labor-management conflicts. To the surprise of many, they found that businessmen were often genial companions. In many instances, particularly in relations between officers and local business, professional, and civic leaders, both groups discovered a common background and a like-mindedness. Officers' attitudes toward organized labor and immigrants did not differ materially from those of other middle and upper middle-class people in the towns and cities where the Army operated during the strike.[47]

Oftentimes, convivial social relations developed between officers and leading local citizens. While General Miles's troops were in Chicago, his officers were invited to use the facilities of local men's clubs, including the prestigious Union League Club. Before the First Infantry left Los Angeles, Colonel William R. Shafter and his officers were feted at a banquet at which "all the surroundings of the occasion were appropriate and handsome, and the prominent civil and military element of the Pacific coast was well represented."[48]

The necessities of strike duty meant that officers had to work closely with railroad managers, mayors and other local politicians, officials of communications agencies, and local merchants. Although in some places the relations between officers and civic leaders were strained, many others were cordial. After the strike the department commanders, their officers, and the War Department received many wires and letters from local people praising the conduct of officers and enlisted men. Colonel Zenas R. Bliss, for example, reported, "I was much gratified to receive a very flattering communication signed by his Honor the Mayor of Trinidad [Colorado], the Chief of Police, Aldermen and other city officers and many prominent citizens."[49] Even some of those who opposed the use of federal troops during the strike admitted that the regulars had conducted themselves admirably. *The Anaconda [Montana] Standard* commented, "Leaving out of consideration the question of the advisability of ordering out the troops, it is generally admitted that the conduct of soldiers during the time that they were on duty here was exemplary."[50]

The expressions of admiration for the conduct of the troops and the letters of commendation for the officers indicate the factor that undoubtedly contributed most to the favorable reactions the Army received. With the exception of General Miles, the department commanders carried out their part of the strike duty with efficiency and little publicity. These generals were well qualified for dealing with civil disorders and civil authorities. Except for General Otis, all had been generals during the Civil War. All had had some duty during Reconstruction, quite extensive duty for Generals Ruger and Merritt. Generals Otis, Brooke, and Ruger had served during the labor riots in 1877, while Ruger also saw riot duty in the New York City draft riots of 1863.

Many subordinate officers were also experienced in riot duty. The older officers of such regiments as the Third and Twenty-second Infantry and the Fifth Artillery served in 1877, and units from Otis's department had gone into the Coeur d'Alene mining region in 1892 to put down a labor riot. Captain Lockwood, the bane of Livingston, for example, dealt with riots in New Orleans in 1874, in the 1877 railroad strikes, and in Coeur d'Alene. Finally, the experience of the troops in the industrial army disorders provided precedents for officers at all levels. The overall leadership exerted by General Schofield ensured central control and strict military command of the troops. As a result, the experience gained in previous upheavals and the role of Schofield eliminated the confusion and inefficiency that attended the use of federal troops in the 1877 outbreaks. This efficiency and good management were not lost on those classes who feared to lose so much in 1894. As a result, at least in some segments of America, the Army gained new friends in 1894.[51]

Notes

1. U.S., Department of Justice, Attorney General, *Annual Report of the Attorney General of the United States, 1896: Appendix,* 54th Cong., 2nd sess., House Executive Document 9 (Washington, D.C., 1896), p. 60, hereafter referred to as Atty. Gen., *Appendix to 1896 Report.*
2. Bennett M. Rich, *The Presidents and Civil Disorders* (Washington, D.C., 1941), pp. 93-109; Allan Nevins, *Grover Cleveland: A Study in Courage* (New York, 1932), pp. 611-23; Horace Merrill, *Bourbon Leader: Grover Cleveland and the Democratic Party* (Boston, 1957), pp. 193-97; Henry James, *Richard Olney and His Public Service* (Boston, 1923), pp. 50-54, 201-04; Almont Lindsey, *The Pullman Strike* (Chicago, 1942), pp. 136-55, 168-70, 180-85; Gerald Eggert, *Railroad Labor Disputes: The Beginnings of Federal Strike Policy* (Ann Arbor, 1967), pp. 153-70. The importance of the General Managers' Association in the strike and its close relationship to the officials of the Justice Department in Chicago is clearly seen in U.S. Strike Commission, *Report on the Chicago Strike*

of June-July 1894, 53rd Cong., 3rd sess., Senate Executive Document 7 (Washington, D.C., 1895), pp. xix, xxviii, xxx-xxxi, xl-xliii.

3. July 9, Atty. Gen., *Appendix to 1896 Report,* p. 76. See also Walker to Olney, July 3, *Ibid.,* pp. 67-68.

4. In James, *Richard Olney,* p. 201. The full story on Olney's efforts to have federal troops sent to Chicago may be found in *Ibid.,* pp. 50-54, 201-07; U.S., Department of Justice, Attorney General, *Annual Report of the Attorney General, 1894* (Washington, D.C., 1894), pp. xxxi-xxxiv; Eggert, *Railroad Labor Disputes,* pp. 162-72; Lindsey, *The Pullman Strike,* pp. 142-50, 170-73; Nevins, *Grover Cleveland,* pp. 615-21.

5. Eggert, *Railroad Labor Disputes,* pp. 167-74; Lindsey, *The Pullman Strike,* pp. 163-68; Atty. Gen., *Appendix to 1896 Report,* pp. 64-66.

6. Eggert, *Railroad Labor Disputes,* pp. 167-74; Nevins, *Grover Cleveland,* pp. 620-22; Lindsey, *The Pullman Strike,* pp. 173-74; James, *Richard Olney,* pp. 50-51, 202-03; Rich, *The Presidents and Civil Disorders,* pp. 96-98; John M. Schofield, *Forty-Six Years in the Army* (New York, 1897), p. 494. It should be pointed out that in his memoirs, *Serving the Republic* (New York, 1911), pp. 253-54, Miles asserted that he vigorously argued for sending troops into Chicago in order to prevent a mass insurrection. The evidence does not support that contention, and Miles's own argument is weakened by the fact that he argues that *he* was the one who, after great effort, convinced Cleveland of the necessity for using troops in Chicago. Such an argument ignores the fact that troops were already in use in the West and displays a total ignorance of the vital role played by Olney and the Justice Department in having troops committed to strike duty. Most likely Miles was attempting to rebut strong criticisms made against him in Schofield's memoirs published in 1897. This argument is very characteristic of Miles, however, as he was prone to overestimate his importance in any event he participated in.

7. Undated, unsigned memo in folder marked "Command of the Army," container 72, John McAllister Schofield Papers, Library of Congress, Washington, D.C. Undoubtedly prepared by or for Schofield, this memo was probably written sometime in 1895, just prior to Schofield's retirement and Miles's assumption of the commanding general's post. The memo is an evaluation, a very unfavorable one, of Miles's qualifications for the post. This memo also contains criticism of Miles's presence in Washington. For a more temperate but still critical view, see Schofield, *Forty-Six Years in the Army,* pp. 493-95.

8. Schofield, *Forty-Six Years in the Army,* pp. 493-95; Miles, *Serving the Republic,* pp. 253-54; Virginia W. Johnson, Miles's biographer, in

The Unregimented General: A Biography of Nelson A. Miles (Boston, 1962), pp. 304-06, points out that Schofield and Miles never got along well. For the Choctaw incident, see Schofield to Miles, May 19; Miles to Adj. Gen., May 26, and Schofield's endorsement on same; Adj. Gen. to Miles, May 29; Miles to Adj. Gen., May 21; Miles to Adj. Gen., June 10, 14, all in PRD no. 6091, Records of the Adjutant General's Office, 1800-1917, Record Group 94, National Archives. Adj. Gen. to Miles, June 9, no. 2019, June 11, no. 2068, Letters Received, 1894, Department of the Missouri, Records of the United States Army Continental Commands 1821-1920, Record Group 393, National Archives.

    9. See, e.g., *The Outlook* 50, no. 1 (July 7, 1894): 10.

    10. See *The Chicago Tribune,* July 1, 1894, pp. 1, 28, July 2, p. 1, July 3, p. 1, for inflammatory stories. *The Chicago Times,* July 3, p. 4, July 4, pp. 1, 2, attempted to counter the scare tactics of most Chicago papers by pointing out the absence of violence. Lindsey, *The Pullman Strike,* p. 172, clearly shows the lack of violence in Chicago. Eggert, *Railroad Labor Disputes,* p. 172, and Nevins, *Grover Cleveland,* pp. 624-25, point out the scare tactics used by Olney and the GMA to justify the presence of federal troops in Chicago. For other examples of the national press's attack on Debs and the ARU, see *The Independent* 46, no. 2379 (July 5, 1894): 858, 860; *Harper's Weekly* 38, no. 1959 (July 7, 1894): 627; *The Nation* 59, no. 1514 (July 5, 1894), p. 1.

    11. To Adj. Gen., July 4, no. 4441, file no. 10, in Records of the Adjutant General's Office, 1800-1917, Record Group 94, National Archives. (Hereafter AGO 10). See also Schofield to Miles, July 2; Martin to Adj. Gen., July 2; Schofield to Martin, July 3; Martin to Schofield, July 3; Martin to Adj. Gen., July 3; all in *Ibid.* See also report of Colonel Crofton to Headquarters, Department of the Missouri, July 28, no. 3255, Letters Received, 1894, Department of the Missouri, RG393, NA.

    12. See Martin to Adj. Gen., July 4; Miles to Adj. Gen., July 4, in no. 4441, AGO 10. Col. Crofton's July 28 report, pp. 5-12, for details on the large number of requests for troops and the sending out of many small units to answer these requests. For descriptions of the tactical difficulties in moving trains and dealing with crowds, see the testimonies of reporters Malcom McDowell, *Chicago Record;* Ray Baker, *Chicago Record;* Harold Cleveland, *Chicago Herald;* Hubert F. Miller, *Chicago Tribune,* all in U.S. Strike Commission, *Report,* pp. 360-68, 368-70, 377, 406, respectively. Also the reports of Capt. W. T. Hartz, 15th Inf.; 1st Lt. M. F. Jamar, 13th Inf.; to Col. Crofton, enclosures 1, 15, respectively, in Crofton's July 28 report, and a number of requests for troops and re-

ports of officers in the field to Headquarters, Department of the Missouri, for July 5, 6, Letters Received, 1894, Department of the Missouri, RG393, NA.

13. Capt. Lee to Miles, July 5, no. 2348, Letters Received, 1894, Department of the Missouri, RG393, NA.

14. Miles to Schofield, July 5, two wires, no. 4441; *Chicago Tribune,* July 5, p. 1, July 5, p. 1; testimony of Harold Cleveland, reporter, *Chicago Herald,* in U.S. Strike Commission, *Report,* p. 371; *Harper's Weekly* 38, no. 1960 (July 14, 1894): 655-57, for word and picture stories; Frederic Remington, "Chicago under the Mob," *Harper's Weekly* 38, no. 1961 (July 21, 1894): 680-81.

15. Testimony of Malcom McDowell of the *Chicago Record,* in U.S. Strike Commission, *Report,* pp. 360-65; *Chicago Times,* July 6, 1894, pp. 1, 4.

16. 1st Lt. M. F. Jamar to Col. Crofton, enclosure 15 in Crofton's July 28 report, *op. cit.*

17. Testimony of Malcom McDowell, U.S. Strike Commission, *Report* p. 365.

18. Vol. 38, no. 1961 (July 21, 1894). The best source for the attitudes of the strikers and Chicago crowds toward the federal troops is the testimony of several newspaper reporters in U.S. Strike Commission, *Report,* pp. 360-68, 399, 401.

19. In special report of Miles to Adj. Gen., July 18, no. 1348, AGO 10.

20. To Adj. Gen., July 8, in no. 4441, AGO 10. See also Miles to Adj. Gen., July 4; Schofield to Miles, July 4; Miles to Lamont, July 6, two wires, July 7, two wires; Miles to Adj. Gen., July 8, two wires, all in *Ibid.; Sec. War Rept. 1894,* p. 109.

21. July 6, 1894, p. 1.

22. *Chicago Times,* July 5, pp. 1, 2, 4; July 6, p. 1; July 7, pp. 1, 2; July 8, p. 4. *The Times* was joined by *The Chicago Searchlight* in its campaign against the Army, see Vol. 1, no. 5 (July 5, 1894): 1-2. For Walker's complaints, see Walker to Olney, July 6, 14, in Atty. Gen., *Appendix to 1896 Report,* pp. 71, 84, respectively. Everett St. John, general manager of the Rock Island Railroad and chairman of the GMA, testified to the U.S. Strike Commission that the troops had not provided the relief expected in the early days of the strike, see the Commission's *Report,* pp. 216-19.

23. On the numbers, see U.S. Strike Commission, *Report,* p. xix; testimony of newspaper reporters in *Ibid.*

24. No. 2431, Letters Received, 1894, Department of the Missouri, RG393, NA.

25. July 7, no. 477, Letters Sent, 1894, *Ibid.*

26. See Illinois, Adjutant General, *Biennial Report of the Adjutant General of Illinois, 1893-94* (Springfield, Ill., 1895), pp. xxii-xxvii, 116-20, 177-78; testimony of John P. Hopkins, mayor of Chicago and Michael Brennan, superintendent of Chicago police, in U.S. Strike Commission, *Report*, pp. 344-49, 354-55, respectively. *Chicago Tribune*, July 8, 1894, p. 1.

27. To Adj. Gen., July 5, no. 443, Letters Sent, 1894, Department of the Missouri, RG393, NA.

28. In undated, unsigned memo, in folder marked "Command of the Army," Schofield Papers. See also Schofield to Miles, July 5, Miles to Adj. Gen., July 6, no. 4441, AGO 10; Schofield, *Forty-Six Years in the Army*, pp. 494-509.

29. No 487, Letters Sent, 1894, Department of the Missouri, RG393, NA.

30. July 10, in no. 4441, AGO 10. On Miles's attitudes on labor and the ARU, see Johnson, *The Unregimented General*, pp. 304-05; Miles, *Serving the Republic*, pp. 251-52; Lindsey, *The Pullman Strike*, p. 174. On plots and revolution, see Miles to Schofield, July 9, 11, three wires, in no. 4441, AGO 10; Miles, *Serving the Republic*, 255-56. On spies, see no. 2558, July 12, no. 2592, July 13, in Letters Received, 1894, Department of the Missouri, RG393, NA. The best example of Miles's distaste for the ARU, his fear of rebellion, and his anti-foreign prejudice, is Miles's July 18 report to the Adj. Gen., no. 1348, AGO 10.

31. Miles's attitudes towards the people of Chicago, the city police, and the loyalty of the mayor seen in his *Serving the Republic,* pp. 255-58, and in his special report to the Adj. Gen., July 18. *op. cit.* Egan's role in the strike explained in U.S. Strike Commission, *Report*, pp. 269-82, and Miles's testimony on pp. 339-40. The correspondence between Egan and Miles: Egan to Miles, July 4, no. 2324; July 5, no. 2336; July 8, no. 2460; July 9, no. 2460; July 10, no. 2546; July 11, no. 2546, no. 2552; July 16, no. 2653; and several unnumbered reports. See also Everett St. John to Miles, July 7, no. 2422. All in Letters Received, 1894, Department of the Missouri, RG393, NA. Miles to Egan, July 4, no. 421, no. 428, Letters Sent, 1894, *Ibid.*

32. In General Correspondence, no date, vol. 17, Richard Olney Papers, Library of Congress.

33. Contained in Charles Morlock, Attorney at Law, to Miles, no date, no. 2614, Letters Received, 1894, Department of the Missouri, RG393, NA. See *Chicago Times,* July 9, 1894, p. 1; *Chicago Tribune,* July 9, 1894, p. 1; on the request for troops in Indiana, see Atty. Gen., *Appendix*

to 1896 Report, pp. 104-07; Schofield to Miles, July 8; Miles to Schofield, July 8, two wires; Miles to Sec. of War Lamont, July 8; all in no. 4441, AGO 10. On the Illinois National Guard, Adj. Gen., Ill. N.G., *Biennial Report, 1894-95,* p. 178, *passim.*

34. To Col. Crofton, enclosure 16, in Crofton's July 28 report, *op. cit.* For a similar description, see testimony of Ray Baker, *Chicago Record,* in U.S. Strike Commission, *Report,* pp. 368, 370.

35. Capt. Charles H. Conrad to Col. Crofton, enclosure 33, *op. cit.;* Conrad to Col. Crofton, July 10, no. 2520, Letters Received, 1894, Department of the Missouri, RG393, NA. See also Adj. Gen., Ill. N.G., *Biennial Report, 1893-94,* pp. 83-84.

36. Remington, "Chicago under the Mob," p. 681, and "Chicago under the Law," *Harper's Weekly* 38, no. 1962 (July 28, 1894): 703, presents the soldiers' view of frustration with this duty. In "Chicago under the Law," Remington wrote, "The regulars hate the scum. The scum taunts the soldiers across the street with vile language."(p. 703).

37. July 16, 1894, p. 12. For a graphic description of life in the camp, see Frederic Remington, "Chicago under the Mob," pp. 680-81, also comments in *Army and Navy Register* 16, no. 2 (July 14, 1894): p. 19. On the reinforcements, see Miles to Schofield and Major General Oliver O. Howard, commander of the Department of the East, from which the Ninth Infantry came, in no. 4442, AGO 10.

38. Capt. Humphrey's report to Col. Crofton, enclosure 4 in Crofton's July 28 report, *op. cit.;* Capt. J. F. Stretch, 10th Inf., used a similar system with his company at Grand Central Depot, see his report to Crofton, enclosure 28, *Ibid.*

39. Bailey's report to Crofton, enclosure 8, *Ibid.* Units from the Ninth Infantry also guarded railroad property, see July returns of Ninth Infantry, in Returns of Regular Army Infantry Regiments, AGO RG94, NA.

40. In no. 4441, AGO 10.

41. See Miles's report to Schofield, July 13, *Ibid.;* Lindsey, *The Pullman Strike,* pp. 178, 214, 239; Eggert, *Railroad Labor Disputes,* pp. 174-75, 192-94.

42. July 14, no. 4441, AGO 10.

43. Schofield to Miles, July 14; Miles to Schofield, July 16; Miles to Sec. of War Lamont, July 17; Adj. Gen. to Miles, July 17; Lamont to Miles, July 17; Adj. Gen. to Miles, July 18; all in *Ibid.*

44. In Miles's July 18 report to the Adj. Gen., no. 1348, AGO 10.

45. See Olney to Walker, July 17; Arnold to Olney, July 18; Walker and Arnold to Olney, July 18; Walker to Olney, July 19; all in Atty. Gen., *Appendix to 1896 Report,* pp. 86-93; Stuyvesant Fish, president of Illi-

nois Central RR, to Schofield, July 19; Charles F. Mayer of the B & O
RR to Hugh L. Bond, July 19; Wm. M. Spring, representing the Rock
Island RR, to Lamont, July 19; all in no. 4441, AGO 10. D. B. Robinson,
Santa Fe RR, to Miles, July 19, no. 2733, Letters Received, 1894, De-
partment of the Missouri, RG393, NA. Roswell Miller to Lamont, July 19,
General Correspondence, vol. 40, Daniel S. Lamont Papers, Library of
Congress. All of these telegrams argue that removal of troops would bring
a new outbreak of violence against the railroads and their new employees.
Miles's special report of July 18 reflects these arguments, *op. cit.*

46. See Miles' comments in *Sec. War Rept. 1894,* pp. 108-09. Frederic
Remington, "The Withdrawal of the U.S. Troops," *Harper's Weekly,* 38,
no. 1964 (August 14, 1894): 748-49, on the explosion of the artillery
caisson. Also see Miles to Adj. Gen., July 20, no. 4441, AGO 10.

47. A full discussion of the public's reaction to the role of the Army
in the Pullman strike and of labor's perceptions of the event will appear
in Chapter Eight, below. For a discussion on anti-foreign attitudes in this
period, particularly as they related to labor problems, see John Higham,
Strangers in the Land: Patterns of American Nativism, 1860-1925 (New
Brunswick, N.J., 1955), pp. 30-32, 54-58, 69-78. On the similarity in
attitudes, origins, and social classes of officers and middle-class business,
professional, and civic leaders, see Richard C. Brown, "Social Attitudes
of American Generals, 1898-1940" (Ph.D. diss., University of Wisconsin,
1951), pp. 223-25, 262, 369-70; on labor, pp. 1-16, 34-35, 50-52; on
social class backgrounds and social attitudes of officers. Also, William B.
White, "The Military and the Melting Pot: The American Army and
Minority Groups, 1865-1924" (Ph.D. diss., University of Wisconsin,
1968), pp. 305-11, 376-78.

48. *Army and Navy Journal* 31, no. 53 (August 25, 1894): 913. On
the use of social clubs in Chicago by officers, see *Chicago Times,* July 15,
1894, p. 5, and Walter H. Wilson, Sec., Union League Club of Chicago,
to Miles, July 9, no. 2544, Letters Received, 1894, Department of the
Missouri, RG393, NA.

49. To Gen. McCook, Sept.6, 1894, no. 5864, AGO 10. For similar
commendations, see letter from Roswell K. Colcord, Gov. of Nevada,
to Col. John S. Poland, in Poland's personnel file ACP 4871-81, AGO,
RG94, NA. Several letters from California citizens and civic groups praising the conduct of Col. William M. Graham, in Graham's personnel file,
ACP 1718-72, *Ibid.;* letter of Eli Jeffery, pres. of Denver and Rio Grande
R.R., to Sec. of War Lamont, July 31, on conduct of Brig. Gen. McCook
during the strike, in McCook's personnel file ACP 3660-74, *Ibid.* See
Chicago Tribune, July 8, 1894, p. 1 for comment on Miles's meeting with

leading "merchants, property-owners and capitalists," of Chicago. Another aspect of these relations appeared in Chicago when the Chicago and Northwestern Railway built a new passenger station at Fort Sheridan immediately after the Pullman strike in recognition of "the valuable services rendered by the U.S. troops during the recent Chicago insurrection," in *Army and Navy Journal* 31, no. 49 (July 28, 1894): 845.

50. Quoted in *The Army and Navy Journal* 31, no. 58 (August 25, 1894): 906. *Chicago Times,* July 18, 1894, p. 4 has very similar comments.

51. On Gen. Ruger, see personnel file ACP 3468-71, AGO RG94, NA; on Gen. Merritt, see personnel file M991CB63, *Ibid.;* on Gen. Brooke, see personnel file ACP 2832/77; on Gen. Otis, see personnel file ACP 2462-80; on Gen. McCook, see personnel file ACP 3660-74, all in *Ibid.* Examples of other officers with riot duty experience include Lt. Col. John H. Page, 22nd Inf., in personnel file ACP 2104-74, Lt. Col. Francis L. Guenther, G275B63, all in *Ibid.;* Capt. Mott Hooten, p. 223, in no. 5779, AGO 10; on Capt. Lockwood, p. 185, *Ibid.*

7 Miners and Soldiers— The Coeur d'Alene in the 1890s

The U.S. Army intervened in labor-management conflicts in the Coeur d'Alene mining region of northern Idaho three times in the 1890s. These interventions were quite unlike those of 1877 and 1894, and they revealed the dangers of placing the Army solely under the command of state officials in any bitterly contested labor dispute. As in 1877, federal troops went to Idaho at the request of the state's governors, but military activity was confined not just to one state but to a specific region of that state, Shoshone County. The Army's task in Idaho was not to quell a widespread disturbance threatening the larger interests of the national economy or the rights and property of a multitude of people. In the Idaho interventions, the Army entered a contest of wills between well-organized miners and the powerful mine owners' association. The miners sought union recognition, collective bargaining, and maintenance of their already established political control of Shoshone County. The mine owners in turn worked to break the union permanently and establish complete management control of the county.

The power of the State of Idaho lay with the mine owners throughout the acrimonious struggle. State officials used their powers to place the state's small National Guard at the disposal of the owners and acceded to management's demands that the Army be called into the mining districts. Idaho's senators and representatives consistently and vigorously presented the owners' case to presidents and the War Department in Washington. The state tolerated management use of private armed guards and labor spies and accepted two companies of nonunion employees of the Bunker Hill and Sullivan Mining Company into the Idaho National Guard.

When disorders broke out in the Coeur d'Alene in 1892 and 1899, Idaho's governors sent state officials to the region to cooperate with management, not in restoring order but in breaking the union. The publicly stated goal of state and management officials to destroy the union and drive union miners out of the Coeur d'Alene, a task in which the Army played a central part, placed federal intervention in Idaho in a category quite different from that of its participation in the disorders of 1877 and 1894. The Idaho interventions illustrated the necessity management and sympathetic state officials sometimes faced in the late nineteenth century of introducing an outside source of force as the only means of breaking the power of locally entrenched workers.[1]

The miners of the Coeur d'Alene first took the offensive in the spring of 1892. In the face of a prolonged lockout, the importation of strikebreakers, and the presence of owner-employed armed guards, the organized miners of Shoshone County struck in July of 1892. On the 11th, miners attacked armed guards at the Frisco mill in Gem, blew up the mill, and drove the guards and strikebreakers out of the valley. The miners then went to other mining towns in the region, closing them down and forcing out strikebreakers. For the next two days the miners ruled the Coeur d'Alene.[2]

State officials were aware of the growing tensions in the mining region. Governor Norman B. Willey had visited the region himself in the latter part of May and then dispatched James F. Curtis, Inspector General of the Idaho National Guard and a key Republican figure, to investigate further. Willey then issued a proclamation on June 4, ordering an end to unlawful assembly, interference with private property, and intimidation of nonunion men. In the interim, the mine owners obtained a federal injunction prohibiting the union from interfering with local railroads or corporations owned by citizens of other states. In late June, Governor Willey, through U.S. Senator George L. Shoup of Idaho, asked the War Department to send federal troops on a practice march through the Coeur d'Alene as a means of cowing the miners. Willey made the same request to President Benjamin Harrison, who denied it. Willey, however, was not disappointed, as he pointed out to Senator Shoup, for the governor was simply laying the groundwork for the future. "I did not . . . expect that Federal troops would be at once ordered there. . . . but the proper authorities should be advised that such a contingency is possible and that it may become a necessity at any time."[3]

Despite all these preparations, the outburst of violence at Gem, on
July 11, caught the mine owners and the state by surprise. The immediate
response of Willey and the owners was to call for federal troops. General
Curtis returned to Shoshone County and supported the call for the Army.
Out-of-state mine owners, while only vaguely informed on events in Idaho,
deluged Willey with demands for federal troops. Similar wires went to the
Idaho congressional delegation, all of whom called upon President Harrison
to act immediately. The mine owners contended that Shoshone County was
was in flames and that the strikers were liable to kill en masse all strikebreakers and management personnel. The Rocky Mountain press amplified
these rumors of death and destruction. Whether these statements were the
result of anxiety or simply a means of convincing Harrison of the necessity
of federal intervention is unclear, but state and management exaggeration
of the union's propensity for terror tactics became a common method of
countering the organized miners after 1892.[4]

Governor Willey did not hesitate to appeal for troops on July 11.
President Harrison granted the request without attempting to discover
the extent of disorder or the extent to which the state of Idaho exerted
itself in quelling the upheaval. On July 12, he ordered the War Department to send troops to Idaho "to cooperate with the civil authorities in
preserving peace and protecting life and property."[5] Major General John
M. Schofield, commanding general, sent troops from Fort Sherman, Idaho,
to the scene. Unlike his policy in 1894, Schofield made no attempt to
delineate how far the field commander could go in aiding Idaho officials;
despite close supervision of the overall operation, he allowed the commander on the scene to define his relationship with civil authorities on
his own.[6]

Colonel William P. Carlin, once a brigadier general and division commander under William T. Sherman and now commanding the Fourth
Infantry at Fort Sherman, Idaho, assumed command of the operation.
Because of the plethora of lurid reports coming from Boise and Seattle
predicting massive armed resistance on the part of the miners, Colonel
Carlin called for more men, requesting a total of 500. Schofield concurred
and ordered troops from Fort Spokane and Vancouver Barracks, Washington, and Forts Keogh and Missoula, Montana, to reinforce the 160 men
from Fort Sherman and a contingent of 200 Idaho National Guardsmen
serving under Carlin. The colonel approached the mountainous Coeur
d'Alene region with caution. Ironically, Carlin's slow approach raised the

ire of the doomsaying mine owners. W. B. Heyburn, attorney for the owners' association, complained to Senator Fred Dubois of Carlin's delay, caustically commenting, "It looks as though the soldiers would get there in time to act as funeral escorts to our dead if the weather is favorable."[7]

Federal troops arrived in the Coeur d'Alene, at Wardner, on the western edge of the valley, on the morning of July 14. Despite fears of resistance from the miners, the regulars easily occupied the little mining towns dotting the valley floor. Carlin's command found conditions in the region peaceful. Indeed, there had been no disorder in the valley since the attack on the Frisco mill. It became readily apparent as well that the miners had no intention of fighting the regulars. Carlin reported on the 14th "that the rioters had dispersed to their respective mining camps taking their arms with them after sending all non-miners captured out of the country. All is quiet here."[8]

The mere presence of regular troops assured maintenance of order and the assertion of state control. The state, in the person of General Curtis, used federal troops to remove county officials sympathetic to the miners and to return strikebreakers to the region. Governor Willey declared martial law in Shoshone County, and under this authority regulars assisted in arresting every union member and sympathizer and in guarding them in makeshift prisons set up in warehouses at Wardner and Wallace. Federal troops also guarded strikebreakers and mines when work was resumed. It is clear that this duty did not conform to the restrictions of the *posse comitatus* law, but neither Carlin nor General Schofield questioned the way in which General Curtis and other Idaho officials used the Army, not to restore and maintain order, but to break the miners' union.[9]

The easy restoration of order and state authority in the Coeur d'Alene did not lead to an early release of federal troops. Governor Willey demobilized Idaho National Guardsmen on July 29, but refused to say when federal troops could be released. Some regulars returned to station under Schofield's orders on July 25, but mine owners in the Northwest, merchants in the Coeur d'Alene, and Governor Willey, after some hesitation, called for the retention of regulars on a semipermanent basis. Willey wrote to President Harrison, "I cannot view, without grave apprehension, the entire withdrawal of the military force."[10] Late in October, he maintained that "martial law and the occupation of the district by a body of troops should continue for some time yet."[11]

When Willey established martial law in July, almost every union member had been arrested and imprisoned. Many were released in a few days, but others were held for a longer time and then set free without going to trial. Federal and state courts failed to obtain convictions against any of the participants in the raid on the Frisco mill. Despite the lack of convictions, the mass arrest policy carried out under Army protection broke the strike, disrupted the union, and drove many union miners out of the region. A state offer to free imprisoned miners who would resign from the union failed, but until the fall, nonunion men worked the mines. The need for skilled miners forced some owners to reemploy union members late in 1892, over the objections of state officials.[12]

Regulars remained in the Coeur d'Alene until November 12, 1892. The number of troops in the area was gradually reduced throughout the fall. There were 500 present until the end of September, but by the time of their final withdrawal, only four companies remained. The troops had little to do during their stay for there was no hint of disorder or resistance. Their presence was intended as a means of intimidating the union men, and it worked. When Governor Willey lifted martial law on November 18, the union had not been destroyed completely, but its ability to challenge the mine owners had been greatly circumscribed.[13]

President Harrison, General Schofield, and Colonel Carlin had allowed the Army to be used to this end. None of them questioned the state's policy of mass arrest or its intent to destroy the union. The activities of Captain John G. Ballance, Twenty-second Infantry and assistant judge advocate of the Department of the Dakota, illustrated the myopia of the Harrison administration and the officer corps in the breaking of the union. Ballance worked actively to aid the state of Idaho in imposing martial law in the Coeur d'Alene. At the request of Governor Willey, Captain Ballance was detailed temporarily to the Idaho National Guard. He represented the state in a federal court suit instituted by the miners, challenging martial law in Shoshone County. Ballance's arguments won federal judicial support for martial law. In October, General Curtis, who supervised martial law in the county, left the Coeur d'Alene. Willey then appointed Captain Ballance to replace Curtis and, according to the *Idaho Daily Statesman*, he "had entire charge of the administration of affairs in Shoshone County under martial law." [14] The county's commissioners later passed a resolution that noted that "the thanks of the people of this country are due to Captain Ballance for his able, energetic and conservative course."[15]

If the Army's presence in northern Idaho had served merely to preserve order, its temporary occupation of the region might have contributed greatly to peace in the long run. The conditions under which they entered Idaho, however, precluded neutrality. State officials requested troops; they defined criminal acts and identified law breakers; then they determined when so-called normal conditions had been restored. All these acts were predicated on destroying the union. Although the state of Idaho conceived and directed the destruction of the miners' unions, the Army carried out the policy. No one in the service questioned this policy.

The Army aided immensely in breaking the strike and in the systematic destruction of the locals. By providing the armed manpower that state officials believed they needed to overcome miners' resistance, regular troops ensured the return of nonunion workers, protection of mine property, and the arrest of all union members. Regular officers who commanded federal forces in Idaho displayed an almost slavish respect for state officials and made no attempt to exert independent action. Colonel Carlin's deference to General Curtis's every request, Captain Ballance's willingness to oversee the legalities of martial law for the state, and General Schofield's silent acceptance of the state's intent to destroy the union in the name of law and order made clear the officer corps' acceptance of the mine owners' perception of conditions in Idaho. Schofield's silence, given his strenuous actions in 1894 to ensure correct military control of forces aiding civil authorities, was most puzzling. Either he lacked interest in the proceedings in Idaho or he believed that he had met the letter of Harrison's order to aid state officials.

The impetus for a harsh state policy against the miners' union and the use of federal troops to back the actions of Idaho officials came from the mine owners. The state government and the Army were simply the tools the owners used to combat an increasingly militant and active union movement which was spreading throughout the Rocky Mountain mining region and was incorporated in the Western Federation of Miners. At the height of the Pullman strike, owners and their allies exhibited their intents by capitalizing on the prevailing disorders. Using their political clout at the federal level, the owners had troops sent once again into the Coeur d'Alene and resumed their lobbying for the establishment of a semipermanent post there.[16]

By the summer of 1894, the miners' union had recovered from the disaster of two years earlier. Union miners again worked most of the mines and, between July 3 and 5, rose up to drive out nonunion workers from Shoshone County. As in 1892, local law enforcement officials failed to impose order, and Rocky Mountain newspapers reported another reign of terror. Governor J. J. McConnell made no attempt to use state forces to deal with the disorders but succumbed quickly to mine owner pressure, calling for federal troops on July 7. After some delay and considerable pressure from the Idaho congressional delegation, the Cleveland administration ordered troops to Idaho.[17]

Troops from Brigadier General Elwell S. Otis's Department of the Columbia, a company of the Fourth Infantry, arrived at Wardner on July 10. The unit found no disorder and no state official met it to direct its operations. General Otis was under the impression that the troops in northern Idaho were to guard the Northern Pacific Railroad as part of the overall railroad strike operation. He sent two more companies to Wardner on July 27 for that purpose. After a peaceful ten days in the region, Otis ordered the companies to return to station. Much to his surprise and confusion, Secretary of War Daniel S. Lamont overruled Otis's order. The general reported to Lamont that no disorder threatened the railroads, let alone the mines. He noted that he had no idea his troops were to aid state officials in the miners' strike. The officer in command at Wardner had reported that "certain parties wish our executive . . . to believe that the state of affairs in this section of two years ago still prevails, which is false."[18] Otis concurred and added that if the troops were needed at one time to assist the state "even then I think that the section could now be given back to the state" and that "the troops should be recalled."[19]

Despite Otis's strong recommendation, federal troops remained in Idaho until September 9. It is apparent that neither General Otis nor General Schofield understood the purpose for which Secretary Lamont had ordered troops to the Coeur d'Alene on July 10. In the ensuing two months of residence in Idaho, regulars had done nothing that could be classified as restoring order. Army officers on the scene readily discerned the purpose of the troops' presence, however. First Lieutenant George B. Duncan observed, "There were no disorders and I could see no reason for our presence except to overawe the striking miners."[20] Mine owners and their newspaper allies explained the lack of violence as a ploy by the miners to deceive federal officials. "It is the play of the unions to make a show of peace and order," the *Spokesman-Review* of Spokane explained.[21] Once federal troops left the area, the explanation went, the

miners would resume their terrorism. The *Spokesman-Review* took up
the owners' call for a military garrison in the Coeur d'Alene as a long-
range means of countering the miners. In petitioning Senators Shoup
and Dubois for a post, mine owners and managers argued that a garrison
of regulars would "prevent these outbreaks and would ultimately result
in so discouraging this lawless element that members thereof would scatter
and [break] the force of effective organization."[22]

Undoubtedly the mine owners would have liked that "effective organization," the Western Federation of Miners, and its locals in the Coeur
d'Alene, broken up. Their attempts to use the Army in 1892 and 1894
to achieve this end were only partially successful. The unions were simply
too strong in 1892, and officers present in 1894 refused to act as the
mine owner's strikebreakers. In the years between 1894 and 1899, the
struggle between miners and their employers did not abate. It broke out
again in open warfare in 1899, in the most violent clash yet, and this time
the Army determined the victor.

In 1899, the central issue remained recognition of the miners' unions
in the Coeur d'Alene, locals which now were part of the Western Federation of Miners. By 1899, the WFM had unionized every mine and mill
except the Bunker Hill and Sullivan Mining Company, the largest operation in Shoshone County. The company adamantly refused to bargain
with the union and used all the anti-union tactics of the age to thwart the
WFM. The miners believed it was essential to organize the company because it was the largest operation in the region, and the smaller mining
enterprises threatened to drop union recognition and adopt nonunion
wages unless the Bunker Hill and Sullivan was organized. The latter's intention of refusing union recognition was indicated not only in the use
of labor spies and immediate dismissal of any suspected union miner but
also in its policy of armed preparedness. The Bunker Hill and Sullivan
mine and mill at Wardner was literally fortified, guarded by private armed
guards, and, in late April of 1899, "the mine still resembles a miniature
armory so far as supply of guns is concerned."[23]

The miners' response to Bunker Hill and Sullivan resistance came with
speed, surprise, and violence on April 29. On that morning, between 800
and 1,000 miners arrived in Wardner by train. Many of the men were
masked and armed. The force disarmed the armed guards at the Bunker
Hill and Sullivan mine and mill, then blew up the plant with a thousand-
pound charge of dynamite. Although the mine guards offered no resistance,
some desultory firing followed the explosion, and two nonunion men

were killed. Apparently satisfied with their work, the mob left Wardner and returned to the other mining towns in the valley. On the next day, the other mines in the Coeur d'Alene were in operation, and the daily business of the several mining towns of Shoshone County proceeded as usual.[24]

The state of Idaho, under the leadership of Governor Frank Steunenberg, reacted to the explosion with deliberate but cautious intent. On April 30, Steunenberg sent State Auditor Bartlett Sinclair to Shoshone County to survey conditions and recommend a course of action. Since Idaho's National Guard was in United States' service in the Philippine Islands, Sinclair recommended to Steunenberg that only federal troops could deal with the disorder in the Coeur d'Alene. The governor concurred, indeed he had made such a request to President William McKinley on the evening of the 29th, asking for 500 federal troops. Adjutant General Henry C. Corbin notified the governor on the next day that troops from the Department of the Colorado were on their way to Idaho.[25]

President McKinley and the War Department received troop requests from people other than just Idaho officials. James L. Houghteling, a stockholder, wired Secretary of War Russell A. Alger, "Armed mob of strikers have destroyed our mill at Wardner, Idaho. Governor has appealed for Federal troops. Please do what you can for us and save immense damage and bloodshed."[26] This and other wires reported riot and ruin in the Coeur d'Alene, reports which were repeated in the newspapers of the Northwest. The papers predicted that the riotous miners would use their arms and knowledge of explosives to turn the rough country of the Coeur d'Alene into an impregnable fortress. The reports spurred the administration to action. President McKinley, who was in New York City at the time, and Secretary of War Alger, on vacation in Detroit, wired the War Department requesting information on military developments. Officials in the War Department hurriedly informed all concerned that immediate troop movements were taking place.[27]

Federal troops did not arrive in the Coeur d'Alene until May 2. In the interim, Northwestern newspapers published inflammatory headlines and stories forecasting open warfare between miners and regulars. *The Portland Oregonian*, for example, headlined: "Rioters Desperate. They Are Prepared to Resist United States Troops"; then wrote:

The miners are nearly all armed, and their positions on Canyon Creek and at Mullan are nearly impregnable, while the country is full of men and women who will furnish all possible information to them. These men will hesitate at nothing, should their liberty be endangered.[28]

This became the common theme put forth by newspapers sympathetic to the mine owners, a theme repeated by the mine owners themselves and Idaho officials. The destruction of the Bunker Hill and Sullivan plant was the result of a massive conspiracy in the Coeur d'Alene, a conspiracy fostered by the WFM and supported by the civic officials of Shoshone County and most of the non-mining populace. Only the most drastic measures, the argument went, could quash the plot.

Mine owners and state officials did not panic at the delay in the arrival of federal troops as they had in 1892. Their composure was due in part to the long-range intentions of Steunenberg and his supporters to crush the union once and for all. Furthermore, the condition of the Army in 1899 prevented immediate, full-scale mobilization for riot duty. Although the military establishment numbered close to 100,000, only 17,000 troops of the line were stationed in the continental United States, the remainder serving overseas. The Army was undergoing reorganization in early 1899, mustering out Spanish-American War volunteers and recruiting new regiments for foreign service. The demands for occupation troops in Cuba and Puerto Rico, and for combat in the Philippines, stretched the enlisted manpower resources and put extra demands on the officer corps. The continental military departments were woefully undermanned, and a general officer often found himself in command of two geographical departments at once and faced with the job of mustering out volunteers and preparing new units for service outside the United States.[29]

The high command of the Army was also in disarray. Nelson A. Miles had replaced John M. Schofield as commanding general in 1895. Miles did not have Schofield's intellectual qualities, nor did he share the latter's concern for making the commanding general's post an office of substantive command. Because of his personality and narrow conception of office, Miles was isolated from Secretary of War Russell Alger and President McKinley. Alger, too, had his limitations, and, particularly in light of the criticisms of the War Department's conduct of the late war, was ineffective in his job. As a result, Adjutant General Corbin exercised de facto command of the Army, and McKinley relied on him in all matters concerning the service. As troops were mobilized for duty in the Coeur d'Alene, then, no one in Washington had the time or inclination to exert close supervision over their actions in Idaho.[30]

Brigadier General Henry C. Merriam, commander of the Department of the Colorado, with headquarters in Denver, assumed command of the Idaho occupation. Merriam also acted as commander of the Department of the Missouri, and divided his time between Denver and Missouri head-quarters in Omaha, Nebraska. In the midst of supervising two military departments, mustering out volunteer troops, and preparing regiments for duty in the Philippines, Merriam received orders from the War Department to direct the operation in Shoshone County. On April 30, Adjutant General Corbin wired Merriam, "The Acting Secretary of War directs that you repair at once to the capital of . . . [Idaho], and after conference with the authorities thence you go to the seat of action." These were the only instructions Merriam ever received from Washington.[31]

General Merriam immediately contacted Governor Steunenberg for information on conditions in Shoshone County. Steunenberg reported "apparent calm," but insisted troops were still needed. The governor and Merriam met at Boise, on May 1. Since no disorders existed at the time, they decided the main action would be apprehension of all miners who had taken part in the destruction of the Bunker Hill mine and mill. While the two men talked, troops from posts in Washington, Montana, Utah, and Wyoming moved into the Coeur d'Alene. Most of the troops were units of the Twenty-fourth Infantry, one of two all-black infantry regiments in the Army. Company M, Captain Joseph B. Batchelor commanding, reached Wardner on the afternoon of May 2. As in 1892, the predictions of open war were not borne out. Batchelor reported, "Situation quiet at present. Much apprehension apparent."[32]

Batchelor reported to Bartlett Sinclair and assisted the auditor in a search for arms and munitions. Under Merriam's orders, other troops arriving in the Coeur d'Alene concentrated at Wardner and Mullan, the western and eastern entries to the valley. The troops were to "scrutinize travel outward and detain suspected passengers." "This may be martial law," Merriam reported to General Corbin, "but no other course likely to secure rioters."[33] Governor Steunenberg agreed on the necessity for martial law, and, on May 3, declared Shoshone County in a state of insurrection and imposed martial law there. There was no opposition to the arrival of federal troops, to the policy of Army control of transportation in and out of the area, or to the imposition of martial law.[34]

Steunenberg and Bartlett Sinclair decided that the best method of apprehending the perpetrators of the great explosion was to arrest and incarcerate every known union miner and sympathizer in Shoshone County. The real culprits would be sorted out later on. As soon as enough troops arrived, Sinclair ordered mass arrests in all the mining towns. Merriam expressed no objection to the policy. By May 4, most of the Twenty-fourth Infantry was in the region. General Merriam reported 128 prisoners under military guard that day. By May 6, "Over 700 arrests have been made at different mining camps," he reported. "Many will apparently be released after investigation. . . . So far no signs of any organized resistance." The arrests continued on a lesser scale throughout the month of May.[35]

In order to carry out the arrests legally, Auditor Sinclair appointed a large number of special deputies, mostly nonunion employees of the Bunker Hill firm, to aid the regulars. The arrests began in Wardner, under the protection of Captain Batchelor's company. As *The Idaho Daily Statesman* reported, "While the arrest of men in Wardner was under way search parties of soldiers headed by the newly created constables were sent out all over the surrounding country to pick up the fugitives."[36] When the rest of the Twenty-fourth arrived, Merriam sent them to the smaller mining communities of Gem, Burke, and Mullan. At Burke, the troops made a clean sweep of the town. *Harper's Weekly* described how the Army conducted the sweep:

> The town stretches out for about a mile, at the bottom of a steep canyon. Guards were stationed on the walls of the gorge to prevent escape, . . . then the soldiers made a house-to-house search. At the shafts other soldiers were detailed to seize the miners as they came off shift. In the business portion of the single long street merchants and clerks were taken from their shops. Cooks and waiters were captured in the kitchens, and guests as they sat at table. The postmaster, the superintendent of the public schools, doctors and lawyers, were all alike "rounded up"—a grand total of two hundred and forty-three persons.[37]

The soldiers did not make the arrests themselves but provided protection for the special police officers. In most cases, however, several soldiers accompanied only one deputy, the soldiers assuming the responsibility of guarding the growing number of prisoners. One witness described the arrests: "They would simply point their finger at them and the soldiers would go and take them."[38] In this fashion, Sinclair and Merriam maintained the legal requirements surrounding military aid to the civil authorities. As mentioned in the *Harper's Weekly* article, the authorities made little attempt to distinguish the innocent from the guilty. Daniel N. Gillen, a miner at Gem, later recalled his arrest on May 4: "I was working on my house at the time. . . . I was arrested by soldiers and a deputy. They asked me if I was a union man, and I said I was. They told me to follow along and took me down the street."[39] Despite all the predictions of resistance, the troops and deputies met no difficulty in carrying out the mass arrests.

Once the deputies had made the arrests, soldiers placed the prisoners on trains and sent them down to Wardner. Here, Sinclair and State Attorney General Samuel H. Hays were reorganizing the government of Shoshone County. They removed the county sheriff and county commissioners from office and placed them under arrest. The new sheriff appointed by Sinclair, Dr. Hugh France, an employee of the Bunker Hill and Sullivan firm, was organizing evidence and booking the prisoners. Because Shoshone County possessed only the normal small county jail, the state had to make different provisions for the incarceration of the arrestees, who totaled nearly 1,000 by May 7. Temporarily, the prisoners "were placed in a large building two stories high which had been constructed and used as a warehouse for storage and grain."[40] Prisoners soon filled the makeshift prison to overflowing, and some two hundred miners were temporarily incarcerated in box cars. The men slept on hay, were herded out in squads under military guard to answer nature's calls, and some went hungry for a day or two until the state organized the prison camp. Merriam noted that these were less than ideal conditions but commented lamely, "yet they were not obliged to sleep on the ground, as did the troops who were guarding them."[41]

When it became clear that many of these prisoners were to remain in custody for some time, the state constructed a semipermanent prison and stockade, partly in response to repeated suggestions from General Merriam, who found the makeshift arrangements unsatisfactory. The prisoners were pressed into aiding with the construction of the new prison. If anyone in the Cœur d'Alene doubted that the state of Idaho intended to deal harshly with arrested miners, the construction of the prison helped to remove those doubts. For the thickheaded, State Attorney General Samuel H. Hays made it even plainer:

We have the monster by the throat and we are going to choke the
life out of it. No halfway measures have or will be adopted. It is
a plain case of the state or the union winning, and we do not
propose that the state shall be defeated.[42]

The next step taken to "choke the life" out of the unions came on
May 8. At that time, Bartlett Sinclair notified General Merriam that "notice
had been served upon all of the mine owners of the district, by which, during the continuance of martial law, they were forbidden to employ miners
unless they were able to present permits from the State authorities."[43]
The state required miners to get the work permits from Sheriff France.
The United States Industrial Commission reported that in order to work
the miners "were obliged to deny participation in the riot of April 29, to
declare the belief that the riot was incited and perpetrated by the influence of the miners' unions, to express disapproval of the the riot and to
renounce membership in the miners' unions."[44] Sinclair showed the public
proclamation declaring the policy to Merriam, who without much thought
wrote, "Examined and approved, H. C. Merriam, Brigadier General, U.S.
Army."[45] The state published the proclamation in most Idaho newspapers
and posted it all over the Coeur d'Alene. The document publicly de-
nounced and outlawed the miners' unions, apparently with the approval
of General Merriam.[46]
    Merriam not only displayed lack of forethought in attaching his name
to this document but exhibited a curious ability to say things to the press
that would best have been left unsaid. In off-the-cuff comments to reporters on the role of the federal troops in Idaho, *The Idaho Daily Statesman* quoted General Merriam as saying that the troubles there "largely
originated in hostile organizations known as labor unions" and that it
might be best to have a law "making the formation of such unions or
kindred societies a crime." In certain circles in the Northwest, such an
attitude was highly appreciated, and regional newspapers picked up the
comments and published them.[47]
    Thinking the affairs of the Coeur d'Alene were settled and giving no
thought to the reverberations his actions might cause, General Merriam
set about seeking relief from strike duty. The Twenty-fourth Infantry
was scheduled for shipment to the Philippines in late June, and Merriam
had this and many other duties connected with his departmental commands to attend to. Between May 10 and May 14, the first battalion of

the Twenty-fourth, four companies, left the region, but the adjutant
general denied Merriam's request for personal relief. Corbin instructed
Merriam to confer with Governor Steunenberg before leaving the mining
district. On May 15, the governor came to the Coeur d'Alene, after stopping in Spokane to confer with mine owners, and met with Merriam. The
two discussed the number of troops that should be kept in the area and
the length of their stay. These decisions were governed by the effectiveness of the permit system. All men working the mines had to have a work
permit by May 18 or quit working. At the mines in and near Burke and
Mullan, the miners resolutely refused to submit to the permit system.
Miners in the other towns adopted their example and soon all the mines
were closed. The result, Merriam reported, was "a large number of idle
and sullen men in the mining centers of Wallace, Burke and Mullan."[48]
Fearing trouble from these men, Governor Steunenberg wanted new troops
sent in to replace the units of the Twenty-fourth Infantry. Merriam requested that two troops of cavalry be sent from Fort Robinson, Nebraska.
These men, Troops A and L of the First Cavalry, arrived on May 24.[49]

The troops in the Coeur now carried out two basic duties. Some remained at Wardner, guarding approximately 400 prisoners awaiting trial
in October. Other units were stationed at Gem, Burke, and Mullan to
guard the idle mines and the surrounding property. Because men were
obliged to operate water pumps in many mines to prevent flooding, an
incident occurred which would later cause problems for General Merriam.
On May 28, the pumpmen at the Tiger-Poorman mine at Burke walked
off their posts. The military commander there, Lieutenant Henry G. Lyon
of the Twenty-fourth, believed the Burke union drove the pumpmen
from their jobs. He called a meeting of the idle union men. Lyon's soldiers
had been shot at once or twice while on night guard duty, and the Lieutenant distrusted the miners. He posted sentinels around the union hall,
told his sergeant to hold the rest of the command ready for riot duty,
and went in to speak to the union men. Lyon gave the Burke union five
minutes to stop harassing the pumpmen and to order them back to work,
"or else," without stating what "or else" meant. Later Lyon said he told
the miners,

I had been ordered to prevent the destruction of the mines in
Canyon Creek. I stated that I interpreted that order to mean the
destruction from any cause—fire, dynamite or water—and that

I proposed to carry out that order, no matter how disagreeable
it might be.[50]

Not unnaturally, the miners and pumpmen assumed Lyon intended
to use force to make the pumpmen return to work. One employee of the
Tiger-Poorman mine recalled that the pumpmen told him "they had to
go [back to work] and there was no way out of it, and they expected
that negro soldiers would be placed over them with the bayonet."[51]
Lyon had no proof that the Burke union had forced the pumpmen out
of work, but his methods of intimidation put them back to work. It also
planted one more seed of hatred toward the Army in the fertile soil of
the Coeur d'Alene.[52]

Meanwhile, General Merriam prepared to leave the Coeur d'Alene. On
May 25, he reported to Adjutant General Corbin, "Conditions here steadily
improving. Some miners accepting permits to work and others leaving the
district. I think acute state of disorders is passed and nothing now required
but time for restoration of civil functions."[53] Merriam informed Corbin
that some 330 prisoners remained under military guard at Wardner. He
left the mining region the same day, turning command over to Major
Allen Smith, of the newly arrived First Cavalry detachment. In a long
letter of instruction to Major Smith, Merriam pointed out the difficulties
of martial law during an industrial dispute. He informed Smith that the
sole role of the Army was "to aid the State executives in maintaining
order and restoring the State government to its legitimate functions."
The general concluded his instructions by reminding Smith to keep guards
over the powder magazines belonging to the mines and to use any force
needed to end any uprising quickly.[54]

General Merriam left Idaho believing he had fulfilled his task firmly
but justly. The regulars under his command had occupied the region without bloodshed, had carried out the arrests requested by the state authorities with speed and efficiency, and had restored order to the Coeur
d'Alene. Merriam and his officers enjoyed cordial relations with the state
authorities and the business and industrial leaders of the mining region.
In his eyes, the swift arrest and incarceration of hundreds of prisoners
and the inauguration of the permit system were not his concerns but the
state's.[55]

When General Merriam left the Coeur d'Alene he did not realize that
the presence of federal troops and the actions of the Idaho government in

northern Idaho would create a storm of some proportions. In a telegram to Corbin, Merriam showed that he was aware that some newspapers had criticized the conduct of federal troops in Idaho. Before he left the mining region he wired, "Referring to press criticism, I have made no orders. My action limited strictly to support of State authorities."[56] The criticism Merriam referred to was a propensity among unions and the labor press to blame the general for the Idaho authorities' vigorous anti-union policies. Almost from the inception of martial law in northern Idaho, protests and petitions from labor groups against these policies poured in to the president, the secretary of war, and the War Department. The Western Federation of Miners played a crucial role in organizing the protest, but as the details of affairs in Idaho reached the public, more and more unions acted on their own.[57]

From the last part of May and into the first two weeks of June, protests and petitions continued to flow into Washington, and the labor press took up the campaign. Organized labor made several charges against the Army. The most frequent and vehement charge was that General Merriam had initiated the anti-union permit system. The WFM sent copies of the permit proclamation all over the country, pointing out Merriam's signature at the bottom of the document. The Western Federation of Miners charged, "That we stigmatize the order of General Merriam and the civil authorities . . . to be worthy of a despotic ruler, and not worthy of notice by citizens of America."[58] The WFM also broadcast the story of the Tiger-Poorman pumpmen and alleged that the Army had forced free-born Americans to work at the point of a bayonet. The wire services picked up the offhand remarks Merriam made about labor unions to the friendly press corps of Northwestern newspapers. These statements provided more ammunition for the labor press.

At first the petitions and editorials scored only General Merriam, but later they also attacked Governor Steunenberg's role in the Coeur d'Alene. The Central Federated Union of New York City, for example, demanded that Secretary of War Alger "recall General Merriam and notify the Governor of Idaho that the military force of the United States can be used only for . . . constitutional purposes . . . and not for the suppression of legitimate association of workingmen."[59] In the end, most of organized labor put Merriam and Steunenberg in the same class, marking them as pliant tools of an oppressive plutocracy.[60]

Another frequent complaint in the labor protests charged the men of the Twenty-fourth Infantry with excessive brutality when making arrests and with harassment while guarding the imprisoned miners. During all of May and the first two weeks of June, this all-black outfit was the main federal force in the Coeur d'Alene. The use of black non-commissioned officers as commanders of search parties and prison guard details generated deep resentment in the miners. They later charged that the men of the Twenty-fourth had cursed them, used the bayonet unnecessarily, repeatedly stole their personal property, and were generally so brutal as to beggar description. Finally, and inevitably, the miners and their wives insisted that the black infantrymen annoyed the women unmercifully, seeking sexual favors from the wives of imprisoned miners. The deep racism of late nineteenth-century America pervades contemporary accounts of the regiment's occupation of the Coeur d'Alene, making an accurate assessment of their behavior difficult. One of their officers, Lieutenant Henry G. Lyon, defended his men by noting that some people in northern Idaho told him that "I seemed to have a jolly crowd of good soldiers there; that they were always jolly and laughing and singing when they were not on duty."[61]

Leaving aside such standard stereotypes of the laughing, singing black man, some conclusions are possible. It is not too difficult to imagine the hate and disgust stimulated in the miners as the black soldiers entered their homes, union halls, and taverns to arrest and search, then march them off to prison. White soldiers performing the same duty would have been resented, black soldiers performing this duty simply intensified the resentment. There is no evidence, even from the testimony of the women of the Coeur d'Alene, that black soldiers committed forcible sexual assaults. Evidently, kindly words of greeting and the passing of pleasantries by black soldiers were seen as venal, casual flirting as assault. It is difficult, further, to imagine that the white officers of the regiment, imbued with the same racial prejudices as the miners, would have tolerated harassment of white women by black troops. There is no evidence of systematic brutality or sexual attack.

The use of the Twenty-fourth Infantry in the Coeur d'Alene stimulated virulent editorial comments from the most conservative labor journals. *The Railway Conductor,* for example, never took an aggressive stand on any labor issue, yet it savagely attacked the use of black troops. "Fit representatives, indeed, are such hyenas to uphold the law. The reign of terror these imps of darkness have instituted . . . will leave a blot upon the page of our nation's history that has no parallel."[62]

William Haywood, president of the Western Federation of Miners, observed that the presence of any kind of soldiery in the Coeur d'Alene would have produced animosity. Haywood was essentially correct, yet the miners, their families, and the labor press were much more critical of the Twenty-fourth Infantry than they were of the behavior of the white cavalrymen who relieved the black soldiers. Despite the virulent feelings against the regiment, however, it is essential to stress the fact that the miners never met it with violence. Forcible resistance against federal troops, even though they were black, apparently never entered the miners' thinking. Neither did the federal authorities contemplate keeping black troops in Idaho as a means of deliberately provoking the miners into violence.[63]

Labor protests did not end when the Twenty-fourth left the Coeur d'Alene, but the focus of the protest shifted from the behavior of the troops to the War Department policy of maintaining any kind of federal troops in the region. President McKinley and the War Department paid little attention to the first protests. Adjutant General Corbin responded to one of the earliest complaints, from the Pueblo (Colorado) Trades and Labor Assembly, by simply replying that the assembly was misinformed about Merriam's conduct "and that it is not true that he has issued an order that no union men shall be employed."[64] At one point, late in May, McKinley's interest was piqued enough to ask Secretary of War Alger if there was any truth in the labor allegations, to which Alger quickly replied no. Apparently, however, the administration was not aware of the stringent policies adopted by the Idaho officials, and that General Merriam at least tacitly supported them. As the protests continued to come in, McKinley became more concerned. On May 26, Adjutant General Corbin wired Merriam to tell him of union charges that the Army was being used to support the permit system. Corbin added, "The President wishes a statement of facts at once."[65] Merriam replied that the charges were preposterous, as "troops are taking no part in this unless keeping the peace does so." Merriam also noted, "Every mine owner I have seen strongly approves."[66]

But as the protests continued to pour in, Secretary of War Alger and Adjutant General Corbin attempted to answer them and bring an end to the agitation. Finally, on May 31, Alger sent a wire to Merriam which in effect was a reprimand. He wired:

> You will instruct Major Smith, commanding at Wallace,
> that he is to use the United States troops to aid the State
> authority simply to suppress rioting and to maintain order.
> Those were your original instructions. The Army must have
> nothing whatever to do with enforcing rules for the govern-
> ment of miners or Miners' Unions.[67]

These were not Merriam's original instructions, for the April 30 message which ordered him to report to Governor Steunenberg said nothing about the simple suppression of rioting and maintenance of order. The order merely told Merriam to consult with the governor and then proceed to the Coeur d'Alene region to oversee the activities of the troops. Intended primarily for public consumption, Alger's message was sent as an answer to any labor protest he received. If the secretary of war had intended to end the misuse of troops in Idaho, he would have worked for their withdrawal for there never had been any rioting and order had been maintained with the first arrival of federal troops. General Merriam was rightfully disturbed by the message and wrote to Corbin saying that since he did not have any record of "instructions to the particular purpose named, I beg to be supplied with the paper to which reference is made." He never got it. The War Department's only concern was to shift blame for the protests on to Merriam. It had no interest in ending the federal presence in Idaho.[68]

Merriam believed he was being persecuted. He was obviously hurt and confused by the labor press criticism and the rebuke in Alger's wire. As a result, his special report on duty in the Coeur d'Alene, published in July of 1899, was essentially an apology for his conduct in the affair. Merriam argued that the permit system, the conditions in the prison, and the continued existence of martial law in the Coeur d'Alene were the result of policies laid down by Governor Steunenberg. The troops' actions in support of these measures, he added, were carried out in the name of preserving peace and at the request of the governor. As to the permit system, Merriam reported, "It was not intended that the troops under my command should assume any part whatever in carrying into effect these rules, . . . nor have they done so in the remotest degree."[69] Merriam ended his report by saying that he interpreted Alger's May 31 telegram as a reprimand and by protesting its release to the press. He said that he had never strayed from his original orders and implied that Alger was amiss in suggesting that he had.[70]

One of the main reasons Merriam used this special report to justify his actions was that the labor press would not leave him alone. In past labor-Army incidents, union journals had refrained from sharp personal attacks on federal military leaders, but not in this instance. When Merriam's report appeared, labor papers attacked again, accusing the general of attempting to use Idaho authorities as scapegoats for his own misdeeds. In a speech at Denver, Samuel Gompers declared sarcastically that "Gen. Merriam [has] . . . done more for organized labor than all the speeches we could make. He ought to be arrested as a labor organizer and agitator."[71] The attacks continued throughout the summer and fall, and well into 1900. Merriam wrote to Adjutant General Corbin,

> I write to assure you . . . that the abuse that has been put upon
> me by the sympathizing labor unions all over the land has made
> it very hard for me not to strike back—in other words to write
> my report from the cold-blooded standpoint of utter indiffer-
> ence to persons.

Yet his July report, and a slightly modified departmental annual report published in late August, were attempts to exonerate himself.[72]

Merriam's protestations did little to put an end to labor criticism of the Army's presence in Idaho. It soon became clear that federal troops would remain there for some time to come. Inquiries from the secretary of war revealed that Merriam and his officers believed the troops would have to stay for several months. Statements made by Governor Steunenberg and Bartlett Sinclair made it clear that Idaho intended to keep the troops as long as they could. Nonunion miners were now being imported into the region, and the mine owners and state officials argued that the union men were just waiting to get revenge and that only the presence of federal troops forestalled them, an argument which had been heard repeatedly since 1892.[73]

Because of this, the mine owners of northern Idaho again pushed for the establishment of a military sub-post in the region. F. W. Bradley, president of the Bunker Hill firm, maintained in a letter to Senator

George L. Shoup that "it is absolutely necessary, in order to make a clean up, that the State for a long time to come, have the assistance of Federal troops."[74] Although the Idaho authorities did not particularly favor the establishment of a permanent post in the Coeur d'Alene, they did want troops kept there for some time. Bartlett Sinclair wrote General Merriam in mid-August that the troops should be retained for at least six months. "The Western Federation has by no means ceased its efforts to incite the Dynamiters to revolt in opposition to the State laws. I do not think that the State could maintain order twenty-four hours without the presence of the troops."[75]

In response to these pleas, General Merriam, with the approval of the War Department, sent 200 men of the Sixth Cavalry from Fort Riley, Kansas, to replace the departing Twenty-fourth Infantry. The new forces, with the two troops of the First Cavalry, made up the semipermanent garrison. The soldiers settled down to routine guard duty at the prison and around the mines and conducted casual patrols of the mining district. In contrast to the time when black troops were in the region, the cavalrymen got along well with most of the local folks. One labor critic of the Twenty-fourth Infantry, *The Pueblo Courier,* did not seem to mind the horse soldiers, pointing out that "nobody objects to them because their appearance on horseback pleases the children and they are good baseball players."[76] Of course, many union men had left the district and approximately three hundred miners still languished in the prison, now referred to as the bullpen.[77]

No one would tell General Merriam how long the War Department intended to keep troops in Idaho. He was concerned because there were no winter quarters for them. Late in September, the department surgeon reported to the Army surgeon general, "The enlisted men eat their meals under a thatched shed which offers no protection to the cold and must soon be abandoned. As the guard duty is very ardous they are not able to keep their clothing and bedding dry."[78] Merriam met with Governor Steunenberg to consider how much longer troops would be needed. In late September, 140 prisoners remained in the bullpen, but Steunenberg was more worried about possible violent outbreaks than about the security of the prisoners. Merriam, in early October, reported on his conference with the governor that he "expects us to continue guarding prisoners and desires troops to remain in district as now to end of his term with con-

tinued martial law." Despite Steunenberg's desires, the adjutant general
told Merriam to prepare to withdraw the bullpen guards on October 20.[79]

On September 28, the new secretary of war, Elihu Root, wrote Governor Steunenberg in an attempt to persuade him to release the troops as
he was "much disinclined to have the troops of the United States continued
longer" as guards over civilian prisoners. Root told the governor that if
he could not agree to release the troops from duty in the Coeur, at least
he could "substitute civil guards as their custodians and relieve the troops
from further performance of that duty."[80]

Governor Steunenberg answered Root's request with a long letter in
which he sketched the entire history of labor in the Coeur d'Alene.
Steunenberg blamed the miners' unions for every instance of crime and
disorder that had occurred between 1892 and 1899. He branded them as
criminal organizations so deeply entrenched in the Coeur that only martial
law could root them out. Steunenberg maintained that the citizens of
Shoshone County were afraid of these criminal groups and needed military
protection before they would testify against them. Because of these factors,
the governor insisted that "the necessity still exists for the detention of
troops . . . and I ask that they be permitted to remain."[81]

In order to impress Secretary Root further with his arguments, Steunenberg went to Washington to present Idaho's case for keeping the troops.
Although it is apparent that Root wanted the troops removed, there was
little he could do when the governor maintained that law and order would
collapse in northern Idaho the day the last federal soldier left. Steunenberg's trip to Washington was successful. Root agreed to keep the troops
in the region if Idaho assumed custody of the prisoners. On October 31,
a newly raised company of the Idaho National Guard took charge of the
twenty-four prisoners remaining in the Wardner bullpen. One-half of the
federal command left Wardner and set up semipermanent camps at Wallace
and Osburn. Late in November, the state of Idaho closed the seven-month-
old bullpen.[82]

The maintenance of the bullpen for seven months under federal military
protection stimulated organized labor to continue its attack against Gen-
eral Merriam and the Army throughout July and August. The Western
Federation of Miners sent an appeal "To the Members and Friends of
Organized Labor who are battling for the Perpetuation of Human Rights
Against Tyranny and Oppression."[83] This appeal pointed out the brutality

of the black troops, the indignities of the bullpen, the oppression of the permit system, and attacked Merriam as anti-labor. Above all, the WFM's plea stressed the bullpen and its military guards, maintaining that the food and health conditions in the prison bordered on the barbaric. The WFM appeal ended with this reminder to its union brothers: "Remember that four hundred men are held prisoners in the Standard Oil Stockade at Wardner under Federal rifles."[84]

The WFM's plea for help paid off admirably. Not only did many labor journals print the official appeal in toto, but many increased their editorial attacks on Governor Steunenberg, General Merriam, and the Army. In line with the WFM, these journals focused on the bullpen. Many of the prisoners were held without bail for months, yet the state of Idaho indicated no desire to bring them to trial. Living conditions in the prison were crowded, uncomfortable, and unsanitary. The suspension of the right to trial engendered more protest from labor than did the anti-union permit system. *The Pueblo Courier,* official newspaper for the Western Labor Union, instituted a weekly "Remember the Bull-Pen" column. Many an editorial pen within labor circles excoriated the prison, but few could match *The United Mine Workers' Journal:*

> The moans of neglected and dying sons and husbands in this hell, where they are being detained and punished by the government, has pierced the hearts of the mothers of Idaho and . . . the mothers of American freemen all over these United States.[85]

The miners' campaign also served to increase the flow of petitions and letters of protest to Washington. Throughout July and well into August, the protests came from such diverse unions as the American Flint Glass Workers' Union of Muncie, Indiana, the Cigar Makers' Local #174, Joliet, Illinois, the Coopers' International Union, Cincinnati, Ohio, as well as from practically every affiliate in the Western Federation of Miners, including miners' locals in British Columbia. Adjutant General Corbin wrote to presidential secretary George B. Cortelyou, "Floods of labor union telegrams continue to arrive."[86] Corbin apparently did not feel it was necessary for the War Department to take any action on these protests but he suggested to Cortelyou, "It seems to me that a polite suggestion to these men that the matter rests with the Governor of Idaho would meet the situation and *let them feel* that their telegrams have at least received attention." (Emphasis added)[87] This became standard practice in the War Department and Corbin had this reply sent to all letters and petitions: "The Constitution and laws of the United States required the President to comply with [Steunenberg's] requisition, and any application for relief should be made to the Governor of Idaho."[88]

President McKinley was not unmoved by these complaints. He personally received a series of affidavits from citizens of the Coeur d'Alene charging black soldiers with misconduct and profane language and accusing certain officers of abusive behavior. McKinley wanted Adjutant General Corbin to investigate these charges and report back to him. The President's original request reached the War Department on July 17, was referred to Commanding General Miles on the 29th, then went to Merriam, who passed it on to Major Allen Smith at Wardner. On July 28, Smith gave it to Governor Steunenberg, who returned it to Merriam. On August 31, Corbin finally returned the memo, with the replies, to McKinley. This bureaucratic channeling not only ate up time but also made it possible for the accused to investigate the charges against themselves. In each case, the parties concerned, Merriam, Steunenberg, and Major Smith, denied that any wrongdoing had occurred. Merriam wrote of the affidavits, "they are only a part of a conspiracy to get sympathy and support from the public, from kindred labor unions, and even from the President." Steunenberg too, wrote them off as a product of the leaders of the criminal organizations now under fire in Idaho. Nothing further was done about the charges.[89]

The practice of assigning investigations to the principals involved in the charges was revealed again in a later incident. On September 27, Edward Boyce, president of the Western Federation of Miners, wired President McKinley that prisoners in the bullpen were on a bread-and-water diet. Boyce protested this as inhumane treatment and demanded redress. McKinley immediately wired Secretary of War Root, "Inquire of governor and military commander. This condition, if true, must be stopped."[90] Root sent wires to Merriam and Steunenberg. The governor, without attempting to discover the truth, replied, "Ed Boyce communication is base falsehood in every particular."[91] The charge was not a "base falsehood" at all, as General Merriam's reply made quite clear.[92]

Merriam reported that the commandant of the prison, Captain F. A. Edwards, First Cavalry, did indeed have the entire prison on bread and

water. Edwards had been in charge of the bullpen since the Twenty-fourth
Infantry had left and had proved to be a hard taskmaster. A strict dis-
ciplinarian, Edwards administered the prison as he would a military prison.
When the miners were recalcitrant, Edwards used solitary confinement,
work details, and bread-and-water diets as punishment. Until September
20, this type of discipline had been meted out on an individual basis. On
that date, however, one of Edwards's soldiers discovered an uncompleted
tunnel leading out of the prison. The Captain ordered some prisoners to
fill it in. They refused. Eventually every man in the prison refused to
work on the tunnel. As punishment for this defiance, Edwards put the
entire camp on the punishment diet and removed the hay the prisoners
used for mattresses. For one entire day, he kept the prisoners standing
in the prison yard while troops searched the barracks for digging tools.
The prisoners never did fill in the tunnel. These facts precipitated Boyce's
complaint, facts totally ignored by or unknown to Governor Steunenberg.[93]

The adamant refusal of the officials of Idaho and of Merriam and his
staff to acknowledge any misconduct on their part or to concede to the
prisoners and the miners any just cause for complaint greatly exacerbated
the hostile feelings generated by the military occupation of the Coeur
d'Alene. Union men in and outside Idaho made many charges against
the state of Idaho. They charged that Governor Steunenberg and his aids
were anti-union and were using the powers of the state to destroy organized labor in Idaho. The miners contended that the state unnecessarily
invoked martial law, called in federal troops when they were not needed,
then used that force to carry out illegal mass arrests and unlawful search
and seizure. The union men maintained that Steunenberg, through his
agent Bartlett Sinclair, then instituted the union-busting permit system
and kept union men in the bullpen for months without allowing speedy
trials.[94]

In every instance, Governor Steunenberg and his aides denied the allegations. They held that the miners' unions had used terror and conspiracy
to dominate the mining region since 1892. The state branded the unions
as criminal organizations directly responsible for all the labor difficulties
in the Coeur d'Alene and as the perpetrators of the destruction of the
Bunker Hill and Sullivan mill on April 29. Because Steunenberg and his
staff believed this, they saw no wrong in using any method to eliminate
the unions. Justifying mass arrests, they argued that since the unions
were responsible for all illegal and violent acts in the region, then ipso

facto all union members were also guilty. Nonviolent union men and non-union members were morally guilty, contended State Attorney General Samuel Hays, because they did nothing to prevent union violence. The state justified the permit system for the same reasons. Bartlett Sinclair defended the permit system, saying, "certain organizations in Shoshone County had shown themselves criminal in purpose, and that accordingly mine owners must not employ men belonging to those organizations."[95]

State officials stressed over and over that harsh measures were used in the Coeur d'Alene in order to ensure that all guilty persons were caught and punished. Yet, of almost 1,000 men held in the bullpen at one time or another, only fourteen ever went to trial, and of this number eleven were convicted. Quite obviously, the state of Idaho had set out to destroy the unions and, in the process, had violated the rights of hundreds of persons. This Governor Steunenberg and his staff were unwilling to admit. Nonetheless, the policy did destroy unionism in Idaho for years. In February, 1900, of 7,000 miners working under state permits, only 130 had belonged to the old unions.[96]

The unions also made accusations against General Merriam and the Army. In the miners' eyes, General Merriam was just as guilty of anti-unionism and violation of civil rights as Steunenberg. Very often, union complaints accused the general of ordering the mass arrests and instituting the permit system. They painted Merriam as a labor-baiting, insensitive man who condoned the soldiers' alleged brutal treatment of the miners. Finally, the laborers believed that the Army's presence in the Coeur d'Alene was illegal for after the destruction of the Bunker Hill and Sullivan mill no violence or insurrection occurred. Merriam defended himself and his troops by saying that throughout the affair they were merely following orders. The general consistently held that all he ever did was aid the state authorities in maintaining law and order according to his instructions from the War Department. In this he was supported by Steunenberg, who wrote Secretary of War Root that the mass arrests, the long detention of prisoners, and the permit system were state actions and not those of Merriam or his officers.[97]

Many of the union complaints against General Merriam were misdirected, though their assessment of the state's role in the affair was accurate. Merriam, of course, was in no way personally responsible for the presence of troops in Idaho. He did not initiate the mass arrests or the permit system. Bartlett Sinclair ordered these actions. By signing his name to the permit proclamation and making intemperate remarks to the press, however, General Merriam gave public approval to Steunenberg's anti-union campaign. In private correspondence to Adjutant General Corbin, he revealed a strong bias against the Idaho union, noting, "I have curbed my inclinations and have avoided everything which should give expression to my own convictions as to the . . . miners' unions."[98] Most importantly, Merriam never questioned the anti-union policy or made any attempt to lessen the Army's part in the state's campaign to drive the WFM out of the Coeur d'Alene.

The relationship between Merriam and Steunenberg and the validity of McKinley's policy of placing and keeping federal troops under state control for months came under congressional scrutiny in 1900. Rising labor criticism of the Army in Idaho forced House Republicans to take action to defend the McKinley administration in an election year. The House Military Affairs Committee, with a Republican majority, traveled to the Coeur d'Alene in February to investigate conditions there and take testimony from miners and their families. The committee considered Merriam's role, the charges of brutality, and McKinley's responsibility for the affair. Not surprisingly, the committee's report reflected partisan allegiances as much as objective conclusions. The majority report absolved the general from any wrongdoing and maintained that the president and the War Department "exercised every precaution that the military act solely within the Constitution."[99] In order to sustain this conclusion, the majority accepted the state's contention that the WFM was a criminal organization, and Steunenberg's justifications for the harsh action taken in the Coeur d'Alene appear throughout the majority report. If any wrongdoing took place, the report further implied, it was the fault of the state of Idaho.[100]

The majority support for General Merriam was based on the fact that the military must subordinate itself to civilian authority and, in the case of the Coeur d'Alene, President McKinley had delegated that authority to Governor Steunenberg. In 1894, Major General John M. Schofield rejected such an interpretation of military law. Schofield concluded that when federal troops were sent to the aid of governors or federal marshals, the direct chain of command from the officer in the field to the president had to be maintained. Incorporated into official Army Regulations in 1895, Schofield's interpretation held that troops could not take orders from civil peace officers to arrest or guard prisoners during domestic disorder. The military's responsibility was merely to restore and maintain order so that civil officials could make arrests and enforce the law. Army regulations admonished officers that "troops so employed are directly responsible to their military superiors. Any unlawful or unauthorized act on their part would not be excusable on the ground of an order or request received by them from a marshal or any other civil officer."[101] General Merriam violated these regulations, as did his subordinates left in command in the Coeur d'Alene. The War Department made little effort to correct the violations but merely sought to shift the public blame for the protest arising from labor agitation from the McKinley administration to General Merriam.

The minority report of the House investigation adopted this point of view. The report stated that General Merriam was too slavish in his willingness to carry out any request made by Steunenberg and Sinclair and concluded:

It is no excuse to say that General Merriam was requested to do this thing by the representative of the governor. It was his duty, as commander of the troops to know the law, and the law was and is that when a military commander is sent into a State to aid the civil authorities thereof he cannot act unless those authorities are being resisted.

Furthermore, the minority held, a federal military commander should refuse requests of state authorities if they support illegal acts, which the minority contended was the case in Idaho. The minority accused General Merriam of obeying the illegal orders of Steunenberg and Sinclair, while ignoring the law, common sense, and his own conscience.[102] The majority report recognized to some extent the fact that federal troops should not have been commanded by civilians outside the chain of command but insisted that the president had the power to delegate authority over the Army to whomever he wished. Such an argument went against standing Army regulations, which read,

In the enforcement of the laws, troops are employed as a part of the military power of the United States, and act under the orders of the President as Commander-in-Chief. *They cannot be directed to act under the orders of any civil officer.* [Emphasis added][103]

Inconsistency weakened the majority's support for the Army's activities in Idaho, an inconsistency stemming from the service's conflicting justifications for its actions. For example, Captain F. A. Edwards, commandant of the bullpen, detained one Tom Heney after the state had dropped all charges against him. Captain Edwards did this because Heney had violated some of the prison rules, and Edwards kept the man in prison until he had served out his punishment. The majority justified Edwards's action, as did the captain and General Merriam, on the grounds that the prison was under military command, not state control, and the military commander had the power to mete out punishment as he saw fit. In other words, when the military carried out duties which seemed beyond military authority, it did so under orders from Governor Steunenberg. When Merriam and his officers deemed it necessary to take independent action, they did so regardless of state law because, according to the majority report, "The troops were not under command of the governor . . . but under command of the military officers and the President."[104]

The 1899 Coeur d'Alene affair may be partially explained by military mismanagement. Despite the contention of the majority report of the House Military Affairs Committee, the president and the War Department took little interest in the affair until public protest made them do so. The state of disorganization within the War Department, perhaps best illustrated by the fact that the commanding general, Major General Nelson A. Miles, had nothing to do with the business, precluded proper administration. Secretary of War Russell Alger was also merely a figurehead, while McKinley and Adjutant General Corbin struggled with reorganization of the Army and the increasingly difficult Philippine insurrection.

Lack of guidance from the War Department, including clearly stated orders, placed the onus upon the officer on the scene. The choice of Henry C. Merriam as the officer to command the military force in Idaho was unfortunate. He, too, was faced with the task of reorganization plus the duties of administering two military departments. Further, Merriam demonstrated an ignorance of law governing civil-military relations, and too often he was intemperate in his public remarks. Merriam failed, as well, in providing clear-cut orders for his successors. Ultimately, however, Merriam and the officers who served under him in the Coeur d'Alene acquiesced to the demands of Idaho officials, not because they lacked direction from Washington but because they did not disagree with the larger policy of Steunenberg and his associates. Indeed, no one in the McKinley administration, including the War Department and the officer corps, expressed any doubts about the legitimacy of Steunenberg's actions. Merriam and his brother officers saw nothing fundamentally wrong with using the power of the state and the Army to destroy the miners' union.

There was a certain inevitability to the Army's actions in Idaho in 1899. Since 1892, mine owners and their supporters, acting in collusion with officials of the state, had sought ways of introducing federal troops to the Coeur d'Alene on a semipermanent basis as the best means of breaking the miners' organized efforts. The union's effectiveness and the miners' dominance of civic offices in Shoshone County forced the owners to bring in forces from the outside to defeat the miners. Idaho simply did not possess the finances nor the military power to meet this need; hence the necessity of federal troops. The Harrison, Cleveland, and McKinley administrations made no effort to see that federal intervention in Idaho maintained any semblance of neutrality and turned federal troops over to state officials. The federal leaders did not collude with the mine owners or state officials; they simply shared the same values.

This was true of the officer corps as well, with its perceptions of unions as conspiracies and its deep commitment to the sanctity of private property. A year and two months after the original intervention, in June of 1900, a company of the Seventh Infantry continued to enforce martial law in the Coeur d'Alene. Lieutenant Colonel William E. Dougherty, senior officer on the scene, supported maintenance of martial law, for "if the policy of the Governor is consistently upheld this plague spot of incivism and anarchy will be obliterated . . . and to this end, it will be necessary to maintain in this district a representation of the power of the Federal government."[105] Federal representation remained in the Coeur d'Alene with a company of infantry stationed at Osburn until April, 1901. On April 11, 1901, just a few days short of two years after the destruction of the Bunker Hill and Sullivan mine and mill, Governor Frank Hunt ended martial law, and the War Department withdrew federal troops from the Coeur d'Alene.[106]

Given the geographical isolation of the northern Idaho mining district, the intense hatred that existed between the miners and the mine owners and their nonunion employees, and the state's inability to handle a virulent labor disorder, federal intervention in 1899 was probably necessary. The federal failure, which in large part was the Army's failure, was the

ready acquiesence to state plans to destroy the union and punish *all* of
its members. Governor Steunenberg, Bartlett Sinclair, and State Attorney
General Hays did not set out merely to apprehend the men who blew up
the Bunker Hill and Sullivan plant or the murderers of the nonunion men
but to eliminate the WFM from northern Idaho. General Merriam accepted
this policy without question. It was his fundamental error.

James Sovereign, editor of the union paper the *Idaho State Tribune,*
later testified that at first all classes in the Coeur d'Alene welcomed the
arrival of troops. The potential for widespread violence and bloodshed
in late April, 1899, was real enough. The people of the mining region
saw the Army as a potential neutral guarantee against open warfare. But,
Sovereign contended, Merriam did not use his troops simply to restore
order. In the editor's eyes, Merriam remained idle while "state authorities
employed the military authorities to do acts in all respects un-American,
acts and outrages that could not have been perpetrated by the civil authorities had they not been supported by the military forces."[107] This was
an accurate assessment of the Army's role in the Coeur d'Alene in 1899.
The Army's presence was crucial, for despite the hard-bitten nature of
the long labor struggle in Idaho, despite the fact that the miners had
fought and killed guards employed by the mine owners, they offered no
resistance to the U.S. Army. Soldiers under the national colors, symbolic
representatives of the nation as much as flesh and blood agents of law,
simply were not to be fought.

Notes

1. The background on the bitter labor conflict in the Coeur d'Alene
of the 1890s is taken from the following: Lt. George E. French, Fourth
Infantry, U.S.A., "The Coeur d'Alene Riots," *Overland Monthly,* 2nd s.
vol. 26, no. 5 (July 1895): 32-49: Samuel H. Hays, Idaho State Attorney
General, "Report to the Governor on the Insurrection in Shoshone
County Idaho, Commencing on April 29, 1899" (pamphlet available at
Library of Congress), *passim;* May A. Hutton, *The Coeur d'Alene or a
Tale of the Modern Inquisition in Idaho* (Denver, 1900), pp. 60-63; U.S.
Industrial Commission, *Report on the Relations and Conditions of Capital
and Labor in the Mining Industry,* vol. 12 of the Commission's reports,
57th Cong., 2nd sess., House Document 181 (Washington, D.C., 1901),
passim; Paul F. Brissenden, *The I.W.W.: The Story of American Syndi-*

calism, 2nd ed. (New York, 1957), pp. 40-41; Melvyn Dubofsky, *We Shall Be All: A History of the Industrial Workers of the World* (Chicago, 1969), chap. 2, 3; Vernon H. Jensen, *Heritage of Conflict: Labor Relations in the Nonferrous Metals Industry up to 1930* (Ithaca, N.Y., 1950), pp. 74-80; D. E. Livingston-Little, "An Economic History of North Idaho: Part V, Discovery and Development of the Coeur d'Alene Mines," *Journal of the West* 3, no. 3 (July 1964): 325-35. Selig Perlman and Philip Taft, *History of Labor in the United States 1896-1932* (New York, 1932), pp. 168-83; Robert W. Smith, *The Coeur d'Alene Mining War of 1892* (Coravallis, Ore., 1961), *passim.* On the National Guard companies, see testimony of James R. Sovereign and James D. Young, ex-sheriff of Shoshone County in U.S. Ind. Comm., "Report on Mining Industry," pp. 408, 531-32, respectively; Hays, "Report to the Governor of Idaho," pp. 7-8; letter of Governor Frank Steunenberg to Sec. of War Elihu Root, Oct. 10, 1899, in *Annual Reports of the War Department, 1899,* vol. 4, no. 2, part 1 (Washington, D.C., 1899), pp. 69-70. Herbert G. Gutman, "The Worker's Search for Power: Labor in the Gilded Age," in *The Gilded Age: A Reappraisal,* ed. H. Wayne Morgan (Syracuse, N.Y., 1963), pp. 45-47, discusses the need often evidenced in small town and rural areas for the interjection of outside force to deal with industrial disputes, due to local officials often sympathizing with striking workers.

2. Smith, *The Coeur War of 1892,* pp. 39-46, 63-70; *Heritage of Conflict,* pp. 25-37; French, "The Coeur d'Alene Riots," pp. 32-38.

3. July 5, 1892, in Norman B. Willey Papers, Idaho State Historical Society, Boise, Idaho. Willey's activities in dealing with affairs in Shoshone County may be followed in the Willey Papers, for June; Willey to Harrison, June 25, Harrison to Willey, July 4, 1892, in series 1, reel 36, Benjamin Harrison Papers, microfilm, Library of Congress, Washington, D.C.; French, "The Coeur d'Alene Riots," pp. 34-35; Smith, *The Coeur War of 1892,* pp. 41-42, 47-49.

4. Reactions to events at the Frisco mill discussed in French, "The Coeur d'Alene Riots," p. 36, and Smith, *The Coeur War of 1892,* pp. 74-75, but are best followed in the correspondence in file number 34728, Principal Record Division, AGO, RG94, National Archives, hereafter referred to as PRD no. 34728. This is a consolidated file on the Army's activities during the Coeur d'Alene strike. Pressure for the commitment of troops in Idaho seen in W.H.H. Miller, U.S. Attorney General, to President Harrison, July 11, two wires; Willey to Harrison, July 11; E. W. Halford, private secretary to the President, to Harrison, July 12; Sen. Shoup to Harrison, July 12; Congressman Willis Sweet, Idaho, to Harrison, July 12; all in series 1, reel 36, Benjamin Harrison Papers, Library

of Congress. The reports of terror and destruction in Willey to Gen. Schofield, July 12, W. B. Heyburn to Sen. Fred Dubois, Idaho, July 16, in PRD no. 34728; in reports to Brigadier General Thomas Ruger, Department of the Columbia, July 13, p. 136, Letters Sent, 1892, Department of the Columbia, Records of the United States Army Continental Commands 1821-1920, Record Group 393, National Archives. Also see *Idaho Daily Statesman,* July 13 and 14, 1892.

5. In PRD no. 34728.

6. Willey's July 11 request for troops to President Harrison in series 1, reel 36, Harrison Papers.

7. July 13, PRD no. 34728. The mobilization of troops for duty in the Coeur d'Alene seen in a series of wires, July 12 and 13 with Gen. Ruger and other department commanders from Gen. Schofield in *Ibid.* One example of the near hysteria Idaho officials expressed about conditions in the Coeur d'Alene was Gov. Willey's erroneous report to Gen. Schofield that the "Bunker Hill and Sullivan [mine] being attacked by one thousand armed men." July 12, in *Ibid.* Colonel Carlin's slow approach to northern Idaho followed in Carlin to Gen. Ruger, July 13, pp. 136-40, Letters Sent, 1892, Department of the Columbia, RG393, NA; Gen. Wesley Merritt to Adj. Gen., July 13, 14, Carlin to Schofield, July 15, all in PRD no. 34728. Complaints of Carlin's caution contained in wires of W. B. Heyburn to Sen. Dubois, July 13, *Ibid.; Rocky Mountain News* (Denver), July 15, 1892, p. 2; *Idaho Daily Statesman,* July 15, p. 1; *Portland Oregonian,* July 15, p. 1. Also see French, "The Coeur D'Alene Riots," p. 39.

8. Carlin to Schofield, July 14, PRD no. 34728. On the activities of regulars in Idaho and conditions in the mining region after July 11, see Gen. Ruger to Schofield, July 14; Carlin to Schofield, July 15, *Ibid.;* Smith, *The Coeur War of 1892, passim;* French, "The Coeur d'Alene Riots," p. 39.

9. See Carlin's remarks in *Sec. War Rept. 1892,* p. 112; Carlin to Schofield, July 15, PRD no. 34728; Gen. Merritt to Adj. Gen., July 18, *Ibid.* July returns, 22nd Inf.; July returns, 25th Inf.; July and Aug. returns, 14th Inf.; July, Aug., Sept., and Oct. returns, 4th Inf., in Returns for Regular Army Infantry Regiments, Records of the Adjutant General's Office, 1800-1917, Record Group 94, National Archives, detail troop duty in the Coeur d'Alene. Also of value are *Idaho Daily Statesman,* July 16, p. 1; 18, p. 1; 19, p. 1, 1892; *Rocky Mountain News,* July 18, 1892, p. 2; *Portland Oregonian,* July 16, 1892, p. 1.

10. July 27, series 2, reel 84, Harrison Papers.

11. To State Senator John A. Finch, Wallace, Oct. 27, 1892, Willey

Papers. See Smith, *The Coeur War of 1892,* p. 84, for pressures on Willey
from mine owners to request retention of regulars; Willey's thinking on
troops followed in Willey to Sec. War Stephen Elkins, July 22, Elkins to
Willey, July 23, PRD no. 34728; Willey to Gen. Curtis, July 28, Willey
to V. M. Clement, manager of the Bunker Hill and Sullivan Mine, Sept.
6, in Willey Papers; Willey to Pres. Harrison, July 23, series 2, reel 84,
Harrison Papers. On troop withdrawals in July, see wires between Gen.
Ruger and Gen. Schofield, July 21-26, in PRD no. 34728. For newspaper
agitation for a semipermanent post in northern Idaho, see *Army and Navy
Journal* 29, no. 50 (August 6, 1892): 869; *Idaho Daily Statesman,* July 17,
1892, p. 1, October 20, 1892, p. 1; *Rocky Mountain News,* July 18, 1892,
p. 2; comments in Smith, *The Coeur War of 1892,* p. 84.

12. French, "The Coeur d'Alene Riots," pp. 48-49; Smith, *The Coeur
War of 1892,* pp. 87-90, 97-105.

13. On troop strengths and withdrawals, see Gen. Ruger to Schofield,
Sept. 9; Adj. Gen. to Ruger, Sept. 10; Ruger to Adj. Gen., Nov. 10, in
PRD no. 34728. Headquarters, Department of the Columbia, to Col.
Carlin, Sept. 12, 20, Nov. 12, in Letters Sent, 1892, Department of the
Columbia, RG393, NA, also discuss the removal of troops, as did the
Idaho Daily Statesman, Nov. 15, 19, 1892. For a description of the rela-
tions between soldiers and civilians in the Coeur d'Alene, see Smith,
The Coeur War of 1892, pp. 90-96.

14. Dec. 11, 1892.

15. In John Green Ballance Papers, Illinois Historical Society, Spring-
field, Illinois, which also contains a similar resolution passed by the Board
of Trustees, Town of Wallace, Idaho. Other sources on Capt. Ballance
include a long article in the *Idaho Daily Statesman,* Dec. 11, 1892; Gen.
Schofield to Gov. Willey, July 27, 1892, no. 820, Letters Sent, 1892,
Headquarters of the Army, Records of the Headquarters of the Army,
Record Group 108, National Archives; French, "The Coeur d'Alene
Riots," p. 41; Smith, *The Coeur War of 1892,* p. 83.

16. On the development of the Western Federation of Miners after
the 1892 federal intervention, see Smith, *The Coeur War of 1892,* pp.
110-22; Dubofsky, *We Shall Be All,* pp. 34-35; Perlman and Taft,
History of Labor in the U.S., pp. 172-83.

17. The events leading up to the 1894 disorders, the pressures on the
Cleveland administration for troops, and the outbreak of conflict in early
July, 1894, are described in the following: letter of W. B. Heyburn, now
manager of the Bunker Hill and Sullivan mine, to Sen. Fred T. Dubois,
July 11, 1894, in U.S., Executive, Department of Justice, Attorney
General, *Annual Report of the Attorney General of the United States,*

1896; Appendix, 54th Cong., 2nd sess., House Executive Document 9 (Washington, D.C., 1896), pp. 216-217. Heyburn complained, among other things, that the miners' union planned a celebration of the 1892 destruction of the Frisco mill. "If this is not travesty upon law and order, then my judgment is at fault." Newspaper coverage of events in Shoshone County reflected Heyburn's strong dislike for union miners, as seen in *Idaho Daily Statesman,* July 5, 8, 10, 11, 1894; *Spokesman-Review* (Spokane) July 5, 8, 9, 10, 12, 1894.

18. Quoted in Gen. Otis to Adj. Gen., Aug. 10, 1894, Letters Sent, 1894, Department of the Columbia, RG393, NA.

19. *Ibid.* Otis's August 10 report to the Adj. Gen., and another report on August 3, in *Ibid.,* provide the chief sources for the 1894 intervention of federal troops in the Coeur d'Alene. Other correspondence in Letters Sent, 1894, Department of the Columbia, RG393, NA, particularly for late July and early August, is also important. Schofield to Otis, and Otis to Schofield, July 9, and Adj. Gen. to Otis, August 3, 6, all in no. 4445, consolidated file 10, AGO, RG94, NA, contain War Department orders for troops in the Coeur d'Alene. Also see Attorney General Richard Olney to Secretary of War Daniel S. Lamont, July 30, 1894, in consolidated file no. 6370, AGO, RG94, NA.

20. In Duncan, "Reminiscences, 1882-1905," p. 55, manuscript in the possession of Henry T. Duncan, Lexington, Kentucky.

21. July 11, 1894.

22. July 23, no. 5216, in consolidated file 10, AGO, RG94, NA. *The Spokesman-Review's* editorials calling for retention of federal troops are in the following issues: July 8, 9, 12, 16, 21, 1894. The fact that both Generals Otis and Schofield were confused as to why troops were sent to Idaho is evident in Schofield to Sec. War Lamont, Sept. 6, 1894, no. 1625, Letters Sent, 1894, Headquarters of the Army, RG108; Otis's correspondence with Schofield and the Adjutant General, cited in note 19 above, and Adj. Gen. to Otis, Sept. 8, no. 2534, Letters Received, 1894, Department of the Columbia, RG393, NA. Activities of troops in the Coeur d'Alene are outlined in July, August and September returns of the Fourth Infantry, in Returns of Regular Army Infantry Regiments, AGO, RG94, NA.

23. *Idaho Daily Statesman* (Boise), April 29, 1899. Also see *Rocky Mountain News* (Denver), April 30, 1899; *The Spokesman-Review* (Spokane), April 29, 1899. For background on the 1899 outburst, see Jensen, *Heritage of Conflict,* pp. 74-80; Perlman and Taft, *History of Labor in the U.S.,* pp. 183-84; Dubofsky, *We Shall Be All,* chap. 3.

24. Descriptions of the April 29 explosion and violence may be found

in the following: "Report of Brigadier General H. C. Merriam, U.S.A., on Miners' Riot in the State of Idaho," 56th Cong., 1st sess., Senate Documents, vol. 4, no. 24 (Washington, D.C., 1900), pp. 15-20; Hays, "Report to the Governor of Idaho," pp. 10-11; U.S. Ind. Comm., "Report on Mining Industry," p. xvii; *Idaho Daily Statesman,* April 30, 1899; *Rocky Mountain News,* May 1, 1899; *The Spokesman-Review,* April 30, 1899. (Merriam's report hereafter referred to as Merriam, "Coeur d'Alene Mining Troubles.").

25. Sinclair's presence in the Coeur d'Alene and his actions reported in *Idaho Daily Statesman,* April 30; and U.S. Ind. Comm., "Report on Mining Industry," p. xvii. The request for troops and the decision to send troops found in the following: Steunenberg to McKinley, April 29, 1899; George B. Cortelyou to Adjutant General Henry C. Corbin, April 29; Benjamin F. Montgomery to McKinley, April 29, all in series 1, reel 6, microfilm, William McKinley Papers, Library of Congress, Washington, D.C. Also see Corbin to Steunenberg, April 30; Corbin to commanding officers Dept. of Dakota, Dept. of Missouri, Dept. of Calif. and Columbia; Dept. of the Lakes, April 30, all in "Report of Brig. Gen. H. C. Merriam, U.S.A., Commanding Department of the Colorado," in *Annual Reports of the War Department 1899,* 56th Cong., 1st sess., House Document 2 (Washington, D.C., 1899), pp. 52-53. There are three basic sources for the military decisions and actions taken in the 1899 Coeur d'Alene affair. The primary source is file no. 231071, Adjutant General's Office, RG94, National Archives, Washington, D.C. This is a large consolidated file containing correspondence from the initial request for troops in April 1899 through mid-1900. Some of this correspondence, along with other useful information, was published in Merriam, "Coeur d'Alene Mining Troubles." Additional correspondence was published in General Merriam's annual report on the Department of the Colorado, cited above, and hereafter referred to as Merriam, "Report on Miners' Riot." Two other sources are useful, the evidence and testimony found in U.S. Industrial Commission, "Report on Mining Industry," and U.S., Congress, House, Committee on Military Affairs, *Coeur d'Alene Labor Troubles,* 56th Cong., 1st sess., H. Rept. no. 1999 (Washington, D.C., 1900).

26. April 30, in Merriam, "Report on Miners' Riot," p. 53.

27. For requests for troops from mining officials, see D. O. Mills to Sec. of War, April 30; James L. Houghteling to John Addison Porter, Sec. to the Pres., April 30; W. S. Crocker to McKinley, April 30; Herman B. Butler to Porter, April 30; A. Ryerson to Alger, April 30, all in *Ibid.,* pp. 53-54. On newspaper reports, see *The Spokesman-Review,* April 30, 1900, pp. 1, 4; *Idaho Daily Statesman,* May 1, 1899, p. 1; *The Rocky*

Mountain News, May 1, 1899, pp. 1, 2; *Portland Oregonian,* May 1, 1899, pp. 1, 4. For administration response to these reports, see G. D. Meikle-john, Acting Sec. of War, to Mills, Ryerson, and Houghteling, May 1, in Merriam, "Report on Miners' Riot," p. 54; Geo. B. Cortelyou to Adj. Gen. Corbin, April 30; Benj. Montgomery to McKinley, April 30; Alger to Corbin, May 1, Corbin to Alger, May 1, all in series 1, reel 6, McKinley Papers.

28. May 1, 1899. See also *Idaho Daily Statesman,* May 1, 1899. The Denver *Rocky Mountain News* presented the most inflammatory predictions of miner resistance, in May 1, 2, 3, 1899, issues.

29. Russell F. Weigley, *History of the United States Army* (New York: 1967), pp. 305-12, and Graham A. Cosmas, *An Army for Empire: The United States Army in the Spanish-American War* (Columbia, Mo., 1971), chaps. 2, 3, discuss the Army's general condition during and after the war. Also see Adj. Gen. Corbin's resume to the President, May 31, 1899, series 1, reel 7, McKinley Papers, and comments of General Miles in *Sec. War Rept. 1899,* pp. 23-25, 74-76, 383-84.

30. For a succinct comment on the relationship between Alger and Miles, see *Idaho Daily Statesman,* May 22, 1899. On the lack of leadership in the War Department, Cosmas, *An Army for Empire,* chap. 2. Edward Ranson, "Nelson A. Miles as Commanding General, 1895-1903," *Military Affairs* 29, no. 4 (Winter 1965-66): 179-200, discusses the irascible Miles.

31. In Merriam, "Coeur d'Alene Mining Troubles," p. 1. For Merriam's role as dual departmental commander, see "Report of Brig. Gen. H. C. Merriam, commanding the Department of the Missouri," *Annual Reports of the War Department 1899,* 56th Cong., 1st sess., House Document 2 (Washington, D.C., 1899), pp. 14-17, and Merriam, "Report on Miners' Riot," pp. 25-27.

32. To Merriam, May 3, in Merriam, "Coeur d'Alene Mining Troubles," p. 3. Also see Steunenberg to Merriam, April 30; Merriam to Adjutant General, May 2; and his comments on the meeting between the general and the governor, in *Ibid.,* pp. 2-3.

33. In Merriam to Corbin, May 2, *Ibid.*

34. *Ibid.,* pp. 3-5. See *Idaho Daily Statesman,* May 3, on the arrival of troops and their reception.

35. In Merriam, "Report on Miners' Riot," p. 54. Also see Merriam to Corbin, May 5, and his comments on the arrest policy in his "Coeur d'Alene Mining Troubles," pp. 4, 5, 6, respectively. Also, *Idaho Daily Statesman,* May 5.

36. May 4, 1899.

37. Vol. 43, no. 2213 (May 30, 1899): 498. See similar descriptions in *Idaho Daily Statesman*, May 5, 1899, and Hutton, *The Coeur d'Alenes*, p. 135.

38. Testimony of F. P. Matchette, of Wardner, in U.S. Ind. Comm., "Report on Mining Industry," pp. 436-37.

39. In *Ibid.*, p. 421. See similar testimony of Levi Miller, of Burke, *Ibid.*, p. 430. Also see descriptions in the *Idaho Daily Statesman*, May 6, and *Rocky Mountain News*, May 4, 1899.

40. Merriam, "Coeur d'Alene Mining Troubles," p. 7.

41. *Ibid.;* for descriptions of life in the makeshift prison, see testimony of several miners in U.S. Ind. Comm., "Report on Mining Industry," *passim.* On further arrests, see *Idaho Daily Statesman*, May 7, 1899.

42. *Idaho Daily Statesman*, May 9, 1899. See Merriam, "Coeur d'Alene Mining Troubles," p. 7, and *Idaho Daily Statesman*, May 16, 1899, p. 1, on the new prison.

43. Merriam, "Coeur d'Alene Mining Troubles," p. 8.

44. In U.S. Ind. Comm., "Report on Mining Industry," p. xx.

45. In Merriam, "Coeur d'Alene Mining Troubles," p. 9.

46. On the proclamation, see *Ibid.*, pp. 8-10; *Idaho Daily Statesman*, May 8, 1899, p. 1.

47. *Idaho Daily Statesman*, May 7, 1899, p. 1; *Rocky Mountain News*, May 30, 1899, p. 4, for comments on this.

48. Merriam to Adj. Gen., May 17, in Merriam, "Coeur d'Alene Mining Troubles," p. 11.

49. See Merriam to Adj. Gen., May 12, 16, 17; pp. 10-11, and his comments on pp. 12-15, all in *Ibid.* On the governor and the miners' reaction to the permit system, see *The Spokesman-Review*, May 13, 15, 18, 19, 1899.

50. In Committee on Military Affairs, "Coeur d'Alene Labor Troubles," p. 116. On the prisoners, see *Idaho Daily Statesman*, May 20, 1899; *The Spokesman-Review*, May 17, 1899. On the duty of the troops, see May and June returns, Twenty-fourth Infantry, Returns of Regular Army Infantry Regiments, AGO, RG94.

51. Testimony of Allen F. Gill, in U.S. Ind. Comm., "Report on Mining Industry," p. 520. Similar testimony given by miner A. C. Cleary, who was at the meeting, *Ibid.*, p. 529.

52. For more on this incident, see *Ibid., passim;* Committee on Military Affairs, "Coeur d'Alene Labor Troubles," pp. 115-17.

53. In Committee on Military Affairs, "Coeur d'Alene Mining Troubles," p. 11.

54. Merriam to Smith, May 24, *Idid.*, p. 12.

55. *Ibid.*, pp. 12-13.

56. May 16, *Ibid.*, p. 11.

57. See copy of Western Federation of Miners appeal to labor in the May 9 material, series 1, reel 6, McKinley Papers. See the Omaha *Western Laborer* 8, no. 45 (May 20, 1899): 1-2, for comments on the growing labor attacks on General Merriam.

58. In the *Pueblo [Colo.] Courier* 7, no. 358 (May 26, 1899): 4.

59. June 6, 1899, in AGO no. 231071.

60. For examples of labor press reaction, see *Iron Molders' Journal* 35, no. 7 (July 1899): 355; *American Federationist* 6, no. 4 (June 1899): 92; *Denver Industrial Advocate* 6, no. 354 (May 12, 1899): 1, 2; *The United Mine Workers' Journal* 10, no. 9 (June 8, 1894): 4; *The Pueblo Courier* 7, no. 358 (May 26, 1899): 4, 7, no. 359 (June 2, 1899): *The Typographical Journal* 14, no. 12 (June 15, 1899): 500, 515; *The Carpenter* 19, no. 7 (July 1899): 4; *Journal of the Knights of Labor* 19, no. 4 (August 1899): 1. A few of the labor petitions protesting Merriam's role in the Coeur d'Alene appear in the published sources, see, e.g., The Pueblo Trades and Labor Assembly to McKinley, May 11, and to Adj. Gen. Corbin, June 3, San Francisco Labor Council to McKinley, June 14, in Merriam, "Report on Miners' Riot," pp. 55, 57, 58, respectively; references to petition from Western Labor Union in Corbin to Merriam, May 26, *Ibid.*, p. 56. In AGO no. 231071 there is a very large packet containing well over one hundred petitions, most of them addressed to the president or the secretary of war. Although many came from WFM affiliates in Montana and Colorado, they reflect a genuine nationwide movement. Such union groups as the Galveston (Texas) Labor Council, the Hoboken (N.J.) Typographical Union, the San Francisco Building Trades Council, the United Labor League of Philadelphia, and many other non-mining unions sent protests to Washington.

61. Committee on Military Affairs, "Coeur d'Alene Labor Troubles," p. 118.

62. Vol. 16, no. 11 (Nov. 1899): 849.

63. See the *Pueblo Courier* 7, no. 360 (June 9, 1899): 2, and 7, no. 369 (August 11, 1899): 3; *Journal of the Knights of Labor* 19, no. 4 (August 1899): 1; *The Carpenter* 19, no. 11 (November 1899): 9; William D. Haywood, *Bill Haywood's Book: The Autobiography of William D. Haywood* (New York, 1929), p. 87; Hutton, *The Coeur d'Alene*, pp. 134, 146-50. In U.S. Ind. Comm., "Report on Mining Industry," there is considerable testimony from miners and townspeople

about the brutality of the black troops, but not one witness could swear that he personally suffered mistreatment. Most testified that they heard that someone else was bayonetted, that they saw someone else pushed around, or that it was just common knowledge that the troops were unnecessarily rough. See pp. 416-17, 422, 425, 429, 513-18, 539.

64. May 25, in Merriam, "Report on Miners' Riot," p. 55.

65. In Merriam, "Coeur d'Alene Mining Troubles," p. 11.

66. Merriam to Corbin, May 30, *Ibid.* See also Geo. B. Cortelyou to Alger, May 26; Alger to McKinley, May 29, in Merriam, "Report on Miners' Riots," p. 55. Reports from Major Allen Smith, commanding at Wallace, to Adj. Gen., May 30, indicated that troops were merely guarding prisoners and keeping the peace, *Ibid.,* p. 56.

67. In Merriam, "Coeur d'Alene Mining Troubles," p. 12.

68. June 6, no. 243149 in AGO no. 231071. See Alger to Central Federated Union, N.Y.C., May 22, 421, vol. 18, and Alger to Muskegon Typographical Union, Muskegon, Mich., 430, vol. 19, Semi-official Letters, Russell A. Alger Papers, William L. Clements Library, University of Michigan, Ann Arbor, Michigan. See *Army and Navy Journal* 36, no. 39 (May 27, 1899): 918, for replies to labor. On the new complaints, see Geo. B. Cortelyou to Alger, May 31; Corbin to Merriam, June 12; Merriam to Corbin, June, in Merriam, "Report on Miners' Riot," p. 58.

69. Merriam, "Coeur d'Alene Mining Troubles," p. 9.

70. *Ibid.,* pp. 9-13.

71. Quoted in *American Federationist* 6, no. 5 (July 1899): 110.

72. August 18, series 1, reel 7, McKinley Papers. For labor attacks on Merriam, then on his report, see many petitions cited below and *The Pueblo Courier* 7, no. 356 (May 12, 1899): 1; *The Industrial Advocate* 6, no. 360 (June 23, 1899): 2; *International Woodworkers* 8 (June 1899): 61; *The Typographical Journal* 15, no. 1 (July 1899): 10, 31-32; *Cigar Makers' Journal* 24, no. 10 (July 1899): 8; *American Federationist* 6, no. 5 (July 1899): 107-08, 111-12; *Journal of the Knights of Labor* 19, no. 7 (November 1899): 4; *The Locomotive Firemen's Magazine* 27, no. 2 (August 1899): 139; *Miner's Magazine* 1, no. 1 (January 1900): 18-21, 1, no. 2 (February 1900): 1-3.

73. See Adj. Gen. to Commanding Officer, U.S. troops at Wardner, June 3; Capt. Benjamin W. Leavell to Adj. Gen., June 3; Merriam to Adj. Gen., June 5; Merriam to Adj. Gen., June 12, all in Merriam, "Report on Miners' Riot," pp. 56, 57, 58, respectively. For plans of the Idaho officials see *The Spokesman-Review,* July 5, 1899, p. 1. On the importation of strikebreakers and lack of union men working, see *The Spokesman-Review,*

May 19, 1899, p. 1, May 28; and the *Pueblo Courier* 8, no. 369 (August 11, 1899): 3.

74. May 9, 1899, in AGO no. 231071.

75. August 18, 1899, in *Ibid*. For other requests for permanent retention of troops in the region, see Frank N. Beebe to McKinley, May 5; Mrs. F. A. Wright to McKinley, May 10, in *Ibid.;* James L. Houghteling et al., stockholders in Bunker Hill and Sullivan, to Alger, June 10; J. W. Babcock to Alger, June 12; Geo. L. Shoup to McKinley, July 23; C.T.P. Bass to McKinley, June 23; J. A. Kebler to John D. Long, Sec. of the Navy, July 26, all in Merriam, "Report on Miners' Riots," pp. 58-59, 61-63.

76. Vol. 7, no. 360 (June 9, 1899): 3.

77. On the Sixth Cavalry, see Merriam to Adj. Gen., June 16; Merriam to Adj. Gen., June 18, in Merriam, "Report on Miners' Riot," pp. 60, 61, respectively. For description of daily life in the Coeur see *Idaho Daily Statesman,* June 30, 1899, p. 3, July 5, p. 1.

78. C. H. Fisher to Surgeon General, September 22, in AGO no. 231071.

79. Merriam to Corbin, October 8, *Ibid*. See Corbin to Merriam, October 5; Merriam to Corbin, October 11; Corbin to Merriam, October 12, all in *Ibid*.

80. In Merriam, "Report on Miners' Riot," p. 28.

81. *Ibid.,* p. 73. For entire letter, see pp. 66-73.

82. On Steunenberg's visit to Washington, see his wire to Root, October 12, AGO no. 231071. Root's resistance to retention of troops partly seen in his note to U.S. Attorney General, October 12, in *Ibid*. The conference between Root and Steunenberg and their respective arguments followed in *Idaho Daily Statesman,* October 24, 1899; October 27, November 8; *The Spokesman-Review* October 22, 24, November 2, 3. On the relief of federal troops at the bullpen, see Merriam to Adj. Gen., November 4, and Adj. Gen. to Merriam, November 13, in AGO no. 231071; *Idaho Daily Statesman,* November 3, 1899; *The Spokesman-Review,* November 3. On closing of the bullpen and transfer of federal troops to Osburn and Wallace, see Steunenberg to Root, November 29; Root to Steunenberg, December 9; Merriam to Adj. Gen., December 6, all in AGO no. 231071; and *The Spokesman-Review,* December 3, 1899.

83. In *The Boilermaker and Iron Shipbuilder* 9, no. 7 (July 1, 1899): 196.

84. *Ibid.,* p. 200. The WFM maintained, despite convincing evidence to the contrary, that the Standard Oil Corporation owned the Bunker Hill and Sullivan mine and mill. For other labor journals that

printed the appeal, see *The International Woodworkers* 3 (June 1899): 62, 66; *The Typographical Journal* 15, no. 2 (July 15, 1899): 56; *American Federationist* 6, no. 5 (July 1899): 105; *Railroad Trainmen Journal* 16, no. 8 (August 1899): 763-64; *Locomotive Firemen's Magazine* 27, no. 3 (September 1899): 263-65.

85. Vol. 10, no. 12 (June 29, 1899): 4; See also 10, no. 21 (August 31, 1899): 4. See the *Pueblo Courier* 7, no. 359 (June 2, 1899): 3; 8, no. 36 (June 16, 1899): 3; 8, no. 377 (October 6, 1899), for examples of the "Remember the Bull-Pen" column. Other journals that attacked the bullpen were *International Woodworker* 8 (August 1899): 90, 8 (October 1899): 112; *The Typographical Journal* 15, no. 2 (July 15, 1899): 54-55; *American Federationist* 6, no. 5 (July 1899): 105, 6, no. 9 (November 1899): 221-22; *Locomotive Firemen's Magazine* 27, no. 3 (September 1899): 263-65; *Railroad Trainmen's Journal* 16, no. 8 (August 1899): 763-65; *The Cleveland Citizen* 9, no. 18 (May 27, 1899): 2, 9, no. 20 (June 10, 1899): 1; *Iron Molders' Journal* 35, no. 7 (July 1899): 355; the bullpen was also excoriated at the convention of the Knights of Labor, see *Proceedings of the General Assembly of the Knights of Labor, Twenty-Third Regular Session, 1899* (Washington, D.C., 1900), pp. 15-16, 21-24. The bullpen became a standard ax to grind for labor polemicists; see, e.g., Hutton, *The Coeur d'Alenes,* pp. 152-53, T. A. Hickey of the Socialist Labor Party, *The Story of the Bull-Pen at Wardner Idaho* (New York, 1900), *passim.*

86. July 28, 1899, in AGO no. 231071.

87. *Ibid.*

88. Corbin to Wm. Hagerty, Butte Miners' Union, August 5, 1899, *Ibid.* Some of these petitions and protests were published in Merriam, "Report on Miners' Riot," pp. 63-64, but many, many more may be found in AGO no. 231071, from which the names of unions cited in the paragraph were taken. Corbin's ploy of pushing the protestors off on Gov. Steunenberg seen also in his wire to Steunenberg, July 17, *Ibid.*

89. Merriam to Corbin, August 24, *Ibid.* Information concerning the affidavits is bound in one packet in AGO no. 231071. Significant pieces of correspondence are Geo. B. Cortelyou to Corbin, July 17; Maj. Smith to Merriam, July 28; Steunenberg to Merriam, August 17; Merriam to Adj. Gen., August 24; memo of Corbin to Pres. McKinley, August 31.

90. September 27, in Merriam, "Report on Miners' Riot," p. 64.

91. September 30, *Ibid.,* p. 65.

92. For Boyce's wire, see *Ibid.,* p. 64. See also Root to Steunenberg, September 29, p. 65; Corbin to Merriam, September 29, p. 65.

93. Full details on this incident may be seen in Merriam to Adj. Gen., October 1, *Ibid.,* pp. 64-65, and Edwards's testimony in Committee on Military Affairs, "Coeur d'Alene Labor Troubles," pp. 98-102; pages 99-100 give the details on the tunnel incident, while the other pages of testimony not only provide information on Edwards's approach to management of the prison but also insight into his personality.

94. These charges may be seen not only in the labor journals cited above but in testimony to the U.S. Industrial Commission in July 1899. See the Commission's "Report on Mining Industry," *passim.*

95. *Ibid.,* p. 20. See also pp. 18-21, 544-46; Committee on Military Affairs, "Coeur d'Alene Labor Troubles," pp. 28-58, 67-75, 84; Hays, "Report to the Governor of Idaho," pp. 11-20; Steunenberg to Root, October 10, in Merriam, "Report on Miners' Riots," pp. 67-73.

96. On the trials, see Idaho, Executive, *Biennial Message of the Governor of Idaho 1901* (Boise, n.d.), pp. 11-12, statement by Governor Frank W. Hunt, Steunenberg's successor. On the effects of the permit system, see Committee on Military Affairs, "Coeur d'Alene Labor Troubles," p. 114.

97. Steunenberg to Root, October 10, in Merriam, "Report on Miners' Riot," p. 73. Merriam's defense of his actions seen in his report, "Coeur d'Alene Mining Troubles," pp. 11-13, and in testimony in Committee on Military Affairs, "Coeur d'Alene Labor Troubles," pp. 68-69, 73-75, 112-13.

98. August 18, series 1, reel 7, McKinley Papers.

99. Committee on Military Affairs, "Coeur d'Alene Labor Troubles," p. 121.

100. See *Ibid.,* pp. 1-2, for condensation of majority conclusions; see also pp. 9, 84, 125.

101. U.S., Executive, War Department, *Regulations of the Army of the United States, 1895* (Washington, D.C., 1895), article 52, section 490, p. 69. Also see *New York Times,* July 7, 1894, for a statement that Schofield's general orders of 1894 had been incorporated into the Army Regulations.

102. Committee on Military Affairs, "Coeur d'Alene Labor Troubles," pp. 127-32.

103. War Department, *Regulations of the Army,* p. 69.

104. Committee on Military Affairs, "Coeur d'Alene Labor Troubles," p. 103. On the majority argument concerning delegation of control of the military by the president, see *Ibid.,* pp. 61-67. On the Heney incident, *Ibid.,* pp. 102-03. For labor reaction to the investigation and attacks on

the majority conclusion, see *Miners' Magazine* 1, no. 4 (April 1900): 7-9; 1, no. 5 (May 1900): 6-7; 1, no. 7 (July 1900): 45-56; *Journal of the Knights of Labor* 19, no. 12 (April 1900): 4, and 19, no. 13 (May 1900): 1.

105. Dougherty to Adj. Gen., June 9, 1900, in AGO no. 231071.

106. On the cessation of martial law, see *Miners' Magazine* 2, no. 5 (May 1901): 2; Perlman and Taft, *History of Labor in the U.S.*, p. 187. On the withdrawal of troops, see *Sec. War Rept. 1901*, p. 275.

107. In U.S. Ind. Comm., "Report on Mining Industry," p. 395.

8 The Army, Labor Disorder, and the Public

Federal military intervention in labor disorders generated greater public interest in the Army between the end of Reconstruction and the outbreak of the Spanish-American War than any other duty the service performed. The nature of the interventions, not their numbers, governed the character of public response. This was particularly the case in the railroad strikes of 1877 and 1894. Since the railroad strikes were exceptional, being the closest equivalents to general strikes the nation ever experienced in the age of industrialism, the Army's central part in ending them brought temporary attention to an otherwise ignored institution. While the railroad strikes occasioned the most publicity, any federal military intervention was always decisive and came in crucial tests of strength between labor and property. Contemporaries recognized the importance of the struggles and devoted considerable attention to them and the Army.

The Army moved into labor disputes in an atmosphere of general public approval for strong presidential action. In 1877 and 1894, both Presidents Hayes and Cleveland were deluged with laudatory and supportive telegrams. Commercial associations, important businessmen, and ordinary citizens all offered praise and advice. One Elliot F. Shepard of New York City advised President Hayes to levy a "heavy chastisement" upon strikers at a single point, perhaps Pittsburgh, setting an object lesson that would "save life, property and law everywhere else."[1] Richard W. Gilder, editor of *Century Magazine,* wrote Cleveland, "On every hand, and from old enemies as well as old friends, nothing is now heard but praise and the expression of intense satisfaction at your patriotic and fearless action."[2] During the railroad strikes, Civil War veterans from both

North and South ostentatiously tendered their services to suppress the rioters if the Army failed to do the job.[3]

Above all, the public press supported the use of federal power to crush those who interfered with the property rights of management and the rights of non-strikers to work. At the very outbreak of disorder in 1877, *The Philadelphia Inquirer* demanded that strikers and rioters be suppressed and punished and, "if this can only be done by the aid of the United States troops, those troops will never have aided in a better cause."[4] No major newspaper or journal disagreed with the *Inquirer*. "With very few exceptions," *Public Opinion* reported in 1894, "the leading newspapers of the country, Democratic, Republican and independent, heartily endorse the action of the President in massing troops at the points of disturbance."[5] The press all too often indulged in lurid headlines and exaggerations of violence and bloodshed. Underlying the depictions of riot and ruin, however, was a deep anxiety over what seemed to be a nascent class warfare. "The days are over," lamented *The New York Times* at the conclusion of the first railroad strike, "in which this country could rejoice in its freedom from the elements of social strife which have long abounded in old countries."[6]

Just as threatening was the disregard strikers displayed for the rights of private property. In reporting the use of militia at Homestead, Pennsylvania, and federal troops in Idaho in 1892, the *Portland Oregonian* asserted that the issue was not labor's needs but the law. And it was clear as to whether "nonunion men are to have the protection of the law when they take the places vacated by strikers. . . . Moreover, the owners of the property, the employers of labor, have the unquestionable right to keep possession of their works and to protect the men whom they employ."[7] The real issue of the Pullman strike, according to *The Outlook,* was "whether the American Railway Union shall determine when, under what conditions, on what railroads, and in what sort of cars the people of the United States may travel." Since the ARU had taken unto itself to dictate to Americans how they would use their property, time, and money, the contest was not between railroad workers and railroad management but "between the American Railway Union and the American people."[8]

In elevating significant labor struggles into battles for the preservation of society, the press inevitably called for harsh measures to suppress strikes and urged on presidents and the Army a policy of sternness. *The*

Philadelphia Inquirer called for an Army of 100,000 in 1877 to deal with
striking railroaders who had not merely stopped the conduct of business
and destroyed property but had "declared war against society."[9] Again
and again the call was for "the stern repression of all mob violence. . . .
The quicker, the sharper, the more thorough . . . the more secure society
is for the time to come."[10] *Harper's Weekly* reflected the same attitude
in 1894:

> The lesson of the supremacy of law must be taught promptly.
> . . . If the first lesson must needs be given by the bayonet and
> the bullet, it will be in every way cheapest and best to administer
> it in the first clear case of resistance to authority.[11]

At times, some elements of the press could be bloodthirsty in the extreme.
In 1894, the *Chicago Tribune* warned strikers that if they continued to
resist regular soldiers they "will be fired upon, they will be bayoneted,
will be tampled under foot by cavalry, and mowed down by artillery."[12]

The Army's efficient work in suppressing the two great railroad strikes
and the apparent ease with which the service cowed militant miners of the
Coeur d'Alene brought the highest accolades from the public press. Editors
and commentators were impressed with the Army's discipline when con-
trasted with that of the police, special deputies, and the National Guard.
The Nation depicted the Army as a machine, "the most terrible of all
machines invented by man, by which the wills of thousands are wielded,
even unto death, by the will of one."[13] A Chicago newspaper also used
the image of the machine to describe a federal regiment, then abruptly
shifted metaphors and wrote, "The regiment is a devil-fish—one body
with 500 arms."[14] The *New York Times* saw it as natural that when the
nation needed drilled and reliable troops it turned to the Army. "One
thousand of them are worth all the militiamen . . . brought into the
service" in 1877.[15] The value of regulars was that they were "soldiers
everyday of their lives; they ask for nothing but their orders, and their
moral influence is double that of" citizen soldiers. "Mobs appreciate the
difference so clearly that as a rule regulars are able to effect without
firing a shot what militia could not accomplish without severe fighting."[16]

The press was particularly impressed with this fact that the presence
of federal troops almost invariably meant an "end [to] trouble without
bloodshed."[17] Mobs succumbed to regulars not simply because they were

impressed with Army discipline and efficiency but because federal troops "have no sympathy with any class. They are colorless in sentiment. They belonged to the class of men who have neither 'politics nor religion,' sympathies nor selfishness."[18] If in fact regulars were not the neutral arbiters most editors claimed they were, press supporters of the service insisted nonetheless that "even the men against whom they are . . . called upon to act will recognize the fact that no feeling of hate or self-interest animates the officers and men of the National Army."[19] The Army was seen as a more effective agency of social control than police or militia because it was not subject to local influences, loyalties, or conflicts, and hence it was less likely to act in favor of one side over the other in a violent labor conflict.[20]

Above all, the Army was successful in the face of angry mobs and determined strikers because regular soldiers were seen as "representatives of the irresistible power of the National Government."[21] *The Philadelphia Inquirer* maintained that one platoon of regulars was worth ten times that number of National Guardsmen because the platoon represented "the power, authority and prestige of the nation."[22] The Army carried the national flag and represented the national will. The law it enforced was not the law of any special interest groups but the law of the land. The Army succeeded because "there is a profound respect for the Army in every American breast as the force that represents a Government of all the people—at once powerful, beneficient and just."[23]

An efficient, disciplined, neutral federal military force was far less likely to use unnecessary force or shed wasted blood, unlike poorly controlled and easily influenced police or militia. Most important to the press analysis, however, was a strong belief that as the representative of the national government, the Army presented to strikers and even unreasoning mobs a force not to be resisted. The potential killing power of federal troops was not the deterrent, it was the moral power of the federal government that regulars symbolized that stopped angry strikers and rampant rioters. "The gleam of a single bayonet representing the authority of the National Government" was more often than not sufficient to inspire "respect for the majesty of the law in the most turbulent localities."[24] While something of an exaggeration, this observation was essentially sound. The legacy of Civil War nationalism played as large a role in the restoration of order and law as did the number of regular troops used in any labor upheaval of the period.

Given the fears and anxieties fostered by the railroad strikes and violent labor conflicts of the Gilded Age, many newspapers and journals advocated an expansion of the Army as the best means of suppressing, or even forestalling, future disorders. The Army's evident ability to end violence quickly and bloodlessly was appealing, as was the generally accurate belief that federal troops would not side with the strikers as National Guardsmen sometimes did. Neither would regular troops stimulate a public outcry as the use of Pinkerton and other private security guards so often did. Sometimes the call for an enlarged Army with constabulary responsibilities smacked too much of special pleading. In 1877, Thomas A. Scott, president of the Pennsylvania Railroad, called for a larger federal service with permanent garrisons near important transportation centers to prevent future disruptions of railroad traffic.[25] The continued agitation in the Pacific Northwest in the 1890s for a permanent sub-post in the Coeur d'Alene was another instance of a particular industry seeking direct federal assistance in controlling a turbulent labor force.[26]

More generally, portions of the press urged a larger federal military force in anticipation of future labor and urban disorders, whatever their causes and wherever they occurred. *The Nation* took the lead in 1877. In calling for an additional 25,000 regulars, the journal justified its position by arguing that not only were regulars the most effective force for ending disorder but were "able to *prevent* such disturbances, while the militia, at best, serve only to suppress them after they have run a more or less destructive course."[27] *The Nation* developed its argument more fully in an editorial "Why the Regular Army Should be Increased," maintaining that the nation's large industrial cities needed to be guarded by a federal force, for "it is in great cities only that rioting is most effective for destruction and disorganization."[28] In a more jingoistic vein, the *St. Louis Post-Dispatch* cried, "If there were no army . . . the country [would] become, as General Sherman has proclaimed, not a nation of law-abiding people, but, in the absence of the army, a stupendous mob!"[29] Other journals and journalists repeated the refrain, and were particularly adamant in their calls for an increase in 1877, when Democrats in the House attempted to reduce the service because of its role in Reconstruction.[30]

In 1894, the *Army and Navy Journal* was foremost in calling for an expanded Army. During the peak of the strike, the *Journal* assessed "The Army and Public Sentiment" and concluded that at last conditions were favorable for a necessary increase.[31] General press support for the Army and editorial calls for expansion seemed to confirm the *Journal*'s optimism. Not untypical was the *New York Commercial Advertiser*'s editorial statement: "We not only need a Regular Army of 50,000 men, but we need these troops where they are most wanted—near the large centers of population."[32] According to the *Review of Reviews,* "A moderate increase in the Army would endanger no man's liberty, and might conduce much to the maintenance of law and order."[33] Although the Army's 1899 intervention in Idaho did not stimulate a general press assessment of the Army's place in society, as had been the case in 1877 and 1894, the *New York Times* saw the event as proof once again of the need to expand the service, for "we must have a regular army as a National Police."[34]

Not unnaturally, the soldiers and civilians who oversaw the administration and finance of the Army viewed press support for the service as an opportunity to further its interests. Perpetually shorthanded and underfinanced, the Army sought to exploit what it saw as a most favorable public attitude to move an ever parsimonious Congress to meet at last its many needs. As the 1877 riots came to an end, General Philip Sheridan wrote to William T. Sherman, "There has been a complete revolution in public sentiment on Army and other matters and I think it best for you to come [to Washington] between now and the meeting of Congress."[35] Colonel Emory Upton made a similar suggestion to Major General John M. Schofield. In the aftermath of both railroad strikes, Secretaries of War George W. McCrary and Daniel S. Lamont wrote strong pleas for increased expenditures and manpower. The annual reports of commanding generals and department commanders stressed the Army's fidelity and effectiveness in the disorders, while noting its lack of troops.[36]

The attempts to further the interests of the Army while favorable public attention was focused on it was understandable. The nature of the appeals was unfortunate and lamentable. Service advocates played on the fears generated by the railroad upheavals as a means of winning the favor of Congress. Secretary McCrary offered the same arguments found in the *Nation* and other press statements in 1877, by stressing the constabulary role of an expanded Army:

> The great value of a strong Federal force stationed in the
> vicinity of our great cities would be seen in the prevention

of mobs and violence . . . far more than in their suppression.
The Army is to the United States what a well-disciplined and
trained police force is to a city, and the one is quite as necessary
as the other.[37]

Daniel Lamont did not fall prey to fanning the flames of class conflict
in 1894, but his generals did. Major General Oliver O. Howard, in his annual
report as Commander of the Department of the East, urged doubling the
Army's enlisted strength, the service thus being "like an adequate police,
the best method of preserving the peace."[38] One of Howard's colleagues,
Brigadier General Elwell S. Otis, Department of the Columbia, recommended that federal troops in his department be garrisoned near potential
trouble spots, particularly Seattle, Spokane, and the Coeur d'Alene. Major
General John M. Schofield, commanding general, was the most outspoken
in the need for more men to deal with future domestic disorders:

> The Army has recently been required to deal with an enemy
> far more numerous and dangerous to the country than any
> savage enemy which it has heretofore been called upon to meet.
> It seems clear that the effective strength of the Army should
> now be considerably increased.[39]

The opportunism of military leaders, with their emphasis on preventing future troubles and cowing the enemy within, was an unfortunate
pandering to public anxiety. It was not reflective of their professional
opinions either. General Sherman, in late 1877, groused to his brother
that congressional refusal to expand the Army left the property owner
defenseless, but nonetheless he opposed Secretary McCrary's policy of
keeping troops in the Division of the Atlantic in anticipation of further
trouble on the railroads. In Sherman's professional judgment, the need
for troops along the Mexican border and in the Dakotas was far more
pressing. Not one general testifying before the Burnside Committee for
the reorganization of the Army in 1878 used strike duty as a justification
for reorganizing or expanding the service. The witnesses included Generals
Hancock, Schofield, and Pope, all of whom had been intimately involved
in suppressing the recent strike.[40]

Professional considerations of efficiency and effectiveness were behind
Lamont's and Schofield's 1894 recommendations for a larger enlisted

corps. The Army had sought additional men per regiment for some time in order to adopt a three-battalion regimental organization. Schofield dropped this recommendation in 1894, and used the domestic disorder argument in its stead. Clearly he believed the latter would more likely win results, noting to a friend that "the experience of last summer strongly impressed the necessity of some increase, even in quarters where such impression was difficult to make."[41]

For years, professional leaders of the Army had recommended abandoning small military posts and concentrating units of regimental size near key transportation centers. The concentration of troops, they argued, would reduce the cost of maintaining the Army and facilitate administration and training. Congress refused to approve the policy for fear of losing the pork barrel benefits of small posts scattered throughout congressional districts. In the fall of 1894, Lamont and Schofield closed several small Western posts and transferred nineteen companies of infantry and cavalry to the Department of the East. They proposed carrying out further concentrations. In his communications with Lamont, General Schofield implied that the policy was to ensure ready aid for civil officials in suppressing disorder. When influential organs of the press, especially the *New York Times* and *Army and Navy Journal*, explained the shift of troops as serving the purpose of "maintaining the respect of all classes for the laws of the United States," Schofield did nothing to discount such an interpretation.[42] He clearly intended to forestall congressional opposition to current concentration and gain approval for later consolidation. Moved primarily by professional requirements of the Army, Schofield, was willing to use the divisions created by labor disorder to further the needs of his service.[43]

Calls for a larger Army and a more active federal role in policing industrial disorders failed. Consistent Democratic opposition in Congress to enlarging the Army, a legacy of Reconstruction, was one reason for the failure. Republicans never strongly advocated a larger Army until the turn of the century in any event. In the immediate setting of the tumultuous railroad strikes, a large Army readily available for constabulary duty seemed very appealing, but the attraction did not last long. Most Americans of whatever political stripe, regardless of their momentary fears of an uncontrollable industrial proletariat, preferred in the long run to keep a small standing Army and use state and local agencies to enforce law and order.[44]

A *Harper's Weekly* editorial in 1894 expressed the prevailing American view of the role of the Army in civil disorder. The journal accepted the fact that an increase in the Army was needed for professional reasons, a goal military leaders had sought for years. Unfortunately, it went on, Generals Schofield and Howard "have sought to advance their cause by appeals to the timidity of capital. Their reports are therefore tainted by a rather high degree of demagogy." The generals had erred by entering the realm of politics, "a field of discussion which they plainly do not understand." *Harper's Weekly* urged the military men to stick to their own province and present the Army's needs in purely professional terms. The journal pointed out that whatever its problems, the service had been able to suppress the Coxey movement and Pullman strike with the resources at hand. More importantly, the editorial stressed that continual use of the Army to control civil disorder was an indication that

> republican institutions have so far failed. . . . It is for the well-being of any republic that it should not trust to a standing army, but to its citizen soldiers and its civic police for the suppression of lawless outbreaks. Dependence on the army . . . for the putting down of riots would destroy the essential republican viture of self dependence.[45]

The journal intuitively touched on the crucial point. The magazine could, and did, support federal intervention in specific instances when state and local agencies failed to quell extensive disorder. Consistent use of federal troops, however, would have eroded the moral power that accompanied the Army in the field and would almost assuredly have led to resistance and bloodshed. Familiarlity could indeed have bred contempt.[46]

Labor did not become contemptuous of the Army in the late nineteenth century. It did come to fear the service, however, recognizing that the Army was the most potent of all governmental tools available for suppressing labor. State and federal courts, police and militia, federal marshals and federal troops, "every element and force at the command of the capitalist class is being utilized and strained in order to humiliate, defeat and destroy" the efforts of workingmen.[47] But from the 1877 outbreak through the mid-1890s, the Army suffered little from laborite journalistic attack. Labor journals conducted scathing attacks on capitalists who sought an expanded Army and used their influence with government to obtain federal military intervention in labor disorders. Railroad officials, particularly Thomas Scott of the Pennsylvania Railroad, received the most attention in 1877. "What Col. Scott and the railroad kings want is that the Federal power should stand guard over this special property of theirs . . . and furnish troops . . . to shoot down strikers," the *Locomotive Firemen's Magazine* asserted.[48]

The disastrous labor failures of 1892 intensified the journalistic attacks. One journal erroneously predicted the imminent crash of capitalism, a collapse capital knew was coming. And in preparation for the cataclysm "the American capitalists have already made a compact with the National and State governments to furnish them soldiers for the expected combat."[49] Eugene Debs surveyed the defeats of that year and caustically concluded,

> We have reached that blessed era when poverty and progress, plutocrats and piracy, guns and gospel are in happy alliance. The capitalist and the scab are on top, and the armies of the Union, with shotted guns, stand guard to see that they remain on top. *Sic tiger gloria bulldog.*[50]

The Cleveland administration's use of federal courts, marshals, and troops to break the ARU strike in 1894 served to evidence the alliance between capital and government. Yet labor editorialists focused primarily on capitalists, President Cleveland, and Attorney General Richard Olney rather than the Army. Despite its opposition to the strike, the *American Federationist* branded Cleveland "Our King-President."[51] The great injustice of 1894 was that "the United States Government, through the intervention of Trust-Attorney General Olney, intervened to aid the companies by ordering troops to Chicago."[52] One of the most disturbing signs of the "increased power of the aggregated capital [was] shown in the eagerness of political and military masters to serve it without questioning."[53]

In the vitriolic assaults upon the railroads and the Cleveland administration, the Army was the last to be attacked. The *Chicago Times*, a strong supporter of the ARU and critic of government policy, even offered praise for the conduct of regular troops. The *Times* and most Chicagoans were pleased to say farewell to regulars, "the more so as they can say it in cordial, friendly tones to guests who, though they came uninvited, have done themselves naught but credit during their stay."[54]

By the conclusion of the strike, however, the tone shifted in many labor editorials assessing the use of federal military forces in labor disorders. Increasingly, editors used the term militarism, attaching a precise meaning to the phrase. Militarism meant the use of the Army to subdue organized labor in its efforts to further its interests. In a letter to President Cleveland, Eugene Debs of the ARU and James R. Sovereign of the Knights of Labor emphasized "that a deep-seated conviction is fast becoming prevalent that this government is soon to be declared a military despotism."[55] George W. Howard, vice-president of the ARU, testified to the United States Strike Commission, "I tell you the people of America have been treated so unfairly . . . that the very sight of a blue coat arouses their anger; they feel it is another instrument of oppression."[56] Despite the Socialist polemics common to radical journals, *Chicago Labor* reflected the fears of the labor movement that 1894 was a prime example of a capitalist attempt "to develop the American militarism in a most effective manner and to bring about a military rule as stringent as that of the Czar of Russia."[57]

Labor discussions of an impending militarism continued to emphasize capitalist domination of American political institutions. Nonetheless, specific attacks on individual military leaders appeared for the first time. Major General John M. Schofield, labeled "a senile old man" by the *Journal of the Knights of Labor,* was most severely criticized for his comments on the need for a larger Army to police internal enemies and his recommendations to concentrate regular troops near railroad centers.[58] The labor press also attacked General Miles. If in the past the Army had served as a tool of property, the service had been a silent instrument. Now, public comments of generals suggested that the Army was openly siding with the oppressors of workingmen. Schofield's comments implied that "he wrote every line of his report in the imaginary gore of untold millions, soon to be massacred on bloody fields of carnage and death by the barbarous vandals of organized labor."[59]

The fears expressed in 1894 appeared to be confirmed by events in 1899. Military suppression of the miners' riot in the Coeur d'Alene under a general who publicly condemned unions indicated that a restless military service was all too willing to serve at the capitalists' beck and call. Events following the Spanish-American War added to the dismay. While labor generally supported the war, it fiercely opposed imperialist expansion and increasing the Army. Union journals were gravely concerned with congressional maintenance of the 65,000 men in the regular Army raised to fight the war and the addition of 35,000 two-year volunteers in March of 1899. A larger Army could be used against American workers just as easily as it could against Filipino insurrectionists. Military expansion in 1899 seemed a final confirmation that military despotism had become entrenched in America.[60]

Federal intervention in the Coeur d'Alene and General Henry Merriam's approval of Idaho's stern policy of destroying the Western Federation of Miners engendered caustic editorial denunciation of militarism in action. In referring to the miners' fate, the *Locomotive Firemen's Magazine,* once the organ for Eugene Debs's fiery editorials, exhibited that fire again:

> If the United States military authorities treat American
> citizens in this manner, God pity the poor, ignorant
> wretches of foreign lands who fall into their power. This
> is but a taste of what is in store when militarism is in the
> saddle. Plutocracy demands an immense standing army.[61]

Government, the Army, and capital were now cooperating to the fullest. "It is the beginning of the end. Large standing armies, a party pledged to protect the trusts and combinations . . . and civil and military authority ever ready to crush labor organizations."[62]

Some editors coupled conspiracy with their doomsaying. "Farseeing reformers predict that the Cuban war was simply an excuse to increase our standing army so that the toilers could be overawed in any struggle they might inaugurate for justice."[63] The suppression of Filipino resistance was merely a warm-up for militarism at home. Intervention in Idaho had "its inspiration and justification in the policy of the Government toward its 'subjects' in the Philippines. . . . Wardner is merely the sequence of Manila."[64] In the spring of 1899, the military governors of Cuba and Puerto Rico suppressed several strikes on the two islands. They arrested native labor leaders and broke up their unions. Few union spokesmen in the United States failed to make the point that when given a free hand, American generals did not hesitate to use military force to destroy organized labor. The fact that the generals who ended strikes in the islands justified their action by making anti-labor tirades to the press further excited American labor.[65]

Labor's opposition to imperialism, its outrage at the Coeur d'Alene intervention, its fear of an enlarged Army, and above all its sense of futility brought forth the most severe attacks on the Army and its personnel during the late nineteenth century. General Merriam was subjected to the harshest attack the labor press ever conducted against an individual military figure. Milder charges compared the general to a Prussian or Russian autocrat, called him a despotic ruler, and named him a "high dignitary of American militarism."[66] The *Journal of the Knights of Labor* explained Merriam's behavior as a quest for glory. He "got no renown out of the Spanish-American War. He did not get a chance to murder the helpless natives of Luzon. But military glory he must have, and the Coeur d'Alene riot afforded the only opening."[67] It was left to the *Miner's Magazine* to savage "this pusillanimous tool in the hands of the mine operators." While Merriam's "black brutes" terrorized the imprisoned miners and their families, the general, "although far past that age . . . held high carnival in 'Wardner society' with women whose cheeks had long since lost the blush of shame." For these reasons, Merriam's name was now "synonymous with that of Benedict Arnold."[68] Merriam would never escape the shame of the Coeur d'Alene. "When he is dead working men will utter his name with contempt, for he, above all men in the United States, deserves the scorn of every working man and woman."[69]

Most of the vituperation fell on General Merriam, but professional soldiers in general came under attack in 1899. The *Pueblo Courier* described officers serving in Idaho as "reptiles who are lower in the scales of decency and morality than are the privates." They served in Idaho because "this aggregation of whisky bloats" was unfit for service in the Philippines.[70] Professional soldiers were "public paupers, better known as the 'military gentlemen' whose principal business . . . is to do the bidding of aggregated capital and 'crush out organized labor.' "[71] The demands of warfare were brutal. "To do this work . . . requires a species of half ape, half tiger, to whom the sight of suffering makes happy."[72]

The strident labor critique of the Army at the turn of the century was partly the product of twenty-five years of sad experience. Working-class perceptions of the service were shaped not only by the experiences of 1877, 1892, and 1899, but by the frequent use of the National Guard. Guardsmen, after all, were garbed in the official uniform of the U.S. Army and often instructed by regular officers at summer camp. Labor feared the "military," not simply regular soldiers. Their fears were grounded in reality. The Army's participation in the destruction of the WFM in 1899, was the latest in a long chain of civics lessons on the locus of power in industrial America. The fact that overseas expansion coincidently brought increases in the Army's manpower during a flagrant misuse of the service intensified long-standing working-class worries about the military.

Underlying the sharp rhetoric of class conflict, however, were older attitudes that persisted throughout the late nineteenth century. Even the events of 1899 did not lead to clarion calls to the barricades to resist the hated "blue coats" or to destroy a plutocratic-dominated government. In part, labor leaders were constrained to issue calls for resistance because experience had taught them that it would lead to bloodshed and likely defeat. Far more important was the fact that most union spokesmen and the vast majority of workingmen eschewed violence as a tactic and revolution as an end. Their views of the military were only partly the products of the struggles associated with rising industrialism. To a great extent, labor opposition to an enlarged Army intervening directly and frequently in civil disorder came from the same sources that led *Harper's Weekly* to oppose a permanent federal industrial constabulary.

Labor journals expressed mistrust for the military in terms that were as old as the nation and far removed from a conscious Marxian analysis of a standing army as a suppressor of the proletariat. Reflecting a distaste for a regular army that had been voiced in pre-Revolutionary tracts and again during Andrew Jackson's tenure as president, the National Labor Union spoke out against the Army a decade before the first great railroad strike, maintaining that "standing armies are dangerous to the liberties of the people, that they entail heavy and unnecessary burden on the productive industries, and should be reduced to the lowest standard."[73] In 1900, the Western Federation of Miners condemned the Army in similar tones. "Aside from the enormous expense a large military establishment imposes on the producers of the nation," the miners argued, history and recent experience proved once again that a standing army was "the chosen weapon of tyrants, a deadly foe to the individual rights of the common people and incompatible with free institutions."[74] Standing armies, with their overprivileged officer corps, were simply a refuge for "hundreds and thousands of lackeys, dressed up at the expense of the people, bowing and scraping to the Commander-in-Chief of the Army, and all following the teachings of military governments of Europe."[75]

A large professional military service threatened the fundamental values of the United States. Unless watched carefully, regular soldiers would interfere in the civilian affairs of the republic, prostituting the constituted political processes. The Army should be kept small, subservient to civilian authority, and sent back "to their commands at the sea-coast fortifications and frontier posts, where the display of arms is in accord with original intent—that of the 'prevention of armed invasion.' "[76] Because military officers were idlers, aristocrats contemptuous of ordinary folk, it was far better to

> hide out of sight the whole business of strutting gilt lace, sword jingle and circus trapping that makes every West Point cadet and small officer swell up in pompous arrogance, as if he were a little tin god looking down in sneering contempt on the whole work-a-day world below![77]

When the professional soldier's moral life was examined, "we find that invariably his life is one of debauchery. Licentiousness everywhere."[78] Regulars could undermine both the political and moral values of the country.

More dangerous was the fact that regulars were unthinking mercenaries "governed by articles of war . . . regulations, orders and unwritten usages . . . applied by court martial made up of officers . . . answerable to their military superiors only."[79] They were mindless professionals "who know and care nothing about the grievance of the people."[80] The end product was a General Merriam who

> only knows how to kill people in the most effective way. He understands nothing but brute force. He has been educated to believe himself the instrument of his superiors to kill, slay, imprison or otherwise destroy upon the order to do it. It is not his duty to reason why. He is not of the people. He belongs to the army.[81]

Although such stereotypes were given greater impetus by military intervention in labor disputes, they were also stock images from a long-standing Anglo-American dislike for regular soldiers. Like past critics of the military, labor did not call for abolition of the Army but for a reduction in its forces or at most maintenance of the 25,000-man enlisted strength. The functions of a regular force were to be defense and policing the frontier, not the suppression of civil disorder. If war were to come, labor's prescription was the same as past opponents of a standing army, the citizen-soldier volunteer. In opposing calls for a larger Army in 1894, the *National Labor Tribune* reiterated this old theme. "The citizen soldiery saved the Union . . . in 1861-5, . . . a soldiery made up of the militia of the states and recruited from all conditions of citizens. A similarly constituted soldiery can save the republic again if necessity arise."[82]

In 1899, the *Western Laborer* rejected "a hireling and mercenary army in the hands of satraps like Otis and Merriam." It called for a return to past policies, for "our armies have always been of and from the people, and volunteers have always been called in emergencies."[83] Except for the Mexican War, volunteers had served only in the defense of the nation. Volunteers had a vested interest in society, as they owned property, earned their living, and cared for their country and government. Such was not the case with regulars, as could be seen in the type of men being recruited for the newly expanded Army of 1899. The new recruits had none of the virtues of volunteers. After 1898, "the places of these volunteers are now being taken by a mercenary army . . . Hessians in every sense of the word." Plutocrats desired an Army of this sort, "an army not drawn from the homes of people but off the streets and out of the slums . . . who care nothing about the country or its institutions."[84]

However incongruous labor support for volunteers seemed, incongruous because the hated state militias made up the core of the 1898 volunteer force, and National Guard officers commanded the units, the support was heartfelt nonetheless. The editor of that virulently anti-military journal *Miner's Magazine* praised volunteers in terms that could have come from the pen of any ardent National Guardsman in the late nineteenth century. "The glory of our republic has been written with the valor and blood of our volunteers. They founded it and they have defended it and made it great."[85] The endorsement of volunteers carried over into war in 1898, when the labor press supported the war effort and laboring men joined state regiments. Disillusionment set in when imperialism led to demobilization of the volunteers and a corresponding increase in the regular service for overseas duty. John Peter Altgeld attacked the McKinley administration's new military policy in traditional phrases:

> The volunteer carries a conscience as well as a gun. That kind
> of soldier is invincible when fighting for liberty and his country,
> but is not considered absolutely reliable when it comes to doing
> dastardly work. For this purpose we must have regular soldiers.[86]

Traditional attitudes towards American military practices in general
and the Army in particular shared by most of the larger society contributed
substantially to labor's perception of military institutions. The experiences of the immediate past intensified long-standing fears of a regular
army as a potential source of tyranny and suppression. Despite the class
conflict tone of labor press rhetoric, most working-class assessments of
American society did not see government or the Army as inherently anti-
labor, as institutions enmeshed in the hegemony of industrial capitalism.
It was obvious that capitalists controlled governmental institutions and
that the Army served solely the interests of property. But labor saw the
Army as a mindless, mercenary instrument misused by a government
temporarily captured by plutocrats, not as a service officered by men
who were the social and political peers of capitalists and imbued with
corporate values.

The *Iron Molder's Journal* called for vigorous political action in 1877,
to place men in office who would not kowtow to the likes of Thomas
Scott.

> When a government founded on the great principle of
> equal and exact justice to all men, can, at the dictation
> of one man, and he a railroad king, launch the United
> States troops into a State . . . then the boasted name of
> a free government loses all its prestige.[87]

The massive use of federal force in 1894 led another labor journal to urge
working men to act "with ballots, not bullets, and with undeviating patriotic
purpose to restore equality."[88] Once control of government was wrenched
from the privileged few and returned to the people, the abusive use of
judicial and military power by one group against another would end. "The
function of the federal jurisdiction is most essentially that of a judge or
umpire between all parties," a labor reformer wrote in 1894. The shame
of that year was that "the government has acted as though the railroads
alone had rights." Government was supposed to be neutral, justice blind.[89]

The Army was expected to act neutrally as well. In Chicago, *Twentieth Century* argue, "With the very first order for the troops to march, there ought to have been a proclamation calling the railroads as well as the strikers to account. . . . Then the soldiers would have been simply suppressors of violence, not ex parte hirelings of one side."[90] Grand Master Workman of the Knights of Labor, James R. Sovereign, offered the same complaint.

> The wickedest part of the strike was the part played by the government. We do not refer to its putting down of violence. That was well. All true friends of labor wish violence put down. We refer to the way in which it did it.[91]

Eugene Debs, in his comments on Nelson A. Miles's actions in Chicago, echoed the plaintive refrain. "It was believed his mission here was to preserve and maintain order, not to take an active part in the strike, nor to defeat the strike. . . . But the fact is, he was in active alliance with the general managers, not only to maintain order, but to suppress the strike."[92]

Labor's reaction to the Army's role in industrial disorders indicated ambiguity. Union spokesmen simultaneously depicted the service as a tyrannical, pliant tool of plutocracy and yet expressed disappointment when it failed to show neutrality. In part this was a legacy of past conceptions of a standing army, which presupposed that society as a whole would not tolerate military intervention in civil affairs. There was little in the traditional view that explained a circumstance in which *civilian* leaders ordered out the Army to act against a segment of civilian society. Nominally, laboring men desired a federal force which had, to cite the *Chicago Tribune* again, "no sympathy with any class" and was "colorless in sentiment."[93] The *Tribune,* however, praised regular troops in this manner precisely because they did not side with strikers, as the National Guard sometimes did. Both the labor and the popular press perceived the Army as highly disciplined and efficient, but to the former this meant harsh, unsympathetic suppression, and to the latter a ready restoration of order. The labor and popular press shared a common rhetoric which expressed fears of too large a standing army but agreed not at all as to what was a "large standing army." Fundamentally, it was not the Army at all but the law and changing values that were at issue. Labor looked to a legal and value system which emphasized the rights of individuals.

Industrial capitalism and a large portion of the public press stressed property rights. The Army served as the arbiter in crucial struggles between these two views, an arbiter committed to the latter perspective.[94]

While testifying to a Senate investigating committee, a Chicago laborer recalled that during the 1877 railroad strike, strikers quickly submitted to federal troops after defying National Guardsmen. When asked why, he replied, "I believe the reason they submitted to the national [troops] was owing to them knowing that they knew they were regular soldiers, and not hired men, as they thought this militia was."[95] By the end of the century, as evidenced in the emotional outburst from the labor press at the actions of the Army in the Coeur d'Alene, most workingmen saw the Army as hired men. While the service was not solely responsible for this development, the actions and statements of officers helped to confirm in labor's eyes the belief that in the struggle over values the Army clearly favored capital.

Notes

1. July 23, 1877, in Executive Mansion Telegrams, book I, 236, Rutherford B. Hayes Papers, R. B. Hayes Library, Fremont, Ohio.

2. July 11, 1894, series 2, reel 85, microfilm, Grover Cleveland Papers, Library of Congress.

3. Hayes received numerous telegrams and petitions during the strike. The Hayes Library has collected all correspondence pertaining to the strike and placed them under one heading. The library also has on microfilm a variety of newspaper clippings and miscellaneous correspondence relating to the strike. For 1894, similar correspondence may be found in series 2, reel 85, microfilm, Cleveland Papers; and in the Walter Q. Gresham Papers and the Daniel S. Lamont Papers, Library of Congress. Tenders of service from National Guardsmen and Civil War Veterans are scattered throughout the Adjutant General's Office consolidated file 10, 1894, Record Group 94, National Archives. Also see Wallace E. Davies, *Patriotism on Parade: The Story of Veterans' and Hereditary Organizations in America* (Cambridge, Mass., 1955), pp. 288-95, 339-40; and Mary Dearing, *Veterans in Politics: The Story of the G.A.R.* (Baton Rouge, La., 1955), pp. 441-43.

4. July 19, 1877.

5. Vol. 17, no. 15 (July 12, 1894): 329.

6. July 25, 1877. The role of the press during the two great railroad

strikes is noted in Robert V. Bruce, *1877: Year of Violence* (New York, 1959), pp. 162-64, *passim;* Almont Lindsey, *The Pullman Strike* (Chicago, 1942), chap. 13.

7. July 13, 1892, p. 4.

8. Vol. 50, no. 1 (July 7, 1894): 8. Editorial condemnation of labor's threat to property rights was widespread in the late nineteenth century. See, as examples, *Harper's Weekly* 21, no. 1077 (August 18, 1877): 638; *Unitarian Review* 8, no. 3 (September 1877): 311-13; *The Independent* 46, no. 2379 (July 5, 1894): 858; *Leslie's Weekly* 75, no. 1924 (July 28, 1892): 74.

9. July 23, 1877, p. 4.

10. *Unitarian Review* 8, no. 3 (September 1877): 312-13.

11. Vol. 38, no. 1960 (July 14, 1894): 651.

12. July 5, 1894, p. 1. Underlying the harsh editorial calls for the repression of working-class protests and incipient violence was a deep fear that social disorder would spread, that the dissolution of society was likely to be the end result of labor upheavals. Morton Keller, *Affairs of State: Public Life in Late Nineteenth Century America* (Cambridge, Mass., 1977), pp. 404-05, 486, 489, 491, contends that the tension between old values and the burgeoning new industrial order was the source of middle and upper-class concerns for social order. The history of the labor movement reinforces Keller's thesis. The labeling of labor protests as basic threats to society was ironic considering that the vast majority of unions, labor leaders, and working people eschewed violence as a valid tactic. See Philip Taft and Philip Ross, "American Labor Violence; Its Cause, Character and Outcome," in *Violence in America: Historical and Comparative Perspectives,* A Report to the National Commission on the Causes and Prevention of Violence, June 1969, ed. Hugh D. Graham and Ted R. Gurr (New York, 1969), pp. 270-76. Also of value here are Gerald N. Grob, *Workers and Utopia: A Study of Ideological Conflict in the American Labor Movement 1865-1900* (Chicago, 1969), *passim:* Herbert Gutman "Work Culture and Society in Industrializing America, 1815-1919," *American Historical Review* 78, no. 3 (June 1973): 567-80.

13. Vol. 25, no. 631 (August 2, 1877): 68.

14. *Chicago Tribune,* July 26, 1877, p. 4.

15. July 24, 1877, p. 4.

16. *Boston Evening Transcript* as quoted in *Army and Navy Journal* 31, no. 47 (July 14, 1894): 804. Surveys of major newspapers and magazines for 1877 and 1894 indicate that praise for the efficiency and discipline of regular troops was the most common editorial observation on the Army's role in the railroad strikes.

17. *Army and Navy Register* 16, no. 1 (July 7, 1894): 9.

18. *Chicago Tribune,* July 26, 1877, p. 4.

19. *Army and Navy Register* 16, no. 1 (July 7, 1894): 9.

20. See, as well, *Philadelphia Inquirer,* August 1, 1877, p. 4; *Army and Navy Journal* 36, no. 46 (July 7, 1894); 789.

21. *Chicago Tribune,* July 26, 1877, p. 4.

22. August 1, 1877, p. 4.

23. *Army and Navy Register* 16, no. 1 (July 7, 1894): 9. Also see *The Nation* 25, no. 631 (August 2, 1877): 68, and 59, no. 1516 (July 19, 1894): 40.

24. *Philadelphia Inquirer,* July 23, 1877, p. 4.

25. "The Recent Strikes," *North American Review* 125, no. 528 (September-October 1877): 351-62.

26. See a series of editorials in the *Spokesman-Review* (Spokane), July 8, 9, 12, 16, 1894, and the relevent discussion in Chapter 7.

27. Vol. 25, no. 632 (August 9, 1877): 85.

28. Vol. 25, no. 635 (August 30, 1877): 131. Also see 25, no. 630 (July 26, 1877): 50.

29. July 27, 1877, p. 2.

30. *The Army and Navy Journal,* a staunch Army supporter, reviewed editorial calls for a larger service in vol. 14, no. 51 (July 28, 1877): 813, and 15, no. 2 (August 18, 1877): 26-27. The *New York Times, Philadelphia Inquirer,* and *Chicago Tribune* supported this increase in editorials in July and August. As other examples, see Goldwin Smith, "The Labour War in the United States, *The Contemporary Review* 30 (September 1877): 539; F. Whittaker, "The American Army," *The Galaxy* 24, no. 3 (September 1877): 396; James Harrison Wilson, "The Size and Organization of Armies, *International Review* (July 1878): 515. Among many denunciations of the Democrats' attempt to reduce the Army, the most critical were *The Nation* 25, no. 646 (November 15, 1877), and *Harper's Weekly* 21, no. 1092 (December 1, 1877): 939, 948.

31. Vol. 31, no. 47 (July 14, 1894): 798.

32. As quoted in *Public Opinion* 17, no. 17 (July 26, 1894): 384.

33. Vol. 10, no. 3 (September 1894): 252.

34. June 24, 1899, p. 6. From May through August of 1894, the *Army and Navy Journal* conducted a strong editorial campaign to expand the Army. Merely as examples, see vol. 31, no. 37 (May 5, 1894): 629, and 31, no. 53 (August 25, 1894): 913. Favorable press opinion on the necessity for a military increase was reviewed in *Public Opinion* 17, no. 17 (July 26, 1894): 384; 17, no. 29 (October 18, 1894): 689; 17, no. 33 (November 8, 1894): 789. Lester D. Langley, "The Democratic Tradition

and Military Reform 1878-1885," *Southwestern Social Science Quarterly*
48, no. 2 (September 1967): 200, notes that an influential minority of
the press of the 1870s and 1880s was "prepared to *accept* and *use* the
army for *national* needs."

35. August 1, 1877, in consolidated file 4042, AGO, RG94. NA.

36. See McCrary's comments in *Sec. War Rept. 1877,* pp. iv-vi; Lamont's
in *Sec. War Rept. 1894,* pp. 6-11. The comments of Schofield, Major
General Oliver O. Howard, and Brigadier General Elwell S. Otis in *Sec.
War Rept. 1894,* pp. 58-62, 102-03, 151-53, respectively, are revealing.
Upton's recommendation in a letter to Schofield, July 28, 1877, in series
4, Letters Received, John M. Schofield Papers, Library of Congress, Washington, D.C.

37. *Sec. War Rept. 1877,* p. v.

38. *Sec. War Rept. 1894,* p. 102.

39. *Ibid.,* p. 59.

40. See Sherman to John Sherman, November 12, 1877, in M.A. De-
Wolfe, ed., *Home Letters of General Sherman* (New York, 1909), p. 387;
Sherman to General Philip Sheridan, November 29, 1877, Letterbook,
September 19, 1872-February 15, 1878, p. 364, in William T. Sherman
Papers, Library of Congress; Sherman's comments in his annual report,
Sec. War Rept. 1878, p. 7. On the Burnside Committee, see U.S., Congress,
Joint Committee on the Reorganization of the Army, *Report and Papers
on Bill S. 1491,* 45th Cong., 3rd sess., S. Rept. 555, pts. 1, 2 (Washington,
D.C., 1879), pp. 426-44, 245-47, 451-52, comments by Hancock, Scho-
field, and Pope, respectively.

41. To John Bigelow, October 29, 1894, in Letters Sent, 1894, pp.
508-10, Headquarters of the Army, Record Group 108, National Archives.
See similar arguments by Schofield to William F. Draper, Member of the
House, July 7, 1894, and Senator James McMillan, October 3, 1894, in
Ibid., pp. 325-26, 550, respectively.

42. *New York Times,* September 25, 1894, p. 2.

43. A review of the annual reports of Secretaries of War and Commanding
Generals from the late 1870s through the 1890s indicates that concentrating regiments near railroad centers was a goal long sought by Army leaders.
Only Schofield used domestic disorders as a justification for the policy.
The policy was briefly noted in *Sec. War Rept. 1894,* pp. 10, 60. General
Order No. 45, as printed in *Army and Navy Register* 16, no. 12 (September 22, 1894): 185, announced the policy to the Army. Schofield's explanation for concentration to Lamont in a letter, September 5, 1894,
no. 623, Letters Sent, 1894 HQA, RG108, NA, and memo dated September
15, Miscellaneous Memoranda, lot D, Schofield Papers. Press comments

on the policy included *New York Times,* September 25, 1894, p. 2, September 29, 1894, p. 4; *Harper's Weekly* 38, no. 1971 (September 29, 1894): 915; *Army and Navy Journal* 31, no. 13 (November 24, 1894): 198.

44. For examples of this position, see *Review of Reviews* 10, no. 2 (August 1894): 132-33; D. McG. Means, "Principles Involved in the Recent Strikes," *The Forum* 17 (August 1894): 638.

45. Vol. 38, no. 1975 (October 27, 1894): 1011.

46. *Harper's Weekly* was by no means the only journal that supported the use of federal troops for specific outbreaks of disorder but opposed the adoption of a general federal military policing policy. See, e.g., *Unitarian Review* 8, no. 3 (September 1877): 311-17; *Chicago Times,* July 31, 1877, p. 4; statements excerpted from the *Washington Capital* and *Baltimore Evening Bulletin* in *Army and Navy Journal* 15, no. 2 (August 18, 1877): 4; *San Francisco Chronicle,* July 18, 1894, p. 4; *The Outlook* 50, no. 23 (October 1894): 971-72; *The Omaha Bee,* cited in *Public Opinion* 17, no. 33 (November 2, 1894): 788. Two-thirds of the newspapers excerpted in *Public Opinion,* and vol. 17, no. 29 (October 18, 1894): 689, opposed Schofield's concentration policy for reasons similar to the *Harper's Weekly* editorial. The American preference for state and local control of public affairs remained strong in the late nineteenth century despite the centralizing tendencies evident in economic activities. Morton Keller, in *Affairs of State,* especially pp. 289-97, makes a strong argument for viewing the federal government in the Gilded Age in these terms.

47. Comments of Samuel Gompers to the American Federation of Labor in convention, 1892, as quoted in *Iron Molder's Journal* (November 1892): 5.

48. Vol. 1, no. 12 (November 1877): 368. Organized labor played only a small part in the conflict between working people and employers in the late nineteenth century. The consequence of this fact makes it difficult to determine how workers viewed the role of the Army in suppressing labor disorders. Periodicals published by unions nonetheless provide one means of gauging workers' reactions to the presence of federal military forces in labor upheavals and are the main source for this section.

49. *Journal of the Knights of Labor* 13, no. 12 (September 15, 1892): 1.

50. *Locomotive Firemen's Magazine* 16, no. 9 (September 1892): 780. Other examples of union attacks on capitalistic use of the instruments of government to thwart workers found in *National Labor Tribune* 5, no. 38 (September 22, 1877): 2; *Locomotive Engineer's Journal* 11,

no. 9 (September 1877): 418; *Twentieth Century* 9, no. 5 (July 28, 1892): 1; *Cleveland Citizen* 2, no. 81 (August 13, 1892): 3.

51. Vol. 1, no. 8 (October 1894): 173.

52. *Journal of the Knights of Labor* 15, no. 3 (July 12, 1894): 1.

53. *Cleveland Citizen* 4, no. 183 (July 28, 1894): 2.

54. July 18, 1894, p. 4. Not surprisingly, the labor journalistic attack on the Cleveland administration was widespread, led by Eugene Debs in the pages of the *Locomotive Firemen's Magazine,* as in 18 (October 1894): 974-75. See as well, e.g., *Twentieth Century* 13, no. 3 (July 19, 1894): 3; *Chicago Searchlight* 1, no. 7 (July 19, 1894): 2; *Cigar Makers' Journal* 19, no. 10 (July 1894): 8; *Journal of the Knights of Labor* 15, no. 9 (August 23, 1894): 2. Also see comments of Samuel Gompers in *Report,* Proceedings of the Fourteenth Annual Convention of the American Federation of Labor, December 1894 (New York, 1895), p. 11.

55. *Journal of the Knights of Labor* 15, no. 3 (July 1894): 1.

56. In U.S. Strike Commission, *Report on the Chicago Strike of June-July 1894,* 53rd Cong., 3rd sess., Senate Executive Document 7 (Washington, D.C. 1895), p. 39.

57. Vol. 2, no. 14 (October 20, 1894): 4. As other examples, see *Journal of the Knights of Labor* 15, no. 17 (October 18, 1894): 2; B. O. Flower, "Fostering the Savage in Our Young," *Arena* 10, no. 57 (August 1894): 422-32, and idem, "Plutocracy's Bastiles: Or Why Our Republic is Becoming an Armed Camp," *Arena* 10, no. 59 (October 1894): 601-21.

58. Vol. 15, no. 17 (October 18, 1894): 2.

59. Comments of James R. Sovereign, in *Proceedings of the General Assembly of the Knights of Labor,* 18th reg. sess., 1894 (Philadelphia, 1894), p. 5. See also *National Labor Tribune* 22, no. 39 (September 20, 1894): 1; *Twentieth Century* 13, no. 24 (December 13, 1894): 2; *Locomotive Firemen's Magazine* 18 (October 1894): 974; John Swinton, *Striking for Life: Labor's Side of the Labor Question* (n.p., 1894), pp. 220-22, 225-26.

60. For labor reactions to the war and the Philippine Insurrection, see John C. Appel, "The Relationship of American Labor to United States Imperialism 1895-1905" (Ph.D. diss. University of Wisconsin, 1950), pp. 11-19, 82-83, 122-23, 155-56, 262-67. Appel also discusses labor reactions to increases in the Army. Also see Philip S. Foner, *History of the Labor Movement in the United States,* vol. 2 (New York, 1947), pp. 413-29, and David Levin, "Organized Labor and the Military, 1897-1917" (Master's thesis, University of Wisconsin, 1950), pp. 30-41, 44-59. Russell F. Weigley, *History of the United States Army* (New York, 1967),

pp. 307-09, notes the military expansion. Most labor journals condemned both imperialism and military growth, e.g., *American Federationist* 6, no. 5 (July 1899): 7; *Locomotive Firemen's Magazine* 26, no. 4 (April 1899): 379-85, which includes citations from many other labor journals.

61. Vol. 27, no. 1 (July 1899): 44.

62. *Denver Industrial Advocate* 6, no. 354 (May 12, 1899); 2. Also see *Boilermaker and Iron Ship Builder* 11, no. 6 (June 1899): 163; *American Federationist* 6, no. 7 (September 1899): 147-50; *The Pueblo Courier* 8, no. 376 (September 29, 1899): 1; *Cleveland Citizen* 9, no. 17 (May 20, 1899): 2. *Miner's Magazine,* official organ for the Western Federation of Miners, which began publication in 1900, was the most caustic and consistent labor critic of the military; see, e.g., Vol. 1, no. 7 (August 1900): 13-15, 3, no. 1 (January 1902): 30-33.

63. *Industrial Woodworker* 8 (May 1899): 49.

64. *Coast Seamen's Journal* 12, no. 35 (May 31, 1899): 7.

65. Appel, "Labor and Imperialism," pp. 190-95, 206-09, 216-19, 220-35; Foner, *History of Labor in the U.S.,* vol. 2, pp. 430-32. Labor's growing distrust of the Army noted in comments of General Secretary-Treasurer John W. Hayes, Knights of Labor, in *Proceedings of the General Assembly of the Knights of Labor,* 23rd reg. sess., 1899 (Washington, D.C., 1899), pp. 21-24; *American Federationist* 6, no. 5 (July 1899): 97-100; *Western Laborer* 8, no. 53 (July 18, 1899): 1; *Coast Seamen's Journal* 12, no. 34 (May 24, 1899): 6; Comments of Samuel Gompers, American Federation of Labor, in *Report,* of the 19th Annual Convention of the American Federation of Labor, 1899 (Washington, D.C., 1899), p. 16.

66. *Typographical Journal* 14, no. 10 (May 15, 1899): 418; *Pueblo Courier* 8, no. 358 (May 26, 1899): 5; *Locomotive Firemen's Magazine* 27, no. 2 (August 1899): 139, respectively.

67. Vol. 19, no. 13 (May 1900). Similar view in *Miner's Magazine* 1, no. 2 (February 1900): 1.

68. Vol. 1, no. 2 (January 1900): 19.

69. Vol. 2, no. 12 (December 1901): 22. Levin, "Organized Labor and the Military," pp. 61-63, notes militant anti-militarism of the *Miner's Magazine* and the WFM. As noted in Chapter 7, labor attacks on General Merriam were widespread. See, e.g., *Journal of the Knights of Labor* 19, no. 11 (March 1900): 1; *United Mine Workers' Journal* 10, no. 9 (June 8, 1899); 4; *Industrial Advocate* 6, no. 360 (June 23, 1899): 2; *Iron Molder's Journal* 35, no. 7 (July 1899): 355; *International Woodworker* 8 (October 1899): 112.

70. Vol. 8, no. 378 (October 13, 1899): 1.

71. *Denver Industrial Advocate* 6, no. 357 (June 2, 1899): 2.

72. *Miner's Magazine* 2, no. 3 (March 1901): 7. Also see *Coast Seamen's Journal* 12, no. 38 (June 21, 1899): 6.

73. In U.S. Industrial Commission, "Labor Organizations, Labor Disputes and Arbitration," vol. 17 of the commission's reports, 57th Cong., 1st sess., House Document 186 (Washington, D.C., 1902), p. 2.

74. *Miner's Magazine* 1, no. 6 (June 1900): 16.

75. Remarks of General Secretary-Treasurer John W. Hayes, Knights of Labor, in *Proceedings of the General Assembly of the Knights of Labor,* 24th sess., November, 1900 (Washington, D.C., 1900), p. 20. See Don Higginbotham, *The War of American Independence: Military Attitudes, Policies, and Practice, 1763-1789* (New York, 1971), chaps. 1-3, on pre-Revolutionary military attitudes. General discussions of American conceptions of a standing army and professional soldiers are found in Arthur A. Ekirch, Jr., *The Civilian and the Military* (New York, 1956), especially chaps. 1, 4, 5, 8; and C. Robert Kemble, *The Image of the Army Officer in America: Background for Current Views* (Westport, Conn., 1973), sections 2, 4, and chap. 15.

76. Resolution adopted by the American Federation of Labor, in *Proceedings of the American Federation of Labor,* 16th Annual Convention, 1896 (Washington, D.C., 1896), p. 87.

77. *Cleveland Citizen* 2, no. 81 (August 13, 1892): 3.

78. *Miner's Magazine* 1, no. 10 (October 1900): 9.

79. *Boilermaker and Iron Ship Builder* 11, no. 6 (June 1, 1899): 162.

80. *National Labor Tribune* 5, no. 38 (September 2, 1877): 2.

81. *Western Laborer* 8, no. 45 (May 20, 1899): 2. As examples of traditional opposition to standing armies expressed by labor journals throughout the period, see *National Labor Tribune* 5, no. 32 (August 11, 1877): 1; *Cleveland Citizen* 4, no. 196 (October 27, 1894): 1; *Coast Seamen's Journal* 2, no. 37 (June 14, 1899): 6; *Cigar Maker's Journal* 24, no. 10 (July 1899): 8; *Railroad Trainmen's Journal* 16, no. 3 (March 1899): 285-86.

82. Vol. 22, no. 38 (September 13, 1894): 1.

83. Vol. 8, no. 45 (May 20, 1899): 2.

84. *Ibid.* 9, no. 3 (July 29, 1899): 2.

85. Vol. 1, no. 9 (September 1900): 31.

86. Quoted in *Ibid.* For other examples of labor calls for a return to the volunteer policy, see *Locomotive Firemen's Magazine* 27, no. 1 (July 1899): 26; *Pueblo Courier* 8, no. 368 (August 4, 1899): 1; resolution adopted by American Federation of Labor at its 1899 convention, in *Report,* Proceedings of the 19th Annual Convention, p. 33.

87. August 10, 1899, p. 418.

88. *National Labor Tribune* 22, no. 38 (September 13, 1894): 1.

89. "A Review of the Chicago Strike of '94," *Arena* 10, no. 58 (September 1894): 525, 515, respectively. Also see E. H. Heywood, "The Great Strike: Its Relation to Labor, Property and Government," *Radical Review* (November 1877): 556, 563; *Twentieth Century* 9, no. 5 (July 28, 1892): 1.

90. Vol. 13, no. 3 (July 19, 1894): 1.

91. *Journal of the Knights of Labor* 15, no. 9 (August 23, 1894): 1.

92. In U.S. Strike Commission, *Report on the Chicago Strike,* pp. 144-45.

93. July 26, 1877, p. 4.

94. Keller, in *Affairs of State,* part 2, discusses the conflict between old values and the new industrial order at length.

95. Testimony of Richard Powers, in U.S., Congress, Senate, Select Committee, *Facts in relation to the employment for private purposes of armed bodies of men, or detectives, in connection with differences between workmen and employers,* 52nd Cong., 2nd sess., S. Rept. 1280 (Washington, D.C., 1892), p. 112.

9 The Army and Civil Disorder

The political-military context within which the Army intervened in labor disorders contributed substantially to working-class perceptions of the service as "hired men" throughout the late nineteenth century. Federal labor policy was poorly defined, and lack of an established policy was a significant cause of the 1899 debacle in Idaho. Congress's failure to provide either the president or federal courts with guidelines to follow when intervening in labor disputes forced officials to make policy on an ad hoc basis. Federal judges worked to fill the void of statute law. Fearful of state interference with property rights as well as labor's challenge to the will of property owners, federal judges relied increasingly on constitutional interpretation and the injunction to preserve the rights of property and restrain labor. Judges were mainly responsible for what little federal policy there was that dealt with labor problems.[1]

Presidents did not have the advantages of interpretive authority or legal precedent, and there was little carry-over of the processes and purposes determining federal military intervention in labor from administration to administration. In the War Department, the Adjutant General's Office drew on past experience to guide secretaries of war and presidents. All too often, however, the only advice the adjutant general offered was procedural; that is, he informed his superiors on the mechanics of how federal troops had been committed to domestic duty in the past. Lacking law and consistent practice as guidelines, presidents relied on others— state governors, federal judges, cabinet members, or corporate officials— to define the necessity for federal intervention.[2]

Reluctance marked presidential commitment of federal troops in the late nineteenth century. Presidents, however, rarely exercised supervision of the conduct of troops in the field to ensure discreet use of federal power. The chain of command was neglected, and others actually determined the purpose and manner in which troops were used. No president expressly set out to destroy unions, rather each justified intervention on the grounds of maintaining order or enforcing the law. Given the nature of the American legal system and the values governing the use of property in the Gilded Age, the mere enforcement of law and maintenance of order would have broken most strikes whatever the intent or sympathies of presidents. Yet, since Hayes, Harrison, Cleveland, and McKinley dispensed with supervising the activities of federal forces, federal marshals and soldiers too often ended up serving wealth and property openly.

This implicit support for corporate values did not lead to unrestrained violence on the part of regular Army officers. As veterans of the Civil War, the men who led the Army on federal strike duty knew full well the results of applied firepower and displayed little inclination to use such tactics on disorderly strikers. The opportunity for the use of firearms by the Army was always present, particularly in such tense places as Johnstown, Pennsylvania, Baltimore, and Chicago, in 1877; in Chicago, Sacramento, Livingston, Montana, and other Western railroad towns in 1894; and in the Coeur d'Alene in 1892 and 1899, where the striking miners were known to be well armed. Yet the Army did not succumb to indiscriminate violence. The war experience had taught these men that to kill on a mass scale was not only ugly and costly but also highly unlikely to produce a change of heart in one's fellow citizens. War had taught as well the necessity, in the face of great pressure and danger, to keep calm, to assess the situation fully before acting, and to act prudently. There was no immediate applicability of skills and experience gained in combat to the suppression of civil disorder, but the discipline and command responsibility learned in war were sound guides to restoring civil peace.

More applicable was the background Army officers acquired in wartime occupation duty and during Reconstruction. Throughout the war, officers found themselves responsible for supervising the policing of occupied Southern cities and regulating civil affairs pending the restoration of civilian governments. They performed the same functions during Reconstruction. Within the postwar service there was a large reservoir of officers acquainted with what could only be called government, and they had learned that armed force had very distinct limitations as a method for governing.

The experienced Civil War commander had learned as well that in the American military system pure military authority was consistently diluted by civilian political demands. State governors insisted that commanders take care of their volunteer troops properly. The volunteers themselves brought essentially civilian ideas with them to the Army and refused to surrender all of those attitudes. The wise commander made the best of both conditions for they were unavoidable. Civilian political leaders interfered in the conduct of military operations, far too often and ineptly in the eyes of many officers, but that interference could neither be stopped nor ignored. The nature of American civil-military relations forced military leaders to consider non-military factors in all their actions and embedded in the officer corps a concern for civilian opinion that could not but act as a restraint upon their activity, be it the conduct of war or the suppression of civil disorder. This was the strength of the American system, whatever its occasional weaknesses, and most military men still in the Army after 1865 had learned it.

The value of Civil War duty at the higher levels of command to the conduct of strike duty is best seen by comparing the performance of Brigadier General Henry C. Merriam in 1899, with that of Winfield S. Hancock in 1877, and that of John M. Schofield and his department commanders in 1894. Merriam, by any measure, made a mess of the entire Cœur d'Alene operation. That he had had no significant command experience during the war showed in his supervision of the Idaho intervention. Even the erratic Nelson A. Miles managed to restrain his actions in 1894, regardless of the violence of his rhetoric. Merriam's failure was a compound of many factors, one of which was his lack of command responsibility in the Civil War.

Bereft of a well-defined presidential policy and cut loose from direct civilian supervision, General Merriam had no other guide to follow but his own background, instincts, and notions. They failed him. A military system that relied upon the intuitive abilities and sagacity of its officers gained in a war now three decades in the past was a flawed system. But ultimately the burden of responsibility fell on President McKinley, where it rightly belonged, and McKinley's failure was one shared by the other presidents who committed federal troops to strike duty in the late nineteenth century. This becomes more evident when early twentieth-century presidential policy is examined. The use of regulars in labor disorders increased in frequency in the first two decades of the twentieth century, but their role was more impartial than had been the case in the previous twenty-five years. First and foremost, either the president or secretary of war exercised close supervision of regulars on duty in industrial upheavals. Secondly, both Theodore Roosevelt and Woodrow Wilson sent personal representatives into states requesting federal troops to investigate the nature of disturbances and determine the necessity for federal intervention. Presidential representatives, unlike agents of state governments, relied not only on owners and managers for information but also conferred with labor and uninvolved third parties. Consequently, Roosevelt and Wilson received accurate descriptions of conditions at the scene of disorder. Finally, partly as a consequence of the general staff reforms in Army administration, federal troops in twentieth-century interventions were kept completely within the federal chain of command and never placed under the direct control of state governors.

Direct presidential participation in the use of federal troops and maintenance of the military chain of command prevented state officials and corporate officers from using the Army as a tool to crush striking workers, regardless of the officer corps' private inclinations and biases. Progressive reforms, which enhanced the power of the presidency and stimulated the federal government to attempt to resolve labor-capital conflicts outside the courts and without the use of force, as seen in Roosevelt's role in arbitrating the 1902 anthracite coal strike, altered the nature of federal intervention in labor disputes in the twentieth century.[3]

The twentieth-century approach to federal intervention may be seen briefly in two instances, one under Roosevelt, the other during Wilson's first term. Roosevelt sent federal troops to Nevada in 1907, at the request of the state, to suppress violence attending a miner's strike at Goldfield. The president ordered Brigadier General Frederick Funston to preserve order but to respond only to orders from Washington. The desires of Nevada officials were to be ignored, Roosevelt noted. "Better 24 hours of riot, damage and disorder than illegal use of troops."[4] Under the direct oversight of Secretary of War Elihu Root, federal troops were instructed not to guard mines, protect strikebreakers, or participate in the arrest of strikers. Roosevelt sent an investigating committee to Nevada to assess the situation. The committee concluded that the governor of Nevada had exaggerated the extent and nature of disorder, and it recommended withdrawal of troops. Regulars left the state in March, 1908. They had preserved order but had not interfered in the final outcome of the conflict.[5]

Wilson displayed the same concern for impartiality when he sent federal troops to Colorado in April, 1914, to end disorder attending a long and violent coal strike. Prior to the commitment of troops, several presidential aides visited Colorado, and all advised federal troops as the best means of preserving order in an extremely tense and potentially violent situation. Secretary of War Lindley M. Garrison supervised troop activity, assuring that federal troops remained neutral, as Wilson had insisted. Wilson refused a request to place troops under the governor and obtained the demobilization of the National Guard. After the guard left, federal troops disarmed miners, private guards, and even local law enforcement officials. As in Nevada, the president kept regulars from guarding mine property, and Garrison refused to allow the importation of strikebreakers. The miners' union praised the Wilson policy. In both instances, federal troops preserved order but refrained from direct participation in ending the strikes.[6]

Presidents Roosevelt and Wilson were responsible for the changes in federal military intervention after 1900. Significantly, the Army did not call for the changes, nor did it question the new approach. The service simply followed its orders. Before Progressive Era reforms, however, Army officers did not have strong presidential guidance and were left to themselves to figure out the dilemma of concomitantly obeying the president and yet responding to requests of civilians outside the military chain of command, which seemed to go beyond what presidential orders denoted. It was partly this concern that led General Winfield S. Hancock to protest the placement of federal troops under the governor of Pennsylvania in 1877. Influenced by the Reconstruction experience, when at times the use of the Army to suppress disorders had smacked of political intimidation, officers approached the question of military intervention in civil disorders with great care. Many were worried about the possibilities of civil court action against them if they overstepped what were poorly defined bounds. These fears were not wholly unfounded; in 1886, labor leaders in Seattle brought suit against General John Gibbon for his action in enforcing martial law as declared by the governor of the Territory of Washington. The suit was dropped, but the example was there nonetheless.

Officers were fully aware that the *posse comitatus* act of 1878 had been passed with the intent of lessening the future possibilities of a federal military presence in a political setting. Doubts persisted, however, as to the proper legal standing of federal troops in labor disorders. Colonel

Elwell S. Otis feared that "the army was not rightfully employed in suppressing the labor riots of 1877, and that the act of 1878 with its severe penalties was placed upon the statute-book to prevent a recurrence of similar action."[7]

While Otis erred in surmising that the 1878 act was intended to curb drastically the uses of troops in industrial disorders, the threatened "severe penalties" contained in the law bred caution in many officers. Above all, they were disturbed by the paucity and vagueness of laws and regulations governing the use of troops in civil upheavals, and the likelihood of legal action against officers who violated the rights of civilians while suppressing disorder. Captain James Regan admonished fellow officers that military duties "in civil commotions are of the most delicate character. The position in which [officers] are placed is, to say the least an unenviable one." The officer on riot duty had many obligations, none of which relieved him from "liability to prosecution in civil and criminal suits, and his every act is subject to the strictest legal scrutiny. Hence great caution must be exercised not to overstep the strict legal bounds."[8]

Most officers desired an explicit statutory statement that when the military appeared to suppress disorder, civilian authority was temporarily suspended until the mob was brought under control. Captain Peter Leary, Fourth Artillery, recommended that the United States adopt a state of seige in peace law similar to those of France and Germany allowing martial law to supplant civil law for the duration of civil disorder. "In reality, the army is now a gendarmery—a national police—in its civil relation," Lieutenant William Wallace forcefully argued. "But the fact lacks acknowledgment; and in this lack of sanction by bold laws . . . its action is uncertain, doubtful, and, naturally, curtailed in its power." Wallace, too, called for the implementation of martial law when rioting required the use of military force.[9]

Congress did not relieve officers' anxieties about their legal liabilities. It passed no other legislation after 1878 confronting the issue. In light of this, Colonel Thomas M. Anderson concluded, "The best we can do is to study such laws as seem relevant and to receive warning or wisdom from pertinent examples."[10] Common sense and circumspection remained the soldier's best course given the lack of legal guidelines. Captain Regan advised commanders on riot duty to "refrain from violence and disorder, and guard against any irregularities that might tend to compromise the Army with the public."[11]

All of this was sound advice, but it did not eliminate the nagging questions of what an officer could and could not do. Nor did it make explicit the extent to which an officer should respond to requests from civilians outside the chain of command. The concern for clearly delineated guidelines to govern the Army's behavior in civil disorders indicated an unease in the officer corps. The uncertainty invariably connected with civil disorder was unsettling to a professional group that liked clear-cut orders and direct action. Certainly the Civil War legacy of a strategic approach of annihilating the enemy was a poor guide to the suppression of civil tumult.[12]

Much of the confusion attending the use of the Army in civil upheavals, officers believed, resulted from the timidity of civil officials at the state and local level. "Civil officers will never admit their own incompetency until red-handed war drives them from their seats. Civil machinery encourages rebellion. The State authorities have been timid and rascaldom has found it out. When rulers are timid, rascals are bold."[13] It seemed unfair, furthermore, that when the military was called in to rectify the blunders of civil leaders, it remained circumscribed. "Were the authorities of the country, in the interest of civilization, to boldly acknowledge the evil" of industrial upheavals and "adopt stringent measures," especially giving the Army greater authority, Lieutenant Wallace wrote "those who love law and order would rest more easily."[14] The veiled contempt of many officers for local and state politicians influenced their entire perception of riot duty. Military men tended to view things in an uncomplicated way; disorder called for suppression, not vacillation. Officers, of course, did not rely on voters to retain their jobs, and, as labor critics stressed, neither did officers have a responsibility to answer to the local community socially or economically once the job of suppression was completed.

Given these perceptions, military leaders on riot duty indicated a natural predisposition for those civilians who advocated vigorous action. Surely Governor Steunenberg's policy against the Western Federation of Miners was appealing because it was stern, direct, and final. Corporate officials were less temperate in their calls for action than were many local civic officials and took their suggestions directly to Army commanders. The suggestions did not fall on deaf ears. All too often, Colonel Anderson suggested, the Army was required to do society's dirty work, which politicians sought to avoid. Officers "must be convinced that soldiers are called in as a preventive rather than as a cure, and that the failure of the civil authorities to restore order has been from a neglect to use the means at their disposal."[15]

Such distaste for civilians suggests that the Army chafed under civilian control in the late nineteenth century. This was not the case at all, for the service was deeply imbued with the Anglo-American tradition of military subordination to the civil power. But to most officers, civilian control was embodied in the president, and in him alone. For Lieutenant Wallace, "the lawfulness of an order rests in the originating power. It is this power only that is accountable. The President as commander-in-chief is the repository of all military power."[16] Perceiving the president as the source of the power of command within the Army, officers expressed a strong desire to remain directly under his command when on riot duty. Captain George F. Price, Fifth Cavalry, stated the commonly accepted view. When the Army was ordered by the president to aid civil officials in suppressing disorder

> it is under the command of the President, and that command
> cannot legally be transposed to the Governor, nor can the troops
> be placed under the order or disposition of the Governor; all
> powers and rights of command are vested in the President and
> in the military officers who may be acting under his orders.[17]

Army Regulations of 1895 supported this interpretation, noting that troops in aid of the civil power "act under the orders of the President as Commander-in-Chief. They can not be directed to act under orders of any civil official."[18] Indeed, despite a few officers who disagreed with this interpretation, this view was so widespread by the middle 1890s, that the actions of the service in Idaho in 1899 seem most puzzling.[19]

General Merriam and the other officers who bent to the will of Idaho officials escaped censure, however, because no one in the Army or the McKinley administration called them to account. The latter's ignorance of the law placed the Army in a situation in which presidential orders left officers two options. They could have ignored Army regulations and followed McKinley's orders to cooperate with Governor Steunenberg, which they did, or they could have challenged the legality of the orders. The Army's deep internalization of obedience and its equally strong commitment to the authority of the president negated the possibility of any challenge. Further, Merriam and his officers could just as likely have been ignorant of the law and regulations themselves. The Army had no ongoing program of training or policy review connected with riot duty. A number of officers discussed the topic in professional and popular journals, but there was no guarantee that even a minority of the officer corps read and digested these articles.[20]

Officers' fears of legal reprisals, their perceptions of local and state civil officials as weak and vacillating, and their desires for more explicit laws governing riot duty naturally led them to emphasize the president's role in the chain of command. With the Army operating directly under the command of the president, the actions of civil officers and the legal questions were of far less concern. The president "has been vested largely with the power of determining upon what occasions the Army shall be used," and that was sufficient for most officers.[21] Indeed, many came perilously close to arguing that there was no such thing as an illegal order from the commander-in-chief. "It is conceded," Captain Peter Leary offered, "that no question as to legality of the use of troops in such cases presents itself to a military commander. His proper superiors have predetermined those questions for him."[22]

Consequently, whatever other doubts officers might have had about carrying out the requests of governors and other state officials, or federal judges and marshals during civil disorders, they could take comfort in the fact that their commander-in-chief had ordered them to cooperate with civil officers outside the chain of command. Further, their strong commitment to civilian control of the military acted as a brake on any impulse to question the ways in which civil officials used federal troops. As evidenced in Idaho, there were times when the Army could be too subservient to civil authorities. If they at times felt uncomfortable at serving under governors, judges, and marshals, officers realized that they were simply heeding their chief's command and adhering to the long-standing American principle of military subordination to civilian direction.

Just as importantly, there was no fundamental difference between the military's perception of the threat protesting workers posed to American society in the late nineteenth century, and of the necessity to suppress those protests, and those of the civilian groups that controlled government and the courts. Since most officers did not disagree basically with the purposes for which the Army was used in labor disputes, there was not likely to be any protest from them. The Army, of course, was not a policy-making institution but an action arm of the federal executive. Soldiers were not asked if they wanted to suppress civil disorder. They were ordered to do so. Nonetheless, officers participating in the suppression of civil upheavals exhibited the same fears and concerns about a disorderly American society that so disturbed middle and upper-class civilians in the two and a half decades following the end of Reconstruction.

Optimism alternated with pessimism among the propertied classes in the Gilded Age. Bust followed boom, and workers' protests and farmers' charges of vast social conspiracies accompanied phenomenal economic expansion. For the propertied classes, the waxing of apparent economic progress engendered not confidence in America but a waning of social cohesion. Industrialism seemed to carry nearly as many curses with it as promises. Ugly, strike-ridden cities filled up with aliens who neither understood nor cared about cherished Anglo-American values. Respect for law and order, obedience, and deference to those who owned and ran the nation's business and industry, a commitment to the American promise that hard work and sobriety would lift one out of the throes of poverty, all these seemed to receive less and less respect from the masses at work in factories, mines, and on the farms.

The widespread disorders of 1877 first suggested to the middle and upper classes that anarchy and radicalism were at work. More disturbing were the labor upheavals of 1886, which culminated in the Chicago Haymarket riot. Here was a graphic example of the imported radical, bomb in hand, out to destroy the physical representatives of law by murdering policemen as well as the symbols of American order by preaching anarchy in the streets of America's second city. The tumult of the 1890s, highlighted by Eugene Debs's challenge to the authority of the federal government in 1894, and capped by the Bryan campaign in 1896, confirmed in the minds of many of the propertied classes that the fabric of society was close to being torn beyond repair.[23]

What middle-and upper-class Americans failed to comprehend during the Gilded Age was the fundamental shift in values taking place as a result of the transmutation of the American economic system. The growth of large-scale economic institutions and the accompanying development of a corporate-bureaucratic apparatus to administer them directly challenged preindustrial values and social relations. Working people did not acquiesce meekly to this fundamental change. Labor protests and the violence that often accompanied them resulted not merely from the desire to obtain higher wages, better working conditions, and shorter hours but also from an impulse to resist the advance of corporate-industrial values.

The propertied classes perceived workers' protests, however, as partly the carping of the less able at the success of those whom nature and God had blessed. More threatening was the apparent correlation between the arrival of immigrants from the non-Protestant areas of Central, Southern, and Eastern Europe, and a concomitant rise in industrial violence and radical political and economic ideas. As reflected in the press response to disorder, the middle and upper classes most often reacted to the growing disorder and apparent dissolution of society with calls for law and order to be imposed by force through the police, the National Guard, and, when necessary, the Army as well. Industrial workers, a New Jersey educator lamented in 1879, were so disorderly, undisciplined, and brute-like that "the rich and more intelligent classes are obliged to guard them with police and standing armies, and to cover the land with prisons, cages, and all kinds of receptacles for the perpetrators of crime."[24]

It was not possible for the Army to remain unaffected by the struggle over values in late nineteenth-century America. At crucial times the service was called upon to intervene directly in social conflict. As an instrument of a government controlled by the propertied classes, it was committed to preserve and protect the newly emerging value system. The service performed this duty because it was imbued with the concepts of implicit obedience and respect for civilian control but also because the values of the officer corps did not differ in any significant way from the majority of middle and upper-class Americans in any event. Although in some ways the service stood outside the mainstream of American life, officers retained the middle-class values they brought with them when they entered the service. The professionalizing tendencies evident within the Army by the late 1890s, and its physical isolation from industrializing, urbanizing America did not create within the officer corps a particular view of life or of American society which differed substantially from its civilian counterparts in the larger society. Indeed, the hierarchical, bureaucratic structure of the service and efforts within the institution to emphasize professional specialization resembled similar developments in the maturing corporate economy.[25]

The relationships which Major-General John M. Schofield developed with a segment of the corporate elite in the 1880s and 1890s illustrates the fact that a West Point education and a career in the Army did not isolate officers from other parts of society. Schofield, of course, was hardly a typical officer. He was but one of five men to serve as commanding general from 1865 to 1900 out of an officer corps that numbered at least 2,000. His circle of friends and acquaintances serves as an example, nonetheless, of the commonality which could develop between officers and the propertied classes. It was not that Schofield conspired with his friends to suppress labor, but that he was so much a part of their milieu as to perceive the challenges of workers in the same light as they did. Comfortable in the presence of the corporate elite, General Schofield did not reject the world industrialism wrought.

From at least the time that he commanded the Department of the Missouri, with headquarters in Chicago, 1883-86, until he retired from the commanding general's post in 1895, Schofield corresponded and hobnobbed with some of America's leading business and financial figures. When he left Chicago for Washington, the prestigous Calument Club of Chicago favored the general with an elaborate going away dinner. The Committee of Invitations included Marshall Field, George M. Pullman, and railroad managers J. W. Doane and N. K. Fairbank. Among those who attended and autographed the dinner program were George A. Armour and Cyrus McCormick.

During these years Schofield maintained a lively correspondence with Grenville Dodge, Pullman, and Doane of the Union Pacific Railroad. In the manner of the times, Schofield requested and accepted free railroad passes for himself and members of his family from such railroads as the Chicago and Northwestern and the Chicago, Burlington and Quincy. He held stock in the Illinois Central Railroad, the New York, West Shore, and Buffalo Railway, and the Missouri-Pacific line. Other corporations in which Schofield held an interest included the Bull Run Panorama Company, as well as the American Sugar Refining Company and, interestingly, the Pullman Palace Car Company.[26]

The General sold his Pullman stock in June of 1893, a year before the great strike, and there is no hint of a direct conflict of interest in his role in 1894. Schofield's financial holdings and his relations with corporate managers indicate not conspiracy but the fact that his point of view on strikes and other industrial disorders would inevitably be shaped by his participation in corporate stockholding and his social class affiliations. The general certainly had rapport and empathy with management, as his correspondence with a variety of industrial figures ranged easily over both large and small matters. For example, letters between Grenville Dodge and Schofield could touch one time on the next expedition of their fishing club and another deal with the placement of troops near the property of Dodge's railroad.[27]

Other generals of the period developed similar affiliations. When Nelson A. Miles became commanding general in 1896, a group of prominent businessmen, including Collis P. Huntington, raised $50,000 to purchase a suitable home for Miles in Washington. As part of its appeal, the group sent a circular to businessmen emphasizing "the extent of the influence of Gen. Miles in having the regular army sent to subdue the riots in Chicago."[28] Brigadier General Henry C. Merriam was reported, both by the labor and popular press, to have held important pieces of business property in Seattle and a cordial relationship with businessmen there.[29]

More indicative of officers' perceptions of the social struggle over values in the late nineteenth century were the observations and comments they made in professional and popular periodicals. While this body of material represented only a minority of officers in the service, it is the best source for revealing the reactions of the men who led federal military forces in suppressing labor disorders. The majority of articles appeared in the *Journal of the Military Service Institution of the United States,* the foremost military professional journal during these years. When added to the reactions officers made during strike duty itself, these published remarks suggest strongly the similarity between the officer corps's perception of industrial upheavals and those of the propertied classes.

In a textbook on military law published in 1892, Lieutenant William E. Birkhimer stressed, "The instances of disorder show unmistakeably that there is abroad in the land a spirit of reckless defiance of authority."[30] Many of Birkhimer's military compatriots shared his concern over the prevalence of disorder in post-Reconstruction America. One military commentator predicted four years earlier that "riots of the future are likely to be both more frequent and more formidable than those of the past."[31] An infantry captain describing the Army's role in the Pullman strike saw it as "but a symptom of a disease—a sign of the times; not a mere incident in our history; but one indicative of a condition that confronts us."[32]

The condition that confronted American society and concerned Army officers was readily recognized by them. While occasionally an officer would indict "professional politicians" who, "by reason of incompetency or venality . . . bring the law into disrepute," most saw social upheaval as a direct product of economic change.[33] Lieutenant William Wallace wrote perceptively that great forces and passions were at work in American society which were causing "if not the birth of a new civilization, at least the death of the present one."[34] Wallace recognized that the shift to industrial factory work in crucial areas of the economy was responsible for these changes. Colonel Thomas Anderson more directly noted that "of late there has been a great change in business methods and social relations which may be followed by serious complications." Both men reluctantly conceded, as Wallace put it, that "the capitalist and the laborer have been created."[35]

It was one thing to comment on the obvious and quite another to comprehend the larger meanings of such dramatic changes to those who were affected the most by it. A few officers complained of the arbitrary way in which corporations used their power and lamented the "ghoul-like despotism of capital" along with the "brutal tyranny of labor."[36] Most, however, focused their attention on the working class and its behavior and ideas.

Officers commenting on organized labor generally expressed benevolence towards unions and workingmen. "My heart goes with all workingmen in every lawful effort they make to better their condition," General O. O. Howard stressed.[37] General Nelson A. Miles, in the aftermath of 1894, also expressed his sympathy for organizations that sought to improve workers' lives. Beneath the benevolence was a deep distrust of unions when their activities went beyond fraternal intentions. Collective bargaining and the quest for the closed shop were contrary to American values. Most disturbing to the *Army and Navy Journal* were "the arrogance and spirit of dictation, governing the labor organizations," which led to the intimidation of nonunion workers.[38] "The shameful lengths to which these societies have gone . . . in violation of law and in trampling upon the rights of others" disturbed one officer.[39]

The strike bothered officers considerably. Sooner or later unions turned to this tactic, "and without stopping to inquire into their merits . . . the fact remains that out of strikes will come riots."[40] By resorting to strikes, unions were responsible for disorder. "A great strike . . . not to be accompanied by violence, is an impossibility in fact," the chaplain of the Twenty-fifth Infantry argued, "and an absurdity in idea. And its violence if unorganized is riot, and if organized, *war*!"[41] General Miles believed the ARU boycott and strike were "red hot anarchy, insurrectionary and revolutionary!"[42] The commander of federal forces in California in 1894, General Thomas Ruger, also viewed "the actions, manner of procedure and intent" of the railroad strikers as "distinctly insurrectionary."[43]

Strikes and the methods used to support them violated property laws, and the rights of non-strikers, and threatened the public peace. When the worker turned to intimidation and destruction, "he places himself as much outside the protection of the law as if he were a foreign adversary. In fact he becomes a public enemy."[44]

Most dangerous of all was that any labor induced turbulence was liable to unloose uncontrolled mobs of ignorant, vicious people who had no stake in society. As did civilian observers, military commentators on civil disorder stressed the presence in American society of a large mass of people who lacked commitment to a stable and lawful social order. The advance of the suffrage, for example, had gone so far "till now the criminal and ignorant classes are as powerful man for man, at the polls as are the law-abiding and intelligent classes."[45] Lower-class voting meant bad laws and weak leaders. Then, when violence came, "in every instance of tumult there is a class engaged who are not honest strikers—the turbulent element, having nothing to lose and everything to gain by riot, arson, and pillage."[46] A deeply pessimistic soul like Lieutenant William Wallace could paint the lower classes in the darkest of hues. "Their strength and minds are brutish and they have miniature hells for souls. Famine, pestilence, and war, are truly their deities. There is but one thing they fear, and that is death."[47]

Military observers also looked upon direct action by labor unions with skepticism because of the presence of immigrants in large numbers in the American work force. To Colonel Anderson, "the practice of forming combinations to resist constituted authority is a foreign importation," indicating a feeling in the Army that unions and their tactics were un-American.[48] Altogether, immigrants made up an idle, dangerous class not given to work, or were virulent agitators on the fringes of the labor movement urging honest workers to form combinations to defy authority. And still the unsavory outsiders kept coming, causing one captain to contend, "The class of emigrants [sic] flocking to the United States has deteriorated, and has been found to contain a larger proportion of criminals and paupers than in the past."[49] In his *North American Review* article, General Miles urged ending "the importation of the vast hordes of cheap and degraded labor on our Atlantic coast."[50] Immigrant workers were easy prey for demagogic union organizers. The officer in command of the federal force in Idaho in 1900 reported of union members there that

> about 80 per cent of the dupes of these men [union organizers]
> are foreigners, mostly ignorant of our laws and institutions and in-
> capable of recognizing the existence of any obligation of obedi-
> ence or duty to the state.[51]

Perhaps most frightening of all was the fact that immigrants seemed to
introduce alien ideas into the labor-capital conflict. One of Miles's officers
saw the upheavals in Chicago as the harbinger of "a social revolution either
now or in the near future. The lower order of the foreign element is making the strike an excuse for social upheavals. Immigration should be at
once prohibited and the strong force of arms extended to repress this
menace to the country's safety."[52] The labor struggle was in reality, then,
but a "pseudo-combination," "a noxious compound of French commu-
nism, German socialism, Irish agrarianism, Russian nihilism, American
trampism."[53] One part American to four parts foreign, that is. In the
final analysis, most officers believed the real cause of social disorder lay
with "the ceaseless and untiring energy displayed by the restless and im-
placable association of Socialists, Communists, and Nihilists that have
taken root in our midst."[54] Far too readily, the officer corps and the
propertied classes in civilian life interpreted the turbulence of industrializing America in terms of anarchy and alien philosophies. To them disorder *was* anarchy.

In assessing the threat of disorder in the United States in the 1880s,
Lieutenant Richard Young saw the anarchists as the crucial threat to
society. "Rioting may be said to be their profession. They will prepare
for it by posing as the friend of labor, by widening the breach between
capital and labor, and intensifying hatred between classes."[55] It was the
anarchist who manipulated the discontented worker, the "honest" worker
officers so often wrote about, who was so easily misled by evil agitators.
The anarchist worked upon the ignorance and discontent of the immigrant. The impatient worker, native or foreign-born, was "in a mood to
lend ear to the communistic and anarchist theories of today and do away
with justice, property, and rights."[56] While it was possible for officers
to see the changes taking place in American society and to sympathize
with the difficulties workers faced in adjusting to change, nonetheless
"anarchy is the great danger of the day."[57] Here was the crucial point
for the Army, Lieutenant Wallace insisted.

In this way only is the army brought into the question of
capital and labor. And its status towards labor depends entirely upon labor's status towards anarchy. The army is opposed
to the anarchist; and if labor makes him an ally, not only does the
army maintain the imputation of siding with capital, but the
laborer must find arranged against him all notions of right, justice, and reason.[58]

The Army thus sided with capital, not because it favored one class over
the other, but because it stood for law and order. Essentially middle-class
in background and social values, officers held a strong respect for the
rights of property, law and order, and social stability. Few would have
disagreed with *Leslie's Weekly's* contention that "this is a country of law,
and law, resting upon and embodying a sound public conviction is with
us, and will remain, the supreme force."[59] Unable to comprehend the
constraints that law placed upon labor, unwilling to confront the forces
that drove workers to disorder, the Army fell in line with the propertied
classes in condemning those who displayed a "mistaken impatience of
and resentment against the conservative legal restraints needful for the
general order."[60] The problem, Captain James Regan wrote, was "what
do the lawless or the mob care for such laws, the anarchists, their friends,
want chaos or the destruction of all law and order."[61] Change must proceed slowly and through the constituted processes. The use of force was
totally unacceptable to remedy the ills of the discontented.[62]

A deep respect for order and stability motivated the officer corps to
speak out strongly against labor related disorders. As with Lieutenant
Wallace, other officers strove to make the point that they were not anti-
labor, but pro-order. To Captain A. H. Russell, the service was "the con-
servator of law and order and of the rights the people have to peacefully
change the law. . . . The army is the supporter of no classes and of no
party. It stands for the united nation."[63] Colonel Thomas Anderson
stated the Army view succinctly.

No organizations are in any danger in this country if they do not
violate some law. We of the army are the instruments used in the

last resort to support and enforce the law. If the laws made in the
interests of labor were forcibly violated by capitalists, we should
be used on the side of labor and should act as willingly. If there
is any law which presses unfairly upon the rights of labor, the
remedy under our theory of government is not resistance but repeal.[64]

There was, of course, no federal military intervention to suppress a capitalist's riot in the late nineteenth century. This fact, however, served
merely to reinforce the prevailing view: disorder, riot, and violence came
from an overaggressive labor movement.

Officers not only accepted the continuance of the existing order of
things but exhibited a strong respect for private property. While he
lamented some of the actions of the wealthy, Colonel John Hamilton,
Fifty Artillery, nonetheless conceded, "The truth is that the proud-of-
wealth man rides into protection on the high conception that the soldier
holds of the sacredness of property and peace."[65] Unlike Hamilton, Lieutenant Wallace expressed admiration for capitalists and also accepted the
need to protect their property. "Had there never been a capitalist," he
wrote, "the laborer as well as the rest of the human race, would have been
running around eating roots, in a most savage state."[66] Support for law
and order implicitly meant, above all, the protection of the property of
capitalists, whether soldiers admired them or not.

Inevitably, officers assessing the nature of social disorder in the late
nineteenth century raised the question of the role of the Army in future
upheavals. Many suggested a policy of containment by urging the creation of large garrisons near industrial cities. Lieutenant Arthur L. Wagner
recommended posting full regiments at five different points in the country
with easy access to the largest industrial centers. "These posts . . . should
be chosen with a view to their strategic positions in domestic warfare."[67]
The presence of troops in these "industrial" garrisons could easily serve
as a deterrent, according to another officer. "The strong hand should be
visible. Mere absactions are rarely respected and never feared. A national
force, sufficiently strong not only to suppress, but to prevent rioting,
should therefore be maintained near every great city."[68] In this view, a
new role for the Army would be developed. "The red savage is pretty well
subdued," the *Army and Navy Register* editorialized, "but there are white
savages growing more numerous and dangerous as our great cities become

greater." The Army should be used to deal with the white savages as it had with the red ones.[69]

Officers anticipated a further role for the Army in civil disorders. "It is predicted that the elements of discord which have caused these domestic disturbances are with us to stay, at least for a generation or so," one commented in 1896, "and the future will bring forth many painful occasions for the use of the Army as a police force."[70] The Army, some argued, would have its hands full for some time to come because the discordant elements in society would not quickly fade away. Local police and the militia had shown that they often could not cope with the challenges of civil disorder. "The causes that brought forth the whirlwind of lawlessness that swept through the land, in 1877, still exist," Lieutenant Wagner posited in 1884, "and will continue to exist." Consequently, "all thinking men and good citizens will recognize the existence of reliable troops at convenient points as one of the greatest of our military necessities."[71] If, as General Miles contended a decade later, Americans had to choose between anarchy and mob violence, or the supremacy of law and the maintenance of order, then the Army had a job to do. So asserted a junior cavalry officer. "Cavalry has, heretofore, been the advance guard of civilization; it must now perform the equally important duty of rear guard."[72]

Rear guard duty was necessary because of the activities of labor unions. The struggle over values would continue; the agitators would keep up their pernicious work. Labor would not be quiet. And, "Have we any guarantee that its demands will always be reasonable? When its demands become extravagant, then what? Is it not the duty of government to provide adequate means for preventing, not strikes, but the illegal results?"[73] To Army officers, the authority of the government was the key. If law were to be mocked, if force were to win out over constituted authority, then indeed the struggle for civilization would be lost. The Army placed great emphasis on stability and order, and its duty to ensure their maintenance. Lieutenant Colonel William Ludlow argued forcefully:

> To be worthy of respect a government should be able to command it and, since the preservation of order is the object to be attained, there is needed so much of an organized force at the disposal of the government as should be able not only to restore peace, but forbid its breach.

Ludlow warned that if the United States did not maintain and use the Army for this purpose it "presently would find itself at the mercy of the criminal and violent classes."[74]

Officers took Ludlow's fearful predictions seriously. In a prize-winning essay for the *JMSI*, Lieutenant Wagner asserted that the containment and suppression of domestic disorder was "of scarcely less importance than the measures to be taken for national defence against foreign enemies."[75] The need to control the enemy within placed one more demand on the Army's already overtaxed resources, and younger officers took up the refrain of their superiors, calling for military expansion to meet the need for a "national police." Colonel Emory Upton prefaced his critical analysis of U.S. military policy with the observation that "the military policy of a republic should look more to the dangers of civil commotion than to the possibility of foreign invasion." Upton referred first to the anarchy that preceded the collapse of the Roman Empire, then briefly recalled the history of civil disorder in the United States, from Shays's Rebellion to the railroad strikes of 1877. "It should be our policy," he concluded, "to suppress every riot and stamp out every insurrection before it swells to rebellion. This means a strong government," with a larger Army.[76]

The *Army and Navy Journal* consistently editorialized for an increase in the service in order to meet the threat of civil disorder. Whenever the civilian press or labor journals accused the Army of serving the interests of capital in suppressing workers, the *Journal* responded, stridently at times, in support of the Army and repeated past appeals for a larger military force to deal with dissidents.[77] As had General Schofield, some officers argued that in 1877 and 1894 the service had been stretched to its limits. Rather than risk a failure of federal authority, it was far wiser to provide an adequate force to avoid a future humiliation of the federal government. Did not this potential threat, one officer asked, "suggest a necessity for a reasonable increase in the Army? Heretofore the Army has without much difficulty suppressed such mobs as it has come in contact with in the line of duty. But it has accomplished this by moral force—not physical force."[78]

Military advocates of increasing the service in order to deal with domestic disorder were well aware of the traditional American fears of a large standing army. By arguing that manpower in the service should be established on a pro rata basis to population, usually one soldier for every 1,000 civilians, Adjutant General Henry C. Corbin sought to ease these fears. "There can be no menace to the Republic in a standing army of proportions so meagre when compared with the total population."[79] Perhaps more effectively, supporters of an increase asked whether a large, well-trained Army was a greater threat then an enraged mob filled with foreigners inflamed by alien ideas. Certainly, General O. O. Howard emphasized, the Army was no threat. "Naturally, as we wish it to be, the Army is a conservative body; and, in the hands of the President, a preserver of order. In times of rebellion, in hours of mob-law and riot; in brief during all dangers to the Republic from within or without, its history is a most flattering one."[80] An Army greatly outnumbered by civilians, yet strong enough to deal with riot, rebellion, or revolution, posed no threat to the nation.

Not all officers agreed with the calls for a larger Army serving in a more active constabulary role. Those who demurred were a minority of the published officers, however. Captain Otho Michaelis despaired over the turmoil in the nation but believed that "suitable education and wise legislation seem to be our only hope for overcoming the terror of the future." The solution to labor-capital conflict was "the statesman's province," not the soldier's.[81] Another military author, reflecting Michaelis's somber tone, saw riot and tumult as inevitable but cautioned against using the Army except in "cases of instant and imperious necessity." Unless there was no other recourse "the Army should not be used against the people."[82] These attitudes were similar to those of the vast majority of civilian Americans. Military expansion came at the end of the century due to external military needs, not internal ones.

There was an element of special pleading present in both civilian and military suggestions for an increase in the size of the service and an expansion of its role in domestic disorder. Tom Scott's bombastic calls for a larger Army to keep order among dissident railroad workers was too self-serving for most to take seriously. Similar statements by entrepreneurs and their public mouthpieces did not manage to overcome the inherent American distrust of a large, professional, peacetime army. The National Guard, whatever its faults, became proficient enough to handle most disorders. The Guard's local and state orientation made it more susceptible to the control and use of the propertied classes than was the Army in any case.

Professional soldiers all too often relied on the domestic disorder argument as an expedient to solve a larger problem. The end of Reconstruction and the tapering off of the Indian wars presented professional military men with a fundamental issue: how to justify the Army's existence. Military reformers sought to reconcile the conundrum of the traditional American dislike for a standing army and the absence of external threats with the great advances in European military administration, command, promotion, training, and size. While Upton's suggestions contained valid technical points, his demand for military reforms failed to produce an authentic external threat to justify the expense of change. As did many other officers writing in the same vein, Upton sought to exploit temporary fears of labor turbulence in order to further institutional interests.[83]

Institutional provincialism accounted for much of the stridency in officers' commentary on domestic disorder and their calls for larger forces to meet the threat of anarchy and industrial rebellion. In their analyses of military needs in the late nineteenth century, military authors almost invariably devoted greater detail and space to the purely professional needs of the service than to necessities for keeping the civil peace. In a single article an officer could recommend a moderate increase in manpower and justify the increase on the grounds of meeting foreign threats, improving career opportunities, and preventing internal disorder.[84]

As Russell Weigley has shown, a significant portion of the officer corps in the late nineteenth century suffered a deep sense of pessimism about their professional way of life. The Army's place in American society was poorly defined and, in the soldiers' eyes, totally unappreciated, at a time when European military institutions were undergoing profound change. Europe's soldiers stood at the right hand of kings and premiers; millions of dollars went into continental army budgets; and men in uniform received the praise of the public in all the great nations of Europe. In America, however, professional soldiers despaired of ever being taken seriously. Unable to attract attention to the many needs of their service, Army officers were willing to pander to fears of social upheaval to draw attention to their institution. To call for more money and men to meet the needs of civil disturbances and to recommend more stringent laws governing the conduct of riot duty were part of a larger intellectual effort to justify the Army's existence as a professional calling worthy of respect and as a significant element in the nation's government.[85]

Beyond service parochialism, however, was an evident concern for social turmoil and a strong identification with the prevailing values and interests of the propertied classes. Perhaps officers wished they could have avoided involvement in riot duty because of the lack of defined policy and law. They had no choice and obeyed their orders. It was more than a question of obedience, however. No officer ever challenged the validity of an order to suppress labor-related disorders. When the question of social disorder was elevated to the level of a struggle for the survival of society, as in 1894, then officers not only obeyed orders but came down firmly on the side of property.

Soldiers knew in general terms what their civilian superiors wanted when ordered to riot duty. But military men had to decide what measures to take and whose advice should be heeded when they reached the field of action. Policy decisions that should have been made at the federal level were not, due to the awkward administrative system of the Army and the lack of leadership on the part of presidents and their cabinets. As a result, when left on their own, soldiers went looking for advice and counsel. Usually they turned to civilians of authority and prestige outside the federal chain of command. When governors, mayors, marshals, railroad managers, and mine owners proved aggressive and urged vigorous action, officers acceded. In the 1877 railroad strikes, Major General Winfield S. Hancock more often acted on the suggestions of Governor Hartranft and Thomas Scott than on any from President Hayes. During the Pullman strike, General Schofield and his department commanders acted in concert with railroad managers throughout the episode. In the Coeur d'Alene interventions, Army officers never questioned the union-busting requests of Idaho officials. They did so, above all, because officers perceived society as did their civilian associates.

Given the social origins of the officer corps, underlying sympathies with property were inevitable. Yet, in an age when class consciousness was so evident, it behooved the officer corps to be aware of both its actions and its words. The Army was one of the few genuine national institutions in the late nineteenth century touching all regions and all classes. Abetted by its role in the Civil War, the service stood above all federal agencies as a representative of the nation *in toto*. Officers who argued that it was the moral rather than the physical force of the Army that suppressed mobs were quite correct. This moral force emanated not from the professional purity of the service, as some officers smugly implied, nor from its serried ranks of disciplined enlisted men. The Army's moral force derived from its symbolic representation of the entire nation.

A potential existed for an agency of the federal government to ameliorate relations between working people and their employers because that government presumably represented everyone. Labor leaders and union journals apparently expected the Army to act in such a way, judging from their obvious disappointment when the service failed to serve as a neutral force for order. When officers commanding federal military intervention not only suppressed disorderly strikers but conferred regularly with management and carried out anti-union activities, labor hopes of an impartial federal role turned to fear and suspicion. The greater failure was not the Army's but that of its civilian leaders. Nonetheless, the bulk of the officer corps, unable or unwilling to temper their natural sympathies, perceived no necessity to divorce themselves from open identification with property. Furthermore, military advocates of Army reform relied upon demagogy to promote their institutional interests. In the process, they alienated a large portion of the working class. Only when the nation as a whole participated in the military effort of World War I did the Army recapture the public esteem it had held after the Civil War.

Notes

1. Arnold M. Paul, *Conservative Crisis and the Rule of Law: Attitudes of Bar and Bench, 1887-1885* (Ithaca, N.Y., 1960), pp. 6-18, 105-07, chap. 2; Gerald G. Eggert, *Railroad Labor Disputes: The Beginnings of Federal Strike Policy* (Ann Arbor, 1967), pp. 2-22, *passim.*

2. Eggert, *Railroad Labor Disputes,* pp. 19-21, 229-32.

3. Edward Berman, *Labor Disputes and the President of the United States* (New York, 1924), pp. 46-59.

4. Frederick T. Wilson, "Federal Aid in Domestic Disturbances, 1787-1922," 67th Cong., 2nd sess., Senate Document 263 (Washington, D.C., 1922), p. 310.

5. *Ibid.,* pp. 310-12; Berman, *Labor Disputes and the President,* pp. 64-69; Bennet M. Rich, *The Presidents and Civil Disorders* (Washington, D.C., 1941), pp. 125-35.

6. Wilson, "Federal Aid in Domestic Disturbances," pp. 312-315; Berman, *Labor Disputes and the President,* pp. 76-99; Rich, *The Presidents and Civil Disorders,* pp. 136-50.

7. In "The Army in Connection with the Labor Riots of 1877," *Journal of the Military Service Institution of the United States (JMSI)* 6, no. 22 (June 1885): 117. Other statements of concern for the legal prob-

lems officers faced when on riot duty noted in Colonel Thomas M. Anderson, "Duties in Connection with the Enforcement of Civil Law," *JMSI* 26, no. 89 (September 1897): 265-75, which is a thoughtful and literate discussion of the necessity for officers to be cognizant of all the legal ramifications of riot duty. Interestingly, Anderson's article originally was a lyceum lecture delivered to the officers of his Fourteenth Infantry Regiment; Major Wallis O. Clark, "The Use of Regulars During Civil Disorders," *Infantry Journal* 1, no. 3 (January 1905): 41; Lt. Richard W. Young, "Legal and Tactical Considerations Affecting the Employment of the Military in the Suppression of Mobs; Including an Essay on Martial Law," *JMSI* 9, no.33 (March 1888): 73. Hereafter the latter will be referred to as "The Mob and the Military." The suit against General Gibbon is recounted in Lt. William E. Birkhimer, *Military Government and Martial Law* (Washington, D.C., 1892), pp. v, 401-02.

8. Captain James Regan, *Military Duties in Aid of the Civil Power: For the Regular Army, National Guard, etc., and Police Forces Generally* (New York, 1888), p. 36. Other comments noting the need for care in keeping with the laws governing riot duty are Captain James Chester, "Martial Law and Social Order," *JMSI* 17, no. 76 (July 1895): 57-58; Captain Peter Leary, "Certain Laws Concerning the Use of Troops in Civil Disorders," *JMSI* 22, no. 85 (January 1897): 83-86; Major Robert N. Scott, "Martial Law in Insurrection and Rebellion," *JMSI* 4, no. 16 (1883): 408-09. Also, Anderson, "Enforcement of Civil Law," pp. 269-75; Clark, "Use of Regulars During Civil Disorders," pp. 43-49; Young, "The Mob and the Military," pp. 67-70.

9. "The Army and the Civil Power," *JMSI* 17, no. 77 (September 1895): 255, but also see pp. 254-59. Leary's recommendations in "Certain Laws Concerning Use of Troops in Civil Disorders," pp. 111-12. Chester, "Martial Law and Social Order," pp. 58-61, echoed the call for martial law. Otis, "The Army in Connection with the Labor Riots of 1877," p. 139, called for laws but did not go as far as the former.

10. "Enforcement of Civil Law," p. 275.

11. *Military Duties in Aid of the Civil Power,* p. 26. Also see Clark, "Use of Regulars During Civil Disorders," pp. 43-45.

12. Russell F. Weigley, *The American Way of War: A History of United States Military Strategy and Policy* (New York, 1973), pp. 145-52, chap. 8.

13. Chester, "Martial Law and Social Order," pp. 62-63.

14. "The Army and the Civil Power," p. 254.

15. "Enforcement of Civil Law," p. 268. Also see comments by regular

Army officers in Gen. E. L. Molineux, N.Y.N.G., "Riots in Cities and Their Suppression," *JMSI* 4, no. 16 (1883): 361, 369-70.

16. "The Army and the Civil Power," p. 256. Also Regan, *Military Duties in Aid of the Civil Power,* pp. 24-25. Young, "The Mob and the Military," p. 81, is a succinct statement of the Army's commitment to the ultimate authority of the civil power over the military.

17. "The Necessity for Closer Relations Between the Army and the People, and the Best Method to Accomplish the Result," *JMSI* 6, no. 24 (December 1885): 307, hereafter referred to as "The Army and the People." Similar statements in Regan, *Military Duties in Aid of the Civil Power,* p. 25; Chester, "Martial Law and Social Order," pp. 61-62; Leary, "Certain Laws Concerning Use of Troops in Civil Disorders," p. 87; Clark, "Use of Regulars During Civil Disorders," p. 42; Anderson, "Enforcement of Civil Law," pp. 264-67; Capt. William N. Blow, 15th Inf., "The Use of Troops in Riots," *JMSI* 25, no. 100 (July 1899): 45-57; Editorial, "The Use of The Army in Riots," *Army-Navy Journal* 32, no. 46 (July 13, 1895): 76. Otis, "The Army in Connection with the Labor Riots of 1877," pp. 123-27, 133-35, discussed the question of the president's power in this matter in detail.

18. U.S., Executive, War Department, *Regulations of the Army of the United States, 1895* (Washington, D.C., 1895), p. 69.

19. Young, "The Mob and the Military," pp. 74-75, and Birkhimer, *Military Government and Martial Law,* p. 395, both argued that the president could delegate command of the Army to governors.

20. Chester, "Martial Law and Social Order," p. 63, on the officers' lack of knowledge of the law pertaining to civil disorder.

21. Young, "The Mob and the Military," p. 70.

22. "Certain Laws Concerning Use of Troops in Civil Disorders," p. 84. Also see Anderson, "Enforcement of Civil Law," pp. 275-76; Wallace, "The Army and the Civil Power," p. 255, who contended, "Duty is an army's highest law and supersedes all other law"; Clark, "Use of Regulars During Civil Disorders," p. 42.

23. The following works have been of particular value in reconstructing the reaction of the middle and upper classes to social change and social disorder in the late nineteenth century: Howard M. Jones, *The Age of Energy: Varieties of American Experience, 1865-1915* (New York, 1971), pp. 36, 200-15, 338, 351-71, 379-80; John Higham, *Strangers in the Land: Patterns of American Nativism 1860-1925* (New Brunswick, N.J., 1955), pp. 30, 54-58, 69-74, 77-78; Frederic C. Jaher, *Doubters and Dissenters: Cataclysmic Thought in America, 1885-1918* (New York, 1964), pp. 35-59; Arnold M. Paul, *Conservative Crisis and the Rule of*

Law: Attitudes of Bar and Bench, 1887-1895 (Ithaca, N.Y., 1960), pp.
229-33; Matthew Josephson, *The Politicos, 1865-1896* (New York, 1938),
especially book 3, despite its polemicism is valuable for catching the
flavor of the times; Edward C. Kirkland, *Industry Comes of Age: Business,
Labor and Public Policy, 1860-1897* (Chicago, 1967), chap. 15-19.

24. As quoted in Herbert Gutman, "Work, Culture, and Society in
Industrializing America, 1815-1919," *American Historical Review* 78,
no. 3 (June 1973): 585. Gutman has provided an invaluable conceptual
framework within which the turmoil of the late nineteenth century may
be better understood. Of most use here, see *Ibid.,* pp. 567-80, and "The
Worker's Search for Power: Labor in the Gilded Age," in *The Gilded Age:
A Reappraisal,* ed. H. Wayne Morgan (Syracuse, N.Y., 1963), pp. 40-41.
Supporting Gutman's conception of a struggle over values, although with
a different emphasis, are Louis Galambos, "The Emerging Organizational
Synthesis in Modern American History," *Business History Review* 44, no.
3 (Autumn 1970): 287-88, and Robert Wiebe, *The Search for Order, 1877-
1920* (New York, 1967), chap. 1-6. Gutman's contention that elite groups
perceived workers and immigrants as disorderly and a distinct threat to
the new corporate-industrial value system is supported by Jones, *Age of
Energy,* p. 374; Paul, *Conservative Crisis and the Rule of Law,* chap. 2,
and Edward C. Kirkland, *Dream and Thought in the Business Community,
1860-1900* (Ithaca, N.Y., 1956), pp. 19-23, 121-24.

25. The middle-upper class makeup of the officer corps has already
been discussed in Chapter 2. Russell F. Weigley, "The Elihu Root Reforms and the Progressive Era," in *Command and Commanders in Modern
Warfare,* ed. William Geffen, 2nd ed., Proceedings of the Second Military
History Symposium, United States Air Force Academy (Washington, D.C.,
1971), pp. 15-17 has suggested the similarities between the corporate structure of the Army and civilian institutions of like ilk and the shared professionalizing tendencies in the service and certain civilian occupations. Other
historians have noted the shared values of the officer corps and the middle
and upper classes, particularly Allen Guttman, *The Conservative Tradition
in America* (New York, 1967), chapter 4, "Conservatism and the Military
Establishment"; Richard C. Brown, "Social Attitudes of American Generals" (Ph.D. diss., University of Wisconsin, 1951), chaps. 1, 6; William
B. White, "The Military and the Melting Pot: The American Army and
Minority Groups, 1865-1924" (Ph.D. diss., University of Wisconsin, 1968),
pp. 305-11, 376-78. Samuel P. Huntington, *The Soldier and the State:
The Theory and Politics of Civil-Military Relations* (Cambridge, Mass.,
1957), pp. 226-39, 257-60, 266-68, has argued with great intellectual
vigor that in the late nineteenth century the American officer corps de-

veloped a set of conservative philosophical-social values that set it apart from almost all social groups in the United States. Huntington's contention is based on the argument that while the vast majority of Americans from all socioeconomic classes were imbued with the values of classical liberalism, Army officers rejected this optimistic view of man and society and marched to the beat of classical conservatism with its emphasis on authority, loyalty, order, and subjection of the individual to the will of the group, especially the nation-state. Upon close examination, Huntington's theoretical constructs do not hold up well for Gilded Age America. See Allen Millett's discussion of the professionalization of the Army for the era in *The General: Robert L. Bullard and Officership in the United States Army, 1881-1925* (Westport, Conn., 1975), pp. 3-12, 27-29.

26. The John McAllister Schofield Papers, Library of Congress, the source here. On the Chicago going-away party, see Miscellaneous Memos, lot C. On Schofield's stock holdings and correspondence with leading corporate figures, see letters in Letters Received, series 4-5, and Miscellaneous Memos, lot A, B.

27. See correspondence between Dodge and Schofield in Letters Received, series 4-5, espejcially Dodge to Schofield, September 19, 1894.

28. Quoted in *The Army and Navy Journal* 34, no. 24 (February 13, 1897): 427.

29. On this, see *The Spokesman-Review* (Spokane), May 23, 1899, p. 1, and *Miner's Magazine* 1, no. 1 (January 1900): 21.

30. *Military Government and Martial Law*, p. 403.

31. Young, "The Mob and the Military," p. 249.

32. Capt. J. J. O'Connell, 1st Inf., "The Great Strike of 1894," *United Service*, n.s., vol. 15, no. 4 (April 1896): 301. For similar comments, see Wallace, "The Army and the Civil Power," p. 242; Lt. Arthur L. Wagner, "The Military Necessities of the United States, and the Best Provisions for Meeting Them," *JMSI* 5, no. 19 (September 1884): 265-66; Major George S. Wilson, "The Army: Its Employment During Time of Peace, and the Necessity for its Increase," *JMSI* 18, no. 81 (May 1896): 482-83; Lt. Colonel Harry C. Egbert, 6th Inf., "Is An Increase of the Regular Army Necessary?" *United Service*, n.s., vol. 16, no. 5 (November 1896): 380.

33. Young, "The Mob and the Military," p. 253.

34. "The Army and the Civil Power," p. 237.

35. Anderson, "Enforcement of Civil Law," p. 266, and Wallace, "The Army and the Civil Power," p. 261. Other commentators made the same point. See, e.g., *Army and Navy Journal* 34, no. 29 (March 20, 1897): 527; Major General Nelson A. Miles, "The Lesson of the Recent

Strikes," *North American Review* 159, no. 453 (August 1894): 181; Col. James M. Rice, Ill. N.G., "The Proper Military Support to the Civil Power," *United Service* 11, no. 2 (August 1884): 125; Thomas B. Nichols, "The Pittsburg Riots," *United Service* 1, no. 2 (April 1879): 262; Captain Otho E. Michaelis, Ordinance Dept., "The Military Necessities of the United States, and the Best Provisions for Meeting Them," *JMSI* 5, no. 19 (September 1884): 288; Egbert, "Is an Increase of the Army Necessary?" p. 380.

36. Michaelis, "Military Necessities of the U.S.," p. 288. Also See Young, "The Mob and the Military," p. 253.

37. Maj. Gen. Oliver O. Howard, "A Plea for the Army," *The Forum* 26 (August 1897): 646.

38. October 10, 1885, p. 198.

39. Young, "The Mob and the Military," p. 251. For expressions of sympathy for a docile labor, see *Ibid.;* Captain T. G. Steward, "Starving Laborers and the 'Hired' Soldier," *United Service,* n.s., vol. 14, no. 4 (October 1895): 363, 366; George B. McClellan, "The Militia and the Army," *Harper's New Monthly Magazine* 72, no. 428 (January 1886): 298; Leary, "Certain Laws Concerning Use of Troops in Civil Disorders," p. 83; O'Connell "The Great Strike of 1894," p. 299; Miles, "The Lesson of the Recent Strikes," pp. 181-86.

40. Wilson, "The Army During Time of Peace," p. 491.

41. Rev. and Capt. T. G. Steward, "The Strike in Montana," *The Independent* 46, no. 2384 (August 9, 1894): 1017. Emphasis in the original.

42. "The Lesson of the Recent Strikes," p. 186.

43. *Sec. War Rept. 1894,* p. 115.

44. Wallace, "The Army and the Civil Power," p. 264. Also see Young, "The Mob and the Military," p. 251; O'Connell, "The Great Strike of 1894," pp. 301-02; Fitz-John Porter, "How to Quell Mobs," *North American Review* 141, no. 347 (October 1885): 351, 358-59. Officers in the field during the 1894 strikes often expressed a dislike for the strike tactic. See, e.g., Col. J. C. Bates, Second Infantry, to Department of the Platte, August 1, 1894, enclosure 2, in AGO 10, Adjutant General's Office, Record Group 94, National Archives; Col. Zenas R. Bliss, to Department of the Colorado, August 30, 1894, no. 5864, in *Ibid.;* letter of Col. William R. Graham, Fourth Artillery, writing from San Francisco, to *Army and Navy Journal* 33, no. 1 (September 7, 1895): 2, 9; comments of officers in General Miles's command in Chicago, in their July 18, 1894, reports, Letters Received, 1894, Department of the Missouri, Record Group 393, National Archives; remarks by Capt. Charles J. Crane,

24th Inf., in his memoirs, *Experiences of a Colonel of Infantry* (New York, 1923), pp. 205-07. See, as well, observations of Lt. Col. William E. Dougherty, 7th Inf., to Adj. Gen., June 9, 1900, in AGO no. 231071, RG94, NA. The *Army and Navy Journal* reflected the anti-labor, anti-strike feelings of the officer corps, as seen, e.g., in vol. 32, no. 18 (December 1894): 297, and vol. 32, no. 33 (April 13, 1895): 621.

45. Price, "The Army and the People," p. 319.

46. Leary, "Certain Laws Concerning the Use of Troops in Civil Disorders," p. 83.

47. "The Army and the Civil Power," p. 265. Also see Nichols, "The Pittsburg Riots," p. 262; Otis, "The Army in Connection with the Labor Riots of 1877," pp. 293-94; *Army and Navy Journal* 34, no. 29 (March 20, 1897): 527.

48. From a letter to the editor of the *Portland Oregonian,* found in PRD 1892 no. 39611, AGO, RG94, NA.

49. Capt. E. L. Zalinski, 5th Artillery, "The Army Organization Best Adapted to a Republican Form of Government, which will Insure an Effective Force," *JMSI* 14, no. 65 (September 1893); 949.

50. "The Lesson of the Recent Strikes," p. 188, also p. 186.

51. Lt. Col. Dougherty's report to the Adj. Gen., June 9, 1900.

52. In no. 2860, Letters Received, 1894, Dept. of the Missouri, RG393, NA.

53. Michaelis, "Military Necessities of the U.S.," p. 288.

54. Molineux, "Riots in Cities and Their Suppression," p. 336. Anti-foreign sentiments grew within society as well as within the Army in the years following the 1877 railroad strike. For the Army, see as examples, *Army and Navy Journal* 15, no. 2 (August 18, 1877): 24-25; vol. 30, no. 8 (October 15, 1892): 122-23; and vol. 30, no. 34 (April 1893): 565. Also see O'Connell, "The Great Strike of 1894," pp. 300, 304; Wallace, "The Army and the Civil Power," pp. 265-66; Egbert, "Is An Increase of the Army Necessary?" pp. 381-82; Wilson, "The Army During Time of Peace," p. 492; Miles, "The Lesson of the Recent Strikes," p. 188; McClellan, "The Militia and the Army," p. 297; comments of Brig. Gen. John Gibbon, in *Sec. War Rept. 1886,* p. 189; Maj. George W. Baird, "The Army as the Guardian of Peace," *Century Magazine,* n.s., vol. 27, no. 6 (April 1895): 959; Lt. Col. William Ludlow, "The Military Systems of Europe and America," *North American Review* 160, no. 458 (January 1895): 83. Higham, *Strangers in the Land, passim,* and White, "The Military and the Melting Pot," pp. 305-11, 376-78, provide important background material here. Officers' perceptions and fears of immigrants were quite similar to those of other middle-class, native-born Americans, despite the high percentage of immigrant enlisted men.

55. "The Mob and the Military," p. 250.

56. Wallace, "The Army and Civil Power," p. 264.

57. Chester, "Martial Law and Social Order," p. 57.

58. "The Army and the Civil Power," p. 244. The officer corps's deep fear of anarchy is seen in the pertinent references immediately above, and also in *Army and Navy Journal* 23, no. 38 (April 17, 1886): 765; Price, "The Army and the People," p. 323; Wagner, "Military Necessities of the U.S.," p. 265; Rice, "Military Support to the Civil Power," p. 125; and Capt. James Regan, 9th Inf., "Military Duties in Aid of the Civil Power," *JMSI* 18, no. 80 (March 1896): 292. Also see C. Robert Kemble, *The Image of the Army Officer in America: Background for Current Views* (Westport, Conn., 1973), pp. 122-24, on the similarity of views of officers and civiliams as to the threat of anarchy.

59. Vol. 75, no. 1924 (July 28, 1892): 74.

60. Ludlow, "The Military Systems of Europe and America," p. 83.

61. "Military Duties in Aid of the Civil Power," p. 292.

62. On this, see Capt. A. H. Russell, "What is the Use of a Regular Army in this Country?" *JMSI* 24, no. 98 (March 1899): 217; Wallace, "The Army and the Civil Power," pp. 247-48; *Army and Navy Journal* 32, no. 23 (February 2, 1895): 295.

63. "What is the Use of a Regular Army?" p. 218.

64. From letter to *Portland Oregonian*. Similar views in Wallace, "The Army and the Civil Power," pp. 235-36; Russell, "What is the Use of a Regular Army?" p. 217; Ludlow, "The Military Systems of Europe and America," pp. 83-84. The concern for respect for the law and social stability seen in the above and in Gen. Gibbon's comments in *Sec. War Rept. 1886*, p. 189; Howard, "A Plea for the Army," pp. 641-642; Egbert, "Is An Increase of the Army Necessary?" p. 382; Birkhimer, *Military Government and Martial Law*, p. 403; *Army and Navy Journal* 21, no. 17 (November 24, 1883): 334; and Capt. James Chester, 3rd Art., "Standing Armies a Necessity of Civilization," *United Service* 9, no. 6 (December 1883): 661. For background, see Brown, "Social Attitudes of American Generals," pp. 369-70.

65. In Molineux, "Riots in Cities and Their Suppression," p. 370.

66. "The Army and the Civil Power," p. 262. Most of the citations in note 64 include statements on the need to protect property. Also see Lt. John H. Parker, 13th Inf., "The Army Problem: Questions of Size, Organization and Administration," *The Outlook* 61, no. 11 (March 18, 1899): 638-39, for appreciative comments on the methods of industrialists, and Miles, "The Lesson of the Recent Strikes," p. 186. Brown, "Social Attitudes of American Generals," pp. 40-42 is relevant here.

67. "Military Necessities of the U.S.," pp. 265-66.

68. Chester, "Standing Armies a Necessity of Civilization," p. 666.

69. Vol. 13, no. 51 (December 17, 1892): 816. In this same vein, see Miles, "The Lesson of the Recent Strikes," p. 181; O'Connell, "The Great Strike of 1894," pp. 315-16; Egbert, "Is An Increase of the Army Necessary?" pp. 382-84; Price, "The Army and the People," p. 329; Wallace, "The Army and the Civil Power," p. 265; *Army and Navy Journal* 23, no. 38 (April 17, 1886): 765; comments of Brig. Gen. Elwell S. Otis, in *Sec. War Rept. 1894,* pp. 149-51.

70. Wilson, "The Army During Time of Peace," p. 483.

71. "Military Necessities of the U.S.," p. 266.

72. Lt. Alonzo Gray, 5th Cav., "Uses of Cavalry in Time of Riots," *JMSI* 19, no. 82 (July 1896): 112. Miles, "The Lesson of the Recent Strikes," p. 187. For other predictions that the Army would continue to play a part in industrial disorders, see *Army and Navy Register* 13, no. 28 (July 9, 1892): 445; Capt. H. C. Cochrane, U.S.M.C., "The Naval Brigade and the Marine Battalion in the Labor Strikes of 1877," *United Service* 1, no. 1 (January 1879): 116; Gen. J. C. Kelton, Adj. Gen., "Requirements for National Defense," *The Forum* 8 (November 1889): 317; George B. McClellan, "The Regular Army of the United States," *Harper's New Magazine* 55, no. 239 (October 1877): 782; Brig. Gen. Wesley Merritt, "The Army of the United States," *Harper's New Monthly Magazine* 80, no. 478 (March 1890): 507; Chester, "Standing Armies a Necessity of Civilization," pp. 664-65; Michaelis, "Military Necessities of the U.S.," p. 273; Price, "The Army and the People," p. 323; O'Connell, "The Great Strike of 1894," p. 302; Wallace, "The Army and the Civil Power," p. 249.

73. Chester, "Standing Armies a Necessity of Civilization," p. 665.

74. "The Military Systems of Europe and America," p. 83. Also see Chester, "Standing Armies a Necessity of Civilization," p. 665; O'Connell, "The Great Strike of 1894," p. 302; Wallace, "The Army and the Civil Power," pp. 236, 250-51.

75. "Military Necessities of the U.S.," p. 59.

76. *The Military Policy of the United States* appears in 62nd Cong., 2nd sess., Senate Document 494 (Washington, D.C., 1912), pp. xiv, also xiii.

77. As examples, see vol. 15, no. 2 (August 18, 1877): 24; vol. 21, no. 17 (November 24, 1883): 334; vol. 32, no. 13 (November 24, 1894): 198; vol 34, no. 29 (March 20, 1897): 527.

78. Wilson, "The Army During Time of Peace," p. 492. Also see Baird, "The Army as Guardian of Peace," pp. 958-59; Capt. H. R. Brinkerhoff, 15th Inf., "A Plea for the Increase of the Army," *United Service,* n.s.,

vol. 14, no. 6 (December 1895): 491-95; Chester, "Standing Armies a
Necessity of Civilization," p. 666; Bvt. Major Gen. A. V. Kautz, "Our
National Military System: What the United States Army Should Be,"
Century Magazine 36, no. 6 (October 1888): 934-38; Ludlow, "The
Military Systems of Europe and America," p. 84; O'Connell, "The Great
Strike of 1894," pp. 303, 315; Wagner, "Military Necessities of the U.S.,"
pp. 249-50, 252-54; Wallace, "The Army and the Civil Power," pp. 255-
58; Wilson, "The Army During Time of Peace," p. 492; Zalinski, "Army
Organization," p. 949. Even a National Guardsman could make such an
appeal, see Harry P. Mawson, "The National Guard," *Harper's Weekly*
36, no. 1863 (September 3, 1892): 858.

79. In "The Army of the United States," *The Forum* 28 (January
1899): 519. Similar proposals in Parker, "The Army Problem," p. 637;
Howard, "A Plea for the Army," p. 646; *Army and Navy Journal* 32, no.
19 (January 5, 1895): 313; Lt. George B. Duncan, "Reasons for Increasing the Regular Army," *North American Review* 166, no. 497
(April 1898): 453-55.

80. "A Plea for the Army," p. 651. See strikingly similar statements
in Chester, "Standing Armies a Necessity of Civilization," p. 661, and
Russell, "What is the Use of a Regular Army?" p. 218.

81. "Military Necessities of the U.S.," p. 290.

82. Lt. Lyman V. Kennon, 6th Inf., *The Army: Its Employment During
Time of Peace, and the Necessity for Its Increase,* Monograph of the U.S.
Infantry Society, no. 2 (n.p., 1896), p. 14.

83. See *The Military Policy of the U.S., passim;* and Upton, *The Armies
of Asia and Europe* (New York, 1878), p. 367. Also of value, Stephen
Ambrose, *Upton and the Army* (Baton Rouge, La., 1964), pp. 105-07;
and Russell F. Weigley, *History of the United States Army* (New York,
1967), pp. 271-80.

84. Parker, "The Army Problem," pp. 636-38.

85. Russell F. Weigley, *Towards an American Army: Military Thought
From Washington to Marshall* (New York, 1962), pp. vii-viii, 100-20,
137-47, 156-61.

Bibliography

Manuscripts

The John McAllister Schofield Papers, Library of Congress, Washington, D.C., were the most useful private military papers. This extensive collection covers Schofield's entire military career from the early 1850s until his retirement in 1895. The Schofield Papers are particularly useful for the period following Reconstruction. The general correspondence not only concerns military matters but gives a clear picture of Schofield's many non-military friends and acquaintances and his extensive financial involvements. A key figure in the post-Reconstruction Army, Schofield corresponded with leading figures of the Army, Congress, and industry. His papers provide a useful overview of Schofield's role in the service as well as the Army's connection to other institutions in American society. Other manuscript collections of Army officers used here were:

Thomas M. Anderson Papers, University of Washington Libraries, Seattle

John Green Ballance Papers, Illinois State Historical Society, Springfield

William F. Barry Papers, Maryland Historical Society, Baltimore

William F. Barry Collection, Buffalo and Erie County Public Library, Buffalo, New York

Henry C. Corbin Papers, Library of Congress, Washington, D.C.

George W. Getty Papers, Library of Congress, Washington, D.C.

Winfield Scott Hancock Papers, Pennsylvania State Library, Harrisburg

William R. Shafter Papers, Stanford University Libraries, Palo Alto, California

Philip H. Sheridan Papers, Library of Congress, Washington, D.C.

William T. Sherman Papers, Library of Congress, Washington, D.C.

While invaluable for an overall understanding of the period and the particular labor disputes involved, the papers at the Library of Congress of Daniel S. Lamont (secretary of war 1894), Richard Olney (attorney general 1894), Walter Q. Gresham (secretary of state 1894), and Elihu Root (secretary of war 1899) failed to provide anything significant on the role of the Army in labor strikes. Microfilm copies produced by the Library of Congress of the papers of Grover Cleveland, Benjamin Harrison, and William McKinley were most useful. They not only revealed the circumstances under which each president decided to commit troops to strike duty but also helped to reconstruct public reaction to each commitment.

The Rutherford B. Hayes Library, Fremont, Ohio, has separated all material pertaining to the 1877 upheaval from the rest of Hayes's papers and placed them in a single "Strike File." The library has also prepared a microfilm, "Papers pertaining to the Railroad Strike of 1877," which contains many newspaper clippings on the strike and the use of the Army in the dispute as well as letters from citizens praising Hayes's action. The Hayes Papers were most valuable in preparing the 1877 chapters. The papers of Norman B. Willey (governor of Idaho in 1892) are meager but give some insight into the first federal intervention in Idaho. They are held by the Idaho State Historical Society, Boise.

National Archives

The bulk of the source material used here came from military records held by the National Archives. No student of American military affairs in the nineteenth century can approach his subject without reference to the Records of the Adjutant General's Office, 1800-1917, Old Military Records Division, Record Group 94. The most important and useful part of the vast records of this office is the "Document File," which contains all general correspondence that passed through the Adjutant General's Office. Each of the major military interventions examined here has a consolidated file in RG94, as indicated in the footnotes. For the 1877 strikes, AGO file no. 4042 (1877), available on National Archives microcopy no. 666, "Letters Received by the Office of the Adjutant General, Main Series, 1871-1880," reels 347-57, was most useful. See PRD no. 34728, 1892, for the Coeur d'Alene activity and PRD no. 6091 (1894) for the coal strike of that year. See AGO no. 6370 (1894) for the Coxey affair. Material on the Pullman strike is found in AGO no. 10 (1894), and AGO no. 231071 (1899) is the consolidated file for the 1899 Coeur d'Alene intervention.

The consolidated files are most useful. They not only contain orders for the deployment of troops, all orders from the adjutant general, secretary of war, and commanding general to troops in the field, reports from commanders in the field, and final reports submitted by these commanders, but they also have communications from governors, senators and representatives, and businessmen interested in federal military intervention in labor disputes. Almost all correspondence received by federal departments and bureaus relating to the Army and strike duty usually ended up in the consolidated files.

Besides the document file of RG94, the Appointment, Commission, and Personal branch of the Adjutant General's Office provided useful information on officers involved in strike duty. The ACP files were consolidated personnel files on officers. Also useful were Returns from Regular Infantry Regiments, June 1821-December 1916, National Archives microcopy no. 727, and Returns from United States Military Posts, 1800-1916, National Archives microcopy no. 617. These returns of monthly reports often indicated the nature of strike duty for individual military units.

After Record Group 94, the most useful set of records from the National Archives came from Record Group 393, Records of United States Army Continental Commands 1821-1920. These are records of military divisions and departments and sometimes of individual military posts. RG393 provided a day-to-day detailing of strike duty not found in the correspondence at higher levels. Record Group 107, Records of the Office of the Secretary of War, and Record Group 108, Records of the Headquarters of the Army more often than not contained correspondence duplicated in the RG94 consolidated files. Sometimes a useful piece of information from the Secretary's office or HQA was discovered but not often.

One set of non-military records in the National Archives, Record Group 60, General Records of the Department of Justice, proved useful. In the central files of RG60, year file no. 4017 (1894) contained valuable information on Richard Olney's policy toward the Coxey industrial army movement. Also in the central files, file 16-1-23, section 3.4, contains the same sort of information on the Justice Department's approach to the Pullman strike.

Published Documents

Federal Government

The annual reports of the Secretary of War, which appear in the House Executive Documents of the regular serial set of congressional documents, contained the reports of the secretary of war, the commanding general, the adjutant general, the heads of other logistics bureaus, and the department commanders. The secretaries' annual reports from 1870 to 1900 provided a sketch of the general operations and conditions of the Army. They also showed the thinking of Army leaders on the crucial problems of the service. Finally, in the years in which strike duty took place, the reports contained general information on the use of troops in civil disorder. Usually, the department commanders' reports on strike duty appeared as part of the regular departmental reports. In 1899, however, General Merriam submitted two separate reports which give significant detail on the Coeur d'Alene incident. Both reports were published as congressional documents. They are: "Report of Brig. Gen. H. C. Merriam, U.S.A., on Miners' Riots in the State of Idaho," 56th Cong., 1st sess., Senate Documents, vol. 4, no. 24 (Washington, D.C., 1899); and, in 56th Cong., 1st sess., House Documents, vol. 4, no. 2, part 1, (Washington, D.C., 1899), entitled "Report of Miners' Riot in the State of Idaho."

A most useful government document was Frederick T. Wilson, of the Adjutant General's Office, "Federal Aid in Domestic Disturbances 1787-1903," 57th Cong., 2nd sess., Senate Documents, vol. 15, no. 209, (Washington, D.C., 1903), later updated in 1922 under the same title but extending coverage to that year and appearing as 67th Cong., 2nd sess., Senate Documents, vol. 19, no. 263 (Washington, D.C., 1922). Wilson makes no attempt at historical interpretation but merely sketches the outlines of each case of federal intervention in a domestic disturbance and provides illustrative documents from the Adjutant General's Office for each instance. Nonetheless, the work is valuable as an outline for the Army's role in suppressing civil disorders.

A variety of federal documents, as indicated in the chapter notes, were used in this study besides the annual reports from the War Department. Several congressional reports of investigations into labor conditions as well as the reports of the U.S. Industrial Commission were relevant to the question of labor and the Army. Reports from the attorney general for 1894 supplemented War Department reports.

State Governments

State documents do not appear in this study to any great extent since the main focus is at the federal level. The use of the reports of state adjutants general, particularly from Pennsylvania in 1877, and Illinois and California for 1894, has added to an understanding of the problems faced by state forces when called out to control their fellow citizens. The state reports on the militia/National Guard also reveal the ambiguity with which some state officials viewed the arrival of federal troops to suppress disorder. Again, the Illinois and California reports for 1894 are particularly relevant. Idaho state documents, including reports of the adjutant general for the state and the governors' annual messages, were of value.

Newspaper, Magazines, and Journals

Contemporary articles and newspaper coverage were an important source for reconstructing the views that military officers had of American society and the place of the Army in that society in the nineteenth century as well as the attitudes they held toward labor, management, and industrial upheaval. Popular magazine and newspaper comments provided source material for civilian views of the military. Finally, labor journals served as a source for the reactions to the military, both the Army and the National Guard.

For the military perspective, *The Journal of Military Service Institution of the United States* was of greatest value. Also perused extensively were *The United Service Magazine* (Philadelphia), *The Army and Navy Journal* (New York), and the *Army and Navy Register* (Washington, D.C). Chapter notes indicate the extent of material taken from these sources and their overall value to the study.

Popular periodicals used throughout the study were

> *Arena*
> *Century Illustrated Monthly Magazine*
> *The Christian Union*
> *The Forum*
> *Frank Leslie's Illustrated Weekly*
> *Harper's New Monthly Magazine*
> *Harper's Weekly*
> *The Independent*
> *The Nation*
> *North American Review*
> *Public Opinion*
> *Outing*
> *The Outlook*
> *The Penn Monthly*
> *The Review of Reviews*
> *Twentieth Century: A Weekly Radical Magazine*

Newspapers:

Baltimore American and Commercial Advertiser
Chicago Times
Chicago Tribune
Idaho Daily Statesman (Boise)
New York Times
Philadelphia Inquirer
Philadelphia Public Ledger
Portland Oregonian
Rocky Mountain News (Denver)
St. Louis Dispatch
San Francisco Chronicle
The Spokesman-Review (Spokane)
The Washington Evening Star
The Washington News
The Washington Post

Labor journals and newspapers surveyed and their publishers were

The American Federationist. Magazine of the American Federation
    of Labor.
The Boilermaker and Iron Ship Builder. Journal of the Brotherhood
    of Boilermakers and Iron Ship Builders.
The Carpenter. Official Journal of the United Brotherhood of Car-
    penters and Joiners of America.
Chicago Labor. Official Organ of the Socialist Labor Party of
    Chicago.
The Chicago Searchlight. Edited and published by Henry Vincent,
    reform and Populist leader.
Cigar Makers' Official Journal. Issued by the Cigar Makers' Inter-
    national Union of America.
The Cleveland Citizen. Published by the Central Labor Union of
    Cleveland, Ohio.
Coast Seaman's Journal. Organ of the International Seaman's Union
    of America.
The International Woodworker. Official Journal of the Amalgamated
    Woodworkers' International Union of America.
Iron Molders' Journal. Official Organ of the International Iron
    Molders' Union of North America.

Journal of the Knights of Labor. Official Magazine of the Knights of Labor.

Locomotive Engineers' Journal. Published by the Brotherhood of Locomotive Engineers.

Locomotive Firemen's Magazine. Published by the Brotherhood of Locomotive Firemen.

The Miners' Magazine. Published by the Western Federation of Miners.

The National Labor Tribune. Official Organ of the Amalgamated Association of Iron and Steelworkers of the U.S.A.

The Pueblo Courier. Official Newspaper of the Western Labor Union.

Railway Carmen's Journal. Official Journal of the Brotherhood of Railway Carmen of America.

Railroad Trainmen's Journal. Official Organ of the Brotherhood of Railroad Trainmen.

The Railway Conductor. Published by the Order of Railway Conductors.

St. Louis Labor. Official Paper of the Socialist Labor Party of St. Louis.

The Typographical Journal. Official Paper of the International Typographical Union of North America.

The United Mine Workers' Journal. Published by the National Executive Board of the United Mine Workers of America.

The Western Laborer. Privately published newspaper of strong labor leanings, Omaha, Nebraska.

Books and Memoirs

Books did not contribute substantially to this study. A considerable number of memoirs and reminscences by officers who had served in the late nineteenth century were read. The vast majority of them, however, shed little light on the use of the Army in domestic disorders. The most useful memoirs were John M. Schofield's *Forty-Six Years in the Army* (New York, 1897); Nelson A. Miles, *Serving the Republic: Memoirs of the Civil and Military Life of Nelson A. Miles* (New York, 1911); George B. Duncan, "Reminiscences 1882-1905," unpublished manuscript in the possession of Henry T. Duncan, Lexington, Kentucky. Other books of use were

Crane, Charles J. *The Experiences of a Colonel of Infantry.* New York, 1923.

DeWolfe, M. A., ed. *Home Letters of General Sherman.* New York, 1909.

Hancock, Almina Russell. *Reminiscences of Winfield Scott Hancock.* New York, 1887.

Haywood, William D. *Bill Haywood's Book: The Autobiography of William D. Haywood.* New York, 1929.

Hutton, May A. *The Coeur d'Alene or a Tale of the Modern Inquisition in Idaho.* Denver, 1900.

James, Henry. *Richard Olney and His Public Service.* Boston, 1923.

Michie, Peter S. *The Life and Letters of Emory Upton.* New York, 1885.

Parker, James. *The Old Army: Memories 1872-1918.* Philadelphia, 1929.

Regan, Captain James, 9th Inf. *Military Duties in Aid of the Civil Power: For the Regular Army, National Guard and Police Forces Generally.* New York, 1888.

Scott, Hugh L. *Some Memories of a Soldier.* New York, 1928.

Swinton, John. *Striking for Life: Labor's Side of the Labor Question.* N.p., 1894.

Upton, Emory. *The Armies of Asia and Europe.* New York, 1878.

———. *The Military Policy of the United States,* 62nd Cong., 2nd sess., Washington, D.C., 1912.

Articles

If memoirs were of limited value, contemporary articles by regular officers and by civilians sympathetic to the Army form an important part of the source material of this work. Many of the men who ignored the noncombatant role of the Army after 1877 in their reminiscences dealt with the topic in articles written for professional journals and popular magazines. Some civilians expressed an interest in the American military system after Reconstruction, and popular magazines carried many articles on military reform. Some contemporary articles by labor leaders, reform advocates, businessmen, and politicians dealing with the problems of industrial upheaval have been used as well. Taken as a whole, the articles provided a valuable source for assessing the Army's participation in industrial disorders. Specific articles are cited in the chapters, those in Chapters 2 and 9 being the most important. For a full listing of articles used in this study, see Jerry M. Cooper, "The Army and Civil Disorder: Federal Military Intervention in American Labor Disputes, 1877-1900" (Ph.D. diss., University of Wisconsin, 1971), pp. 449-55.

Secondary Works

A detailed bibliography of secondary works may be found in Cooper, "The Army and Civil Disorder," pp. 455-63. Nonetheless, a number of studies must be cited here because of their importance in shaping the interpretations and perspectives presented in this work. American military historians owe a great debt to Walter Millis, whose *Arms and Men: A Study of American Military Policy* (New York, 1956) has pointed the way for a reassessment of the place of military institutions in American history. My debt to Millis's influence is matched by that of Russell F. Weigley. In *Towards an American Army: Military Thought from Washington to Marshall* (New York, 1962), and *History of the United States Army* (New York, 1967), Weigley added scholarly substance to Millis's seminal thinking. Both Millis and Weigley show that in order to understand American military institutions fully, they must be studied in peacetime as well as in war. This work is a direct outgrowth of such thinking. time as well as in war.   This work is a direct outgrowth of such thinking. Other works in this vein that have influenced the perspective of the present volume include

Ambrose, Stephen E. *Upton and the Army*. Baton Rouge, La., 1964.

Brown, Richard C. "Social Attitudes of American Generals." Ph.D. diss., University of Wisconsin, 1951.

Cosmas, Graham. *An Army for Empire: The United States Army in the Spanish-American War*. Columbia, Mo., 1971.

Higham, Robin, ed., *Bayonets in the Street: The Use of Troops in Civil Disorders*. Manhattan, Kan., 1969.

Huntington, Samuel P. *The Soldier and the State: The Theory and Politics of Civil-Military Relations*. Cambridge, Mass., 1957.

Kemble, C. Robert. *The Image of the Army Officer in America: Background for Current Views*. Westport, Conn., 1973.

Millett, Allan R. *The General: Robert L. Bullard and Officership in the United States Army, 1881-1925*. Westport, Conn., 1975.

The social, political, and economic context within which the Army's role in industrial disorders developed has been drawn from a variety of excellent secondary works. The nature of the value struggle and the part organized labor played in it has been taken from the work of Herbert Gutman, particularly his essay "Work, Culture and Society in Industrializing America, 1815-1919," which originally appeared in *American Historical Review* 78, no. 3 (June 1973): 531-588, but is more conveniently available, as are other of Gutman's essays on working people in the late nineteenth century, in *Work, Culture, and Society in Industrializing America: Essays in American Working-Class and Social History* (New York, 1976). I have also benefited substantially from John R. Commons et al., *History of Labour in the United States* (New York, 1923), Selig Perlman and Philip Taft, *History of Labor in the United States 1896-1932* (New York, 1935), and the first two volumes of Philip S. Foner's *History of the Labor Movement in the United States* (New York, 1947, 1955) in understanding labor's position in this era.

Of the studies that have examined the development and application of federal policy to federal intervention in industrial disorders, the most useful by far has been Gerald G. Eggert, *Railroad Labor Disputes: The Beginnings of Federal Strike Policy* (Ann Arbor, 1967). Also of use were Edward Berman, *Labor Disputes and the President of the United States* (New York, 1924), and Bennett M. Rich, *The Presidents and Civil Disorders* (Washington, D.C., 1941). Monographic treatments of individual strikes and industrial problems included:

Brissenden, Paul F. *The I.W.W.: The Story of American Syndicalism.* 2nd ed. New York, 1957.

Bruce, Robert V. *1877: Year of Violence.* New York, 1959.

Dubofsky, Melvyn. *We Shall Be All: A History of the Industrial Workers of the World.* Chicago, 1969.

Jensen, Vernon H. *Heritage of Conflict: Labor Relations in the Non-ferrous Metals up to 1930.* Ithaca, N.Y., 1950.

Lindsey, Almont. *The Pullman Strike.* Chicago, 1942.

McMurry, Donald L. *Coxey's Army: A Study of the Industrial Army Movement of 1894.* Boston, 1924.

Pollack, Norman. *The Populist Response to Industrial America.* New York, 1966.

Smith, Robert W. *The Coeur d'Alene Mining War of 1892.* Corvallis, Ore., 1961.

Index

Alger, Russell A.: response to 1899 labor protests, 183; role of, in 1899 Idaho disorders, 173-74, 194

Army, U. S.: fails to plan for strike duty after 1877, 85, 90, 104-06, 244; illegality of, serving under state officials in Idaho (1899), 192-94; inadequate command system of and influence on 1877 disorders, 48-49, 56-57, 62; lacks plans for strike duty in 1877, 47-48; organized labor's view of, 218-19, 222-28; press support for in labor interventions, 211-13; public demands for increase of, 82, 214-15; public opposition to increase of, 217-18; relation to civil officials outside chain of command, 242-43; relation to president, 242-43. *See also* federal troops; Officers, U. S. Army

Bunker Hill and Sullivan Mining Company, role of in 1899 Idaho disorders, 165-66, 172-73, 177

California National Guard. *See* National Guard

Chicago, 1877 disorders in, 56-59

Cleveland, Grover, approves federal military intervention in: 1885, Wyoming Territory, 87-88; 1886, Washington Territory, 88-90; 1894, industrial armies disorders, 103-07, 114-15; 1894, Pullman strike, 145-46; 1894, supported by press for, 210-11

Corbin, Henry C. (Adjutant General, U. S. Army): responds to 1899 labor protests, 183, 188-89; role of in 1899 Idaho disorders, 173-74, 194

Coxey's Army. *See* Industrial armies

Federal military interventions at state requests: confusion surrounding legalities of in 1877, 49, 62-65, 75; controlled by states in 1877, 79-80, 82-83; in early twentieth century, 239-41; in Idaho (1892), 165-66; in Idaho (1899), 192-93; legalities of, 16-17, 63-64, 77-78, 82-84, 241-43

Federal strike policy, 17-18; in 1877 disorders, 47, 75; remains ill-defined after 1877, 83-88, 91, 237-38

ABOUT THE AUTHOR

Jerry M. Cooper is Associate Professor of History at the University of Missouri at St. Louis. His articles have appeared in *Labor History, Military Affairs,* and other journals.